Based on extensive analysis and deep insider knowledge of the Australian retail energy sector, F.C. Simon builds a powerful and fascinating critique of meta-regulation theory and its practical manifestation. Simon shows how complexity and contested views of compliance and market competition challenge key tenets of meta-regulatory thinking, not least capacities for learning and for responsiveness to reputational risk. *Meta-Regulation in Practice* will be of considerable interest to scholars, policy makers and managers in the energy sector and beyond.

     Michael Power, *London School of Economics and Political Science, UK*

Meta-Regulation in Practice is an excellent case study on the attempt to morally and politically steer the Australian retail energy sector. F.C. Simon shows how such regulation efforts may only result in a growing hiatus between the public self-description of an industry and its actual functioning. Its intricate systems-theoretical reflections connect this book with cutting-edge contemporary social theory far beyond its immediate area.

    Hans-Georg Moeller, *Professor and Subject Convenor, Philosophy and Religious Studies Program, University of Macau, China*

F.C. Simon provides a unique and original perspective on the practice of regulatory organizations and in doing so rejects the enthusiastic claims and uncritical accounts of many academic commentators. She takes as her starting point the contradictions and self-deceptions under which these organizations operate. In the footsteps of Niklas Luhmann, whose systems theory inspired her analysis, she skilfully exposes their taken-for-granted world as an illusion. At the same time she recognizes fully the complexity of the task facing regulation in its attempt to reconcile the demands of politics, law and economics and produce a coherent account of its activities. This is a ground-breaking book which deserves to be widely read.

    Michael King, *Professor Emeritus, University of Reading, UK*

Meta-Regulation in Practice

Meta-regulation presents itself as a progressive policy approach that can manage complexity and conflicting objectives better than traditional command and control regulation. It does this by 'harnessing' markets and enlisting a broad range of stakeholders to reach a more inclusive view of the public interest that a self-regulating business can then respond to.

Based on a 17-year study of the Australian energy industry, and via the lens of Niklas Luhmann's systems theory, *Meta-Regulation in Practice* argues that normative meta-regulatory theory relies on questionable assumptions of stakeholder morality and rationality. Meta-regulation in practice appears to be most challenged in a complex and contested environment – the very environment it is supposed to serve best.

Contending that scholarship must prioritise an understanding of communicative possibilities in practice, this book will be of interest to undergraduate and postgraduate students, as well as postdoctoral researchers interested in subjects such as business regulation, systems theory and corporate social responsibility.

F.C. Simon is a regulatory policy practitioner, having worked in both regulatory and regulated organisations.

Routledge Advances in Sociology

For a full list of titles in this series, please visit www.routledge.com/series/SE0511.

209 **Racial Cities**
Governance and the Segregation of Romani People in Urban Europe
Giovanni Picker

210 **Bourdieusian Prospects**
Edited by Lisa Adkins, Caragh Brosnan and Steven Threadgold

211 **Alienation and Affect**
Warren D. TenHouten

212 **Homeownership, Renting and Society**
Historical and Comparative Perspectives
Sebastian Kohl

213 **Social Class and Transnational Human Capital**
How Middle and Upper Class Parents Prepare Their Children for Globalization
Jürgen Gerhards, Silke Hans and Sören Carlson

214 **Transnational Social Policy**
Social Welfare in a World on the Move
Edited by Luann Good Gingrich and Stefan Köngeter

215 **Meta-Regulation in Practice**
Beyond Normative Views of Morality and Rationality
F.C. Simon

216 **The Sociology of Postmarxism**
Richard Howson

217 **The Precarious Generation**
A Political Economy of Young People
Judith Bessant Rys Farthing and Rob Watts

218 **Human Rights, Islam and the Failure of Cosmopolitanism**
June Edmunds

219 **New Generation Political Activism in Ukraine**
2000–2014
Christine Emeran

220 **Turkish National Identity and Its Outsiders**
Memories of State Violence in Dersim
Ozlem Goner

Meta-Regulation in Practice
Beyond Normative Views of Morality and Rationality

F.C. Simon

LONDON AND NEW YORK

First published 2017 by Routledge

2 Park Square, Milton Park, Abingdon, Oxfordshire OX14 4RN
52 Vanderbilt Avenue, New York, NY 10017

Routledge is an imprint of the Taylor & Francis Group, an informa business

First issued in paperback 2019

Copyright © 2017 F.C. Simon

The right of F.C. Simon to be identified as author of this work has been
asserted by her in accordance with sections 77 and 78 of the Copyright,
Designs and Patents Act 1988.

All rights reserved. No part of this book may be reprinted or reproduced or
utilised in any form or by any electronic, mechanical, or other means, now
known or hereafter invented, including photocopying and recording, or in
any information storage or retrieval system, without permission in writing
from the publishers.

Notice:
Product or corporate names may be trademarks or registered trademarks, and
are used only for identification and explanation without intent to infringe.

British Library Cataloguing in Publication Data
A catalogue record for this book is available from the British Library

Library of Congress Cataloging in Publication Data
A catalog record for this book has been requested

ISBN: 978-1-138-23372-0 (hbk)
ISBN: 978-0-367-22870-5 (pbk)

Typeset in Times New Roman
by Wearset Ltd, Boldon, Tyne and Wear

For my family

Contents

List of illustrations	xi
Preface	xii
Acknowledgements	xv
List of abbreviations	xvi

1 Introduction 1

The machinery of meta-regulation 4
Luhmann's systems theory 8
The Australian retail energy industry 11
The structure of this book 14

**2 The implicit assumptions underpinning normative
meta-regulatory theory** 21

Consensus on values and the public interest 25
Organisational rationality and capacity for learning 43
Conclusion 45

**3 Creating the regulatory framework for the world's most
competitive retail energy market** 58

The early policy vacuum in Victoria 58
*The industry and regulatory response to the policy
  environment 59*
The development of the Retail Code 64
Government intervention in pricing 71
Conclusion 74

x   *Contents*

4   The next thirteen years: complexity, politics and change   78

Overview of the markets: 2003–2015 79
Protecting vulnerable consumers 85
Contingency and unpredictable outcomes 93
Inside the industry 103
Conclusion 108
References 112

5   Contesting compliance in hardship regulation   115

The genesis of the Victorian hardship provisions 116
Drawing out the conflict on roles in energy bill management 127
Conflicts between the ESC and EWOV and wrongful disconnection
*   referrals 136*
The implications for compliance and performance 140
The creation of retailer hardship programmes 145
A surprising turn of events: the ESC proposal to abolish hardship
*   programmes 146*
Conclusion 148

6   Conflicting views of market competition   154

Economic assessments of competition 155
Complicating factors in identifying effective competition 157
Political views of market effectiveness 167
Co-regulation, self-regulation and external enforcement of
*   door-to-door sales 177*
Conclusion 187

7   Rethinking meta-regulation   196

The political need to 'do something' 197
Harnessing the market? 203
The role of the law 211
Assessing the effectiveness of meta-regulation in the Australian
*   energy markets 213*
A different perspective on meta-regulation 222
Some final thoughts 227

Index   232

Illustrations

Figures

2.1	Inputs to business self-regulation under meta-regulation	26
2.2	Stages in the reputation mechanism	40
2.3	The key function and organisational systems for this research	47
4.1	Structural change in the Australian retail energy markets, 2003–2015 inclusive	84
7.1	The regulatory matrix for complex and contested environments	224
7.2	The reputation matrix for complex and contested environments	226

Tables

2.1	Summary of assumptions underpinning normative meta-regulatory theory	46
4.1	Demonstration of meta-regulation in the Australian retail energy markets	80
7.1	Effectiveness of meta-regulation in the Australian retail energy markets	214
7.2	Command and control versus meta-regulation	222

Preface

This book is about the regulation of the Australian retail energy industry and my observation of the industry's experience of regulation over a 17-year period. It is an empirical examination of meta-regulatory processes and outcomes (that is, regulation for self-regulation), with a focus on whether these performed according to the expectations of current regulatory theory. Specifically, my research examines how energy retailers were able to learn about stakeholder needs and the public interest in order to self-regulate within a meta-regulatory paradigm. This was motivated by my belief that theory that depends on significant industry self-regulation should be able to account for the capacity of a regulated industry to receive, interpret and act on the public interest signals through what is often a noisy environment.

I undertook this research as a personal project while working full time in the energy industry. It began in 1999 when I was a PhD candidate and working for the Victorian state regulator engaged in establishing the market and consumer protections for electricity retail competition. My PhD was about this process; my findings were that the public interest was unclear, politics was pervasive in regulatory policy and rule-making (and particularly where stakeholder views were incorporated in rule formation), industry was risk averse and not predictably rational, and regulatory and industry outcomes were unpredictable. Once I had completed my PhD in late 2002 I left the government and became a consultant to the energy and water sectors. From 2005 to the end of 2015 I worked for two energy businesses as a senior regulation and compliance professional.

I led a project for one energy business to improve the retail division's understanding and management of reputational risk. After considerable research and engagement with staff I was initially concerned that there was inadequate awareness and consideration of reputational risk in the organisational culture. I observed no deception or non-compliance but perceived a mismatch between what I believed the organisation should have valued, compared to what it seemed to value as revealed through its everyday actions. Importantly, there was a mismatch between the organisation's apparent rationality and that hypothesised in much of the academic literature. This finding also did not seem unique to my client; anecdotally it appeared to extend to other energy retailers and organisations in other industries.

Preface xiii

The more I spoke to people and considered the issues, the more I realised that the problem was not the rationality of the organisations I had observed but my own mistaken expectations about their values. What I observed was *not* ineffective behaviour or irrationality; it was instead a different and more subtle organisational rationality than I had expected. I was reminded of my own PhD findings and realised that my earlier research still had currency. In fact, I now had several more years of public data to take the arguments further. So I started to write this book.

It is worth addressing some potential issues straight away. First, it is possible that my employment within the industry may be considered by some as an impediment to independent research. However, I suggest that it can also be argued that my research allows an insider's explanation of how industry views others' efforts to steer it, and specifically how industry observes the messages communicated to it by stakeholders about appropriate organisational behaviour. Usually scholars' access to industry views on regulation are limited: surveys and interviews can provide insight but are likely to demonstrate how organisations want to see themselves and want to be seen rather than how they actually behave. They may also reflect a snapshot of one time and place, and the views of the individual rather than the broader culture or actual decision-makers. Even extended and embedded research is unlikely to penetrate the veil of how businesses really observe and think about regulation: many business staffers themselves are often not privy to how business decision-makers observe their environment, and business self-talk and actions do not regularly align. My own experience supported this; it was hard to get to the kernel of these matters even when directly employed by an organisation, engaged in the subjects, and asking targeted questions as an insider.

At the time of writing I would have participated in well over 2,000 hours of formal and informal discussion on the various issues with industry members (not including day-to-day business discussions with staff), regulatory and departmental staff at all levels, representatives from consumer organisations, consultants, government ministers and their advisors. This input provided a strong foundation for observing the whole regulatory environment and thus the 'toothpaste-tube-like' characteristics common to regulatory systems, where a squeeze in one place may cause a bulge in another (Hood, Rothstein and Baldwin, 2001: 15). These characteristics may have gone unnoticed in a different environment.

A second potential complication for this book is that it owes a heavy debt to a sociologist whose work is generally unpopular with English-speaking audiences for both its opaque style and apparently pessimistic conclusions. The writing of Niklas Luhmann resonated with me as a way of understanding the behaviour of those around me, and it is my interpretation of his systems theory that permeates much of the analysis here. My introduction to Luhmann was via Gunther Teubner's more normative take on Luhmann's work in the field of sociology of law, and Paterson and Teubner's (1998) article on regulation 'Changing maps: empirical legal autopoiesis'. These works were instrumental in giving me confidence to look more deeply into Luhmann's theory and apply it to my own observations when I was undertaking my PhD. As I started this book I then went on to read everything xiv *Preface*

I could find of Luhmann's writing in English, as well as analysis from Luhmann specialists. Luhmann's scholarship across law, politics, economics, protest organisations and the media provided the broad theoretical coverage I was seeking. His books *Risk: a sociological theory* (Luhmann, 2002) and *Ecological communication* (Luhmann, 1989) also provided practical explanations of how different systems view events, and these were invaluable in developing my own thoughts about similar topics. In this time I moved away from Teubner's normative reflexive law perspective and aligned myself with the more 'orthodox' Luhmann scholars who believe that Luhmann's theory was not intended to make the world a better place but instead improve sociological insight. Luhmann did not hold much hope for successful social planning, noting the contingency and unpredictability of outcomes within a complex society, and the presence of operationally closed societal sub-systems that reflect their own versions of reality:

> Luhmann's is a none-too-reassuring message, and one which flies in the face of all idealist utopian solutions to the world's problems. Politics and law, which, according to idealistically inclined commentators on the human predicament, should be working symbiotically and in tandem to solve the world's problems, are reflected in Luhmann's mirror as operating very much within their own frameworks upon a reality which they themselves have created. And these operations, far from embodying a spirit of co-operation and mutual understanding, all too often conflict with one another and limit each other's effectiveness.
>
> (King and Thornhill, 2003: 183)

This is difficult to accept and harder still to turn into positive regulatory prescriptions for the future. However, the empirical data from this research support Luhmann's premise and so should not be ignored. While I suggest improvements to regulatory practice to try and avoid the worst outcomes, my research does not aim to create better regulation in practice but *better regulatory theory that accounts for practice*. This is actually *not* pessimistic or hopeless; in contrast, I hold great hope that this research might benefit theorists and practitioners by providing the opportunity for a new conversation to begin.

References

Hood, C., Rothstein, H. and Baldwin, R. (2001) *The government of risk: understanding risk regulation regimes*, Oxford University Press: Oxford.

King, M., and Thornhill, C.J. (2003) *Niklas Luhmann's theory of politics and law*, Palgrave Macmillan: Basingstoke.

Luhmann, N. (1989) *Ecological communication*, trans. J. Bednarz, Jr., University of Chicago Press: Chicago.

Luhmann, N. (2002) *Risk: a sociological theory*, trans. R. Barrett, introduction: N. Stehr and G. Bechmann, Aldine Transaction: New Jersey.

Paterson, J. and Teubner, G. (1998) 'Changing maps: empirical legal autopoiesis', *Social and Legal Studies*, vol. 7, no. 4, pp. 451–486.

Acknowledgements

I have been fortunate to receive advice from senior scholars in each of the regulatory and the systems theory fields. My great thanks go to Robert Baldwin, Fiona Haines, Michael King, Hans-Georg Moeller and Mike Power for their reviews of early chapter drafts. Of course, all errors remain my own.

Michael King was particularly generous, reviewing my early chapters on Niklas Luhmann's systems theory in detail and helping me with my portrayal of Luhmann's work. Michael also invited me to a conference on Luhmann in September 2014, where I was able to talk with others about Luhmann's work for the first time. It was a wonderful experience, and the Luhmann scholars were very kind.

I acknowledge use of King and Thornhill's *Niklas Luhmann's theory of politics and law* (2003), Palgrave Macmillan, with permission of Palgrave Macmillan.

My family has been tolerant of this project beyond all reasonable expectations. Thank you for your patience and support, and your always helpful encouragement.

Abbreviations

ACCC	Australian Competition and Consumer Commission
AEMC	Australian Energy Market Commission
AER	Australian Energy Regulator
CALC	Consumer Action Law Centre
CIWG	Customer Issues Working Group
CMA	Competition and Markets Authority (UK)
CUAC	Consumer Utilities Advocacy Centre
EAL	Energy Assured Limited
ERAA	Energy Retailers Association of Australia
ESC	Essential Services Commission (Victoria)
ESCOSA	Essential Services Commission of South Australia
EWOV	Energy and Water Ombudsman of Victoria
FRC	Full retail competition
NECF	National Energy Customer Framework
NEM	National Electricity Market
QCA	Queensland Competition Authority
SECV	State Electricity Commission of Victoria

1   Introduction

Until the mid-1980s, the primary focus of regulatory theory and practice was on 'command and control' regulation, which refers to the prescriptive nature of the regulation (the command) supported by the imposition of some negative action by the regulator (the control) (Gunningham, 1998: 4). If adequately enforced, command and control regulation is dependable; it can specify operational parameters and regulatory obligations with clarity and immediacy (Gunningham, Sinclair and Grabosky, 1998; Baldwin and Cave, 1999). However, the command and control approach has been criticised on several fronts.

First, the informational requirements of regulators are very high under command and control regulation, creating problems with setting appropriate standards and calling into question the likely effectiveness of adequate enforcement (Gunningham, Sinclair and Grabosky, 1998; Baldwin and Cave, 1999). For a regulator to be fully informed about an industry and about regulated businesses' behaviour, it ideally has an ongoing relationship with regulated businesses and carries out regular inspections and audits. However, this leads to the second criticism of command and control regulation, which is that this need for a close relationship makes the regulator vulnerable to manipulation by the organisations it regulates. This argument is also the basis of theories about 'regulatory capture' as proposed by Stigler (1971), where regulation itself is seen as a commodity that is traded between industry and the regulator, and the regulator is manipulated by private interests to 'equate the public good with the interests of the industry it regulates' (Kay and Vickers, 1990: 232).

The third criticism of command and control regulation is that it can lead to an over-abundance of unnecessarily complex and inflexible regulation (Bardach and Kagan, 1982; Baldwin and Cave, 1999). The proliferation of such regulation can result in 'counterproductive regulatory overload' (Gunningham, Sinclair and Grabosky, 1998: 46). Finally, the legalistic style of command and control regulation can lead to a loss of trust between the regulator and the regulated business (Bardach and Kagan, 1982; Ayres and Braithwaite, 1992). Legalistic enforcement strategies destroy rather than build cooperation, where a business's disposition to comply can turn to resentment of the regulator and an organised culture of resistance (Bardach and Kagan, 1982; Gunningham, Sinclair and Grabosky, 1998).

2 *Introduction*

In response to these criticisms, the challenge for scholars and regulatory practitioners was to find a regulatory form that could deliver better public outcomes. The solution posed was to introduce a 'regulatory mix' of private and public actors to assist the regulator and regulated business (see Boyer and Meidinger, 1985; Gunningham, 1993, 1998). The vista was broadened to take in the 'regulatory space' (Hancher and Moran, 1989; Shearing, 1993), requiring regulators and regulated businesses to consider all parties with a stake in outcomes (that is, stakeholders)[1] and to focus on using their expertise to develop more responsive regulatory programmes. A key theme was harnessing the private interest for the public good through innovative regulatory techniques (see Bardach and Kagan, 1982; Grabosky, 1994a, 1994b; Gunningham, 1998; Braithwaite, 2000, 2008). This also meant engaging with markets. As Gunningham and Sinclair (1998: 409) wrote in relation to the field of environmental regulation:

> it is desirable to work with markets rather than against them. This is not to be interpreted as a retreat into 'free market environmentalism'. Rather, it is a recognition of the latent power of markets to change industry behaviour and the extent to which this potential influence remains unexploited. In many cases, harnessing the power of markets will, necessarily, be achieved through the vehicles of second and third parties rather than by direct government regulation.

In this vein, writers in the regulatory field emphasised *regulation for self-regulation*, where regulated industries are encouraged to police their own behaviour under the supervision of a regulator, potentially even consulting with stakeholders to write their own rules. The 'responsive' regulatory literature (in particular, Ayres and Braithwaite, 1992) was instrumental in embedding this idea within the academy, calling it 'enforced self-regulation'. Other scholars have since developed and explored related concepts, such as 'smart regulation' (Gunningham, Grabosky and Sinclair, 1998),[2] 'management-based regulation' (Coglianese and Lazer, 2003, 2006), 'regulatory capitalism' (Braithwaite, 2005, 2008) and 'process-oriented regulation' (Gilad, 2010).

'Meta-regulation' has been used to describe regulation for self-regulation in different ways. At its most basic, it relates to corporate self-audits and safety cases where businesses develop their own rules and reporting for the regulator to assess (Haines, 2006; Gunningham 2011). Consistent with the normative literature on responsive regulation and smart regulation, Christine Parker (2002, 2007) uses the term in a broader sense which explicitly prioritises the roles of third parties in industry learning and self-regulation. Parker's focus is how the corporation should and could be made permeable to external values and stakeholders via the principles of deliberative democracy. Quoting Morgan (1997: 40), Parker (2002: 214) describes the 'open corporation' as 'understood empirically and normatively as an "open system"', with a continuous cycle of input, internal transformation, output and feedback. For Parker, 'the group of stakeholders whose interests are considered by management should be made as broad

Introduction   3

as possible in order to make strategic corporate decision-making reflect the broader deliberative democracy as well as possible' (ibid.). The 'deliberative politics of social activism' (ibid.: 300) also has an important role in driving improved corporate behaviour, where social movements and consumer activists 'tend to be good at prompting commitment through publicity and shame' (ibid.: 212; see also Braithwaite and Drahos, 2000: 611; Braithwaite, 2008: 184, 198). Parker sees a business's desire to maintain a positive reputation (or at least avoid a negative one at the hands of activists) as a key source of motivation to meet social needs, which is a view shared by many writers in the regulatory field.

I also use the term 'meta-regulation' in this book. This is because the 'meta' neatly indicates the one step removed from direct command and control regulation that has evolved over recent decades. It also makes sense to respond to existing concepts rather than create new ones. I use the term in a similar way to Parker and others who see regulation for self-regulation as not only about regulatory flexibility and self-regulation but the need to account for third parties and the market in driving outcomes in the public interest. The characteristics of this version of meta-regulation are as follows:

i   Formal rules are based on principles, not prescription, to allow for the necessary flexibility in regulatory practice.

ii   Law (the regulator) is reflexive and responsive (although this means different things in the detail), in order to learn about what works to meet the public interest and to include relevant stakeholders in regulatory processes.[3] Meta-regulation is intended to relieve pressure on a regulator's resources by allowing the regulator to step back and observe self-regulation, taking investigative action only where a regulatory breach is identified.

iii Third parties such as non-government organisations and activists support regulation by acting as 'civil regulators', providing further relief for regulatory resources as well as reducing the chance of regulatory capture by industry. Third parties are involved in consultation for policy formation, to make sure that the right values are embedded in rules. They are also involved in enforcement, via monitoring and using business reputation in markets to force business self-reflection and culture change.

iv   Business self-regulates within the above context (and is also reflexive and responsive). In addition to the threat of formal regulatory penalties for breaches, reputational damage – and by extension, market losses – is a threat where businesses do not respond appropriately. Businesses are expected to be aware of this and accordingly incentivised to prevent breaches of their 'social licence'.

v   Transparency in business performance is promoted, specifically compliance and performance reporting (both self-reporting and regulatory reporting) to provide for third parties to have information to act upon under (iii) above and for industry self-reflection under (iv).

4   *Introduction*

The machinery of meta-regulation

Meta-regulation has been presented as progressive policy design that works effectively with markets and promotes stakeholder inclusion in order to reach a more informed view of the public interest and how the public interest can be met by business. The normative literature on meta-regulation implies that it is the best way to deal with highly complex regulatory problems.[4] This book challenges these claims. Meta-regulation may still be the best of the regulatory options available, but we need to examine the theory more closely. Meta-regulation in practice may not work as intended, and may actually trigger undesirable side-effects.

Others have also made the point that meta-regulation requires scrutiny; for example, Baldwin, Cave and Lodge (2010: 618) have questioned whether the newer regulatory forms have been adequately assessed in the past:

> for some time, the academy has exhibited a tendency to be too fascinated with the description of the latest initiatives and regulatory tools rather than an inclination to engage in critical analysis. Similarly, too much confidence has arguably been placed in so called 'alternative forms of regulation', so that there has been an over-playing of the potential problem-solving capacities of self-regulatory or market-based systems. In the search for the 'regulatory state beyond the state', important questions regarding the capacities of these systems to develop standards, to enforce them, and to gather robust information might have been investigated further.

This book addresses these questions, and in doing so it seeks to identify and bridge the gap between the normative case for meta-regulation and its effectiveness in practice. I look beneath the surface of the normative meta-regulatory language to reveal and test the underlying assumptions.

The primary assumption in the normative meta-regulatory literature relates to the inherent morality of the entities in the regulatory space. Morality is at the heart of meta-regulatory theory, with firms seen to require moral guidance,[5] and third parties and consumers through the market considered to be moral and good by definition. The assumption about the moral inclinations of entities in the regulatory space provides the foundation for a further assumption about the meta-regulatory process itself. The meta-regulatory process is to allow third parties and consumers to guide business towards a better morality; that is, to bring business behaviour into alignment with the public interest. Meta-regulation 'holds business organisations accountable for putting in place corporate conscience processes that are aimed at substantive social values' (Parker, 2007: 209). This seems to assume that meta-regulation can create consensus between different entities, whether through well-meaning communicative discourse or hard lessons learned by business as a result of reputational damage and consumer boycotts. Further, there are assumptions about the ways in which regulators and regulated businesses respond to the messages received through meta-regulation: these

Introduction 5

organisations are perceived to be predictably rational, acting in accordance with the tenets of the theory.

These assumptions tend to not be explicitly discussed in the literature; they are part of the normative hope for meta-regulatory outcomes and so their contingency in practice can be avoided. However, Parker (2013) provides an exception to this in her later writing. In describing Ayres and Braithwaite's responsive regulation theory (which I have included as part of the meta-regulatory literature in its tripartite version),[6] Parker (ibid.: 9) notes the difficulties in achieving optimal outcomes:

> responsive regulation assumes that there are enough regulators, regulated businesses, and third parties who are genuinely committed to the public interest, willing and able to communicate with one another to resolve problems, imaginative enough to come up with 'win–win' solutions to make it possible, and that they then have sufficient capacity and an appropriate substantively just law to enable them to implement those solutions. One sometimes wonders whether any sort of explicit 'regulatory' system would be needed at all if we lived in the sort of world where this was really possible on a regular basis. In pessimistic moments it barely seems possible at all, ever. To be more optimistic, the point is that responsive regulation, like all theories of just law and deliberative democracy, can only ever be incrementally and inchoately implemented in the real world.

Parker's rather circumspect appraisal of the likelihood of effective responsive regulation implicitly acknowledges the theory's underlying assumptions about consensus and rationality. She also identifies (at a high level) the moral dimension, where actors' good intentions provide the driving force for success. We can see this in her statements about the relevant entities being 'genuinely committed' and 'willing'. Even in this critical and reflective mode, Parker continues the normative regulatory theme that some progress through shared meaning would be possible if only actors were well-intentioned and tried hard enough (with support from the law), and, further, that observers of regulation would be in agreement about what this means.

The basic principles of meta-regulation have merit. It makes sense to identify that all regulation is ultimately *self*-regulation, and that businesses and regulators should be receptive to the needs of a broad stakeholder base. I also acknowledge Parker's statement above that the theory cannot translate fully into the real world. However, I consider that the meta-regulatory theory *itself* is underdeveloped relative to what it promises. The normative expectation of predictable shared meaning between diverse interests (that is also desirable from the meta-regulatory scholars' perspective) seems unlikely to regularly occur in practice, and for more complex reasons than those identified by Parker. There is a naïveté in the normative scholarly assumptions about organisational motives and dynamics (across all organisation types) which extends at times into a lofty salvationist and somewhat anti-corporate idealism. The literature also does not

6   *Introduction*

examine how markets work and provides no meaningful account for how market reputation is to be effective as a regulatory tool.[7] This is not helpful for practitioners seeking direction from the theory.[8]

Furthermore, it is unclear how we might test the effectiveness of meta-regulation. If a business was to internalise external values, this would, by definition, be recast by the business as a sensible corporate decision taken on the business's own terms. There is no way to prove it originated from external regulatory design. The examples of meta-regulation in the literature not only do not account for this but also tend not to cover outcomes at all: many scholars merely observe that some regimes have meta-regulatory characteristics, such as stakeholder inclusion and corporate self-regulatory reporting, and then assume this must be good. Given the ambitions of the theory, this would seem a low threshold to suggest an effective regulatory approach. Good policy intent or well managed public relations are not the same as meaningful meta-regulatory outcomes.

My argument in this book is that if the normative meta-regulatory theory is to be progressed, and particularly if it is to be useful to practitioners, scholarship must move beyond assumptions about the moral intent of those in the regulatory space and the apparent power of superior morality to transcend communicative barriers. We should instead focus on how meta-regulation might work practically, and how it might be observed to work, with an aim to create a more reflective and meaningful normative view. Effective meta-regulation seems to require unambiguous and direct communication between all relevant parties – via consultation, reporting, informal discussion, lobbying and market relationships – as well as via information intermediaries such as activists and the news media. Given this, the good intentions of entities in the regulatory space are *irrelevant* if communications cannot occur between the 'right' entities about the 'right' issues on the 'right' terms at the 'right' times. This machinery of meta-regulation is complex and requires examination. This is all the more so because the meta-regulatory theory itself introduced the complexity.

Observing the machinery of meta-regulation requires a more critical look at the meta-regulatory roles of all parties in the regulatory space. Questions include: What is the role for government? Who are the 'third parties' in meta-regulation and who and how do they influence? What do consumers and investors value and act upon in the market and how do they access information? To what degree can communications from various sources be relied upon as the 'truth' for any purpose? This is where the issues of assumed consensus and rationality come to life. There is also the temporal dimension of the relationships between entities: Do the various parties' perspectives on timeframes for necessary action align? What impact does this have on effecting change? This is particularly important where the intentions of businesses are more complicated: the threat of reputational damage as a means of keeping a business virtuous surely relies upon a shared and synchronous understanding of issues and risk.

I do not propose we remove morality from normative theory. I am not sure this would be possible in any event. I do propose that we move our attention

Introduction   7

away from the notion of corporate redemption and instead focus on communicative possibilities. Meta-regulation already gives us a way of considering regulated businesses (and regulators) without needing to use ambiguous value or moral categories about their intentions. The normative meta-regulatory narrative anticipates businesses to be *responsive* self-regulators, whether by acting 'responsibly' in the first place or by changing their behaviour in response to perceived reputational damage where they do not. (In contrast, a business that does not respond to its market or to a regulator will eventually find itself bankrupt or subject to legal penalty; attempts to regulate it will be useless.) Responsive businesses are receptive and responsive to communications about their behaviour – enabling such communications is the role for regulation. There is no need to further differentiate responsive businesses across the compliance intention spectrum between good and bad, at least not before we have grappled with whether the machinery of meta-regulation can work for *anyone*. The key question for meta-regulation is whether responsive businesses of all stripes have direct access to (and an ability to respond to) uncontroversial, clear and commercially meaningful directions from the multiple sources in their environment about how to meet the public interest.

I go on to argue that meta-regulation is not particularly effective at supporting responsive businesses in this task, and certainly not if we are depending on social responsibility and compliance decisions being driven by third party involvement and the market. I provide significant evidence that undisciplined third party stakeholder participation in contested policy areas leads to political outcomes that do not support organisational learning (for either the regulator or a regulated business) or compliance improvements. It creates uncertainty and business risk aversion rather than an atmosphere of positive innovation. Stakeholder contest over meaning also undermines the notion of reputation as a means of clear communication to a business about how to meet its 'social licence'. This is assuming consumers in the market even care enough to act on social or compliance issues, which is far from guaranteed.

These are not easy or appealing conclusions, and they run counter to the normative intent of meta-regulatory theory to date. Critics may reasonably respond by arguing that regulatory regimes across different industries and jurisdictions will exhibit a range of complexities and will have various degrees of success, and that we should not let this deter us from our normative aspirations. However, I do not believe that the argument 'but the theory is normative' is adequate for those seeking meaning and direction from theory. Normative assumptions should have some alignment with practice to be meaningful. It is my view that we should not let society's predictable complexities constitute an escape clause for a theory that perpetuates unobtainable regulatory objectives for the majority of situations. The quote from Parker above already identifies the low likelihood of meta-regulation in its current conception achieving its aspirations in practice. It is on this basis that I suggest a rethink of the theory.

8 *Introduction*

Luhmann's systems theory

The theoretical foundations for this book lie primarily with the German sociologist Niklas Luhmann (1927–1998) who wrote extensively on communicative systems. Luhmann's approach was strictly non-normative, and he had significant concerns about the notion of consensus and rationality bringing parties together to improve society. Luhmann's work is not well cited in English-speaking sociological circles,[9] and it also represents a departure from much of the established scholarship. For this reason, I will provide a brief summary before progressing any further.

Luhmann (1995, 1989, 2002b, 2013) describes the process of modernisation where modern society (the overall system) functionally differentiated into communicative sub-systems as it became more complex. Functional differentiation[10] for Luhmann is not a rational development based on design but a natural evolutionary outcome of increasing societal complexity. Function systems assist in the management of increased complexity in advanced societies by allowing issues to be dealt with in specialised ways. The reduction of complexity is the 'cosmology' of Luhmann's work (Borch, 2011: 7), where the function systems 'create order out of chaos' (King and Thornhill, 2003: 9) by giving meaning to events.

The function systems are communicative systems of meaning that are self-referencing and self-reproducing; their boundaries are marked by the application of particular binary codes that form a distinction between each system and its environment, and these codes and the programmes that underpin them provide for the ongoing self-reference and self-reproduction of each system. For the purposes of this book, the key systems are economics, which uses the binary code of payment/non-payment; politics, which uses the binary code of government/opposition; and law, which uses the binary code of legal/illegal or lawful/unlawful. Using law as an example, the basic code of legal/illegal needs to be activated for the legal system to observe an event in its environment as having meaning.

The function systems are cognitively open (they are able to adapt) but operationally closed (they are defined by their functions). This means that every system can observe events but no one system can truly control or steer another. A system's communications are produced within the system itself based on its function, and so while a system can observe an event in its environment, the system alone determines how it constructs its own reality and how it treats the event within its own communications. For example, a government can observe the economy, and may try to influence it, but it does this in terms of power and via the code of government/opposition. Political attempts to control the economy will in turn be observed and responded to within the economic system according to its code of payment/non-payment, which may create market outcomes that bear little relation to the desired outcomes of politicians. Market outcomes can then re-enter the political domain as a further problem to be 'solved' politically, but only if the 'solution' is viewed through a political lens given that systems cannot transcend their own boundaries and steer one another. Market outcomes

Introduction 9

may also enter the legal system if questions about legality of market behaviours are raised. Through this conceptualisation of systems and their differing perspectives on events and time (including risk), systems theory has been shown to be valuable in explaining complex, modern problems such as the global financial crisis of 2007–2008 (see Esposito, 2011; Moeller, 2012).

Luhmann also considers organisations as self-referencing and self-reproducing systems (influenced by the work of March and Simon, 1958; see Hasse, 2005: 254–255 for a discussion), where organisations reproduce their communications based on decisions (Luhmann, 2003). The boundaries of organisations are determined by membership: this distinguishes organisations from function systems, which are characterised by their functions. Organisations can communicate within any of the function systems but they often take on the functional primacy and binary coding of the systems, such as public agencies within the political system and corporations within the economic system:

> there is no disputing that, if not most, then at least the most important and largest organizations form within functional systems and therefore adopt the functional primacies of these systems. In this sense, we can distinguish between economic organizations, state organizations and other political organizations, school systems, science organizations, and organizations of the legislature and administration of justice.
>
> (Luhmann, 2013: 149)

Several elements of Luhmann's systems theory and its use in this book need to be clarified at this stage. First, the theory does not relate to individuals, a fact that has created concerns for some in the sociological community. Systems do not comprise people; rather, they relate to communications. I will not develop the issue further here other than to note that this research is also not about individuals, but organisations and the function systems of communication most used by these organisations.

Second, the theory is not about accessing reality but about observing observations. Each function system observes its environment as a *virtual reality*, through the application of meaning according to its code and programming. Different systems may have quite different perspectives on 'the environment' and their own performance within it; this is because each system essentially has its own virtual environment and self-image. Examples of the differences in perspective between systems include the self-image of politics as asserting control over society, when it actually has no primacy over other systems, and the self-image of science as presenting the 'truth', which may not be a perspective on science that is shared by the religious system (King and Thornhill, 2003: 10). Each function system also has a blind spot: although it 'sees' itself in its virtual world it cannot see that its own construction of reality (including its self-image) is merely a construct. As described by King and Thornhill (ibid.: 20): 'Through its operations the system repeatedly and continuously reaffirms its vision of the external world and its own situation within that constructed world, and so

10 *Introduction*

forever conceals the paradox of its own existence'. In this book I apply a similar concept to organisational systems, which is consistent with systems theory overall.

Third, I am not using Luhmann's theory in the same way as it has been used by certain legal sociologists. Gunther Teubner and John Paterson have together (Paterson and Teubner, 1998) and separately (see Teubner, 1983, 1985; Teubner, Nobles and Schiff, 2003; Paterson, 2006) built on Luhmann's systems theory to write about reflexive law and its capacity to better steer regulatory outcomes. Leading from this, Rogowksi (2013: 39) explicitly links his notion of reflexive law to Ayres and Braithwaite's (1992) responsive regulation, as well as to corporate social responsibility and Parker's (2007) meta-regulation (Rogowski, 2013: 252–253). However, Luhmann himself took issue with the notion of reflexive law as proposed by Teubner and others, responding that 'reflexive law could only be self-reflexive law' (Luhmann, 1992: 397), and stating further that 'the legal system simply does not get the opportunity to reflect upon legalization and delegalization. It is not asked' (ibid.: 404). He also responded to the issues in Luhmann (2002a), where again he made the point that any system steering is self-steering only. The debate continued later in a response from King (2006) to Paterson (2006), where King was sceptical that Luhmann's theory could be used in the way implied by Paterson, saying that Luhmann 'quite simply was not in the business of prescribing ways of improving the regulatory operations of law and politics' (King, 2006: 45). My use of Luhmann's theory is consistent with Luhmann's and King's perspective in the above citations, which is known in some Luhmannian circles as the 'orthodox' position.

Finally, and related to the previous point, Luhmann's approach is not about prescriptions for a better society; rather it reflects a radically new theoretical sociological programme that 'confronts humankind with the "sociological insult", the insight into the limits of social steering' (Moeller, 2012: 116). A key theme of Luhmann's is that of *contingency*, where everything can always be different (Luhmann, 2003: 37), which can also be applied to the use of the theory itself. Importantly, Luhmann rejects the notion of better, more rational ways to analyse (and so progress) society through beliefs and values, as described by King and Thornhill (2003: 3):

> Holding beliefs and values, and feeling the need to express them, may be necessary to convince ourselves and others of our humanity, our commitment to the well-being of others and our essential 'goodness', but, according to Luhmann, it has nothing at all to do with sociology or the analysis of *society*. More than that – when such beliefs and values become formulated as 'theories' they interfere with or block entirely access to sociological understanding for two reasons. Firstly, they rely upon an 'individualized', 'anthropocentric' or 'psychologized' notion of society by making it appear that satisfactory accounts of the causes of historical events are possible through explanations which focus upon individuals or groups of individuals, and seek to analyse their actions and their decisions by referring to their

Introduction 11

personalities, their motives, beliefs and values. In a similar vein, they often give the impression that the future may be brought under control through controlling or regulating people's personal beliefs and values, and inducing them to act in ways which are likely to lead to a better society than exists at present.

These themes are highly relevant to the discussion of the meta-regulatory literature above and are developed further through this research.

The Australian retail energy industry

The data I use to develop and support my case relate to the meta-regulatory programme for Australian retail energy markets from 1999 to 2015 inclusive. The policy foundation for the Australian energy markets was a package of microeconomic reforms in 1995 known as National Competition Policy. Part of the competition policy reform agenda was the creation of the National Electricity Market (NEM) which was intended to reduce barriers to trade in electricity across the inter-connected states of Victoria, South Australia, New South Wales, Queensland, the Australian Capital Territory and Tasmania (which was later linked to the mainland). The eastern Australian energy sector subsequently changed from a series of state monopolies to a largely privatised industry with competitive generation and retail functions. Electricity generation operates on a national level, where generation output is traded in the NEM via a spot market in electricity traded in half-hourly intervals. The spot price is determined by the balance between electrical load (demand) and available generating capacity for each half-hour. Electricity cannot be stored, so spot prices are extremely volatile; at the time of writing they could vary from –$1,000 to $13,800 (AUD) a megawatt hour (these are price constraints imposed by the market operator). Electricity retailing involves retailers competing against each other to bill consumers. The transport of electricity through the transmission network and distribution networks (the 'poles and wires') remains a regulated monopoly activity, with all retailers authorised to sell electricity having equal right of access.

This books focuses on the retail aspect of the supply chain. The electricity retailer is essentially the manager of risk on the behalf of its customers;[11] it is the interface between the consumer and the rest of the market. The retailer buys electricity from the market at the prevailing spot price (although traders make significant use of contracts that hedge spot price changes) and pays for use of the networks to be able to deliver supply to its customers. It then bills its customers and manages credit risk. Retail service offerings have evolved as the retail markets have developed, with many consumers receiving extra features packaged into the contract, tailored and dynamic prices and fees, and/or consumption information via internet portal access.

A key aspect of the electricity retail sector for this research is the generally accepted notion within the Australian industry and community that electricity is an *essential service* for small consumers. This means provision of electricity

12 *Introduction*

meets a basic public need, particularly for residential consumers. Gas supply has been through similar reforms and is considered an essential service in some Australian states. I use the term 'energy' in this book to refer to both fuels.

Regulation of the reformed energy industry began with new economic regulators in each Australian state and territory, where these operated independently from the state energy departments and supplemented the activities of the existing competition and consumer protection regulators. Economic regulation was first and foremost about regulating for the existence of markets and regulating the behaviour of parties in the market. In Victoria, one of the first Australian jurisdictions[12] to open its retail market, the economic regulator was called the Office of the Regulator-General and later rebadged in 2002 as the Essential Services Commission (ESC). This is where I worked from 1999 to 2002, when the ESC created the regulatory framework for competition in the retail electricity market. At the time of the shift to becoming the ESC in 2002, the ESC's objectives prioritised the protection of the long-term interests of Victorian consumers with regard to the price, quality and reliability of essential services, and the promotion of competitive market conduct. The ESC's legislative objectives changed in subsequent years but not so as to fundamentally alter this remit.[13]

The ESC implements its retail objectives under the legislation by issuing retail licences that require licence holders to comply with Codes and Guidelines in a variety of areas, such as billing, disconnection, marketing and use of consumer information. Importantly, the regime requires retailers to self-report compliance breaches and performance statistics, and to carry out formal self-audits. This group of requirements constitutes the consumer protection regime for energy retail – the focus for this book. Until 2012, the regulatory environment in most Australian jurisdictions reflected the Victorian ESC approach, albeit with some difference in the detail. From 2012, most jurisdictions then switched from state regulation to a similar national regulatory regime enforced by the Australian Energy Regulator (AER), which is discussed in this book.

Energy retail regulation (whether state or national) in the Australian competitive retail energy markets fulfils all the criteria for meta-regulation: it works with the market and is a principles and process-based approach overseen by independent regulators; it was developed (and continues to be modified) in consultation with key stakeholders; and energy retailers self-audit and provide regular compliance and performance data to the relevant regulator, who subsequently releases reports to the public. On face value, the regulation of the sector could be seen as an example of effective meta-regulation, as compliance has generally been high.

However, a more comprehensive assessment suggests that any claim of regulatory success in the retail energy market through a meta-regulatory approach is premature at the least, and most likely unfounded. Compliance problems may be minimal, but the regulation of the retail energy markets does not demonstrate achievement of the commonly accepted benchmarks for 'good' regulation, such as: low cost, unobtrusive methods; evidence-based decision-making; processes that are 'transparent, accessible, fair, and consistent'; and regimes that

Introduction 13

'encourage responsive and healthy markets where possible' (Baldwin, 2010: 262–263). The Australian retail energy regulatory environment has been uncertain, with legislation and regulation often modified or supplemented for political reasons. Competing and unresolved claims about the acceptability of compliance and performance outcomes continue. Although reported non-compliance has been low and self-regulatory and co-regulatory models have existed, these have not been central to any party's evaluation of the effectiveness of regulation, and anything other than strong and publicly demonstrated enforcement of breaches has not been acceptable to key stakeholders.

These outcomes at the least indicate that the meta-regulatory approach in the Australian energy markets needs to be better understood, which this book attempts to do. However, in doing this we face a problem: as discussed above, meta-regulation fundamentally lacks a conceptual framework against which to assess either its mechanisms or its success. Importantly, despite the significance of functioning markets in providing the context for meta-regulation, the meta-regulatory literature shows no consideration of the market conditions required to elicit the desired outcomes, other than a necessary presence of a range of stakeholders who can report on performance and potentially influence consumer transactions. These elements may not be enough, and we need to further examine the implicit assumptions that link markets to retailer self-regulation on standards. Australian energy retail markets are among the most competitive globally, with Victoria holding the title of the most competitive energy retail market in the world from 2005 to 2011 inclusive according to annual switching statistics (VaasaETT, 2012). In addition, competition in the Australian retail energy sector has been reported as higher than in other Australian industries such as telecommunications products, insurance, pay TV and superannuation (Simshauser and Laochumnanvanit, 2011). The retail energy sector is extremely sensitive to shifts in customer numbers, and the vast majority of consumers are customers of energy retailers. Brokers of reputational information are also active, such as consumer advocates and the media, with regular reportage of consumer energy issues. Despite all this, the role of the market in driving retailers' compliance and performance is questionable. If, in this environment, market forces cannot provide for measurably positive meta-regulatory effects, the assumptions about the capacity to harness the market via meta-regulation should be reassessed.

There are two important points that need to be drawn out at this stage. First, the industry I examine in this book is highly complex, with often competing public interest goals. Many scholarly studies to date have focused on environmental regulation or occupational health and safety regulation, where harms are clearly defined and there is some shared understanding about ultimate objectives, if not operational practices. In energy consumer protection the harm to be avoided is less clear and is regularly debated by stakeholders with conflicting world views. The public interest goals relating to the environment (energy conservation and full cost-reflectivity, including the cost of carbon) often conflict with social objectives (guaranteed access and bill affordability for an essential service). Environmental and social objectives often conflict with economic

14 *Introduction*

objectives (efficient competitive market outcomes, which require profits and flexibility for market participants). The regulators discussed in this book are economic regulators and are regularly expected to trade off public interest objectives, particularly the social and economic. This book thus provides a new perspective, allowing an examination of the contest over regulatory objectives and consideration of the flow-on effects of conflict and uncertainty for industry self-regulation.

Second, this book is not about how the policymakers and regulatory practitioners may have understood (or misunderstood) academic theory and applied it. Rather, this book offers a critique of meta-regulatory theory, based on practice. Australian retail energy regulation had many of the characteristics espoused by the group of perspectives I have called meta-regulatory theory. How practice came into being is addressed to some degree in the early chapters but the overall point is that regardless of its policy origins, this book demonstrates how meta-regulation in a complex environment performed over time. If we *are* to consider how policymakers interpreted theory, I observed very few regulatory policymakers who appeared to be familiar with academic regulatory theory, including during my time working for a regulator. In the later years, there was some limited evidence that regulators were familiar with Ayres and Braithwaite's (1992) enforcement pyramid (for example, ESC, 2012: 17 which references the increasing penalties only), but this was the extent to which theory attracted attention. This means that the likelihood of practice being built on the prescriptions of academic regulatory theory was low, and any similarity related more to broader societal forces that the theory and practice mutually observed, such as market liberalisation and management fads. Regulatory practice was also contingent in any event: although this book addresses programmes of consultation and stakeholder inclusion as per meta-regulatory theory, these developed naturally and could just as easily not have happened. In fact, as described in Chapter 3, consultation in Victoria occurred despite the political environment not supporting it, and this practice was not repeated in the other Australian state opening a market at the same time.

The structure of this book

Chapter 2 describes in more detail what I have characterised as the meta-regulatory literature. Specifically, it discusses the challenges inherent in the normative approach which assumes that a consensus on values and the public interest can be effected through meta-regulation, and assumes a predictable rationality on the part of both the regulator and those regulated. This chapter concludes with the finding that these conditions are unlikely to be met, citing substantive research that supports this perspective. Chapter 2 also includes a description of the Luhmannian perspective used throughout the book.

Chapter 3 describes the development of the competitive market in Victoria, Australia's leading state for energy retail competition. This chapter explores the behaviour of the energy industry and other stakeholders from late 1999 to 2002.

Introduction 15

This exploration is based on my experience at the regulator's office and data I collected for my PhD. Chapter 3 shows that the industry was ill-placed to establish the rules for the market, despite this being a core expectation of policymakers. Retailers had no clear sense of their own objectives, let alone the objectives of the market, and their governance role was not supported by prominent consumer advocates who saw the industry as necessarily compromised. In the end, the regulator had to take control to ensure that the market did open, albeit with delay. The approach taken by the regulator was meta-regulatory: it depended on principles over prescription, process over outcomes, stakeholder participation in rule-making, and industry self-reporting on compliance breaches and performance measures. Chapter 3 also shows that the state government intervened in the market when this was politically expedient.

Chapter 4 provides an overview of, and case studies for, 13 years of retail energy policy, 2003 to 2015 inclusive. This chapter shows that the tensions and issues that were present when the market was being established in Victoria continued across the years and presented in other Australian jurisdictions as they developed their energy markets. The industry was in a state of flux for much of this time, building to a crescendo in 2012 when multiple energy policy changes left retailers deeply uncertain about the markets and their value. The meta-regulatory principles-based approach left conflict unresolved: politics was ever-present, and key stakeholder perspectives of industry compliance were largely informed by subjective views of performance through anecdotal tales rather than by objective assessments of compliance with the rules as they were written. A theme of Chapter 4 is the interventionist and fundamentally unpredictable behaviour of various governments and the effect this had on the regulatory framework and energy stakeholders. The industry seemed unable to understand which of its decisions were ultimately political and which were not, resulting in poor outcomes for all.

Chapters 5 and 6 examine in depth the most contentious aspects of the market and policy environment: bill affordability and energy marketing methods. The affordability and hardship debates in Chapter 5 were about regulation as a means of reducing harm to vulnerable people who could not afford to pay their energy bills, putting into effect the principle that disconnection of supply should only be a last resort. Most of the discussion in Chapter 5 relates to one period: Victoria from 2004 to 2006. However, the consumer hardship debates from this time replayed to various degrees across all states for the entire research period and continue to do so. This chapter shows that there was no consensus on what constituted compliance. The industry and regulator were cast as poor performers despite industry compliance being found to be high, and the government used a narrative of regulator mismanagement to pursue new (and technically unnecessary) legislation to bolster its political reputation for action. The industry did not receive clear messages from stakeholders about appropriate actions to support the public interest and many stakeholders seemed to require industry action that was uncommercial to a material degree. Industry co-regulation and self-regulation were not supported by stakeholder talk or behaviour.

16 *Introduction*

Chapter 6 discusses the state of competition itself and the means by which consumers engaged with the market. Conflict was present at all levels of the discussions on competition, including fundamental disagreement about whether competition was actually effective, what constituted appropriate sales tactics, and the expectations of consumer cognitive capacity. Chapter 6 also explores the experience of co-regulation and self-regulation for door-to-door sales, which was a particularly vexed issue for the industry and its stakeholders. The industry took years to take a proactive stance on door-to-door sales despite long-standing negative views from consumer advocates, and eventual retailer self-regulatory actions in this space were more related to threats from government and the competition regulator than from lobbying by consumer advocates. However, even when a new industry self-regulatory scheme was developed, it was actively discouraged by leading consumer advocate groups, who saw the only valid rule enforcement as being public actions by regulators.

Chapter 7 concludes the book by arguing that meta-regulatory theory needs to be revised if it is to be practically useful. Most notably a number of the underlying assumptions need adjustment. Meta-regulation in practice appears to be most challenged in a complex and contested environment; the very environment it is supposed to serve best. This is because conflict between stakeholders creates problems for governments and regulators, who then act politically in order to be seen to be 'doing something'. This undermines the intent of responsive regulation, creates uncertainty for businesses, and further feeds the cycle of political behaviour from stakeholders who see that lobbying reaps results. Stakeholder contest over meaning also complicates the value of reputation as a market regulatory mechanism. Although the reputation mechanism relies on stakeholder passion about contested issues, this same element has the added, contradictory effect of undermining the mechanism because the strong, plural views of stakeholders do not provide clear messages to consumers or investors. Further, the ambitions of normative meta-regulatory theory need to be checked; externally adjusting corporate morality to something other than basic economic value seems unlikely, and cannot be measured in practice. The best we can look for is behaviour that is compliant, which in most environments should be good enough.

Notes

1 I use the term 'stakeholder' in this book to potentially mean any party in the regulatory space. This is because I am observing and writing about the stakeholders of policy processes and outcomes.

2 'Smart regulation' has been presented as picking the right regulatory approach from a range of options, which may include command and control. While this may be true to some degree, the argument made in Gunningham, Grabosky and Sinclair's (1998) book *Smart regulation* is that the regulatory burden on government can and ideally should be reduced, and that 'recruiting a range of regulatory actors to implement complementary combinations of policy instruments, tailored to specific environmental goals and circumstances, will provide more effective and efficient policy outcomes' (Gunningham, 1998: 15; see also Gunningham, 2011: 211).

Introduction 17

3 Parker's version of meta-regulation does not necessarily have a place for the state: it can be regulation of self-regulation via any party. However, she identifies an important meta-regulatory role for the law to 'connect the private capacity and practice of corporate self-regulation to public dialogue and justice' (Parker, 2002: 289). Where businesses cannot be relied upon to adequately engage with stakeholders, the regulator should facilitate stakeholder inclusion and debate through identifying 'legitimate stakeholders for particular issues', guaranteeing them access and information, brokering opportunities for engagement and contestation, and providing sanctions and enforcement to 'back up the informal regulatory tools available to stakeholders' (ibid.: 300–301, see also pp. 40, 225). Further, the regulator holds businesses accountable and supports 'triple loop learning' to require companies to 'evaluate and report on their own self-regulation strategies so that the regulator can determine whether the ultimate substantive objectives of regulation are being met' (ibid.: 245). See also Parker (2007) for her views on how law can meta-regulate for business social conscience.

4 Coglianese and Mendelson (2010: 163) specifically state this may be the case, although they also note that meta-regulation and self-regulation may be 'much less than ideal' (ibid.: 153), also a theme of this book.

5 Business is considered necessarily compromised, whether it is because profit motives are viewed as detrimental to the public interest, or because business is just not seen as aligned with what society values.

6 The best known component of responsive regulation is the enforcement pyramid involving the regulator and regulated organisation and a 'tit for tat' strategy between the two parties (Ayres and Braithwaite, 1992). My reference to the tripartite version is to account for the often neglected element of the theory that includes third parties and the market. Braithwaite has also built on this element since the original theory was published, further developing and explicitly incorporating principles of restorative justice (Braithwaite, 2008).

7 It is interesting that consumer behaviour via the market is initially considered inadequate for regulatory purposes (which is why we need meta-regulation), but then seen as a powerful tool to 'harness the market' in the public interest. This seems to come back to third party morality and communications: the difference in market effectiveness under meta-regulation is due to the presence of consumer activists to provide information to consumers about what is right and good.

8 I note later in this chapter that energy policymakers and regulatory practitioners were not particularly aware of academic theory. This may be a reflection of this particular industry and so I leave the hope open that regulatory practitioners will reflect upon and seek direction from academic theory.

9 Luhmann's oeuvre is large, and only a fraction of his writing has been translated into English. The breadth and depth of his analysis is also impressive, with its origins across a number of diverse areas, including biology, sociology, organisational theory, philosophy and logic. His ambition was to create a grand theory of everything (Moeller, 2012: 12), which he completed with his two-volume work *The theory of society* (Luhmann, 2012, 2013). In my own explanation of Luhmann's writing I do not go into the detail of the theory's origins or even use many of the terms that those familiar with Luhmann might expect, such as *autopoiesis*. This is because this book is already complex and I am trying to make Luhmann's core concepts accessible for those who may be unfamiliar with his work. For readers who would like to discover more about Luhmann's theory I recommend his books *Risk* (Luhmann, 2002b), and *Ecological communication* (Luhmann, 1989). I also recommend the books about Luhmann and his work written by King and Thornhill (2003, 2006), Moeller (2006, 2012), Borch (2011) and Seidl and Becker (2005).

10 Note that Luhmann's concept of functional differentiation is not the same as that of other sociologists such as Durkheim and Weber. Luhmann refers to functional

18 *Introduction*

differentiation according to *meaning* where other functional analysis is about the organisation of labour or social action (King and Thornhill, 2003: 11).

11 I use the terms 'consumer' and 'customer' in this book, with 'consumer' generally referring to any consumer of services, and 'customer' to denote the transactional relationship a consumer has with its retailer.

12 This is the generic term used for the Australian states and territories.

13 At the time of writing, the objective had been changed for the ESC to *promote* the long-term interests of Victorian consumers, having regard to the price, quality and reliability of essential services. Market competition had been relegated to a matter the ESC was to 'have regard to'.

References

Ayres, I. and Braithwaite, J. (1992) *Responsive regulation: transcending the deregulation debate*, Oxford University Press: Oxford.

Baldwin, R. (1995) *Rules and government*, Clarendon Press: Oxford.

Baldwin, R. (2010) 'Better regulation: the search and struggle', in R. Baldwin, M. Cave and M. Lodge (eds) *The Oxford handbook of regulation*, Oxford University Press: Oxford, pp. 259–278.

Baldwin, R. and Cave, M. (1999) *Understanding regulation: theory, strategy and practice*, Oxford University Press: Oxford.

Baldwin, R., Cave, M. and Lodge, M. (2010) 'The future of regulation', in R. Baldwin, M. Cave and M. Lodge (eds) *The Oxford handbook of regulation*, Oxford University Press: Oxford, pp. 614–626.

Bardach, E. and Kagan, R.A. (1982) *Going by the book: the politics of regulatory unreasonableness*, Temple University Press: Philadelphia.

Borch, C. (2011) *Niklas Luhmann*, Routledge: Abingdon.

Boyer, B. and Meidinger, E. (1985) 'Privatizing regulatory enforcement: a preliminary assessment of citizen suits under federal environmental laws', *Buffalo Law Review*, vol. 34, pp. 833–964.

Braithwaite, J. (2000) 'The new regulatory state and the transformation of criminology', *British Journal of Criminology*, vol. 40, pp. 222–238.

Braithwaite, J. (2005) *Meta-regulation of justice*, RegNet Occasional Paper 4, September, Australian National University: Canberra.

Braithwaite, J. (2008) *Regulatory capitalism: how it works, ideas for making it work better*, Edward Elgar Publishing: Cheltenham.

Braithwaite, J. and Drahos, P. (2000) *Global business regulation*, Cambridge University Press: Cambridge.

Coglianese, C. and Lazer, D. (2003) 'Management-based regulation: prescribing private management to achieve public goals', *Law and Society Review*, vol. 37, pp. 691–730.

Coglianese, C. and Lazer, D. (eds) (2006) *Leveraging the private sector: management-based strategies for improving environmental performance*, Resources for the Future: Washington.

Coglianese, C. and Mendelson, E. (2010) 'Meta-regulation and self-regulation', in R. Baldwin, M. Cave and M. Lodge (eds) *The Oxford handbook of regulation*, Oxford University Press: Oxford, pp. 146–168.

ESC (Essential Services Commission) (2012) *Compliance policy statement for Victorian energy businesses*, January, C/11/25490, Melbourne.

Esposito, E. (2011) *The future of futures: the time of money in financing and society*, Edward Elgar: Cheltenham.

Gilad, S. (2010) 'It runs in the family: meta-regulation and its siblings', *Regulation and Governance*, vol. 4, issue 4, pp. 485–506.

Grabosky, P.N. (1994a) 'Beyond the regulatory state', *The Australian and New Zealand Journal of Criminology*, vol. 27, pp. 192–197.

Grabosky, P.N. (1994b) 'Green markets: environmental regulation by the private sector', *Law and Policy*, vol. 16, no. 4, October, pp. 419–448.

Gunningham, N. (1993) 'Thinking about regulatory mix – regulating occupational health and safety futures markets and environmental law', in P. Grabosky and J. Braithwaite (eds) *Business regulation and Australia's future*, Australian Institute of Criminology: Canberra, pp. 133–150.

Gunningham, N. (1998) 'Introduction', in N. Gunningham, P. Grabosky and D. Sinclair (eds) *Smart regulation: designing environmental policy*, Clarendon Press: Oxford, pp. 3–36.

Gunningham, N. (2011) 'Strategizing compliance and enforcement: responsive regulation and beyond', in C. Parker and V. Lehmann Nielsen (eds) *Explaining compliance: business responses to regulation*, Edward Elgar: Cheltenham, pp. 199–221.

Gunningham, N. and Sinclair, D. (1998) 'Designing Environmental Policy', in N. Gunningham, P. Grabosky and D. Sinclair (eds) *Smart regulation: designing environmental policy*, Clarendon Press: Oxford, pp. 375–453.

Gunningham, N., Grabosky, P. and Sinclair, D. (eds) (1998) *Smart regulation: designing environmental policy*, Clarendon Press: Oxford.

Gunningham, N., Sinclair, D. and Grabosky, P. (1998) 'Instruments for environmental protection', in N. Gunningham, P. Grabosky and D. Sinclair (eds) *Smart regulation: designing environmental policy*, Clarendon Press: Oxford, pp. 37–92.

Haines, F. (2006) *Regulatory failures and regulatory solutions: a characteristic analysis of meta-regulation*, Proceedings, Annual Meeting, Law and Society Association.

Hancher, L. and Moran, M. (1989) 'Organizing regulatory space', in L. Hancher and M. Moran (eds) *Capitalism, culture and economic regulation*, Clarendon Press: Oxford, pp. 271–300.

Hasse, R. (2005) 'Luhmann's systems theory and the new institutionalism', in D. Seidl and K.H. Becker (eds) *Niklas Luhmann and organization studies*, Advances in Organization Studies, Volume 14, Liber: Copenhagen, pp. 248–261.

Kay, J. and Vickers, J. (1990) 'Regulatory reform: an appraisal', in G. Majone (ed.) *Deregulation or re-regulation? Regulatory reform in Europe and the United States*, Pinter Publishers: London, pp. 223–251.

King, M. (2006) 'What's the use of Luhmann's theory?', in M. King and C.J. Thornhill (eds) *Luhmann on law and politics*, Oñati International Series in Law and Society, Hart Publishing: Oxford, pp. 37–52.

King, M. and Thornhill, C.J. (2003) *Niklas Luhmann's theory of politics and law*, Palgrave Macmillan: Basingstoke.

King, M., and Thornhill, C.J. (2006) (eds) *Luhmann on law and politics*, Oñati International Series in Law and Society, Hart Publishing: Oxford.

Luhmann, N. (1989) *Ecological communication*, trans. J. Bednarz, Jr., University of Chicago Press: Chicago.

Luhmann, N. (1992) 'Some problems with reflexive law', in G. Teuber and A. Febbrajo (eds) *State, law and economy: regulation and autonomy in a new perspective*, Giuffrè: Milan, pp. 389–415.

Luhmann, N. (1995) *Social systems*, trans. J. Bednarz and D. Baecker, Stanford University Press: California.

20 Introduction

Luhmann, N. (2002a) 'Limits of steering', in C. Calhoun, J. Gerteis, J. Moody, S. Pfaff and I. Virk (eds) *Contemporary sociological theory*, Blackwell Publishing: Malden, pp. 139–152.

Luhmann, N. (2002b) *Risk: a sociological theory*, trans. R. Barrett, Introduction: N. Stehr and G. Bechmann, Aldine Transaction: New Jersey.

Luhmann, N. (2003) 'Organization', in T. Bakken and T. Hernes (eds) *Autopoietic organization theory*, Abstrakt Forlag: Oslo, pp. 31–52.

Luhmann, N. (2012) *Theory of society: volume 1*, trans. R. Barrett, Stanford University Press: Stanford.

Luhmann, N. (2013) *Theory of society: volume 2*, trans. R. Barrett, Stanford University Press: Stanford.

March, J.G. and Simon, H.A. (1958) *Organizations*, John Wiley & Sons: New York.

Moeller, H.-G. (2006) *Luhmann explained: from souls to systems*, Open Court: Illinois.

Moeller, H.-G. (2012) *The radical Luhmann*, Columbia University Press: New York.

Morgan, G. (1997) *Images of organization*, Sage Publications: Thousand Oaks.

Parker, C. (2002) *The open corporation: effective self-regulation and democracy*, Cambridge University Press: Cambridge.

Parker, C. (2007) 'Meta-regulation: legal accountability for corporate social responsibility', in D. McBarnet, A. Voiculescu and T. Campbell (eds) *The new corporate accountability: corporate social responsibility and the law*, Cambridge University Press: Cambridge, pp. 207–237.

Parker, C. (2013) 'Twenty years of responsive regulation: an appreciation and appraisal', *Regulation and Governance*, vol. 7, issue 1, March, pp. 12–13.

Paterson, J. (2006) 'Reflecting on reflexive law', in M. King and C. Thornhill (eds), *Luhmann on law and politics*, Oñati International Series in Law and Society, Hart Publishing: Oxford, pp. 13–35.

Paterson, J. and Teubner, G. (1998) 'Changing maps: empirical legal autopoiesis', *Social and Legal Studies*, vol. 7, no. 4, pp. 451–486.

Rogowski, R. (2013) *Reflexive labour law in the world society*, Edward Elgar: Cheltenham.

Seidl, D. and Becker, K.H. (eds) (2005) *Niklas Luhmann and organization studies*, Advances in Organization Studies, Volume 14, Liber: Copenhagen.

Shearing, C. (1993) 'A constitutive conception of regulation', in P. Grabosky and J. Braithwaite (eds) *Business regulation and Australia's future*, Australian Institute of Criminology: Canberra, pp. 67–80.

Simshauser, P. and Laochumnanvanit, K. (2011) *The price-suppression domino effect and the political economy of regulating retail electricity prices in a rising cost environment*, AGL Applied Economic and Policy Research Working Paper No. 20 – Domino Effect.

Stigler, G.J. (1971) 'The theory of economic regulation', *Bell Journal of Economics and Management Science*, vol. 2, Spring, pp. 3–21.

Teubner, G. (1983) 'Substantive and reflexive elements in modern law', *Law and Society Review*, vol. 17, pp. 239–285.

Teubner, G. (1985) 'After legal instrumentalism? Strategic models of post regulatory law', in G. Teubner (ed.) *Dilemmas of law in the welfare state*, Berlin: De Gruyter, pp. 299–325.

Teubner, G., Nobles, R. and Schiff, D. (2005) 'The autonomy of law: an introduction to legal autopoiesis', in J. Penner, D. Schiff and R. Nobles (eds) *Jurisprudence and legal theory*, Oxford University Press: Oxford, pp. 897–954.

VaasaETT (2012) *World energy retail market rankings report 2012*.

2 The implicit assumptions underpinning normative meta-regulatory theory

Meta-regulatory theory evolved contemporaneously with – and was most likely related to – developments in other policy areas. The meta-regulatory acceptance of, and reliance upon, markets and self-regulation was consistent with 1990s' policy reforms in advanced countries that sought to reduce the role of the state and make better use of market forces (see Osborne and Gaebler, 1992). The concept of third party inclusion in business decision-making is also consistent with the growth of the consumer and environmental movements over recent decades, as well as developments in the corporate social responsibility and business literatures to value and prioritise stakeholder needs (Hoffman, 2001; Vogel, 2005; Freeman, Harrison and Wicks, 2007; Carroll, 2008; Aras and Crowther, 2010).

Despite the appeal of using markets and stakeholder participation in regulation, there is little evidence of the success of meta-regulation in practice. At the least, the global financial crisis of 2007–2008 causes us to question how well economic experts understood the markets they relied upon (Black, 2012, 2013). Empirical studies of meta-regulation have mainly focused on the versions of meta-regulation that do not explicitly include external stakeholders; that is, the regulator and regulated organisation are the sole occupants of the regulatory space. Results of these studies have shown mixed outcomes (Haines, 2009a; Coglianese and Mendelson, 2010; Gilad, 2010; Gunningham, 2011; Black, 2012). This is not surprising because meta-regulation as regulatory oversight of self-regulation with no further stakeholder involvement is likely to demonstrate some of the information asymmetry problems of command and control regulation. Where there have been studies of external stakeholder involvement in meta-regulation, these have often assessed global voluntary codes of conduct and certification schemes. The effectiveness of these schemes has been varied, with the question remaining unanswered about what 'effective' itself means (Meidinger, 2008; Vogel, 2010). However, certification schemes are considered to show value given the lack of state regulatory alternatives.[1]

There are few studies of external stakeholder involvement or influence that might directly inform meta-regulatory scholarship where there is an existing government regulatory regime, which is the version of meta-regulation used in this book. The main examples of this type of study include Nielsen and Parker's

22 *Assumptions underpinning normative theory*

(2008) survey of 999 Australian businesses to see how concerned they were about various third party perceptions of their compliance with trade practices regulation. Although it was found that survey respondents 'worried a lot' about third party perceptions, this worry did not tend to translate into their business operations in practice. Similarly, Hutter and Jones (2007: 40) assessed the influence of third parties on risk management practices in the UK food retail sector, finding that surveyed businesses were 'well aware that there are multiple external influences on their internal risk management practices'. Nonetheless, although their main focus was on maintaining a good business reputation in the competitive market, respondents reported that the influence of activists and the media on business practices was low, and consumer boycotts were not considered a material risk. This was despite activist campaigns against genetically modified food running at the time of the research.

Gunningham, Kagan and Thornton's (2003) study of pulp manufacturing mills is one of the most instructive in the regulatory literature, assessing corporate compliance attitudes toward, and responses to, the business's legal (actual) licence, 'economic licence' and 'social licence'. A key finding was that social licence pressures positively affected corporate compliance attitudes. However, this appeared to be most driven by the mills' host communities protesting against observable pollution: as 'large and ill-smelling' entities, pulp mills loom large in the environment; they draw attention from local residents by being 'industrial elephants' with nowhere to hide (ibid.: 52). This is a specific and localised version of social licence effects. It is not necessarily applicable to circumstances where businesses do not as obviously cause undesirable outcomes and so may require third party intermediaries to make corporate behaviour transparent to relevant stakeholders. It also does not directly relate to the concept of social licence as a business's social acceptance by 'society' that can be affected, and even withdrawn, through consumer responses through mass markets (that is, markets with a broad customer base and mass appeal), which is the way the normative meta-regulatory literature appears to view markets.

In summary, the meta-regulatory means of enlisting third parties and markets to drive business compliance in regulated industries does not seem defined or well-tested in the literature. The roles, responsibilities and capabilities of third parties such as social activists have not been addressed in detail in either the meta-regulatory theory or in empirical studies. An analysis of the form and nature of market responses to social messaging appears entirely absent from regulatory scholarship. Further, where there has been an assessment of business views of third parties and markets, this has tended to rely upon potentially inconsistent[2] self-reporting by (ultimately) self-selected business staff on what is relevant to them at a point in time.

It is important to note that most, if not all, of the regulatory studies to date – including those that consider external factors – focus on corporate morality in self-regulation. These studies seek to identify good and bad business practice, and whether businesses are genuinely committed to compliance. For example, studies have focused on the motivations of regulated businesses to comply with

Assumptions underpinning normative theory 23

regulation (Parker and Lehmann Nielsen, 2011),[3] employees' ethical values (Tyler, 2011) and businesses' managerial styles (Gunningham *et al.*, 2003). These have been found to be more important than other factors, including the compliance system employed by a business (Gunningham *et al.*, 2003; Gilad, 2010; Gunningham, 2011; Parker and Gilad, 2011). The regulatory task has then been to discover and explore what factors influence and shape compliance motivations (Kagan, Gunningham and Thornton, 2011), what makes businesses go 'beyond compliance' (Howard-Grenville, Nash and Coglianese, 2008; Borck and Coglianese, 2011), and how regulatory design can force effective self-regulation (Parker, 2002; Parker and Lehmann Nielsen, 2011).

This scholarly focus on business commitment to compliance and improvement is logical given the shift towards greater business self-regulation in recent decades. Unlike command and control regulation – which assumes that businesses are rational actors who comply with rules if punished severely enough for breaches – self-regulation is 'based upon the activation of internal motivations' (Tyler, 2011: 79). Ayres and Braithwaite's (1992) responsive regulation enforcement pyramid relies on and encourages virtuous behaviour from regulated businesses, where 'ethics and morality are assumed to matter most' (Simpson and Rorie, 2011: 70, see also Haines, 1997; Parker, 2006). Gunningham (2011: 201) notes that research suggests: 'a compliance strategy may be valuable in encouraging and facilitating those willing to comply with the law to do so, but may prove disastrous against "rational actors" who are not disposed to voluntary compliance'.

It is clear that the scholarly focus on business values is essential, and will remain so while assessments of the regulatory space are limited to observing a regulator and a largely self-regulating business. However, this is not the same as the regulatory space under the broader version of meta-regulation examined in this book. A business's pre-existing moral commitment to compliance is only one part of this meta-regulatory picture. In this version of meta-regulation, the business's *environment* – particularly the values and behaviour of its range of stakeholders, including consumers and other transactional stakeholders through the market – is expected to create in the business a desire to self-regulate in the public interest. This was of course the purpose of including third parties and markets in the first place; they were to act as 'surrogates' for at least some aspects of formal enforcement (Gunningham, 2011: 199).

Accordingly, my book takes a different approach from most of the regulatory scholarship to date. Rather than focusing on the internal motivations and reported statements of regulated businesses, this book is a long-term examination of the environment of an industry and how it influenced industry behaviour. Based on my insider's experience, I address how business learning as hoped for by normative meta-regulatory scholars worked in practice. This is an active shift away from the usual moral stance to instead address the *machinery of meta-regulation*, where we consider the perspectives and communications of each of the key organisational entities in the regulatory space, including taking a closer look at how markets work. The everyday experience of meta-regulation – ideally

24 *Assumptions underpinning normative theory*

for all stakeholders of the regulatory process but at least for regulated organisations – needs to be illuminated and contextualised, with a deeper exploration of communicative possibilities in practice, including how meaning is constructed.

I believe that moral categories can effectively be discarded if we assume that businesses are responsive to their environment in both good and bad ways. Under the normative conceptualisation of meta-regulation even the bad guys are expected to become responsible when faced with financial losses from reputational damage. I also believe that we *should* discard moral categories in the investigation of the machinery of meta-regulation, at least as we grapple with the detail of the machinery for the first time. In particular, the apparently unquestioned normative meta-regulatory stereotype of the 'good' activist educating the 'bad'[4] or uninformed business on what is 'right' may be attractive to some,[5] but it blinds us to the complexity of society and of organisations, as well as masking the actual capacity of meta-regulation to bring diverse perspectives together. To suggest a move away from moral judgements in the first instance is not to suggest a descent into complete moral relativism, but to instead suggest that the capacities and perspectives of all parties (including their self-image and perceptions of others) in the regulatory space are more complex than has been assumed. It does no justice to any party to have their point of view simplified to 'good' or 'bad' by outside observers and it certainly does not promote open sociological analysis. This chapter explores some of the reasons why this is the case.

The research programme I am suggesting is clearly ambitious, and is probably not possible in its most complete sense. An observer of social phenomena will always bring their own moral perspective and they will always be limited by their own cognitive and research constraints. My own attempt at a broader analysis of a regulated industry's environment is not immune from these limitations. However, as will be shown, the findings in this book are still sufficient to cause a rethink for normative meta-regulatory aspirations.

Before proceeding, I should note that although the focus of this book is the regulatory literature, the elements of meta-regulation outlined in Chapter 1 (and the unpromising research outcomes) are consistent with scholarship in the fields of reflexive governance and corporate social responsibility.[6] Each field considers increased stakeholder inclusion in policy and business decisions to improve public interest outcomes, particularly where the state has a reduced role in policy-setting and regulation. Reflexive governance is broader in concept than the subject of corporate regulation but shares with meta-regulatory theory the principle of stakeholder inclusion to create learning institutions;[7] it is 'about the organisation of recursive feedback relations between distributed steering activities' (Voss, Bauknecht and Kemp, 2006: xvi). While definitions of corporate social responsibility vary in the detail (see Carroll, 2008), the literature in this area is about businesses going beyond their legal obligations[8] and shareholder responsibilities to take into account the needs of a broader stakeholder base. The study of reputation within the corporate social responsibility field is also highly relevant to meta-regulation, as will be discussed later in this chapter. Overall, these fields of study can be characterised as being about the *empowerment of*

Assumptions underpinning normative theory 25

stakeholders in the development and implementation of reflexive organisational self-regulatory processes oriented toward meeting substantive objectives; that is, for our purposes, corporate behaviour in line with the public interest. It is in this sense that I refer to the normative meta-regulatory literature throughout this book.

I will now address some of the key assumptions underpinning meta-regulatory theory so that we can better understand the normative case in the detail. These relate to the assumed conditions in place for effective meta-regulation, and are:

i   a consensus of values between governments, regulators, third party advocates and activists, and ultimately regulated businesses that can be effected through meta-regulation; and

ii   predictable (classical) rationality of regulators and regulated businesses.

These conditions are rarely discussed in the meta-regulatory literature; in contrast, they tend to be assumed or glossed over. However, there is enough evidence to date to cast doubt on these conditions being in place, or occurring as expected, and as such they deserve specific attention.

Consensus on values and the public interest

We can see that the concept of involving multiple parties in regulation *anticipates* different perspectives, and thus does *not* start from a position of consensus. If everyone had the same values and beliefs then by definition there would be no need to bring any additional parties into the regulatory space. However, the meta-regulatory process itself is then assumed to provide for stakeholder consensus about the substantive objectives – the public interest – to be served by regulation (and ultimately business), through a version of communicative rationality in the Habermasian (1981) sense.[9]

This notion of an objective public interest is open to challenge: scholars have noted that the concept of the public interest is highly contested, and perhaps even impossible to meet in an objective sense (see Holzer, 2010). For example, Hood (1991) argues that the state is subject to competing values which he conceptualises as sigma-type, theta-type and lambda-type values and these have competing 'currencies' of success and failure. The 'sigma' family of values relates to *efficiency* and *parsimony*, the 'theta' family relates to *honesty* and *fairness*, and the 'lambda' family relates to *security* and *resilience*. Given these fundamentally incompatible principles, Hood states that these core values probably could not be satisfied by any one organising principle for administrative design. The notion of conflicting values that cannot be reconciled is not a new one: in his sociological writings on power and the rationality of actors, Weber (1964) argued that differences between values could never be debated rationally and often could not be understood on anything other than a purely intellectual basis.

Although many meta-regulatory theorists also acknowledge the difficulty in achieving consensus, they still presume that further discourse of the right kind

26 Assumptions underpinning normative theory

can overcome the problem of accommodating plural perspectives in public and corporate policy (see Parker, 2002, 2013; Voss *et al.*, 2006; Bernstein and Cashore, 2007; De Schutter and Lenoble, 2010). Deliberative democracy as a concept has also been subtly enlisted by the normative meta-regulatory theorists as a tool for corporate conversion to external values rather than mutual accommodation. For example, although Parker's (2002) version of deliberative democracy allows for conflicts in values, this is ultimately about managing the *corporation's* permeability to *other* values. When combined with Parker's view that social activism is a valid form of indirect corporate regulation through activists inflicting reputational damage when they do not agree with corporate behaviour, it is hard to see how this approach is to provide for acceptable outcomes unless the corporation changes its own values to align with those of its stakeholders (or the most vocal stakeholders).

It is worth examining the relationships that normative meta-regulatory theory implicitly assumes to be in place between the various parties in the regulatory space, and how the parties' interests align with the public interest. Technically, the most complete way of showing these relationships diagrammatically might be a spider web of lines connecting all parties to one another, with direct inputs and outputs (Braithwaite's (2008: 201) 'webs of control'). This is because ideally there are relationships between all parties, with information flowing in both directions in order to facilitate participation and regulatory and business learning. Figure 2.1 instead shows a simple version of these relationships, focusing only on key entities in the regulatory space (and so leaving out other stakeholders such as business partners and consultants) and only at a high level (leaving out parties such as employees). Crucially, and consistent with the

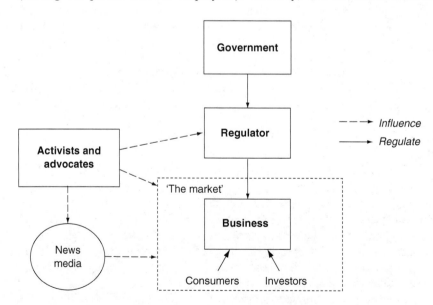

Figure 2.1 Inputs to business self-regulation under meta-regulation.

Assumptions underpinning normative theory 27

underlying theme of a business being permeable to external values, Figure 2.1 shows only inputs, demonstrating what the normative meta-regulatory theory anticipates as inputs to a business's decision-making in order for it to regulate its behaviour in the public interest. Each input is assumed by the theory to reflect the public interest.

As shown in Figure 2.1, the government provides the foundation for the regulator to act but otherwise does not have a role. The regulator then directly regulates the business, and the business is also 'regulated' by consumers and investors through the market. Third parties such as consumer or environmental activists stand to the side, but are seen to have a fundamentally positive role both in influencing rule setting and in enforcement. Rule setting occurs via consultation with the regulator and/or the business. Enforcement occurs either through direct input to these entities or via the reputation mechanism in the market, which is more likely to involve use of the mass media (the news media in particular) to seek to enlist consumers and perhaps investors to change their purchasing or investment decisions to favour or boycott the business.

These relationships are discussed further below. Figure 2.1 also provides a map to this chapter, with the entities' titles in bold corresponding to the sections where these are discussed. It should be noted that my aim is not to describe the ways that the various parties make mistakes or may choose to act against the public interest – such a catalogue would be interesting but beside the point for this analysis. My aim is instead to draw out the theoretical and practical issues with assuming that these groups *necessarily* reflect the public interest in particular ways, or can be made to do so.

The government is a silent enabler of the public interest

Other than elements of the corporate social responsibility scholarship that question the capacity and interest of governments to direct and enforce regulation (particularly in developing nations and for transnational issues), the meta-regulatory literature appears to assume that government does not have separate involvement in rule-making. For some meta-regulatory writers, government has a role to 'shape market orderings and to facilitate the constructive activities of non-governmental institutions' (Grabosky, Gunningham and Sinclair, 1998: 124). Otherwise the literature tends to be silent on the role of government, expecting that governments' and regulators' interests are the same.

Exceptions to this perspective can be found in Baldwin (1995), Hood, Rothstein and Baldwin (2001), and Haines (2009a, 2011). Haines (2011) draws out the differences in actuarial risk, socio-cultural risk and political risk, the contradictions often found in trying to manage all three with one approach, and the importance of political support for regulation. Other regulatory theorists have acknowledged the presence of government in regulation, with the recognition that regulation is 'embedded in the practices of the interventionist state' (Hancher and Moran, 1989: 272), and that the political support available to a regulatory body 'is never beyond question' (Baldwin, 1995: 170). Baldwin

28   *Assumptions underpinning normative theory*

(ibid.: 14) notes that governments may use rules for all the 'right' technical reasons, but may also use rules to suit their own political interests, such as giving the appearance of taking positive action, or as a means to make it more difficult than otherwise to challenge policies. There have been calls to accept the state within the regulatory environment, and bring the role of government out into the open (Baldwin, 1995; Haines, 1997), where 'openness about the politics of rule-making would allow issues to be anticipated or responded to rather than ignored' (Baldwin, 1995: 173).

Niklas Luhmann's systems theory accounts for political decision-making and provides a useful theoretical framework for the data in this research. Luhmann introduces us to the concept of the political function system, which is a constantly self-reproducing system of communication that recognises communications as political where they are concerned with power. In democracies the political system takes the form of a distinction between government and opposition. Politics for Luhmann is about much more than the traditional notion of 'the state'; and it is not really about the state at all:

> Politics is all political parties and every sort of political lobby; all information in the press, on the radio, or television that is politically selected as positive or negative; every intentional or careless unofficial statement by upper echelon officials or politicians; many types of intrigue; being seen and not being seen on certain occasions; promoting or not promoting political careers; and naturally the political election with everything that it reputedly or actually influences.
>
> (Luhmann, 2002: 161–162)

According to Luhmann, the function of politics is the production of collectively binding decisions, much of which is then handed to the legal system as law. Politics presents itself as a system of societal control (Luhmann, 2002: 173); its self-image is one of putting things in order (Luhmann, 1989: 85) which it does through the application of power. According to its own self-image, politics is superior and ubiquitous. However, if one is to observe the political system from outside its boundaries this not the case: politics is not superior to the other systems and its ambitions for societal control cannot be fulfilled. Politics is one system among many, and political decisions do not have any special power to steer other systems through transcending their own coding or otherwise determining their communicative processes.

Luhmann describes politics as being further divided into politicians, administration and public opinion. The political administration allows politicians to unburden themselves from the minutiae of political decision-making, and public opinion is the means by which politics observes its performance in its environment (generally through the mass media). Notably, Luhmann has a particular perspective on political legitimacy: for him legitimacy is not located outside politics as something to be bestowed on the political system, it is a symbolic resource generated by the system itself. Legitimacy is 'simply the formula which

Assumptions underpinning normative theory 29

the political system produces for itself in order to underwrite and give value and plausibility to its operations – so that it might effectively present its "activity as the furthering of interests"' (King and Thornhill, 2003: 73). Legitimacy comes from the politicians, not the administration; this frees the administration so that it may focus on its own tasks.

Luhmann notes the challenges faced by the political system in managing conflicting objectives, particularly given the need for politics to show it is in control while this cannot be so (it has no primacy over the other societal systems). This means that governments often have to employ double talk and hypocrisy to handle situations 'when what is said cannot be done and when what is done cannot be talked about' (Brunsson, 2003a: 214; see also Brunsson, 2003b). The use of the term 'hypocrisy' as used by Brunsson (and referenced by Luhmann) is not a moral judgement but has a particular meaning: it is the necessary reaction of a political organisation to manage conflict between inconsistent norms and present the illusion of conflict resolution in order to take action in some form. This is not an abstract theoretical notion: the hypocritical elements of political decision-making and the way that politics uses the media to make announcements about doing something in a 'post-truth' world (Oborne, 2005: 6) have been the subject of extensive commentary and analysis based on empirical observation and experience (see Edelman, 1988, 2001; Salter, 2007; Hood, 2011). Lindsay Tanner (2010: 105), former Australian federal Labor finance minister, writes in his book *Sideshow*:

> All political behaviour is now governed by the need to look like you're doing something. As long as the appearance of activity is presented, it doesn't really matter if anything is being achieved.

This concept provides the foundation for much of the discussion in the chapters to come and will be described in greater detail using the data.

The regulator's values and actions represent the public interest

Normative meta-regulatory theory presumes that the actions of the regulator[10] reflect the public interest.[11] This is the case almost by definition given the theory is normative, and thus about how things *should be*, and relates to the topic of regulation. The only regulatory failures seen by normative meta-regulatory theory in the achievement of optimal outcomes arise from the natural cognitive limitations for a regulatory agency struggling to come to terms with a complex industry. It is, of course, these limitations that led theorists away from command and control regulation and towards meta-regulation in the first place. The self-regulatory aspect of meta-regulation is a response to complexity in the regulatory environment and the impossibility of the regulator being able to actively monitor the activities of regulated parties.

Under meta-regulation the regulator instead focuses on steering and observing self-regulation, and is able to identify what does and does not work. It also

30 *Assumptions underpinning normative theory*

facilitates stakeholder involvement in rule-making and enforcement as required. The responsive and reflexive regulatory aspects of normative meta-regulatory theory in particular see the law as cognitively open and thus able to learn about, represent and support changing societal norms. This assumes that law through the regulator is capable of picking the stakeholders and the issues that matter, managing outcomes and then embedding learning about agreed values within a logical legal framework (see Parker, 2002, 2008).

Clearly, a regulator operating in alignment with normative meta-regulatory theory has a complex stakeholder management task that extends well beyond past expectations under command and control. Despite this, the normative meta-regulatory theory does not examine the philosophical or practical effects of its doctrines on the regulator and it does not investigate the nature of the regulator's own legitimacy.[12] There is a presumption of legal values in regulation that is not questioned, and while political factors are sometimes recognised[13] their effect on the regulator is not addressed.

It is my contention that the vagueness about the role and capacity of the regulator under meta-regulation is a key deficiency of the theory and warrants attention. This vagueness leaves empirical outcomes entirely open to interpretation based on the normative yearnings of the observer. It will always be easy to point to compliance successes as support for the theory and failures as faults of the regulator or its charter. Sociologists confronting unexpected regulatory outcomes in their data are left with no explanation other than the world is complex and so is regulation.

Systems theory provides a possible framework to understand messy regulatory outcomes: its conception of function systems gives us a means of understanding the role of law, and thus what should be our reasonable (and even aspirational) expectations of it. In Luhmann's systems theory, the legal system uses the binary code legal/illegal to distinguish what is and what is not amenable to law's operations and to give meaning to events. The function of law in society is to stabilise normative expectations over time. This provides for society to 'take precaution against conflict and to provide for stable expectations in the case of disappointment' (Luhmann, 1989: 65):

> A norm stabilizes expectations, also and in particular where conduct is unexpected. Where norms are violated, it is not the expectation but the conduct that is wrong. Although one can have erred in respect of the facts, one has not done so on the normative side of expectation. In other words, the violation of the norm offers no occasion for amending it, no occasion for learning; it condenses and confirms expectations in providing an occasion to activate and confirm it.
>
> (Luhmann, 2002: 54)

This means that the law is not goal oriented: its programme is 'fixed in the future-perfect tense' (Luhmann, 1989: 66), which allows events to happen and to then be treated by law accordingly ('if this has happened then that will happen').

Assumptions underpinning normative theory 31

Law is no more able to steer society than any other function system: it sets the terms for what will be considered lawful, which may (but not necessarily) be accepted by other systems using their own way of observing and making sense of the world.

A systems theory understanding of law does not support law as being an open, learning system as anticipated by normative meta-regulatory theory. In contrast, if law is to effectively set stable expectations about societal norms it *cannot* be highly sensitive to change. This is one reason why regulators are not necessarily in a position to create reflexive or responsive law. A further, and arguably more important, reason is that according to my reading of systems theory, regulators are organisations that primarily reference the political system, not the legal system, at least when acting in a meta-regulatory capacity. This also aligns with the rather optimistic meta-regulatory desire to have regulators act as inclusive facilitators of stakeholder engagement, which is surely more political than legal behaviour (also noted by Haines, 2009b). If regulators are indeed fundamentally political, this bodes well for regulatory learning and change, but only as a political process, not a process of evolving substantive law in the public interest (unless this is valued by politics at the time, but this is contingent and as viewed through a political lens). This book investigates how the Australian retail energy regulators met law's function of stabilising societal norms.

Third party advocates and activists represent the public interest

Meta-regulation supports and seeks to enable the regulatory involvement of third parties in the regulated business–regulator relationship,[14] viewing this as positive by definition. The normative meta-regulatory literature considers that parties such as activists, advocates and other socially or environmentally focused non-government (not-for-profit) organisations[15] are effectively gatekeepers for moral or ethical outcomes – that is, outcomes in the public interest. At its most ideal, meta-regulation provides for businesses to undergo a moral conversion through communication with these third parties. This concept is understandable from a normative perspective, as it is the best way to provide for genuine *ex ante* rather than *ex post* self-regulation, and so harm may be avoided rather than having to occur and then be responded to. However, the apparent assumptions underpinning this are questionable. The notion of activists providing to business a means of access to morality and the public interest has been challenged by scholars who point out that no party has a monopoly on morality or an automatic right to participate in corporate decision-making (see Henderson, 2001; Bob, 2005). While this is acknowledged to some degree by some in the meta-regulatory area (see Conley and Williams, 2005; Wheeler, 2008) it has not been sufficiently developed. This creates a practical problem for businesses that are expected through discourse with stakeholders to arrive at the 'right' or ethical answer.

As stated earlier in this chapter, my objective is not to document all the failures of various parties to reflect the public interest. However, it is useful to

32 *Assumptions underpinning normative theory*

illustrate the difficulties associated with assuming that the actions and communications of third parties such as activists reflect a clear public interest. Reich (2008: 183) provides several examples of actions taken by American activists against businesses which demonstrate the complexity of the issue. These examples include when conservative religious group Focus on the Family urged consumers to boycott Proctor and Gamble products because of the company's support for a Cincinnati ordinance forbidding discrimination against homosexuals. There was also the case where the Action League of Chicago called for a boycott of Mattel's products because Mattel had supplied funding to a programme for disadvantaged girls that provided advice on issues such as pregnancy prevention. Reich also discusses the threats of the National Rifle Association to 'run hundreds of billboards casting oil giant ConocoPhillips as an enemy of gun owners' (ibid.). The NRA did this because ConocoPhillips had joined a federal lawsuit to block an Oklahoma law allowing employees to take guns to their worksites.

It is easy for us as a regulatory community to recognise that deaths at work and environmental devastation are harmful and that it is ethical corporate behaviour to not effect these harms. The more prosaic examples such as those discussed by Reich bring further challenge and ambiguity to businesses trying to follow a moral compass in a pluralistic society. Which parts of civil society should businesses listen to, and on what issues?[16] This is taken to its logical conclusion in a statement made to corporate social responsibility advocate Simon Zadek (2007: 185), where a manager from a British water utility is reported to have said:

> As a water utility we are a major landowner. We have been approached by representatives from the anti-hunting league and asked to stop renting out a parcel of land for use by sports-hunters. To be honest, we don't have a corporate view on hunting, and do not particularly want to have one. Where does all of this end? If there is a church but no mosque on our land, will we eventually have to have a view on God?

One of the most quoted cases of activism and consumer action being said to positively change corporate behaviour is the 1995 Brent Spar case involving Shell and Greenpeace, where Greenpeace activists occupied the Brent Spar oil storage facility in the North Sea as part of a campaign to stop the decommissioned facility from being disposed of at sea. There was significant media on the issue, with the story told as a battle between Greenpeace's David and Shell's Goliath, and Shell cast as an uncaring environmental polluter. The meta-regulatory take on the Brent Spar case is that Shell learned from this (and from another public relations disaster in Nigeria the same year) that it needed to improve its approach to public consultation and public messaging (for example, see Parker, 2002: 165). However, the issues were actually much more complex and I do not agree that it was simply a matter of Shell needing to learn how to better manage risk and understand community values. Given the extent to which this example has been quoted and the body of research that supports the case, I will address the Brent

Assumptions underpinning normative theory 33

Spar case in some depth. This case exemplified 'language games' (Livesey, 2001) that left no party unscarred:

> the 'scientific debate' about the Spar was not a rational argument about what is or is not known, but instead was a confused and fruitless series of exchanges mostly based on misinformation and misunderstandings.
>
> (Rice and Owen, 1999: 43)

Each side of the debate used their version of science to pursue their case regarding the Brent Spar, but Greenpeace made much better use of the media to deliver a rhetoric that turned Shell into a 'modern terrorist' (Livesey, 2001: 70; also Holzer, 2010: 21). Shell was slow to respond to the claims of Greenpeace, and when it did respond its statements were technocratic, defensive and managerial. The absence of useful sound bites made Shell's perspective difficult for the media to pick up (Bakir, 2005). The battle was waged in the media for some weeks, culminating in harmful boycotts on Shell petrol stations in Germany (and two attacks: gunshots in one case and petrol bombs in the other) (Rice and Owen, 1999: 92–93). Greenpeace also made further claims that the Spar contained 50 times more oil than Shell had advised – claims that later proved to be wrong. Some in the television media also subsequently admitted that they had given preferential treatment to Greenpeace during the occupation and had felt 'exploited and embarrassed' by Greenpeace (ibid.: 109). The Brent Spar case raises the issue of how a corporation could get things right under these circumstances, and why its being held to ransom by parties with a specific agenda and misguided accusations was necessarily in the public interest. What even was the public interest? The final studies found that onshore and offshore disposal options presented around the same degree of environmental harm, but onshore disposal was estimated as six times more dangerous for operational staff (ibid.: 100). On this basis, offshore disposal remained the better option in the sense of the net public interest (if such a thing existed).

Perhaps the public interest was served by having the approval processes and science better understood in the end, which is an argument made by Rice (a deep-sea scientist) and Owen (1999) despite their clear concerns about the scientific misrepresentation and politics employed. This is, however, not the same as the meta-regulatory perspective of this case as demonstrating that corporate self-regulation might be improved from stakeholder participation. We need to consider the counterfactual: if Shell had approached Greenpeace from the start to discuss its plans for the Brent Spar, what substantive differences to the outcome would have been likely? I suggest that this action may have muted the initial outrage but not changed the outcome because it seems that the only acceptable outcome for Greenpeace was Shell not disposing of the Spar offshore (a view supported by Rice and Owen, 1999: 139, 147). And yet, taking on Greenpeace's preferred option would have gone against the scientific environmental studies at the time. We might also consider the potential for further damage from onshore processing that was present but not realised: what if Shell

34 *Assumptions underpinning normative theory*

employees had been hurt in the process of bringing the Spar onshore? As an environmental pressure group Greenpeace might not have been concerned about this, but Shell had a responsibility to its people that it could not ignore. If there had been human casualties from the onshore option, how might the business management and meta-regulatory literature have recast this tale of David and Goliath?

Clearly, the public interest in disposing of the Brent Spar was not a matter for negotiation and communicative discourse; rather it constituted 'a forum of competition for public attention' (Holzer, 2010: 21). This is not to say that Shell could not have done a better job of managing the issue and its stakeholders, and it certainly went on a path to conversion as a good corporate citizen afterwards, complete with glossy brochures and breathless public relations statements and reports (see Henderson, 2001). But to view this highly complex and contested case study as evidence that Shell just needed to regulate itself better and listen to third parties to come to an improved outcome is a very limited perspective. It also does not account for the way that stories like this frame the need for business to listen to third parties as a veiled threat rather than as an opportunity: 'in stark contrast to normative theories, stakeholders are a managerial "dread factor" and an explicitly recognized source of risk to the enterprise and its reputation' (Power, 2007: 137).

Systems theory is again useful as a means of describing and explaining the dynamics at play for cases such as the Brent Spar, and particularly the role of the media. Luhmann writes about protest movements, which are not organisations 'because they do not organize decisions but motives, commitments, ties' (Luhmann, 2013: 155), but can be populated by organisations, such as Greenpeace. Protest movements pick an issue and stick with it, rejecting situations 'in which one could become the victim of the risky behaviour of others' (Luhmann, 2002: 136). Protests invoke ethical principles; they are communications addressed to others calling on their sense of responsibility, particularly the political system (Luhmann, 2013: 159). Protesters do not attempt to take the place of or understand those they protest against; they do not have to unless as a means of developing protest tactics (Luhmann, 2002, 2013). This should be considered against the normative meta-regulatory theory that sees consensus as possible from rational debate with those in the protest movement. Protest groups' lack of desire to share ownership of outcomes has also been noted by others, such as Zadek (2007: 22), who writes about when he proposed to UN conference attendees that advocacy organisations ('civil society' organisations) be given decision-making rights and responsibilities:

> The feedback from the assembled civil society leaders was clear and to the point. As one participant explained, 'Our role is to lobby, to influence, to shape thinking. These roles would be compromised by your proposals for us to have a place at the decision-making table'. In proposing that civil society organizations should have greater power, this and others [sic] participants agreed, I clearly did not fully appreciate the importance of protecting ... their role.

Assumptions underpinning normative theory   35

None of this is to say that protest is bad; this is not my personal belief nor the argument I am mounting. Luhmann also suggests that protest fulfils a necessary role to provide an alternative view of society. The argument here is that *the nature of protest is not oriented towards resolving conflict.* Further, there is no natural means of identifying who from among protest movements should participate in decisions. Complex and risky issues have a large range of parties affected by decision-making and unknown further future parties who may be found to be affected only in hindsight (Luhmann, 2002: 110).

The attempt to inject values and morality via protest is also problematic according to Luhmann, who in his discussion on values establishes that they are unlikely to be agreed. The code for morality is 'good'/'bad', and is seen to validate esteem or contempt (Luhmann, 1989). However the terms 'good' and 'bad' are not open to discussion and do not require justification: 'Everybody can choose the programme that favours their own interests and opinions, while despising those who do not adhere to the same programme' (Müller, 2006: 179). According to Luhmann, protest organisations are not inherently virtuous: 'there is nothing to suggest that protest movements know [the environment] better or can judge it more correctly than other systems of society' (Luhmann, 2013: 165). What is good and what is bad is entirely in the eyes of the observer and not always a matter for agreement.

Moving on to the delivery of communications, the Brent Spar example shows the importance of the mass media in how protest movements articulate their cause and seek public attention. Luhmann (2000) considers the mass media as also a recursive and self-reproducing societal communication sub-system, and one particularly used by protest movements. The mass media's code is information/non-information and its operations process new information into non-information using this code:

> Information cannot be repeated; as soon as it becomes an event it becomes non-information. A news item run twice may still have its sense, but it loses its information value. If information is used as a code, this means that the operations in the system are constantly and inevitably transforming information into non-information.
>
> (Luhmann, 2000: 19–20, as translated by Moeller, 2006: 127)

The function of the mass media according to Luhmann is to provide society with a continuous production of descriptions of social reality, which also functions as a form of societal memory (Moeller, 2006). Note that this is not about truth, despite this being part of the self-image of the mass media system. The mass media system selects carefully for its construction of reality, showing a variety of opinions, commentary and versions of issues, and maintaining plural perspectives. It has the ability to constantly recycle an issue already reported (thus turned into non-information) back into 'information' via a new perspective. The mass media system functions via the medium of public opinion, which also plays a role in the political system; the political system uses the mass media

36　*Assumptions underpinning normative theory*

observation of public opinion to observe its performance. Political parties compete to be viewed favourably and so observe the mass media system's representation of issues and public opinion in order to further their political communications to meet their own needs.

The mass media make use of moralising talk, particularly on the basis of scandal, which is always newsworthy: 'The way morality is imagined and its ongoing renovation is linked to sufficiently spectacular cases – when scoundrels, victims, and heroes who have gone beyond the call of duty are presented to us' (Luhmann, 2000: 31). Further, when presented via the mass media, norms are inherently valid and unquestioned, 'almost as though the meaning of the norm was vouched for by sacred powers' (Luhmann, 2008: 33). Luhmann explains further, also referencing the Brent Spar case:

> Communication about ecological problems is a particularly good example for our purposes, because it goes far beyond the individual's world of experience. (Who could say from their own knowledge what would have happened to the contents of the Brent Spar platform, given the pressure operating on the sea bed, if it had been sunk?) The mass media too are unequal to the task, and when they turn to science, they will typically be given more knowledge and more ignorance at the same time. So, we are dependent upon schema formation. It might be normative sentences which are set against a 'virtual reality' and are very typically fashioned metaphorically. For example, the ocean should not be used as a rubbish dump. This is self-evident, so to speak. If one asks further, more scripts are brought to bear.
>
> (Luhmann, 2000: 110–111)

In conclusion, there is cause to question whether activist and other non-government organisations are in a position to signal to industry how it may achieve objectively 'better' outcomes in the public interest, whether this signalling is direct or via the media (and market, which links to reputation as discussed below). The examples provided by Reich demonstrate the problem of identifying one position as somehow more moral or virtuous than another. Further, despite the self-image of the news media as sources of the 'truth', they should not be assumed to provide an adequate perspective on events given their self-selection of issues to report (which will depend on decisions taken within the mass media system), their dependence on scandal, their need to constantly generate new opinions and information, and their own reliance on the information and moral tales as provided to them.

The private corporate interest can be aligned with the public interest

The normative meta-regulatory literature assumes that regulatory design can align a business's private interest with the public interest. The normative belief remains that businesses *should* be made to transcend the short-term pursuit of

Assumptions underpinning normative theory   37

their shareholders' financial needs in order to account for broader social factors. The most idealistic versions of meta-regulation aim for 're-positioning companies as integral social partners from whom good "corporate citizenship" is expected' (Corkin, 2008: 39; see also Waddock and McIntosh, 2009). The less idealistic (and more common) versions appeal to businesses to see corporate social responsibility as positively contributing to the bottom line – this is the 'win–win' school of thought. The literature using this second theme claims that efforts to genuinely engage with stakeholders on their needs will ultimately be in the commercial interests of the business (see Orlitzky, 2008 for a full discussion of the issues). This relies on the notion of political or ethical consumerism, which translates 'political objectives into consumption choices' (Holzer, 2010: 65; also Micheletti, 2003). At its heart is a threat of reputational damage through the media if a business's social or environmental performance does not match activist stakeholder expectations, where consumers will then respond via their purchasing decisions (such as boycotts) to inflict financial loss on the offending organisation. We saw this situation play out in the Greenpeace campaign against Shell.

Despite the apparent importance of the threat of reputational damage as a regulatory tool, the meta-regulatory literature provides no direction about how it might be *relied upon* to work, nor how businesses might actually interpret their environment and construct meaning (see Edelman and Talesh, 2011). Normative meta-regulatory scholars (and recall that this group includes writers on corporate social responsibility) quote from a set of familiar case studies (including the Brent Spar) and then simply assume reputation has an objective value that can generally be used to keep companies in check. Closely related to the corporate social responsibility literature, the strategic management literature on reputation[17] takes this further, claiming reputation to be an essential intangible asset for every business to protect. Referring to the ubiquitous Brent Spar case, Power (2007: 131) notes 'The experiences of Shell and other documented cases have come to be part of a reputational dramatology' where 'the sites for this drama are conferences, surveys and prescriptive texts, and a growing body of advisors exploit reputational concerns to reposition their services as a form of risk management'. In some cases, the claims of those in the reputation management movement reflect unsubstantiated and wishful thinking that is closely related to what we see in the normative meta-regulatory literature, which makes sense given the obvious overlap in topic. It is also probably because both the corporate social responsibility and the reputation management literatures cannot seem to clarify general definitions of terms or means of identifying value (see Crane, McWilliams, Matten, Moon and Siegel, 2008; Barnett and Pollock, 2012). In other cases the claims of writers on reputation are clearly part of a lucrative business model designed to engage with (and in some cases, help create) marketing, brand, risk and public relations corporate functions (see Conley and Williams, 2005; Shamir, 2005). There have been developments in the economic analysis of reputation, but there is still no body of evidence about the conditions that need to be in place for reputation to have material value as a regulatory tool in

38 *Assumptions underpinning normative theory*

non-exceptional cases. The study of reputation to date does not seem fit for purpose for a robust theory of regulation.

Given this, I will draw out what I consider to be the necessary conditions for the reputation mechanism in its meta-regulatory context. While it may seem logical to start with whether a business even values reputation, and at what level of materiality, this is too broad. Reputation is valued and fought on particular issues at points in time, and a business's perspective is likely to be driven by the issue at hand within a specific context. For this reason, it is better to start with the *expectations of stakeholders* and how businesses might observe and respond. I posit that for each issue the price/product (economic) and non-price/product (non-economic) expectations of stakeholders (including activists and other non-governmental organisations as influencers of transactional stakeholders such as financiers, investors, insurance companies, employees, suppliers and partners) must:

i *exist* (including there being clarity on who the relevant stakeholders are) and be *articulated* by stakeholders;
ii be able to be *accessed* and *understood* by business;
iii be largely static and technically *possible for the business to meet* through self-regulation even if they are idealistic and/or onerous;
iv be *commercially valid* from the business's perspective, including an assessment of economic damage/loss of market share: *there needs to be a business perception*[18] *that there can be material net damage*[19] from not meeting the expectations of customers and other transactional stakeholders and them subsequently withdrawing support; and
v be *responded to* by the business in ways that the stakeholders recognise and value, and thus accept.

The above elements depend on some degree of direct input/output, which may occur via media such as the news (and probably has to) but nonetheless can be accessed and understood as intended.

The reputation mechanism must also provide the right outcomes (and ideally supplant detailed rules and enforcement) *in the temporal dimension*. This involves closely timed observations of others and communications about those observations:

i in the first instance, *observations of business performance by stakeholders*, who then *communicate their views or concerns to the business and/or others*; where
ii these stakeholder communications are then *observed by the business in a timely fashion* in order to then prioritise and respond as above and *communicate its response to stakeholders also in a timely fashion*; where
iii the business's communications about its responses to stakeholder concerns are then *observed in a timely fashion by the stakeholders* and are seen by them to meet their expectations so they can *then communicate their*

Assumptions underpinning normative theory 39

acceptance or at least not communicate ongoing dissatisfaction and not cause reputational damage. If the stakeholder expectations are not met the cycle of observation and communication (and potential reputational damage) would begin again.

A key assumption worth drawing out relates to the state of competition in a given market being adequate to act as a regulatory mechanism to manage economic behaviour. This is different from whether consumers actually act to boycott products; rather it is a core question about whether competition on its own terms is even effective and consumer rationality is as expected. The assumption seems to be that markets in any regulatory arena are *effective on objective economic criteria* – that is, market values such as price and product attributes. To my knowledge, there has been no examination of this assumption in either the normative or the empirical writing. In contrast, whether the market to be harnessed 'works' in any objective economic sense is an important question for this book. This is why I have noted the economic expectations as well as the non-economic expectations of stakeholders above.

I have already made the point that the normative meta-regulatory theory starts from a position of value conflict, with the expectation that the conflict can be transformed into consensus via the meta-regulatory process. A further point is that the theory, insofar as it expects stakeholders to effect reputational damage, is underpinned by the potential for *controversial* conflict. To explain, the reputation mechanism inherently depends on relevant issues having meaning for stakeholders. This is about the degree to which parties *care* about corporate behaviour and are prepared to rally for the cause. I have already addressed this issue above from the perspective of stakeholders in the market having views and being able to express these views. Here I want to elucidate a further underlying factor, which is that the reputation mechanism relies on *passionate* views and enthusiasm for action, at least at key times. This must be the case; if it were otherwise, then apathy would mean that no stakeholder could be depended on to communicate what was 'right' to business in order to effect corporate behaviour change (in saying this I am briefly putting aside my concerns that stakeholders do not have a monopoly on what is right). If reputational damage is to be inflicted, some form of scandal must be enacted, drawing in strong views from the community and market.[20]

Figure 2.2 shows the criteria discussed above. I have focused on third parties and their relationship with a business because third parties, such as activists, clearly play a vital role in the meta-regulatory literature as intermediaries in communicating and enlisting support from transactional stakeholders. Third parties appear to be the catalyst for non-economic values (that the market by definition does not recognise) to be transformed via political and media campaigns into transactional stakeholder consumption and investment choices that the market can then see and respond to. (If the stakeholder values of merit were already transactional stakeholder values, the market would theoretically provide adequate self-regulation without the need for engagement with

40 Assumptions underpinning normative theory

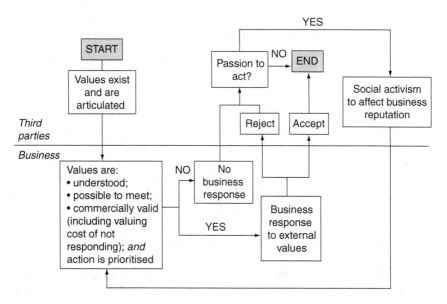

Figure 2.2 Stages in the reputation mechanism.

third parties.) The model in Figure 2.2 shows in a simple way that a business needs to respond to third party values in a way that is accepted by the third parties if they are not to engage in social activism to try to negatively affect the business's reputation. I have included the element of third party passion in this characterisation.

Figure 2.2 does not explicitly address the temporal dimension other than by noting that the business must *prioritise* action. However, if we see the flowchart as relying on perceptions at a point in time, the temporal dimension is implicitly included. For example, if a business does not act soon enough on issues of value, then it may be seen by third parties as *not* providing a response. Perhaps the business was going to act later, but if third parties see insufficient response according to their desired timeframes, they may then consider whether to take action to affect the business's reputation.

The model is at a sufficiently high level that it does not engage with the *likelihood* of different outcomes; this is discussed below. Nevertheless, I have shown the activism pathway as a potential cycle, which *is* related to the likelihood of outcomes and should be clarified. The normative meta-regulatory literature seems to rely on an assumption that activism will cause a business perception of reputational damage, which will then positively change business behaviour in line with activists' values. I suggest that this is not necessarily the case and we cannot justify shutting down the pathway after one or two runs through. Perhaps third party efforts to inflict damage will be persistently misjudged by the business, or perhaps they will be accurately judged as toothless given the

Assumptions underpinning normative theory   41

business's understanding of its customers' rationality and its market. This relates to my statement that the meta-regulatory literature depends on a particular view of effective competition and consumer rationality. Further, perhaps some reputational damage is acceptable to a business if it does not consider the net financial loss (if any) to be material. Although not countenanced by the meta-regulatory literature, it is conceivable that the activism action pathway is constantly repeated.

The range of tacit assumptions and criteria for success outlined above are my views of how the reputation mechanism is expected to work. These have not been previously articulated in the scholarly literature to my knowledge. However, the broader normative hopes for corporate self-regulation on social issues via social and market pressure have been addressed by scholars, with discouraging empirical findings. Even writers who are keenly pro-corporate social responsibility see 'profound contradictions between societal expectations of corporations and what corporations can actually deliver' (Banerjee, 2007: 171). As Kuhn and Deetz (2008: 177) note, 'the marketplace does not work well as a way of representing social values' (see also Burk, 1988).[21] Social and normative pressures have a role to play, but research has shown that they do not easily enlist or harness market forces to create the 'win-win' circumstances so often claimed by the reputation or corporate social responsibility enthusiasts (see Vogel, 2005; Reich, 2008; Steger, 2008; Kagan *et al.*, 2011).

Within the field of environmental regulation, Gunningham *et al.* (2003: 145) found 'little empirical support' for the thesis that what is good for the environment will be good for business; on the contrary, they found that 'win-win solutions do not abound'. Writing about the corporate citizenship theme within the corporate social responsibility literature, Banerjee (2007: 48) states that the assumptions that good corporate citizenship is related to good financial performance and that if a corporation is a bad citizen then its licence to operate will be revoked by 'society', are simplistic, with 'little theoretical or empirical support'. Tellingly, in a meta-analysis of 251 studies across 35 years of academic research on the business case for corporate social responsibility, Margolis, Elfenbein and Walsh (2009: 23) found that 'the preponderance of evidence indicates a mildly positive relationship between corporate social performance and corporate financial performance'. This leads to a question whether 'aside from striving to do no harm, companies have grounds for doing good' (ibid.: 2).

It is worth drawing out the experiences of market or transactional stakeholders, such as consumers and investors, because these are the parties that directly 'regulate' a business via the market. There is little evidence that consumers in mass markets[22] make purchasing decisions based on reputation on non-price factors (see Bhattacharya and Sen, 2004; Vogel, 2005). Consumer willingness to pay for corporate social responsibility may be high in surveys but is limited in practice (Vogel, 2005; Reich, 2008). At the most, ethical consumerism as a basis for consumer purchasing decisions 'appears to be highly contingent' (Smith, 2008: 298; see also Devinney, Auger and Eckhardt, 2010). Evidence of investor responses to reputation is also lacking (Gunningham *et al.*,

42 *Assumptions underpinning normative theory*

2003; Reich, 2008; van Erp, 2011). Data collected by Campbell and Vick (2007) on investor behaviour found that a good reputation did not enhance a company's stock market value. In fact, Campbell and Vick found that during bear markets, 'sin' paid, and the relative returns of the ethical investments they investigated were much worse.

If the research findings discussed above are applied to the reputation mechanism flowchart in Figure 2.2, we can see that the mechanism lets down the normative meta-regulatory hopes at the point where business assesses the commercial validity of taking action to meet stakeholder needs. It is generally not commercially valid for a business to make operational changes based on activist claims that are not supported by transactional stakeholders. It is not clear, but perhaps the mechanism also falters where activists have to make the call about whether they care enough to act. In any event, social activism does not appear to regularly cause enough reputational damage (or benefit) to cause businesses to change their operations. This would imply that the activism cycle can continue unless and until activists give up or compromise. While this does not have to lessen the normative desires to have businesses make moral or socially responsible decisions for non-financial reasons, it does limit the possibilities for meta-regulatory design in a practical sense.

The nature of the private corporate interest and the value of reputation as a regulatory tool are prominent themes in this book, and link into the previous discussion on the role of non-government organisations to communicate the public interest, both directly and via protest and social activism to effect corporate reputation shifts. Given that the retail energy sector relies on a consumer-facing mass market, the capacity for consumers to demonstrate their values through market transactions is particularly relevant, as are business perceptions of this capability. I investigate and explain how the conditions for the reputation mechanism were met in the competitive retail energy industry, and what the findings might mean for meta-regulatory theory more generally.

Systems theory is again of use in this endeavour: systems theory views businesses as organisations that are formed within the economic function system. Events only have meaning within the economic system (and in the organisational systems dominated by the economic system) when they can be translated into the economic terms of payment/non-payment. The stream of meta-regulatory theory that argues for business corporate social responsibility because it is commercially prudent is actually broadly consistent with a systems theoretical approach: both consider the issue based on the terms of the business rather than on externally imposed values. However, systems theory provides greater explanatory power for the empirical outcomes in the field of reputation research once we account for the other societal function systems, protest movements and organisational system rationality.

Organisational rationality and capacity for learning

So far, I have reviewed the implicit assumptions of normative meta-regulatory theory relating to stakeholder values and how they may be brought into consensus through interaction and communication. The second set of assumptions underpinning the normative meta-regulatory literature relates to how businesses and regulators 'see' this process, how they learn and how they adapt. These assumptions fundamentally support a notion of predictable rationality, where it is possible to steer and predict corporate behaviour. Regulators are expected to learn in predictable ways and be rational in an evidence-based way. They are expected to reflect on themselves and on those they regulate in order to learn and improve. Further to Ayres and Braithwaite's (1992) responsive regulation, which I have included as meta-regulation, Baldwin and Black (2008) write that 'really responsive regulation' brings additional challenges for regulators. Really responsive regulators also need to be responsive to 'operating and cognitive frameworks of firms; the institutional environment and performance of the regulatory regime; the different logics of regulatory tools and strategies; and to changes in each of these elements' (ibid.: 59). The normative meta-regulatory theory applies these same assumptions to those who are regulated (and who self-regulate). It is anticipated that businesses will learn in predictable ways and will be rational in an evidence-based way – that is, be responsive to the messages received from their environment, including from the regulators.

We can thus see that the normative meta-regulatory theory anticipates that business and regulatory organisations will observe their environments and themselves within their environments and, in doing so, will also observe how others in their environments are observing them. The organisations can then internalise others' expectations, and plan and adapt their own positions accordingly. Although reasonable in theory, successful meta-regulation in practice appears to require significant capacity to process, reflect, remember and to think creatively about regulatory problems and appropriate responses. This raises questions: Are the relevant entities up to this task? How do we know? Do we need to reconsider these hopes for rationality and learning when applied to highly complex and functionally differentiated organisational systems?

The meta-regulatory assumptions about organisational rationality have much in common with other theoretical and practical approaches, specifically the traditional economic and legal perspectives of rational decision-making in markets and through contracts.[23] As such, rationality has already been critiqued at some length and we can draw on several schools of thought for our own analysis. The organisational literature has been particularly instructive: in the 1950s scholars proposed that the rational decision-maker was more an 'administrative man' in possession of only limited information, or 'bounded' rationality (March and Simon, 1958; Simon, 1961). This view of the decision-maker proposed that instead of 'rationally maximising', or 'optimising', in decision-making, decision-makers 'satisfice', or rather, make do with the best option they can find and adapt to their circumstances to move to their next preferred stage: 'Organizing is

44 *Assumptions underpinning normative theory*

about fallible people who keep going' (Weick, 2001: xi). Organisational theory also progressed analysis of how decision-makers' environments affect their rationality: the field of institutionalism addresses the institutional environment of decision-makers and considers how this shapes their decisions, whether in the social context (see Meyer and Rowan, 1977; Scott, 1981) or through patterns of transactions and exchanges (see Pfeffer and Salancik, 2003).

Linked to the findings of the organisational literature, the field of behavioural economics is also informative, where the core concept is that decision-makers are 'predictably irrational' (Ariely, 2009); they are subject to a range of decision-making biases and use decision-making heuristics to reduce complexity (see Kahneman, Slovic and Tversky, 1982; Gilovich, Griffin and Kahneman, 2002). Brunsson (2007: 37) notes that it is easier to consider few alternatives than many alternatives, which 'makes sense from an action point of view, because considering multiple alternatives evokes uncertainty, and uncertainty reduces motivation and commitment'. In order to satisfice, a decision-maker needs only a self-perception, with basic decision rules, and a conception of his fit with the environment (the external forces to which he is subject) rather than a full comprehension of all alternatives and their ramifications. In fact, and consistent with Weber (1964), several theorists have posited that organisational decision-making can be characterised as rule following behaviour, and have found that organisations create their own rules in times of uncertainty (see Cyert and March, 1963; Heiner, 1983; March and Olsen, 1989; Zhou, 1997). This notion of basic rule following in order to move forward does not sit easily with a perspective that organisations are open and reflexive learners, particularly when feedback comes from many sources in a complex environment. This is especially relevant for this book.

Many organisational theorists also consider organisational rationality to be unpredictable, depending as it does on what an organisation chooses to see or not see in order to reduce complexity in decision-making. Weick (2001: 11) writes about how decision-makers select what they see in their environments and construct their own sense of the world and their options ('sensemaking'), where 'reality is an ongoing accomplishment'. According to Weick, sensemaking is akin to cartography, where there is an 'indefinite number of plausible maps that can be constructed' in an environment where the terrain changes constantly (ibid.: 9). These perspectives on organisational rationality are consistent with systems theory, which views organisations as self-reproducing, self-referencing systems operating in environments of their own creation.[24]

None of this means that business or regulatory organisations can afford to give up the illusion of predictable and traditional rationality; this illusion is a necessary 'mechanism of hope' (Brunsson, 2006). Organisational reform promises that things can always be better, and the management environment regularly produces new technologies of control to be applied, whether through strategic management, reputational analysis or risk management systems (see Brunsson, 2007; Power, 2007). However, although the new organisational technologies may provide necessary hope, this is likely to be a false hope given that the

Assumptions underpinning normative theory 45

environment the organisation is trying to adjust for and to control is by definition external to the organisation. As Power (2007: 144) states about reputation, it is a 'paradoxical management object in so far as intervention increases managerial attention to largely uncontrollable external perceptions'. Similarly, Vos (2005) discusses the strategic management literature and notes that it assumes that an organisation can observe its environment as independent of itself while also reflecting it in its true complexity; however:

> an organization can never capture the full complexity of its environment; every observation of the environment is ultimately just a simplified construction. This leads to the crucial question: what are companies ultimately supposed to adapt to? It cannot be the environment as such because of its incomprehensibility, and it cannot be the organizational construction of the environment because then organizations would just adapt to themselves.
>
> (Ibid.: 368)

Observations of others' rationality are also time dependent. This affects how observers consider and construct stories of outcomes. Rationality is in the eye of the beholder at a particular point in time, with observers who reflect on past events seeing 'an orderliness and inevitability that suggests that the events unfolded in a rational manner and could be managed by a simple application of rationality' (Weick, 2001: 37). This is also the lens through which the normative meta-regulatory literature views past events. The usual tales of corporate social responsibility successes and failures are explained as if the logic had been there for all to see the whole time rather than constructed in hindsight. However, it can be argued that any business is socially responsible until it is not; it is just a matter of time and of what is seen by second-order observers in a highly contingent environment.

In summary, the meta-regulatory assumptions about the capacity of regulated and regulatory organisations to observe and learn from their environments require closer scrutiny and, potentially, adjustment. My research provided an opportunity to undertake such an exercise, and to do so in a complex and real world environment.

Conclusion

Much of the meta-regulatory literature avoids discussing the problem of communicating across conceptual, situational, organisational or temporal barriers to understanding. Plural values are embraced as positive (including recognising corporate needs), but the underlying normative assumption seems to be one of achieving consensus through process, ultimately to change the private interest into a reflection of a 'better' or 'moral' public interest. The keepers and communicators of the public interest include not only regulators and governments but also activists and consumers through the market. All entities are seen as able to provide direct input to other entities about what is good/bad; there is no notion

46 *Assumptions underpinning normative theory*

of interpretative processes and how organisations construct meaning on their own terms. The implicit assumptions or pre-conditions underpinning the normative meta-regulatory literature have been discussed at length in this chapter and are summarised in Table 2.1. If it were not for the fact that much of the meta-regulatory literature is normative, meeting all of these assumptions would seem rather heroic.

The discussion in this chapter leads us to some preliminary conclusions that challenge the assumptions of the normative meta-regulatory theory. First, the public interest is not unitary or stable and, as such, the concept of an organisation 'meeting the public interest' is problematic. Osborne (2009: 99) notes that the 'public interest' is 'often an empty term, mistaken for the evanescent sentiments of whatever majority of special interests happens to prevail today'. Although we can observe obvious examples of corporate negligence and wrongdoing such as deaths at work and chemical spills and know the harm to be avoided (that is, the public interest in its most simple conception), such examples

Table 2.1 Summary of assumptions underpinning normative meta-regulatory theory

---

Consensus on the public interest
1 There is a meaningful public interest.
2 The government is a silent enabler of the public interest.
3 The regulator acts in the public interest.
4 Third party advocates and activists represent the public interest.
5 The private corporate interest can be aligned with the public interest via markets and reputational effects
  a Economic and non-economic stakeholder expectations:

    i exist and are articulated/acted on by stakeholders (including consumers in the market);
    ii can be accessed and understood by business;
    iii are largely static and technically possible for the business to meet through self-regulation even if they are idealistic and/or onerous;
    iv are commercially valid from the business's perspective, and further, the business perceives a material financial loss from negative reputation effects if it does not take action; there must be a net perceived cost of not responding;
    v are responded to by the business in a way the stakeholders recognise, value and accept.

  b The market and reputation mechanism provides the right outcomes in the temporal dimension:

    i stakeholders observe business performance and communicate their views or concerns to the business and/or others;
    ii these communications are then observed and responded to by business in a timely fashion;
    iii the business's communications about its responses to stakeholder concerns are observed in a timely fashion by the stakeholders and are seen to meet expectations, ending (possible) reputational damage.

Rationality
1 The regulator learns in a predictable way and is rational in an evidence-based way.
2 The regulated business learns in a predictable way and is rational in an evidence-based way.

Assumptions underpinning normative theory 47

are not typical of the majority of the political, moral and regulatory minefields that business must navigate. Even understanding these 'obvious' harms does not provide business with a way to reliably assess risk and the many small trade-offs that occur in practice. As Steger (2008: 566) writes about corporate social responsibility, the outcome is a 'pretty sobering' picture:

> in the absence of one or several major (and then likely catastrophic) 'external' events, we are most likely to see a continued 'muddling-through' based on 'more of the same': a public attention cycle here, a progress there, a backlash here, and all within a highly complex and dynamic system in which we really do not know where the limits are and what the potential outcomes might be.

Second, organisational rationality is unlikely to meet the normative demands upon it. Cognitive constraints prevent a full and traditionally 'rational' assessment of options. These constraints apply to both the regulator and the regulated organisations. Further, rationality is not an objective concept: one person's rational behaviour may be another person's irrational behaviour. Rationality is much like morality in this regard.

The notion that communications and connections between societal and organisational systems are fraught is not surprising from a Luhmannian systems theory perspective that sees only systems that cannot steer one another and do not share perceptions of events or time. Unlike Parker's (2002) meta-regulatory ideal of the corporation as an *open* system that receives direct inputs from its environment, Luhmann's systems theory considers systems (including organisational systems) as *closed*. From a systems theory perspective, Figure 2.1 would instead look more like a number of recursive shapes with no direct inputs, as shown in Figure 2.3.

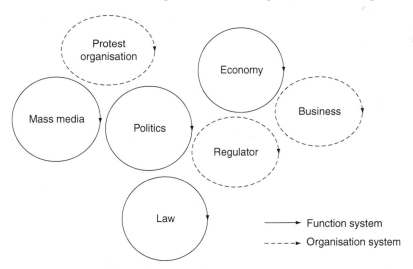

Figure 2.3 The key function and organisational systems for this research.

48 *Assumptions underpinning normative theory*

It is challenging to reproduce systems theory in diagrams such as in Figure 2.3 because the nature of the theory means that the shapes can be grouped in any way; there is no primary system and no direct input or output. Each system 'sees' only its own reproduction of its environment, and any system could occupy any position in the diagram. This diagram also omits other systems, such as religion and science. Nevertheless, the grouping in Figure 2.3 is not entirely random: the systems are arranged to show closer relationships as discussed in this chapter (although this is my interpretation and not necessarily an orthodox systems theory approach). For example, I have positioned business close to the economy. This is because regulated organisations primarily find meaning in economic communications (such as those relating to profits, customer numbers, the cost of capital and debt) and according to economic timescales (such as financial year, budget periods and public financial reporting periods). Legal norms, for example, have meaning in the economic system only insofar as they are attributed meaning via economic coding; law has no special ability to direct behaviour in the economic system. Law does, however, provide stable norms about societal expectations, which economic organisations may internalise according to their own organisational values.

Having outlined the theory, I now turn to the data for my research. The first theme explored through the data relates to how public interest messages were conceptualised and communicated to the industry. As discussed, meta-regulatory theory anticipates that the inclusion of more stakeholders in policymaking and enforcement will help regulators and regulated industries understand and account for different perspectives, ideally to reach consensus. In the Australian energy sector, there are various sources of potential input to retailers' decision-making in addition to the law. Did these send clear messages from which retailers could learn? Importantly, what was the role of the market and of consumer behaviour in regulating retailer behaviour? This relates to the notion of reputation as a regulatory tool. Did competition via the market provide regulatory and compliance messaging? What did customers and shareholders value and listen to? How did they respond?

The second theme relates to how retailers and the regulators behaved in response to the signals received from the environment, and specifically how retailers integrated different sources of information and found means to engage with and understand 'social licence' drivers. How did retailers appear to learn and respond to the inputs received: did they internalise the outside world, and if so, how?

The third and final theme is about the value of meta-regulation as a theory both in a normative and practical sense. What did meta-regulation in the energy market mean for the regulator and the law? What does successful meta-regulation look like?

Chapter 3 commences the exploration of the energy retail markets with a description of the development of one of the first Australian markets to open. It also describes the creation of the Victorian consumer protection framework.

Notes

1 In a comprehensive examination of 'civil regulation' codes of conduct and agreements, Vogel (2010) argues that a realistic assessment of civil regulation should compare outcomes to actual policy alternatives and not an ideal of economic governance. Although civil regulation is 'clearly less effective' than government regulations in developed countries, its effectiveness is 'roughly comparable to that of many intergovernmental treaties and agreements' which also show 'mixed and uneven' effectiveness (ibid.: 44). Vogel states that civil regulations in a range of areas are also *more* effective than their alternatives (which in some cases may not exist) in developing countries. Meidinger (2008) makes a similar point in his discussion of 'multi-interest self-governance', noting that 'there do not seem to be any plausible competitor governance systems' in the areas he studied. Meidinger further suggests that multi-interest self-governance approaches may not 'solve' the problems they seek to address; the greatest strength of such systems of governance may be more in their 'ability to "race" with the problems they confront' (ibid.: 286).

2 Survey and interview-based methods assume that survey respondents and interviewees have a shared sense of the issues and terms used – with one another and with the scholars – including a shared understanding of materiality in statements of motivation (such as a business 'caring very much'). This is unavoidable but should nevertheless be recognised as a source of potential misunderstanding.

3 In their book *Explaining compliance*, Parker and Lehmann Nielsen (2011: 14–15) split corporate motives from organisational capacity, stating that 'motivation to comply is of secondary importance if a firm does not possess the capacity to comply'. Although this is true, the demarcation between motivation and capacity is not actually clear in terms of how the literature deals with the topic. A lack of capacity, for instance in resourcing, can arise from a lack of business commitment to compliance, and much of the literature sees this type of capacity issue in this way, including many of the chapters in Parker and Lehmann Nielsen's book that are apparently focused on 'capacity'. My research takes a view of capacity that addresses organisational system characteristics rather than the outcome of business commitment to compliance.

4 There is an apparent contradiction in the writing of some of the meta-regulatory scholars on this issue. These writers see businesses as potentially 'virtuous' and needing support in self-regulation, but at times they also broadly describe business motivations in negative terms. A particular example is where Parker (2007: 209) refers to the potential 'delight of corporate power-mongers' who can bend law to their interests under self-regulation. Braithwaite (2005: 32) similarly talks about alternative dispute resolution needing non-government organisations to act as a 'countervailing lobby' to the power of corporate interests who 'will attempt to capture, corrupt or politically influence the access to justice accreditation agency when it impacts upon their interests'.

5 Particularly in light of the anti-corporate movement that has had a surge of popularity in recent years. Osborne (2009) describes and explains anti-corporatism (and the data that do and do not support its premises) in detail.

6 Regulatory scholars have also published in these areas, such as Parker (2007) on meta-regulation via the lens of corporate social responsibility, and Scott (2010) and Gunningham (2012) on meta-regulation and reflexive governance. Gunningham (2007) has also applied his findings from Gunningham *et al.* (2003) to corporate social (environmental) responsibility.

7 See Lenoble and Maesschalck (2010: 21) who discuss a range of views on reflexive governance, concluding that they all share the concept of 'expanding the conditions for success of learning operations such that, from the point of view of the actors involved, their effectiveness as normative processes is ensured'.

50 *Assumptions underpinning normative theory*

8 'Going beyond' the law may appear anti-intuitive as a link to regulatory theory but is in fact consistent with the meta-regulatory desire to shift corporate behaviour to meet substantive public interest objectives, and is very much within Parker's meta-regulatory scope.

9 Noting however, that despite how his theory has been represented by others, Habermas himself was not optimistic that communicative rationality was likely to be regularly possible; in his later writing he stated that it was 'not an immediate source of prescriptions' (Habermas, 1996: 4). See Rydin (2003) for a comprehensive analysis of communicative rationality and the issues in the environmental planning context.

10 In this reference I mean state-based regulatory agencies.

11 The degree of actual regulatory involvement varies between the three theoretical strands that I have characterised as meta-regulatory theory. There is debate within the corporate social responsibility field in particular about the role of law and the degree to which there may be a contradiction in requiring the law to have a stronger role in what is predominantly a voluntary approach to stronger social accountability (McBarnet, 2007). However, in each of the meta-regulatory theoretical strands the role of the regulator is presumed to be part of a move toward better substantive law, acting as an agent for the public interest that uses law to achieve its goals.

12 See Black (2008) for a useful discussion of the complexity of regulatory accountability and legitimacy for state and non-state-based regulators. Black's descriptions of polycentric regulation also have much in common with the meta-regulatory perspective (but not in its normative form), where members of 'civil society' are also regulators.

13 For example, see Parker (2006: 615) where she notes that regulatory agencies have their own social, political and regulatory licences, and also Parker (2008: 357), where 'responsive law is intimately connected with politics' and 'continually corrects itself in relation to political discussion'.

14 They can also be seen as third parties to the regulated business–customer or regulated business–investor relationship, which is drawn out in the next section.

15 This book uses these terms interchangeably; the key third parties in the research were low-income consumer advocacy organisations that were non-government organisations and that combined policy advocacy and lobbying with traditional activism around social and media campaigns.

16 Parker (2002: 214) says this is a matter for the community to resolve in the first instance, but she is silent on how this is to happen, noting that setting out a theory for 'for how deliberative law-making and regulatory action can occur' is beyond the scope of her book (ibid.: 300). The role is then passed to the regulator.

17 The corporate social responsibility literature and the reputation management literature are opposite sides of the same coin. Each addresses the need to listen to stakeholders because it is good for business. Corporate social responsibility writing is more focused on business ethics and arguing why businesses should be ethical, with most scholars then forming links to the financial benefits of corporate social responsibility in order to be compelling. Reputation writing on strategic management starts with the financial costs to businesses of reputational loss, viewing the need to be seen to be ethical as strategic risk management.

18 Note that perceptions are required, regardless of whether these perceptions are later borne out by experience.

19 Reputational value may also be about moral status alone, where perceived changes in the business's moral status in the eyes of key stakeholders are sufficiently valued by the business. However, given the implicit links to the market effects of negative reputation in much of the meta-regulatory literature, the commercial perspective is the main focus for this research. It is also the most targeted to what the majority of businesses value – if an appeal to the corporate bottom line does not work it is difficult to say why moral status alone would be more effective in a general sense.

20 Reputational action in a *positive* direction may not require conflict but it still requires that stakeholders care enough to take action. Positive reputational shifts also imply that the subject of the positive action is doing more than its counterparts; it must be superior to the status quo to be singled out for positive views. This then brings us back to the negative side of the distinction that other subjects would be on. In any event, as discussed earlier, much of the meta-regulatory literature relies on a veiled threat of reputational damage rather than positive measures, and scandal-seeking media are also more likely to exploit and reinforce controversy than report on positive stories of consensus between business and stakeholders.

21 Of course, this is not always how businesses sell the story of social responsibility; this is an environment characterised by rhetoric (see Henderson, 2001; Conley and Williams, 2005).

22 Recall this means markets with a broad customer base and mass appeal. Reputation does have demonstrated regulatory value for more niche industries. Scholars have found reputation to have an effect under certain circumstances, such as van Erp's (2008) study of the cotton trade in the American South, the diamond trade, and the Dutch construction industry. The circumstances of these markets involved businesses trading with one another within an environment of high trust, and where there was little to no regulation by the state (or indeed, where business activity was already illegal). Reputation served a purpose as a 'simplifying device' in efficient contractual relations (ibid.: 154), and was certainly better than nothing. Although these findings are instructive, they do not specifically lend support for the broader case for reputation mounted by meta-regulatory scholars, where markets demonstrate looser relationship ties and large-scale transactional stakeholder responses to business behaviour are required.

23 This claim might be refuted by meta-regulatory scholars, many of whom state an awareness of cognitive and operational constraints on regulators and regulated businesses, and who themselves refer to the organisational literature discussed in this section. However, the full implications of the cited organisational theories do not sufficiently translate into the normative meta-regulatory view that clearly anticipates predictably rational and well-informed entities in the regulatory space. These implications also do not fully translate into empirical assumptions: for example, Parker and Lehmann Nielsen (2008) note in their writing about studies on compliance that 'decision-making and behaviour that are not optimally rational will often still be consistent and predictable, and, therefore, amenable to empirical study'.

24 Luhmann's writing on organisations explicitly drew on the work of March and Simon, Weick and Brunsson.

References

Aras, G. and Crowther, D. (eds) (2010) *NGOs and social responsibility*, Emerald Group Publishing: Bingley.

Ariely, D. (2009) *Predictably irrational*, HarperCollins Publishers: New York.

Ayres, I. and Braithwaite, J. (1992) *Responsive regulation: transcending the deregulation debate*, Oxford University Press: Oxford.

Bakir, V. (2005) 'Greenpeace v. Shell: media exploitation and the social amplification of risk framework (SARF)', *Journal of Risk Research*, vol. 8, no. 7–8, pp. 679–691.

Baldwin, R. (1995) *Rules and government*, Clarendon Press: Oxford.

Baldwin, R. and Black, J. (2008) 'Really responsive regulation', *The Modern Law Review*, vol. 71, issue 1, pp. 59–94.

Banerjee, S.B. (2007) *Corporate social responsibility: the good, the bad and the ugly*, Edward Elgar: Cheltenham.

52 *Assumptions underpinning normative theory*

Barnett, M.L. and Pollock, T.G. (2012) 'Charting the landscape of corporate reputation research', in M.L. Barnett and T.G. Pollock (eds) *The Oxford handbook of corporate reputation*, Oxford University Press: Oxford, pp. 1–15.

Bernstein, S. and Cashore, C. (2007) 'Can non-state global governance be legitimate? An analytical framework', *Regulation and Governance*, vol. 1, pp. 347–371.

Bhattacharya, C.B. and Sen, S. (2004) 'Doing better at doing good: when, why, and how consumers respond to corporate social initiatives', *California Management Review*, vol. 47, no. 1, pp. 9–24.

Black, J. (2008) *Constructing and contesting legitimacy and accountability in polycentric regulatory regimes*, LSE Law, Society and Economy Working Papers 2/2008, London School of Economics and Political Science, Law Department: London.

Black, J. (2012) 'Paradoxes and failures: "New Governance" techniques and the financial crisis', *The Modern Law Review*, vol. 75, issue 6, pp. 1037–1063.

Black, J. (2013) *Seeing, knowing, and regulating financial markets: moving the cognitive framework from the economic to the social*, LSE Law, Society and Economy Working Papers, 24/2013, London School of Economics and Political Science, Law Department: London.

Bob, C. (2005) *The marketing of rebellion: insurgents, media, and international activism*, Cambridge University Press: Cambridge.

Borck, J.C. and Coglianese, C. (2011) 'Beyond compliance: explaining business participation in voluntary environmental programs', in C. Parker and V. Lehmann Nielsen (eds) *Explaining compliance: business responses to regulation*, Edward Elgar: Cheltenham, pp. 139–169.

Braithwaite, J. (2005) *Meta-regulation of justice*, RegNet Occasional Paper 4, September, Australian National University: Canberra.

Braithwaite, J. (2008) *Regulatory capitalism: how it works, ideas for making it work better*, Edward Elgar Publishing: Cheltenham.

Brunsson, N. (2003a) 'Organized hypocrisy', in B. Czarniawska and G. Sevón (eds) *The Northern Lights: organization theory in Scandinavia*, Copenhagen Business School Press: Ferndon, pp. 201–222.

Brunsson, N. (2003b) *The organization of hypocrisy: talk, decisions and actions in organizations*, second edition, trans. N. Adler, Copenhagen Business School Press: Herndon.

Brunsson, N. (2006) *Mechanisms of hope: maintaining the dream of the rational organization*, Copenhagen Business School Press: Liber.

Brunsson, N. (2007) *The consequences of decision-making*, Oxford University Press: Oxford.

Burk, J. (1988) *Values in the marketplace: the American stock market under federal securities law*, Walter de Gruyter: Berlin.

Campbell, K. and Vick, D. (2007) 'Disclosure law and the market for corporate social responsibility', in D. McBarnet, A. Voiculescu and T. Campbell (eds) *The new corporate accountability: corporate social responsibility and the law*, Cambridge University Press: Cambridge, pp. 241–278.

Carroll, A.B. (2008) 'A history of corporate social responsibility: concepts and practices', in A. Crane, A. McWilliams, D. Matten, J. Moon and D.S. Siegel (eds) *The Oxford handbook of corporate social responsibility*, Oxford University Press: Oxford, pp. 19–46.

Coglianese, C. and Mendelson, E. (2010) 'Meta-regulation and self-regulation', in R. Baldwin, M. Cave and M. Lodge (eds) *The Oxford handbook of regulation*, Oxford University Press: Oxford, pp. 146–168.

Conley, J.M. and Williams, C.E. (2005) 'Engage, embed and embellish: theory versus practice in the corporate social responsibility movement', *The Journal of Corporation Law*, vol. 31, pp. 1–38.

Corkin, J. (2008) 'Misappropriating citizenship: the limits of corporate social responsibility', in N. Boeger, R. Murray and C. Villiers (eds) *Perspectives on corporate social responsibility*, Edward Elgar: Cheltenham, pp. 39–63.

Crane, A., McWilliams, A., Matten, D., Moon, J. and Siegel, D.S. (2008) 'Introduction', in A. Crane, A. McWilliams, D. Matten, J. Moon and D.S. Siegel (eds) *The Oxford handbook of corporate social responsibility*, Oxford University Press: Oxford, pp. 3–15.

Cyert, R.M. and March, J.G. (1963) *A behavioural theory of the firm*, Prentice-Hall: New Jersey.

De Schutter, O. and Lenoble, J. (eds) (2010) *Reflexive governance: redefining the public interest in a pluralistic world*, Hart Publishing: Oxford.

Devinney, T.M., Auger, P. and Eckhardt, G.M. (2010) *The myth of the ethical consumer*, Cambridge University Press: Cambridge.

Edelman, L.B. and Talesh, S.A. (2011) 'To comply or not to comply – that isn't the question: how organizations construct the meaning of compliance', in C. Parker and V. Lehmann Nielsen (eds) *Explaining compliance: business responses to regulation*, Edward Elgar: Cheltenham, pp. 103–122.

Edelman, M. (1988) *Constructing the political spectacle*, University of Chicago Press: Chicago.

Edelman, M. (2001) *The politics of misinformation*, Cambridge University Press: Cambridge.

Freeman, R.E., Harrison, J.S and Wicks, A.C. (2007) *Managing for stakeholders: survival, reputation, and success*, Yale University Press: New Haven.

Gilad, S. (2010) 'It runs in the family: meta-regulation and its siblings', *Regulation and Governance*, vol. 4, issue 4, pp. 485–506.

Gilovich, T., Griffin, D. and Kahneman, D. (eds) (2002) *Heuristics and biases: the psychology of intuitive judgement*, Cambridge University Press: Cambridge.

Grabosky, P., Gunningham, N. and Sinclair, N. (1998) 'Parties, roles and interactions', in N. Gunningham, P. Grabosky and D. Sinclair (eds) *Smart regulation: designing environmental policy*, Clarendon Press: Oxford, pp. 93–134.

Gunningham, N. (2007) 'Corporate environmental responsibility: law and the limits of voluntarism', in D. McBarnet, A. Voiculescu and T. Campbell (eds) *The new corporate accountability: corporate social responsibility and the law*, Cambridge University Press: Cambridge, pp. 476–500.

Gunningham, N. (2011) 'Strategizing compliance and enforcement: responsive regulation and beyond', in C. Parker and V. Lehmann Nielsen (eds) *Explaining compliance: business responses to regulation*, Edward Elgar: Cheltenham, pp. 199–221.

Gunningham, N. (2012) 'Regulatory reform and reflexive regulation: beyond command and control', in E. Brousseau, T. Dedeurwaerdere and B. Siebenhüner (eds) *Reflexive governance for global public goods*, MIT Press: Cambridge, Massachusetts, pp. 85–104.

Gunningham, N., Kagan, R.A. and Thornton, D. (2003) *Shades of green: business, regulation, and environment*, Stanford University Press: Stanford.

Habermas, J. (1981) *The theory of communicative action*, London: Beacon Press.

Habermas, J. (1996) *Between facts and norms: contributions to a discourse theory of law and democracy*, trans. W. Rehg, MIT Press: Cambridge.

54 *Assumptions underpinning normative theory*

Haines, F. (1997) *Corporate regulation: beyond 'punish or persuade'*, Clarendon Press: Oxford.

Haines, F. (2009a) 'Regulatory failures and regulatory solutions: a characteristic analysis of the aftermath of disaster', *Law and Social Inquiry*, vol. 34, issue 1, pp. 31–60.

Haines, F. (2009b) 'Vanquishing the enemy or civilizing the neighbour? Controlling the risks from hazardous industries', *Social and Legal Studies*, vol. 18, no. 3, pp. 397–415.

Haines, F. (2011) *The paradox of regulation: what regulation can achieve and what it cannot*, Edward Elgar: Cheltenham.

Hancher, L. and Moran, M. (1989) 'Organizing regulatory space', in L. Hancher and M. Moran (eds) *Capitalism, culture and economic regulation*, Clarendon Press: Oxford, pp. 271–300.

Heiner, R.A. (1983) 'The origin of predictable behavior', *American Economic Review*, vol. 73, pp. 560–595.

Henderson, D. (2001) *Misguided virtue: false notions of corporate social responsibility*, Hobart Paper 142, The Institute of Economic Affairs: London.

Hoffman, A.J. (2001) *From heresy to dogma: an institutional history of corporate environmentalism*, expanded edition, Stanford University Press: Stanford.

Holzer. B. (2010) *Moralizing the corporation: transnational activism and corporate accountability*, Edward Elgar: Cheltenham.

Hood, C. (1991) 'A public management for all seasons?', *Public Administration*, vol. 69, Spring, pp. 3–19.

Hood, C. (2011) *The blame game, spin, bureaucracy and self-preservation in government*, Princeton University Press: Princeton.

Hood, C., Rothstein, H. and Baldwin, R. (2001) *The government of risk: understanding risk regulation regimes*, Oxford University Press: Oxford.

Howard-Grenville, J., Nash, J. and Coglianese, C. (2008) 'Constructing the license to operate: internal factors and their influence on corporate environmental decisions', *Law and Policy*, vol. 30, no. 1, pp. 73–107.

Hutter, B. and Jones, C.J. (2007) 'From government to governance: external influences on business risk management', *Regulation and Governance*, vol. 1, pp. 27–45.

Kagan, R.A., Gunningham, N. and Thornton, D. (2011) 'Fear, duty, and regulatory compliance: lessons from three research projects', in C. Parker and V. Lehmann Nielsen (eds) *Explaining compliance: business responses to regulation*, Edward Elgar: Cheltenham, pp. 37–58.

Kahneman, D., Slovic, P. and Tversky, A. (1982) *Judgement under uncertainty: heuristics and biases*, Cambridge University Press: Cambridge.

King, M. and Thornhill, C.J. (2003) *Niklas Luhmann's theory of politics and law*, Palgrave Macmillan: Basingstoke.

Kuhn, T. and Deetz, S. (2008) 'Critical theory and CSR: can/should we get beyond cynical reasoning?', in A. Crane, A. McWilliams, D. Matten, J. Moon, and D.S. Siegel (eds) *The Oxford handbook of corporate social responsibility*, Oxford University Press: Oxford, pp. 173–196.

Lenoble, J. and Maesschalck, M. (2010) 'Renewing the theory of public interest: the quest for a reflexive and learning based approach to governance', in O. De Schutter and J. Lenoble (eds) *Reflexive governance: redefining the public interest in a pluralistic world*, Hart Publishing: Oxford. pp. 3–21.

Livesey, S.M. (2001) 'Eco-identity as discursive struggle: Royal Dutch/Shell, Brent Spar, and Nigeria', *Journal of Business Communication*, vol. 38, no. 1, pp. 58–91.

Assumptions underpinning normative theory 55

Luhmann, N. (1989) *Ecological communication*, trans. J. Bednarz, Jr., University of Chicago Press: Chicago.

Luhmann, N. (2000) *The reality of the mass media*, trans. K. Cross, Stanford University Press: Stanford.

Luhmann, N. (2002) *Risk: a sociological theory*, trans. R. Barrett, Introduction: N. Stehr and G. Bechmann, Aldine Transaction: New Jersey.

Luhmann, N. (2008) 'Are there still indispensable norms in our society?', *Soziale Systeme 14*, vol. 1, pp. 18–37, Lucius & Lucius, Stuttgart.

Luhmann, N. (2013) *Theory of society: volume 2*, trans. R. Barrett, Stanford University Press: Stanford.

March, J.G. and Olsen, J.P. (1989) *Rediscovering institutions: the organizational basis of politics*, Free Press: New York.

March, J.G. and Simon, H.A. (1958) *Organizations*, John Wiley & Sons: New York.

Margolis, J.D., Elfenbein, H.A. and Walsh, J.P. (2009) 'Does it pay to be good ... and does it matter? A meta-analysis of the relationship between corporate social and financial performance', 1 March, available at SSRN: http://ssrn.com/abstract=1866371.

McBarnet, D.J. (2007) 'Corporate social responsibility: beyond law, through law, for law: the new corporate accountability', in D. McBarnet, A. Voiculescu and T. Campbell (eds) *The new corporate accountability: corporate social responsibility and the law*, Cambridge University Press: Cambridge, pp. 9–56.

Meidinger, E. (2008) 'Multi-interest self-governance through global product certification programmes', in O. Dilling, M. Herberg and G. Winter (eds) *Responsible business: self-governance and law in transnational economic transactions*, Oñati Series in Law and Society, Hart Publishing: Oxford, pp. 259–291.

Meyer, J.W. and Rowan, B. (1977) 'Institutionalized organizations: formal structure as myth and ceremony', *The American Journal of Sociology*, vol. 83, no. 2, pp. 340–363.

Micheletti, M. (2003) *Political value and shopping: individuals, consumerism, and collective action*, Palgrave Macmillan: New York.

Moeller, H.-G. (2006) *Luhmann explained: from souls to systems*, Open Court: Illinois.

Müller, A.F. (2006) 'Some observations on social anthropology and Niklas Luhmann's concept of society', in M. King, and C. Thornhill (eds) *Luhmann on law and politics*, Oñati International Series in Law and Society, Hart Publishing: Oxford, pp. 165–185.

Nielsen, V.L. and Parker, C. (2008) 'To what extent do third parties influence business compliance?', *Journal of Law and Society*, vol. 35, no. 3, September, pp. 309–340.

Oborne, P. (2005) *The rise of political lying*, Free Press: London.

Orlitzky, M. (2008) 'Corporate social performance and financial performance: a research synthesis', in A. Crane, A. McWilliams, D. Matten, J. Moon and D.S. Siegel (eds) *The Oxford handbook of corporate social responsibility*, Oxford University Press: Oxford, pp. 113–136.

Osborne, D. and Gaebler, T. (1992) *Reinventing government*, Penguin Books: New York.

Osborne, E. (2009) *The rise of the anti-corporate movement: corporations and the people who hate them*, Stanford University Press: Stanford.

Parker, C. (2002) *The open corporation: effective self-regulation and democracy*, Cambridge University Press: Cambridge.

Parker, C. (2006) 'The "compliance trap": the moral message in responsive regulatory enforcement', *Law and Society Review*, vol. 40, no. 3, pp. 591–622.

Parker, C. (2007) 'Meta-regulation: legal accountability for corporate social responsibility', in D. McBarnet, A. Voiculescu and T. Campbell (eds) *The new corporate*

56 *Assumptions underpinning normative theory*

accountability: corporate social responsibility and the law, Cambridge University Press: Cambridge, pp. 207–237.

Parker, C. (2008) 'The pluralization of regulation', *Theoretical Inquiries in Law*, vol. 9, no. 2, pp. 349–369.

Parker, C. (2013) 'Twenty years of responsive regulation: an appreciation and appraisal', Editorial, *Regulation and Governance*, special issue: 'Twenty years of responsive regulation: an appreciation and appraisal', vol. 7, issue 1, March, pp. 12–13.

Parker, C. and Gilad, S. (2011) 'Internal corporate compliance management systems: structure, culture and agency', in C. Parker and V. Lehmann Nielsen (eds) *Explaining compliance: business responses to regulation*, Edward Elgar: Cheltenham, pp. 170–195.

Parker, C. and Lehmann Nielsen, V. (2008) 'How much does it hurt? How Australian businesses think about the costs and gains of compliance and noncompliance with the Trade Practices Act', *Melbourne University Law Review*, vol. 32, pp. 554–608.

Parker, C. and Lehmann Nielsen, V. (2011) 'Introduction', in C. Parker and V. Lehmann Nielsen (eds) *Explaining compliance: business responses to regulation*, Edward Elgar: Cheltenham, pp. 1–33.

Pfeffer, J. and Salancik, G.R. (2003) *The external control of organizations: a resource dependence perspective*, Stanford Business Books: Stanford.

Power, M. (2007) *Organized uncertainty: designing a world of risk management*, Oxford University Press: Oxford.

Reich, R.B. (2008) *Supercapitalism: the transformation of business, democracy, and everyday life*, Vintage: New York.

Rice, T. and Owen, P. (1999) *Decommissioning the Brent Spar*, E&FN Spon: London.

Rydin, Y. (2003) *Conflict, consensus and rationality in environmental planning: an institutional discourse approach*, Oxford University Press: Oxford.

Salter, D. (2007) *The media we deserve*, Melbourne University Press: Melbourne.

Scott, C. (2010) 'Reflexive governance, regulation and meta-regulation: control or learning?', in O. De Schutter and J. Lenoble (eds) *Reflexive governance: redefining the public interest in a pluralistic world*, Hart Publishing: Oxford, pp. 43–63.

Scott, W.R. (1981) *Organizations: rational, natural and open systems*, third edition, Prentice-Hall: New Jersey.

Shamir, R. (2005) 'Mind the gap: the commodification of corporate social responsibility', *Symbolic Interaction*, vol. 28, issue 2, pp. 229–253.

Simon, H.A. (1961) *Administrative behaviour*, Macmillan: New York.

Simpson, S.S. and Rorie, M. (2011) 'Motivating compliance: economic and material motives for compliance', in C. Parker and V. Lehmann Nielsen (eds) *Explaining compliance: business responses to regulation*, Edward Elgar: Cheltenham, pp. 59–77.

Smith, N.C. (2008) 'Consumers as drivers of corporate social responsibility', in A. Crane, A. McWilliams, D. Matten, J. Moon, and D.S. Siegel (eds) *The Oxford handbook of corporate social responsibility*, Oxford University Press: Oxford, pp. 281–302.

Steger, U. (2008) 'Future perspectives of corporate social responsibility: where are we coming from? where are we heading?', in A. Crane, A. McWilliams, D. Matten, J. Moon and D.S. Siegel (eds) *The Oxford handbook of corporate social responsibility*, Oxford University Press: Oxford, pp. 560–567.

Tanner, L. (2010) *Sideshow: dumbing down democracy*, Scribe Publications: Melbourne.

Tyler, T.R. (2011) 'The psychology of self-regulation: normative motivations for compliance', in C. Parker and V. Lehmann Nielsen (eds) *Explaining compliance: business responses to regulation*, Edward Elgar: Cheltenham, pp. 78–99.

van Erp, J. (2008) 'Reputational sanctioning in private and public regulation', *Erasmus Law Review*, vol. 1, issue 5, pp. 145–161.

van Erp, J. (2011) 'Naming and shaming in regulatory enforcement', in C. Parker and V. Lehmann Nielsen (eds) *Explaining compliance: business responses to regulation*, Edward Elgar: Cheltenham, pp. 322–342.

Vogel, D. (2005) *The market for virtue: the potential and limits of corporate social responsibility*, The Brookings Institution: Washington.

Vogel, D. (2010) 'The private regulation of global corporate conduct: strengths and limitations', paper prepared for the Global Economic Governance Programme, Oxford University, 2007.

Vos, J.-P. (2005) 'Strategic management from a systems-theoretical perspective', in D. Seidl and K.H. Becker (eds) *Niklas Luhmann and organization studies*, Advances in Organization Studies, Volume 14, Liber: Copenhagen, pp. 365–385.

Voss, J.-P., Bauknecht, D. and Kemp, R. (eds) (2006) *Reflexive governance for sustainable development*, Edward Elgar: Cheltenham.

Waddock, S. and McIntosh, M. (2009) 'Beyond corporate responsibility: implications for management development', *Business and Society Review*, vol. 114, no. 3, pp. 295–325.

Weber, M. (1964) *The theory of social and economic organization*, ed. T. Parsons, The Free Press: New York.

Weick, K. (2001) *Making sense of the organization*, Blackwell: Malden.

Wheeler, S. (2008) 'Engaging individuals', in N. Boeger, R. Murray and C. Villiers (eds) *Perspectives on corporate social responsibility*, Edward Elgar: Cheltenham, pp. 224–245.

Zadek, S. (2007) *The civil corporation*, second edition, Earthscan: London.

Zhou, X. (1997) 'Organizational decision making as rule following', in Z. Shapira (ed.) *Organizational decision making*, Cambridge University Press: Cambridge, pp. 257–281.

3 Creating the regulatory framework for the world's most competitive retail energy market

The state of Victoria was the first Australian jurisdiction to privatise its energy assets, with reform occurring in the mid-1990s. After a period where only large business consumers were able to choose their electricity retailer, the retail electricity market was to be fully available to households and small businesses from 1 January 2001. This was called full retail competition, or FRC. Although the Victorian government had set out the broad policy about the industry restructure, it did not explain how the retail market would work. Instead, the industry was expected to identify and develop the necessary arrangements. However, the industry was slow to act: by late 1999 there was still no significant progress made in the market's development and even basic questions about functionality and rules had not been addressed. Given the non-existent policy environment and the industry's apparent inability to take action, the regulator (the Office of the Regulator-General, later called the Essential Services Commission, or ESC) stepped in. From late 1999 to 2002 the ESC undertook a comprehensive consultation process across the industry, community and government sectors to develop what became the consumer protection regime and basic market technical rules.

Regardless of the progress made by the ESC, it was not enough. The industry was fundamentally responsible for its own readiness and it was not ready for the planned market start date of 1 January 2001. FRC eventually commenced on 13 January 2002, with Victoria going on to be known as the most competitive energy retail market in the world from 2005 to 2011 inclusive, according to annual switching statistics (VaasaETT, 2012).

Building on my own experience working for the regulator to establish the consumer protection regime, this chapter describes the policy environment and the energy retailers' risk-averse responses to it. This chapter also illustrates meta-regulation in the rule creation stage, and the unplanned ways that the regulator needed to cope with conflicting objectives. A final theme is the government's need to intervene in the market to protect its own interests.

The early policy vacuum in Victoria

During the initial reform process the then Liberal (conservative) Victorian government's published material set out the broad policy regarding restructuring of the industry but said very little about the retail market that would result. In fact, all that was said about the market post-2000 was that all Victorian electricity consumers would be 'deregulated customers' by 2001 (for example, see Energy Projects Division 1997: 41).

Consistent with this language of deregulation, the government acted as though the absence of government regulation was all that was required to ignite market forces, and that these, in turn, would create any necessary rules. There were consumer protections in place prior to FRC, in the form of the Victorian Supply and Sale Code, which was developed by the regulator in 1994. This Code set out minimum standards relating to the distribution and retailing of electricity, and addressed such matters as payment collection cycles, payment processes and disconnection processes. However, the Code was designed for the monopoly service providers and was therefore scheduled to sunset (that is, cease to have effect) on 31 December 2000 – the original advent of FRC. The task of identifying and developing technical requirements and rules of structure and conduct was then left to the industry. As noted by the government department responsible for the reform, 'The best initial market structure will be developed in an environment where the commercial interests of the different parties within the industry are allowed maximum expression' (Office of State Owned Enterprises, 1994: 6).[1]

Thus the FRC element of the energy reform provided no direction for the industry or the regulator. This lack of direction was reinforced by a change of state government in the election of September 1999, which came as a surprise to all, including the new government. The new Victorian Premier had been in charge of the state Labor Party for less than six months when he came to power as Premier, and he had never served in ministerial office. Only four ministers in his Cabinet had previous experience. The new government found itself having to implement a policy that it had vigorously opposed when in Opposition: the privatisation of the energy industry meant the move toward competition could not be unwound without serious political consequences. Perhaps understandably then, the new government's public stance on FRC was low-key and negative through most of 2000. It took every opportunity to clarify that any problems were a result of the 'flawed' privatisation programme of the previous government (see Department of Natural Resources and Environment, 2000; Office of the Premier, 2001) but was otherwise silent. The policy vacuum of the previous government was maintained, and the industry was still looked to for direction and market development during the key years prior to FRC.

The industry and regulatory response to the policy environment

Under the public sector model prior to privatisation in the mid-1990s the electricity industry comprised the State Electricity Commission of Victoria (SECV) and 11 municipal electricity undertakings (which for ease of reference will be referred to in aggregate as the SECV). Under the SECV, the priorities were system maintenance and security, with customer service provided only as

60   *Creating Victoria's regulatory framework*

required to deliver electricity to customers and have them pay for what they consumed. Risk management was about building excess generation capacity to ensure supply, and disconnecting customers who would not pay.

The process of restructuring the SECV into separate generation, transmission and retail-distribution businesses, and their corporatisation and sale to the private sector, ushered in a new era for Victoria's energy industry. This was an era characterised by private sector management practices, financial risk management, marketing innovations and principles of customer service. The businesses were bought primarily by overseas interests, which promptly sent CEOs to oversee the new enterprises and to develop business strategies consistent with the intent of the parent companies. From all accounts, the intent of the foreign investors in the five retail-distribution businesses was to break into the new world of competitive multi-utilities in Victoria in advance of deregulation initiatives in their own countries, learn from the experience and then apply what they had learned at home. The American CEOs for TXU, Powercor and United Energy were all quoted at various times as stating that their companies had thought Victoria would provide a lucrative testing ground for market liberalisation in energy within the United States.

However, it takes more than an enthusiastic new CEO and new corporate plan to change an organisational culture, particularly one as entrenched as the 75-year-old SECV. CEOs came and went and ownership changes were made; nevertheless, the bulk of the staff responsible for FRC tended to be ex-SECV. Many of these people did not seem convinced of the benefits of the reform and did not appear to fully support their new organisational goals. This is not unexpected given that those who were expected to develop competition were the incumbent electricity businesses: the parties with the most to lose from FRC. It was also not seen as an unreasonable perspective by many in the industry because there was a strong perception that the risks and costs of FRC were sizeable and would continue to increase. For example, the incumbent businesses had to expend significant resources modifying their billing systems for FRC, with the costs of developing the requisite systems estimated by some as being as high as $1 billion across the retail sector (Wilson, 2001). With costs like these, the businesses spent time seriously considering their future and re-evaluating whether it was even worth it. This view was supported by interviews I carried out in 1999 for my PhD, prior to my joining the regulator's office. In their discussions with me most retailers were very careful about their long-term plans and appeared to want to keep their business options open. One senior manager said 'there are a lot of people who would say that the overall benefits perhaps aren't there, given the cost of implementing these systems'. This sentiment was also repeated by the industry in the media (for example, see Myer, 1999; Schulze, 1999).

The process of bringing the retailers together to agree on a solution to anything was described by one interviewee as like 'herding cats'. The only thing that the retailers appeared to agree on was the need for each of them to stay a viable business in an uncertain environment.

Creating Victoria's regulatory framework 61

For example, one interviewee said in 1999:

> Whilst it's profitable to be in there, we'll be in there. You could also say that we want to make money from selling our retail book and we have to have a decent book to sell. So both of those things say that it's an investment we need to maintain. We don't go over the top, but we don't let it die on the vine. I think you'll find all the [businesses] are saying exactly the same, and they'll see how it'll play out in the 2001 market.... So we're into the water as much as we dare go. No one's sort of saying 'dive in the deep end', and no one's sort of saying 'I'm not going to play in the pool'.

This may well have resulted in some (if not all) of the incumbent retailers seeking to create or maintain barriers to customer loss under competition. For example, when asked if customer inertia (that is, a customer unwillingness to switch retailer) was a good or bad thing, an interviewee from 1999 said:

> It's sort of a bit of a dilemma really, because we are putting a lot of effort into this to maybe have very few customers switch, I mean, you're sort of wondering why we've done all this. I guess we're still trying to establish competition, we have to actually create the market if you like; it's not a natural market. There are people within our company and I'm sure other companies that would regard a barrier to competition as being great, provided that there's some value there that we can capture and retain.

Most people I encountered seemed to feel that the whole reform was far more difficult than anyone had first imagined. A phrase used often was 'the devil is in the detail'. The industry as a whole seemed confused by FRC; no one seemed to know what was required of the businesses or of the market. For example, in 1999 a senior manager explained to me the difficulties of trying to develop a metering strategy for FRC:

> The thing that's been the stumbling block is just the fact that the [electricity businesses] are all over the place like a dog's breakfast and the level of understanding and thinking of this stuff was very low. It was just an educational process. It's not that they're a bunch of no-hopers, it's that there are a lot of complex issues in here that are very intertwined, and they didn't have their minds around them.

An issue that compounded this problem was the lack of a physical or conceptual split between the retail and distribution functions in the energy industry. For much of the key FRC development period, there was a lack of clarity about whether personnel were with the distribution arm (a regulated monopoly) or the retail arm (competitive), and this was reflected in general confusion and a lack of innovation.

It is worth describing in detail the key risks that retailers believed they faced. The lack of political direction was certainly a clear risk to retailers. Some of the political changes could not be foreseen, such as the change in state government

62 *Creating Victoria's regulatory framework*

in 1999; however, other changes could have been managed more effectively if government had committed to policy in the energy arena. The volume of regulation in the 'deregulated' market was also significant, and covered everything from market wholesale rules to tax law. There was a perception that the magnitude of the resources to be expended in ensuring compliance could be enough to offset the benefits of operating in the market. Lawyers played an integral role in energy companies' compliance management, and the Electricity Supply Association of Australia even held annual electricity lawyers' conferences in the early 2000s. There was also the risk that further regulation could turn a currently manageable situation into an unmanageable one, with new rules coming from a range of unpredictable sources. For example, national privacy legislation was passed in late 2000 that stopped private sector businesses from using information for any purpose other than the purpose for which it was collected without express customer consent. This restricted the business plans of energy retailers seeking to become multi-utilities and to market bundled various products and services.

An important political risk related to the uncertain potential customer base nationwide. The firms that purchased Victoria's electricity businesses did so in the belief that they would also be able to venture into other Australian states by purchasing electricity assets in those states and/or competing in their retail markets. The limited customer numbers available in each state warranted a national energy strategy if retailers were to make money from retailing electricity (an economy of scale).[2] However, a national approach looked increasingly unlikely as state governments began to turn against FRC. Two key states effectively pulled out of implementing FRC, with Queensland announcing in October 2001 that it would be 'madness' to adopt it (Premier and Trade, 2001) and South Australia delaying FRC until at least 2003. New South Wales also chose to implement a form of pricing that disallowed price signals, which effectively undermined competition in that state. This scenario dismayed the private sector companies that sought to enter the market over those first years in the belief that there were opportunities to make money and exploit economies of scale over the eastern half of Australia. By September 2000 the media reported that off-shore operators were 'prepared to walk away in disgust' (Verrender, 2000).

Other risks were more predictable and controllable, as they were related to the natural risks for a retailer in the wholesale and retail markets. However, the stakes were still high. For example, the risk of loss in the volatile wholesale market was significant, with generation output traded in a spot market in half-hourly intervals. On certain days of the year, when generation capacity was limited and demand was high, the prices paid by retailers to generators through the wholesale market could be as high as $10,000 per megawatt hour,[3] compared with the then average price range of $25–$40 per megawatt hour. An important way in which retailers managed risk was through contracts with individual generators, called hedging contracts. These were financial instruments in which generators and retailers agreed on specific prices, irrespective of the going wholesale rate, and thus hedged their risk. Hedging contracts were still risky, as the retailer had to estimate the likely electricity price for the period in question

Creating Victoria's regulatory framework   63

and choose the best form of hedging available to it. Beside the risk of not obtaining an optimal hedging contract, retailers were also subject to the risk that generators could choose not to provide them. In 2001, there were allegations of Victorian generators withholding forward hedging contracts for high-risk periods, such as the summer months, which led to a greatly increased risk of high spot prices (Myer, 2001a, 2001b; Sharam, 2001).

The risk of losing customers (initially a problem for the incumbents only) and the counter-risk of customer inertia also loomed large for retailers. The possibility of losing customers was intrinsic to the supposed benefits of competition; the risk of loss would keep the retailer attentive to the needs of its customers, whether through low prices or attractive service packages. Indeed, and as implied above, this risk likely had a role to play in the incumbent retailers' difficulty in establishing the market in the first place (surely the most effective barrier to competition). In contrast, the risk of customer inertia was very real for the new entrant retailers (and any incumbent who sought to compete for other retailers' customers). Given the nature of electricity as a homogenous, somewhat intangible and relatively unexciting 'product', consumers were not expected to be highly enthused about having a choice of electricity retailer and there was a concern that consumers would expect significant savings to switch. This was the experience of many overseas electricity markets at the time, as noted by an industry observer:

> Almost without exception, energy retailers trying to make headway into small business and residential markets around the world have found switching rates to be low.... Advertising expenditures yield little return where customer interest remains below the threshold necessary to spur action.
>
> (E Source, 2000: 29)

The risk was that if switching levels were low (say, less than 5 per cent in the first year) new entrant retailers would not be able to obtain enough customers to turn a profit.

The final type of risk that retailers faced related to their dependence on complex systems and agreements that were out of their control. The system capabilities that were required to allow retailers to trade in the competitive marketplace were complex, and were the bane of all who desired an easy and swift progression towards FRC. For example, in addition to the required changes to the billing systems described above, retailers needed significant technology to interact with the national customer transfer system on which they depended, involving yet more in the way of retailer resources. The combined retail-distribution businesses were reported to have spent as much as $40 million each, with interstate companies being 'forced to rework their whole systems' and spend as much as $130 million (Myer, 2001c).

In the face of these risks, the Victorian incumbent retail-distribution businesses endeavoured to share the risks and costs of developing FRC. In 1999, they jointly submitted a proposal to government for metering policy. Then, as

64 *Creating Victoria's regulatory framework*

the date for FRC grew closer, the five incumbents developed an alliance comprising an FRC Project Group with a number of working groups under this (at one time it was reported these numbered 17) and a gatekeeper 'Validation Committee' which approved any material to be released outside the five businesses.

The FRC Project Group (and its sub-groups) released very little public information during the time it ran the FRC processes. It could be surmised that this was because only those matters that were agreed by all in the group managed to get through the Validation Committee, and very little was agreed. The FRC Project Group appeared to be subject to infighting at both inter- and intra-business levels, as even within each business there were different functions with different values. Over time, the FRC Project Group fell apart as each of the incumbents appeared to develop the confidence to go out on their own, and as the retail and distribution arms of the businesses began to separate. Importantly, every topic the FRC Project Group pursued had to be taken over by the ESC for implementation. The original policy expectations that the industry could self-organise in the public interest (and, importantly, prior to FRC) were definitely not met and the result was a delay in the market start date.

The development of the Retail Code

Arguably the biggest issue for the industry, and certainly for consumer advocates, was the replacement for the Supply and Sale Code, which was to fall away when FRC commenced. This was also the area where the industry seemed completely unable to make any progress. In 1999, and under the auspices of the FRC Project Group, the five incumbent retailers established a Customer Issues Working Group (CIWG) to address all customer matters under FRC, including small customer contractual minimum standards. Each of the five incumbent retailers had representation on the CIWG, and the retailers took turns to manage the CIWG and house the contractors hired to staff the project. There was no consumer representation on the CIWG and no non-incumbent retailer representation. No material from the CIWG was made public.

Around the same time as the industry CIWG was being formed, the regulator was considering its options. Allowing minimum standards to completely fall away or to be set solely by industry were not seen as feasible alternatives to regulation, particularly as the regulator had been provided with strong views from consumer representatives supporting a need to investigate and set standards (see Field, Lowe and Nelthorpe, 1999). Although the regulator was not explicitly empowered to act in this role through legislation, it still had legislative responsibility to ensure that customers benefited from competition and it interpreted its ongoing role in customer protection in this light. It did not receive overt support from the government of the time in undertaking this action.

Given this legislative responsibility, and the industry's inability to set standards or consult effectively, the regulator took control of the development of minimum standards for FRC and commenced a consultation process oriented towards developing a replacement for the Supply and Sale Code. The retailers

Creating Victoria's regulatory framework 65

provided little argument against this in concept. The final Electricity Retail Code (later known as the Energy Retail Code) was published in October 2000,[4] and was supported by further guidelines. Together these set the basic terms and conditions with which all contracts with domestic and small business consumers (using less than 160 megawatt hours per year) had to be consistent, and included rules relating to:

- the need for consumers to provide explicit, informed consent to enter a retail energy contract, including the information to be provided to a consumer in marketing material;
- how consumers could vary some of the terms of their contract;
- minimum mandated payment methods and options, including payment plan availability and information about how to access government support;
- detailed information in bills that provided consumers the ability to personally validate that their bill was based on actual and correct consumption amounts and agreed tariffs;
- minimum bill payment dates and disconnection processes, including reminder and disconnection notices with prescribed contents and timeframes; and
- contract termination rights and obligations.

To develop the consumer protections for FRC, in August 1999 the ESC convened and facilitated a Minimum Standards Working Group, which comprised representatives from consumer advocacy groups, the incumbent CIWG, non-incumbent retailers, the Office of the Electricity Industry Ombudsman (as it was known at the time; it later became the Energy and Water Ombudsman of Victoria (EWOV)), and the Concessions Unit from the Department of Human Services (which managed rebates and emergency relief payments for consumers receiving income support). The Minimum Standards Working Group met often to discuss the issues and various drafts of documents. The ESC also provided all stakeholders[5] with opportunities to make submissions on various versions of public issues papers, draft decisions leading to final decisions, and, ultimately, the regulatory instruments themselves. The consultation process for the Electricity Retail Code took more than a year to complete, and during the consultation process the ESC not only held many meetings of its working group but also held public fora and managed smaller sub-groups that addressed specific matters, such as customer financial hardship. The ESC also dealt with individual members at some length. These comprehensive consultation processes were generally well-received by the range of stakeholders, with all apparently pleased that the ESC had stepped in as an independent party. This was meta-consensus according to the definition of Dryzek (2010), where all agreed that something needed to be done for the new market environment even though stakeholders' views on the detail were frequently polarised.

66　*Creating Victoria's regulatory framework*

Retailer participation in the consultation

The retailers' philosophical views as communicated to the regulator were pro-market and anti-regulation, with concerns that regulatory prescription would stifle the innovation that would drive the market. The usual argument put by all retailers was that regulation should be a response to market failure and that the market was not there to solve as-yet-undetermined social issues. Of course, this perspective did not enable action to create rules for a market that had not yet opened, and the retailers seemed to be at a loss when engaging on the issues raised by the regulator.

Further, when the incumbent retailers attempted to work together to minimise costs and efforts for all, they created a bureaucratic[6] system that did not meet the needs of any of them, let alone any party outside of the incumbent group. For the initial few months of the consultation process, when submissions were called for, the five incumbent retailers provided joint submissions to the regulator under the auspices of the CIWG and overall FRC Project Group. Each submission would apparently go through a rigorous sign-off process within the FRC Project Group, which concluded with a final stamp of approval from the Validation Committee. These submissions were somewhat vague, and frequently failed to reflect the variety and strength of opinions voiced by the representatives of the incumbent retailers at meetings of the Minimum Standards Working Group. Over time, this process appeared to fall apart, as various retailers apparently tired of having their needs diluted to this one-size-fits-all approach. The bureaucratic design of the FRC Project Group's validation process also made effective and timely responses to the regulator's consultation papers difficult. As the CIWG began to crumble, the regulator would receive one submission from all incumbents, followed by supplementary submissions from individual incumbent retailers. By August 2000, the FRC Project Group submissions had ceased entirely.

Despite the anti-regulation rhetoric, true flexibility in standards was not pursued by the industry. In fact, retailers spent a great deal of time seeking clarification on the intent of the regulator and attempting to have standards prescribed in more detail to match their own interpretation of what was required, and, of course, their own needs in the market. Whenever the regulator left interpretation of clauses relatively open, it would be subject to individual requests from retailers asking what was *really* intended and what they should do to comply.

The industry's inability to move forward in the then unregulated market was not limited to the incumbent retailers. There were around ten independent or 'second tier' retailers who had no existing Victorian customer base and who should have been keen to compete. However, while these retailers were not generally given the same opportunities by government to participate in the early development of FRC, even when they were given opportunities to provide input they rarely grasped them. The ESC made every effort to include second tier retailers in decision-making and to take their needs into account, but it received very little in response. On the few occasions that second tier retailers provided responses to requests for stakeholder views, these often showed a lack of real understanding (or interest) in the consultation to that point, and rarely did they provide the much needed information about the requirements of an entity trying to break into the market. By late 2001 only two second tier retailers showed any interest in FRC development, with one of these participating at every possible opportunity throughout 2001 (the same individual each time, who also called regularly to ask what the regulator 'really meant' and who asked for more prescription), and the other choosing not to participate, but then criticising the process after lengthy consultation processes had closed. This situation did not change once FRC commenced.

Why did the second tier retailers behave in this way? It should be clarified who the second tier retailers were. Of those retailers who were licensed in Victoria and identified as second tier retailers in the key FRC development period from mid-1999 to mid-2001, only one was not linked to electricity distribution assets from interstate. The rest were the incumbent energy retailers of New South Wales and Queensland, and as such were the interstate contemporaries of the Victorian incumbents. These retailers had their own FRC debates in their home states, and their break into the Victorian market was likely to be peripheral to their overall energy business strategy. They were also not privately owned, as the energy industry in these states was still in the public sector, although corporatised. This meant that they did not have a profit requirement to ensure the businesses survived in Victoria. To speculate, they possibly were not true believers in FRC in any event, given their incumbent interstate head offices probably reacted to FRC in much the same way as the Victorian electricity retail and distribution businesses. Recall that the owners of the interstate retailers, the New South Wales and Queensland governments, each made decisions that stifled FRC in their own states at the time, with the New South Wales government implementing a pricing arrangement that undermined FRC in that state, and the Queensland government choosing to not proceed with FRC at all (although eventually opening the market in 2007).

Consumer advocate participation in the consultation

In contrast with the pro-market and anti-regulation retailer views, many consumer advocates were sceptical of the market and were pro-regulation. There were ten consumer advocacy groups involved in the development of the rules for Victorian FRC: five that specifically advocated on behalf of low-income and vulnerable residential consumers, one farming representative, one co-operative representative and three business customer representatives. There were no environmental groups involved. Each of the consumer advocacy groups was an issues-based policy body; these were not grassroots local community groups but organised entities funded by government, members or welfare groups. The low-income and vulnerable consumer advocacy groups were the only ones to regularly attend meetings of the Minimum Standards Working Group, and they were also the most vocal. Of these groups, only one had a consumer constituency at the time: in the early 2000s the Victorian Council of Social Service had more

68   Creating Victoria's regulatory framework

than 800 members, comprising individuals and organisations that dealt directly with consumers.

Most of the low-income consumer advocacy groups did not support the reform of the energy industry, and consumer advocates formally asked for a public inquiry and analysis of FRC several times (see Scott, Marles and Wise, 1995; Field *et al.*, 1999). Unlike for the larger commercial consumers, the benefits of FRC for residential and small business consumers were said to be unclear; in fact, it was claimed that many low-income or vulnerable consumers were at risk of being seriously disadvantaged (see Field *et al.*, 1999; Sharam, 2001; Consumer Coalition, 2002). There was a view that essential services such as electricity, gas and water should be provided to all consumers even where they could not pay; the basic concern raised by the low-income consumer advocates was that markets would not value social equity. It was also assumed that suppliers would 'race to the bottom' to improve returns to shareholders, leaving all consumers worse off and particularly those consumers who could be seen to be unprofitable or otherwise unappealing.

The low-income consumer advocates' regulatory preference for prescription was also the opposite of the approach put forward by retailers (at least as stated by retailers publicly). While retailers wanted to see evidence of the market failing (and resulting consumer harm) before there was a need for state regulatory intervention, the low-income consumer advocates followed the precautionary principle and wanted evidence of *no* consumer harm before they would entertain the retailers' perspective. The consumer advocates wanted the consumer protection rules written in detail *before* the market had the opportunity to disadvantage consumers. It is in this way that the Victorian rules were written with the anticipated experience of the more vulnerable consumer in mind, although the consultation was never able to draw out what vulnerability meant, except as a general principle that vulnerable consumers were more at risk from disadvantage in the market. Steps to improve clarity were not assisted by the clear differences of opinion even between the low-income consumer advocates about definitions and priorities.

There was also conflict between consumer advocacy groups about the precautionary principle and the likelihood of market outcomes leading to disadvantage. For example, in the early days of the consultation, consumer advocacy group Co-operative Energy supported FRC and sought to develop initiatives where consumers could join forces to access the best prices in the market. Co-operative Energy was scathing in its assessment of the views of two of the low-income consumer advocacy bodies in the FRC consultation, stating that their opposition to FRC 'betrays a discredited view of consumer protection – that consumers can only be protected through legislation and regulation' (Griffiths, 1999: 8). Co-operative Energy eventually bowed out of the process: as the consultation progressed, it was clear that barriers to co-operative arrangements would be in place, albeit unintentionally,[7] and so the organisation ceased its participation.

Although it occurred after the development of the Retail Code, the debate surrounding the creation of the Essential Utility Services Consumer Advocacy

Centre (EUSCAC) in 2002 (which later became the Consumer Utilities Advocacy Centre, or CUAC) is a further illustration of the differences within the consumer sector. In response to the concerns of consumer groups that they did not have the resources to promote well-informed and effective representation in regulatory decision-making processes, the then Victorian government sought to create EUSCAC as a central advocacy body:

> EUSCAC will provide a forum where consumers, including disadvantaged groups, can come together to discuss and exchange information. EUSCAC will also monitor grassroots utility consumer issues with particular regard to low income, disadvantaged and rural consumers. EUSCAC will advocate, with one voice, on issues of concern to utility consumers.
>
> (Department of Treasury and Finance, 2001: 25)

While its intent appeared reasonable, the government was naïve in its belief that a consumer advocacy organisation could 'advocate with one voice'. The Energy Action Group (2001) and the Victorian Council of Social Service (2001) did not support EUSCAC's establishment, and each called for direct financial resourcing of existing consumer advocacy organisations. The Victorian Council of Social Service was particularly critical, saying that EUSCAC was a bureaucratisation of consumer advocacy, and that the differences in objectives and interests were too great to have advocacy through one entity. Importantly, it stated that 'many issues that affect low-income households are contrary to the needs or wishes of the broader consumer movement' (ibid.: 3). Further:

> To advocate with 'one voice' implies that all consumers are united in their opinions regarding issues that affect them. This assumption is inaccurate. For example city energy users may have conflicting interests to regional and rural users, business users different issues to domestic households, environmental issues versus social policy issues, user pays versus cross subsidies, the role and type of concessions offered [–] the list is potentially endless.
>
> (Ibid.: 4)

This extract clearly demonstrates the need to see differences in perspectives even between apparently similar organisations. The point made here that 'many issues that affect low-income households are contrary to the needs or wishes of the broader consumer movement' is also particularly sobering when we consider the ambitions of meta-regulation to have regulated organisations adopt the public interest according to consumer advocacy bodies *and* (or *through*) the market (which includes all consumers).

How the ESC managed the issues

As already noted, neither the government nor the ESC had originally intended that the ESC would develop minimum standards for FRC, and the ESC's

70 Creating Victoria's regulatory framework

inclusive and consultative approach was more a function of the ESC's own style than an expectation from policymakers. The approach was eventually institutionalised by government with the *Electricity Act 2000* but this was based on the precedent set by the ESC in 1999 and 2000. Despite its clear alignment with what I have referred to as meta-regulatory theory, the ESC's approach was not based on academic theory. There was no link whatsoever to meta-regulatory writing (or any other scholarship) on consultation and stakeholder inclusion. This is not supposition: I was particularly aware of the lack of connection between theory and practice given my dual roles at the time as ESC staffer and PhD candidate. The ESC's consultative approach came down to specific personalities in the ESC combined with strong views put forward by the low-income consumer lobby. It could have all been different, and it *was* different in New South Wales, which opened its market at the same time but with a relatively low-key and opaque consultative approach.

It was not only contractual minimum standards that the ESC had to take over from the industry. The ESC's workload increased significantly from 1999 as consultation progressed and more issues were identified. What started as a programme of work to replace the Supply and Sale Code became a programme of work across nine separate topics, including marketing standards, cost recovery, customer transfer rules, metering and new connections, with some topics (such as minimum standards) being split into further consultations. There were initial papers on each of the topics, with all of these receiving submissions, all requiring workshops and briefings and most progressing to position papers or draft and final decisions in 2000 and 2001.

In parallel with meta-regulatory theory (but again, with no relationship) the ESC did not seek to prescribe outcomes but to regulate processes. For example, rather than defining a maximum level of customer disconnections from supply as a percentage, the ESC prescribed the detailed process a retailer had to follow prior to disconnecting a customer. Regulations as processes to meet high-level principles made sense conceptually and were consistent with what later became the normative meta-regulatory literature, but this approach brought with it the problem of stakeholder uncertainty on outcomes. An issue that became particularly contentious in subsequent years was how to assess a customer's capacity to pay the instalments of a payment plan (also known as an instalment plan), which was generally provided when the consumer was experiencing payment difficulties. Consumer advocates wanted the rules to specifically require the payment plan to be set only according to a customer's capacity to pay, as defined by the customer. Retailers said they would consider this but they needed to also ensure payment plans were sustainable and covered ongoing consumption to some degree. In managing this issue, the ESC did not define an approach, leaving it open to retailers to take into account both a customer's capacity to pay a plan and the customer's ongoing consumption. This is returned to in Chapter 5.

There were other unavoidable negative consequences of the regulator's consultation processes, and these involved the sometimes political compromises the regulator felt it necessary to make. The ESC sought to collect evidence and understand issues objectively (from its perspective of objectivity), but the market was not yet open and international experience with competitive retail energy markets was also limited. This meant that the ESC's approach to decision-making often meant trading off different stakeholders' claims to arrive at some reasonable middle ground, and the 'middle' would shift depending on the weight of opinion. Some regulation was only symbolic, provided to placate particularly strong stakeholder views. These were generally the views of the consumer sector, where low-income consumer advocates sought precautionary limitations on retailer behaviour; one consumer representative in particular was known for his threats to make things political and tear up the Retail Code live on a television current affairs programme. The ESC staff thus wrote some rules as a means of managing risk to the legitimacy of the Retail Code development process. As an aside, this is perhaps one of the reasons why energy co-operatives were not provided for: the idea was ahead of its time and not sufficiently supported by vocal stakeholders, and therefore it was not particularly salient for the regulator. The ESC's work programme was significant and while it recognised that providing for consumer aggregation and co-operatives would be desirable, it did not investigate the concept sufficiently because its resources were limited and the supporters of the concept were not as politically active as other stakeholders. State regulatory outcomes did not require external regulatory impact assessments at the time (and the national process was largely absent for energy), and the Victorian government was not engaged, so the only external accountability for the ESC was a more political accountability to demonstrate stakeholders' views were considered.

Although the ESC had intended the Electricity Retail Code to be a slim standalone document of principles, stakeholders' pressure to codify their preferences resulted in a legalistic and detailed regulatory regime. The final 31-page Electricity Retail Code in late 2000 (which grew to over 50 pages to accommodate gas and become the Energy Retail Code in 2003) was more legalistic than the regulations applying to the pre-FRC environment. It also called up two further regulatory guidelines on credit assessments and consumer consent, where compliance was mandatory through the retail licences. There was also the Marketing Code of Conduct, the Transfer Code, the Customer Metering Code, and the Metrology Procedure, all of which were unnecessary before FRC. Irrespective of the best intentions of the regulator, the Victorian retailers were the most regulated in the country.

Government intervention in pricing

It was not only the minimum standards that were regulated; prices were also regulated for several years, despite this not being the intention of the original policymakers. This constituted further financial risk to retailers, as retail input costs were volatile and retail price regulation did not always ensure cost pass-through. Recall that generation spot prices at the time could go to $10,000 a megawatt hour, which happened according to time of the day, day of the week, by season,

72 *Creating Victoria's regulatory framework*

and in relation to overall supply and demand conditions. Electricity retailers purchased energy dispatched into the wholesale market at the spot price, and generators and retailers also formed financial hedging agreements that limited the effects of volatile prices on both parties. The notion that external parties would have a better idea of efficient risk management and pricing was anathema to the industry. However, in 2001, Victorian electricity retailers faced price regulation in what they had believed was going to be a price deregulated market.

The political need to regulate energy prices in 2001

As it became clear that FRC would not start on schedule in 2001, the Victorian government and the electricity retailers agreed that electricity prices for the default 'standing offer' (the price all consumers started on) would not increase in real terms in 2001 above the prices that applied in 2000. This agreement in August 2000 was likely seen by retailers as a short-term political compromise with little risk attached. However, this did not turn out to be the case: the arrangement was enabled through a new 'reserve' pricing power the government gave itself, and set a precedent that was not reversed for some years. It was already a problem for retailers in late 2000, when wholesale prices increased substantially as a result of consumers' high use of air-conditioning and coincident generation shutdowns. Spot prices were pushed to the price ceiling on the hottest days in the summers of 2000 and 2001, where temperatures exceeded 40 degrees Celsius. This resulted in higher costs on average throughout the year to retailers.

With the increases in wholesale prices, in late 2001 the five incumbent retailers sought to increase their regulated standing offer contract prices by around 16 to 20 per cent, to apply from the start of 2002. As each retailer publicly advised its proposed price increase, the government referred the increase to the ESC to report on the fairness and reasonableness of the increase (although the Victorian Premier was frequently quoted in the media at the time as saying the rises were not acceptable). This required the ESC to assess the various factors of retail prices and determine appropriate benchmarks against which to compare the retailers' proposals. This was problematic given the complex components of prices, the inevitable subjective quality of how retailers might manage their hedging contracts and efficiency in the market, and the difficulty of determining reasonable price increases (which may include cost recovery for inefficient or unsuccessful practices) and unreasonable increases that may reflect retailers exploiting their smaller customers. Following a public consultation process, the ESC recommended ranges of acceptable benchmark prices for the retailers. On the basis of this, the government allowed some price increases, but the increases were much smaller than the retailers had requested. The government's media release was highly political, claiming that the price increases were due to the previous government's 'flawed' system and its privatisation of the industry (see Office of the Premier, 2001).

The government also advised that price regulation would be reviewed based on the effectiveness of FRC, upon which the ESC was to report to the government by September 2002. Given that such a report to government would have to go through consultation processes and effectively be completed by August, this meant that the government was expecting the effectiveness of FRC to be judged only six or so months after it had commenced. By choosing such a brief evaluation period, the government had essentially entrenched price regulation. The timing was likely related to the next Victorian election, scheduled for November 2002. The timing of the FRC effectiveness review provided for the government to continue the appearance of maintaining control over the electricity retailers during the election campaign.

It was therefore predictable that the ESC's final report found that competition was not yet effective, despite 'considerable progress' being made (ESC, 2002: 79), and price regulation was maintained.

The problem of regulating prices low in a competitive market

Regulating prices to politically acceptable levels had undesirable implications for the competitive market. As the price regulated standing offer constituted the starting point for small customers in the market, it was the yardstick against which consumers compared alternative offers made by retailers. Expensive standing offers were expected to result in high customer take-up of alternative packages in the market, while low standing offers would provide little opportunity for retailers to compose cheaper alternative offers. Therefore, if competition was to be facilitated, the standing offer needed to be priced at a level sufficient for competition to take hold through cheaper prices. However, this did not account for the important public policy matter of consumer access to supply at reasonable prices. Further, there was the risk that a standing offer priced at a level that included a margin for competition would necessarily discriminate against those customers who were unlikely to be provided with any other contractual offer. At the time, some consumer advocates were concerned this might happen to vulnerable and low-income customers.

The conflict between the concept of electricity as a commodity and the concept of electricity as an essential service is thus obvious. Allowing the price to be high enough to encourage competition would disadvantage consumers who could not obtain a lower price through the market, yet regulating standing offer prices to levels low enough to protect these consumers would undermine competition. The ESC was confronted with this problem when the Victorian government required it to determine benchmark prices in 2001. Other jurisdictions that were implementing FRC at the time also had to grapple with this dilemma, where the level of standing offer price had a fundamental influence on competition. Of the United States jurisdictions, Pennsylvania was the only market to have substantial customer churn at the time, but this was because it set a high retail margin on its standing offer, which it called a 'shopping credit'. Other US states set rates that were too low, and 'established standard offer rates in a way that could not possibly lead to retail competition, especially for small customers' (Rosen, Sverrisson and Stutz, 2000: 87).

74   *Creating Victoria's regulatory framework*

Conclusion

This chapter has discussed the origins of FRC in Australia, where the state of Victoria provided the precedent for the meta-regulatory consumer protection regime that was eventually adopted in various forms across the country. This chapter has set the scene for the chapters to come.

In this chapter we saw that the industry seemed incapable of consulting with stakeholders and writing rules for self-regulation. From a systems theory perspective, we might posit that the retailers were primarily operating within the economic function system, and that with its code of payment/non-payment and programme of prices, the economic system was not able to 'see' (that is, find meaning in) the non-economic requirements of the policymakers, the ESC or the consumer advocates. Therefore the retailers could not create norms or self-regulate on non-economic issues. What the economic system *did* see was financial risk to payments and prices, and so the industry reacted accordingly with risk-averse behaviour. The industry responded to its uncertain environment with bureaucracy, which was logical from a retailer perspective, as it placed a semblance of order on the uncertain environment. Although energy retailers claimed they wanted principles and not prescription, at every point they sought prescriptive rules in order to be able to act.

While the retailers' behaviour may have been rooted in an economic perspective, it was unpredictable in any traditional economic sense. The original policy reform rationale assumed that retailers would act to establish a functioning market with minimal barriers to competition because they were traditionally economically rational (which the reformers took to mean an interest in capturing greater market share). This belief rested on the assumption that the long-term interests of different retailers would coincide, and that retailers would act in these long-term interests rather than perhaps pursuing less predictable short-term interests. This assumption about industry interests is shared by some of the meta-regulatory academic literature. However, the outcomes did not meet these expectations. The objectives underpinning FRC were not consistent with how retailers perceived their interests and so were not internalised as retailers' organisational objectives. There was also no consensus of organisational values across retailers, and there was no agreement about appropriate steps to FRC, which is why the retailer bureaucracy turned out to be inefficient. This is not surprising, with research over many years finding that business interests are not always organised or in consensus (see Bardach and Kagan, 1982: 221; Hood, Rothstein and Baldwin, 2001: 113). Systems theory also explains this outcome, noting that systems, including organisational systems, operate self-referentially according to their own virtual worlds rather than a world that exists in any objective sense.

Ultimately the market could not develop without the regulator taking a stronger role: the ESC and its processes were necessary to get anything done. Following the industry's failure to organise itself there was meta-consensus from stakeholders for the ESC to pursue the necessary work for FRC; the regulator was the one party with the perceived independence and the consultative

Creating Victoria's regulatory framework 75

processes in place. The ESC essentially acted in a political administrative role in that it provided binding decisions, and the various stakeholders accepted this given the lack of alternatives and the need for a regulatory approach for the impending market opening. The ESC's processes also enabled the function of the legal system – in this case, the Electricity Retail Code – to stabilise societal expectations (norms).

However, while there was meta-consensus on the ESC's development of the consumer protection regime, there was no consensus on the detail of the regulations or the underlying values, and further discussion did not help. The lack of consensus was present not only between different stakeholder groups but also within them, and related to the value of markets and of consumer protections for an essential service. The ESC found itself in the difficult position of negotiating irreconcilable world views and eventually handled this through various trade-offs. It also developed symbolic regulation where this was politically necessary.

This chapter has also shown that the government demonstrated that it had the will to intervene directly to affect regulatory outcomes, which it did during 2001 and 2002. The FRC reform programme put in place a clash of economic and political values: the market focus of FRC did not sit easily with the political need of the government to reduce risk to itself and to be seen to be in control of consumer protections. In the end, the government's perception of the political danger of allowing free market forces in the provision of an essential service outweighed any perceived benefits from the market. This is consistent with a systems theory perspective that identifies the political system as coded by government/opposition, and thus government viewing its environment through the lens of public opinion and of staying in government. This finding is, however, inconsistent with meta-regulatory theories that assume the government to be only a benign enabler of policy.

The ESC's approach to consultative regulation was largely successful, becoming a model for future years that most stakeholders viewed positively. That could be the end of the story, where diverse interests came together to create a well-regarded regulatory regime through a participative process (even if there was unexpected political intervention). However, it was just the beginning: of course competition was not yet effective and retailers' compliance with the regime was not yet established.

Notes

1 It is not clear how much of the government's renowned programme of economic rationalism was cynical politics and how much was true faith. In a speech to the Electricity Supply Association in February 2000, the person commonly considered the architect of the Victorian reform programme, Dr Peter Troughton, was reported to call for FRC to be 'scrapped', saying that the push to expose Victoria's residential and farming customers to full competition was driven by ideology rather than good policy (Rollins, 2000).

2 It was said at the time that a retailer needed to be guaranteed of at least 500,000 customers to make any profit, and at least one million customers to give price reductions

76 *Creating Victoria's regulatory framework*

and make reasonable returns (Ward, 1999). This was one-quarter to one-half of Victoria's domestic and small business market, and so was a very high threshold for a new retailer to meet and largely impossible in the short term within the Victorian market alone.

3 At the time of writing this had risen to $13,800 a megawatt hour.

4 By which time the government had enabled the minimum standards under the Code through changes to the *Electricity Industry Act 1993*, and later through the *Electricity Industry Act 2000*.

5 Consistent with my previous broad use of the term, I use the term 'stakeholder' in this book to potentially mean any party in the regulatory space. However, every party was at some point another party's stakeholder. Use of the term should be self-explanatory depending on which perspective one takes; where a particular organisation is mentioned (such as the ESC) everyone else is that organisation's stakeholder for at least that moment or on a particular issue.

6 Using the Weberian (1964) sense of bureaucracy as merely rule creation and routinisation.

7 The requirement for every consumer to personally give their explicit informed consent to the new retailer in order to switch retailer limited the value for co-operatives and aggregators to have a direct role with the consumer, meaning that the business case for these organisations became weak.

References

Bardach, E. and Kagan, R.A. (1982) *Going by the book: the politics of regulatory unreasonableness*, Temple University Press: Philadelphia.

Consumer Coalition (2002) *Submission by Consumer Law Centre Victoria, Consumers' Federation of Australia, Financial and Consumer Rights Council and Victorian Council of Social Service to the Essential Services Commission: assessing the effectiveness of full retail competition for electricity for low-income and vulnerable consumers*, submitted to the Essential Services Commission, June.

Department of Natural Resources and Environment (2000) *Security of electricity supply taskforce report*, State Government of Victoria, September.

Department of Treasury and Finance (2001) *Proposal paper: implementation of the Essential Services Commission, the government's response to consultation and proposals for legislation*, June, Melbourne.

Dryzek, J.S. (2010) *Foundations and frontiers of deliberative governance*, Oxford University Press: Oxford.

E Source (2000) *Customer loyalty and switching: the new dynamics of retail competition*, Strategic Issues Paper XIII, Financial Times Energy: Boulder.

Energy Action Group (2001) *Essential Services Commission: exposure draft, submission by the Energy Action Group*, submitted to the Department of Treasury and Finance, July.

Energy Projects Division (1997) *Victoria's electricity supply industry: towards 2000*, Department of Treasury and Finance: Melbourne.

ESC (Essential Services Commission) (2002) *Special investigation: review of the effectiveness of full retail competition for electricity: Final report*, Melbourne, September.

Field, C., Lowe, C. and Nelthorpe, D. (1999) *Consumer participation and protection in the Victorian electricity market following retail contestability in the below 160 MWh per annum tranche*, Consumer Law Centre Victoria and Consumers' Federation of Australia: Melbourne.

Creating Victoria's regulatory framework 77

Griffiths, D. (1999) *Small consumer empowerment, Co-operative Energy's response to the Consumer Law Centre Victoria and Consumers' Federation of Australia: consumer participation and protection in the Victorian electricity market following retail contestability in the below 160 MWh per annum tranche*, Co-operative Energy: Melbourne.

Hood, C., Rothstein, H. and Baldwin, R. (2001) *The government of risk: understanding risk regulation regimes*, Oxford University Press: Oxford.

Myer, R. (1999) 'Power industry accepts rural charges cap', *The Age*, 9 November, p. C1.

Myer, R. (2001a) 'Power retailers feeling heat', *The Age*, Business News, 23 February, p. 3.

Myer, R. (2001b) 'Prices, insurance bedevil power game', *The Age*, 5 August, p. 3.

Myer, R. (2001c) 'Public urged to consider choice of power supply', *The Age*, 10 October, p. 5.

Office of the Premier (2001) 'Bracks Government acts to limit electricity price rises', Victorian Government, media release, 19 December.

Office of State Owned Enterprises (1994) *Reforming Victoria's electricity industry, stage two: a competitive future – electricity*, February, Department of the Treasury: Melbourne.

Premier and Trade (2001) *Beattie Government acts to stop electricity price rises*, Queensland Government, Ministerial media statement, 3 October.

Rollins, A. (2000) ' "Scrap" power freedom of choice', *The Age*, 22 February, p. A7.

Rosen, R.A., Sverrisson, F. and Stutz, J. (2000) *Can electric utility restructuring meet the challenges it has created?*, Tellus Institute: Boston, November.

Schulze, J. (1999) 'Power of marketing meets new challenge', *The Age*, 9 November, p. C5.

Scott, D., Marles, F. and Wise, G. (1995) *Report of the Independent Public Enquiry into the privatisation of the electricity industry*, People Together Project: Melbourne.

Sharam, A. (2001) *From universal service to no service? The redlining of vulnerable customers in Victoria*, Energy Action Group/Essendon Community Legal Centre, Melbourne, October.

VaasaETT (2012) *World energy retail market rankings report 2012*.

Verrender, I. (2000) 'Power play', *Sydney Morning Herald*, 2 September, p. 23.

Victorian Council of Social Service (2001) *Essential Services Commission: response to proposal paper, submission by the Victorian Council of Social Service*, submitted to the Department of Treasury and Finance, July.

Ward, A. (1999) 'New TU boss sees Australia as attractive investment opportunity', *Electricity Supply Magazine*, no. 53, May, Electricity Supply Association of Australia: Sydney South, pp. 8–9.

Weber, M. (1964) *The theory of social and economic organization*, ed. T. Parsons, The Free Press: New York.

Wilson, N. (2001) 'Pulling the plug on power price reforms: grid and bear it', *The Australian*, 5 October, p. 34.

4 The next thirteen years

Complexity, politics and change

The previous chapter described the development of the electricity regulatory framework for full retail competition, or FRC, in Victoria until late 2002. This chapter looks at the regulatory policy environment over the subsequent 13 years, from 2003 to 2015 inclusive, both in overview and also in the detail of the political environment as it affected the industry. The 13-year period reflects much of my own time in the industry after leaving the Victorian regulator's office. Although Victoria is still a focus, this chapter also covers the other key competitive markets in the National Electricity Market (NEM): New South Wales, Queensland and South Australia.[1]

Consistent with the Victorian experience outlined in Chapter 3, the retail energy policy environment across the states was marked by conflicting values and perspectives. Despite compliance not being a problem in any systemic sense, the regulatory regime itself was highly contested. It was subject to constant and unresolved stakeholder[2] conflict about the degree of harm experienced by consumers in the market, the degree of harm to be tolerated, and who should bear the various risks or costs. There was significant consultation on the issues over the years, but nothing seemed to bring stakeholders together.

Retailers observed their environment with disquiet: it was highly political and became only more so over time. Outcomes were fundamentally unpredictable, with the drivers for policy change percolating up from smaller decisions and perceptions within the political system that retailers were not able to observe. Retailers struggled to manage and account for the contingent nature of decisions and events,[3] with reputation risk management remaining particularly elusive.

To continue a theme from Chapter 3, it should be recognised that none of the stakeholder groups discussed in this chapter – that is regulators, governments, retailers and consumer advocates – were unitary entities. Each of these groups was marked by intra-group conflict, whether this was between the national and state regulators, energy department staff and their political leaders, low-income and mainstream consumer advocates, or incumbent and second tier retailers. Within each sub-group there were also differences on individual issues, based on different parties' contrasting ideological positions, organisational cultures, commercial outlooks and size. However, there were sufficient similarities within groups enough of the time to provide the group characterisations presented here.

The next thirteen years 79

Overview of the markets: 2003–2015

The Victorian electricity FRC framework was replicated for the Victorian gas industry in 2002, and for the South Australian electricity and gas industries in 2003 and 2004 respectively. The New South Wales energy market rules for 2002 were also based on those developed in Victoria. Queensland moved to FRC several years after the other states (2007) and so took what were considered the best parts of the other states' regulations to create the Queensland regulatory framework. The largest customer base was in New South Wales, with more than three million small customers (residential and small business), followed by Victoria with more than two million customers, Queensland with more than 1.5 million customers, and South Australia with less than a million customers.

The states also privatised their retail assets: South Australia was privatised in 2000, Queensland in 2007, and New South Wales in 2010. In response to the opening of the new markets and the privatisations, the retailers integrated significantly across the states, leaving three incumbent retailers, which had incumbency in at least one region in one fuel in most states. The incumbent businesses were Origin Energy, AGL and EnergyAustralia (which had gone through several name changes, from its original TXU to TRUenergy, to EnergyAustralia). There were also around 11 second tier retailers that competed in all or at least several jurisdictions. Most active retailers were considered national to some degree.

The Victorian rules remained the most comprehensive of the state regulatory approaches, eventually forming the basis for the national regulatory approach that was to replace the states' regulatory regimes in 2012. Victoria was also unique in other (related) ways: this is where the strongest consumer advocacy occurred, and this was the market privatised first. As noted previously, Victoria was reportedly the most competitive retail energy market in the world from 2005 to 2011 inclusive, based on customer switching statistics (VaasaETT, 2012). It was also the first Australian state to deregulate retail energy prices, where, from 2009, the standing offer prices were no longer approved by government, although they still had to be published.

The state (and eventually national) regulatory approaches were meta-regulatory, with a combination of principles, competitive markets, self-reporting, consultation and transparent information. Table 4.1 shows how the core elements of meta-regulation were present across the jurisdictions. The detail underpinning the information in Table 4.1 is explained in the chapters to come.

Compliance outcomes

As shown in Table 4.1, retailer compliance largely met regulatory expectations over the period. Retailers demonstrated the core central elements of compliance systems as identified by regulatory scholars (see Parker and Nielsen, 2009), with dedicated compliance functions that trained staff, shared information, maintained relevant breach registers and managed reporting to regulators. The compliance functions in the more sophisticated retailers (and in saying this I mean most

80   *The next thirteen years*

Table 4.1 Demonstration of meta-regulation in the Australian retail energy markets

Core elements of meta-regulation	*How these were demonstrated in the retail energy markets*
i Formal rules are based on principles, not prescription.	The regulatory frameworks used principles and set out processes. Outcomes were not prescribed.
ii Law is reflexive and responsive.	If we take the law as the regulators, they were reflexive and responsive: regulation and its interpretation were regularly assessed and reconsidered in light of compliance outcomes as well as stakeholder concerns.
iii Third parties such as non-government organisations and activists support regulation by acting as 'civil regulators', via	Larger retailers had customer consultative committees, and many retailers also developed informal relationships with consumer advocacy organisations.

• consultation for policy formation, to make sure that the right values are embedded in rules; and
• enforcement, in
  a monitoring, and
  b using reputation in markets to force industry self-reflection and culture change.
	The regulators engaged in public consultation for regulatory development and change, including comprehensive meetings that involved all relevant stakeholders. Low-income consumer advocates were particularly represented in regulatory consultation. The advocates also regularly published reports about retailer performance (outcomes); most were taken up by the media in some form.

iv Business self-regulates within the above context (and is also reflexive and responsive).	Energy retailers self-reported breaches as below; they were proactive in identifying issues. Compliance was generally found to be high. Energy retailers existed in a competitive retail market with high consumer switching rates.
v Transparency in business performance is promoted, specifically compliance and performance reporting (both self-reporting and regulatory reporting) to provide for industry self-reflection under (iii) above, and third parties to have information to act upon under (iv) above.	The retail energy businesses self-reported compliance breaches and reported on performance indicators. Retailers were also required by regulation to periodically bring in external auditors to audit on set criteria. Auditors' reports were also provided to the regulators, and reported on publicly.

retailers) had a focus on continuous improvement, and they worked with the complaints handling functions of the organisations.

The regulators used the retailers' self-reported data to publish regular compliance reports on the industry that showed little in the way of systemic or material breaches, and retailer self-audits provided the same results. As identified in the public reports, where there were breaches, they primarily related to

The next thirteen years   81

information technology (IT) problems. This was most apparent when the three incumbent retailers each experienced billing delays and inaccuracies after they upgraded their IT platforms from around 2008. Each incumbent had inherited incompatible IT systems when they acquired other retailers, resulting in costly processes (such as separate call centres on different systems) and major impediments to effective business and customer analysis. The IT 'transformation' projects were to resolve these issues, but as multi-year, highly complex projects they brought problems of their own. It was also not just the incumbent retailers that had IT issues: incomplete data and/or inflexible IT structures were the bane of most retailers.

Call centre responses were sometimes raised as compliance problems. Call centre agents were at times found to provide deficient advice to consumers on issues such as access to financial hardship programmes and government concessions schemes (which covered rebates and emergency relief). There were also erroneous disconnections of customers. These were not endemic problems, but they were relevant given stakeholder concern about how retailers assisted vulnerable consumers, as discussed in the next section. The issues relating to supporting customers in financial hardship are also the topic of Chapter 5.

The door-to-door sales channel was also regularly the subject of compliance commentary. As the main driver for in-situ customer switching (that is, switching that did not involve a customer moving house), it was used heavily by most retailers for some years, and had a reputation for misleading sales agent conduct. However, it took until 2012 for a punitive regulatory response, when the competition regulator started taking retailers to court. Before then, compliance concerns were handled at the bottom of the enforcement pyramid (see Ayres and Braithwaite, 1992). Chapter 6 discusses the events leading to the incumbent retailers discarding the door-to-door sales channel entirely for residential consumers.

Performance outcomes

Retailers also self-reported on performance indicators, such as numbers of customer disconnections and payment plans, customer debt levels, complaints and call centre call handling times. In contrast with compliance statistics (where breaches could incur penalties) performance statistics were for information only and there were legally no right or wrong outcomes. Retailers were required to provide regular data (generally quarterly) to the relevant regulator and the regulator released annual performance reports that described trends and provided comparisons between retailers. In addition to providing a means for assessing market trends, performance reporting also provided context for compliance findings and Ombudsman complaints. For example, if a retailer's trend on a measure became abruptly worse this might indicate deeper problems – including as-yet-unreported breaches – and warrant closer attention from the regulator.

Although performance reporting was consistent with meta-regulation, it was not planned. In Victoria, performance reporting had carried over from before

82 *The next thirteen years*

FRC when the energy companies were first privatised, and in the early days of FRC the intent in Victoria was to wind it back. However, this did not occur. Over time, external stakeholders (particularly the consumer advocates) were highly supportive of performance reporting because it would help keep the retailers accountable. In 2012, the national regulatory regime adopted the bulk of the Victorian indicators and supplemented these with further topics to assist the regulator to form a view on the state of the market overall (which was part of its remit).

Performance outcomes as reported over the research period are difficult to characterise, other than to say that there were no major or sustained issues identified by the relevant regulators. The data were complex and difficult to compare both across time and between retailers. Regulators' reports tended to provide the numbers for the various indicators and note shifts from previous reporting periods, but they did not draw conclusions. However performance as a *concept* is another matter, with stakeholder concerns about performance not meeting the right objectives driving much of the policy debate discussed later in this chapter and in Chapter 5.

The industry experience

From the industry perspective there were several elements of the Australian retail energy markets that were consistent over the period of this research. Retailers were subject to ongoing regulatory policy uncertainty, with regulatory obligations changed for unpredictable reasons. The period from 2009 was particularly politically tumultuous, with several changes of government across the states and at the national level. These changes created the expected challenges as each new government came up to speed with its remit and considered its own priorities, but they also had a role to play in the far more damaging political nervousness – and even capriciousness – that all stakeholders observed as major reforms were undermined to meet other agenda. The regulatory uncertainty reached a peak from 2012 as policymakers and regulators regularly changed the rules to meet political needs. Regulatory impact statements were noticeably absent from the regulatory environment, particularly in the states.[4]

Price rises also drove unpredictable political intervention: electricity prices increased by 45 to 84 per cent in most jurisdictions (30 to 62 per cent in real terms) over the five years to June 2012 (Australian Energy Regulator, 2012: 4). Energy prices became salient for the community as a whole for the first time, with media reporting focusing on the issue from around 2009. This in turn drove a swell in public opinion about the energy industry, which was exploited by various special interests as they represented the price rises in different ways,[5] including by the governments who were largely responsible for the price rises and sought to reallocate blame to other parties. Price rises were generally caused by government-owned network infrastructure costs and government green schemes, including the short-lived federal carbon price mechanism that was in place for two years from mid-2012.

The next thirteen years 83

Regulatory policy uncertainty was also related to jurisdictional governments *retaining* regulatory obligations beyond their expected use-by period. The key example of this was each government introducing and then retaining retail price regulation. Despite a formal inter-governmental agreement in 2006 for the governments to deregulate prices when competition was found to be effective, the governments did not behave as agreed. The political risk for politicians was too great, particularly in the environment of rising prices.[6] Price deregulation across most NEM states did eventually occur, with the reasons discussed further in Chapter 6. However, until deregulation occurred in each state, standing offer price regulation was the industry's number-one policy issue. It was the largest structural constraint on retailer behaviour, affecting retailer decisions about market entry, prices, and offers made. For the incumbent retailers that provided standing offers, the problem of price regulation was primarily a matter of cost recovery – some price caps (particularly for regional areas) left retailers unable to recover regulated network costs, let alone able to recover wholesale and retail costs and make a profit. Second tier retailers did not have to offer regulated prices but standing offer price regulation still set the prices they had to beat to obtain customers. It was vital to these retailers that regulated prices had the required headroom for their offers to be appealing to consumers. Where prices were set too low in some jurisdictions, second tier retailers left the markets.

Technological advancement was also a key theme for the period. The advent of smart meters in 2011 in Victoria (taking more than three years to be rolled out across the state and playing a role in Victorian price rises) was a fundamental evolutionary step for the industry. Smart meters read consumption on a half-hourly basis and communicated this information to meter data agents, who then provided the data to relevant market participants for customer billing and for network management. Smart meters were read remotely rather than requiring a site visit, and the meters could also be connected and disconnected remotely. The technology enabled consumers to be given near real-time feedback on their energy use, more accurate bills, more frequent bills (if required), better tailored energy services, and reduced fees because site visits were no longer required to read meters. The technology also allowed a range of third parties to enter the market in different ways to compete with retailers. While not a topic for this book, smart meters also provided for industry disruption, where smart meters, combined with household solar panels and battery storage, were expected to fundamentally redesign the energy value chain and the customer experience.

The major structural events through the period 2003 to the end of 2015 are shown in Figure 4.1. This shows the changes that national retailers were expected to anticipate and/or accommodate. As shown in the timeline, the research period can be characterised as a series of phases, from bedding down FRC and privatisations from 2003 to 2009, to preparing for change through 2009 to 2012, to a period of unprecedented change and upheaval from mid-2012 to the end of 2015. Figure 4.1 does not show the many consultations occurring at any given time. There were probably between ten and 20 consultation processes in

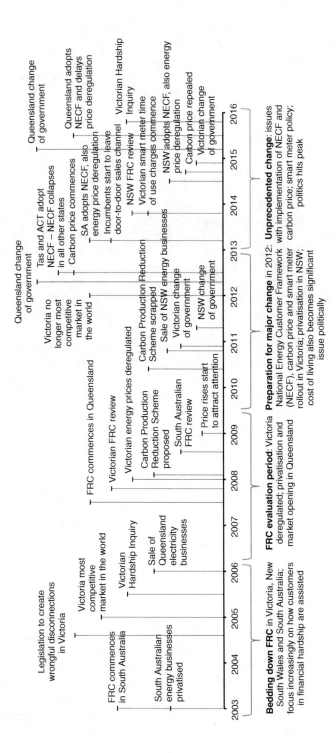

Figure 4.1 Structural change in the Australian retail energy markets, 2003–2015 inclusive.

The next thirteen years   85

play across the issues and jurisdictions at any one time, with industry (and often consumer groups) expected to attend workshops and submit formal responses.

The remainder of this chapter discusses the key events and points of concern for the industry in more depth.

Protecting vulnerable consumers

Retail energy consumer protections existed to protect small consumers in the market from unfair or unreasonable contractual terms and from misleading sales practices in the delivery of an essential service. It is worth reiterating that these protections were comprehensive, with rules on matters such as customer contract entry and termination processes (including consent to transfer and allowable contractual variations), minimum mandated payment methods and retailer offers of payment support, detailed contents of bills, collection cycles and disconnection processes.

As discussed in Chapter 3, the primary group for whom regulation was drafted was the 'vulnerable' residential consumer group, where vulnerable consumers were considered more likely to experience disadvantage in the market. The experiences of vulnerable customers continued to dominate regulatory thinking over subsequent years, with the discussion that commenced in Victoria in 1999 about vulnerable customer needs in the competitive market continuing to play out in cycles of policy consultations across most jurisdictions. A serious complication in these consultations (and a driver of them) was that 'vulnerability' was immune to objective definition, as discussed below.

Of course the meta-regulatory programme itself enabled the cycles of regulatory consultation and debate. With its focus on stakeholder involvement in policy setting and enforcement, meta-regulation provided a logical means for stakeholders to raise issues and seek engagement. Further, the soft terms used in meta-regulatory instruments such as the Victorian Retail Code were interpreted in quite different ways by different stakeholders, and interpretation also varied over time. This in turn meant that policy issues were regularly reinvigorated as people concluded that the regulatory programme (and occasionally the regulator) was not working as it should. The debates took on a strong moral tone, with stakeholders competing to define good or moral outcomes according to their own perspectives.

Chapter 5 examines the debates about bill affordability and the experience of vulnerable consumers in the market. Chapter 6 addresses how retailers sold energy services to consumers (including vulnerable consumers), and the troubling issues with door-to-door sales in particular. This section provides an overview and background to the topics covered in those two chapters.

The definitional problem

As with the pre-FRC days of the Victorian Retail Code development, although people intuitively grasped the concept of vulnerability, the concept was complex

86 *The next thirteen years*

and did not lend itself to definition or codification in rules. There were no definitive public debates about what truly constituted vulnerability, and efforts to address vulnerable customers related more to actions targeted to specific groups by special interests.

In my own participation in policy discussions I observed that there were two categories of vulnerable customer: those who were vulnerable to financial hardship from high bills or inadequate income, and those who were vulnerable to their own poor decision-making and/or exploitation by others due to a limited capacity to understand the market. The 'affordability' group included those with high energy consumption from changing family situations (new babies, long-term visitors, energy for medical use), people prioritising other expenses (house and car repayments, school fees, medical bills), and those with reduced income as a result of unemployment (between 4 and 6 per cent of the population) or in the category of 'working poor'. Bill affordability was also said to be a problem for many tenants of energy inefficient (often public) housing. The circumstances that produced financial hardship were often correlated; for example, an accident could lead to medical bills and result in unemployment, which could give rise to increased energy use for the person due to being at home more.

The 'limited capacity' group of vulnerable consumers included people who entered contracts they did not understand or who agreed to terms they could not manage, people who did not understand their bill (and perhaps paid bills they did not realise were incorrect) and people who did not have the means to discuss problems with their retailer when problems arose. The usual examples of this group included non-English speakers, the elderly and the mentally ill. Low literacy was a particular issue for people engaging with energy contracts and bills, with the Australian Bureau of Statistics (2006) estimating that in 2006 around 46 per cent of the Australian population, or seven million people, had poor or very poor literacy, numeracy and problem-solving skills. These people had difficulty using many of the printed materials encountered in daily life, such as bus timetables and bank statements.

There was no easy way to differentiate causes and effects when addressing consumer vulnerability to disadvantage, and there was also overlap between the two vulnerable consumer categories in practice. For example, a person with very low literacy could be expected to have a lower paying job or be unemployed. The people who struggled to understand their options could also find their energy and other bill affordability problems amplified if they agreed to contracts with higher prices than necessary, paid fees they could have avoided or were not confident to ask for more flexible payment arrangements from their retailer.

Moreover, none of the indicators were definite or stable over time. A consumer could be notionally 'vulnerable' but not have that vulnerability activated (such as a low-income family that rationed well, or a person who had poor English but who never solicited or received an energy contract), or they may have been effective despite the vulnerability (such as a non-English speaker who had information from a marketer translated by a family member). In addition, it might not have been clear when individuals were vulnerable and when they were

The next thirteen years 87

not. For example, a consumer may have been elderly but had no cognitive problems and been perfectly able to represent their own interests. A consumer who was 'vulnerable' on one occasion might not be on another occasion, such as where people experienced temporary financial difficulty or treatable mental illness. This meant it was impossible to meet all the needs of all vulnerable customers ahead of time in a clear operational sense. One could make assumptions about disadvantage, but none of this would be tangible until the disadvantage happened, and, by definition, the disadvantage would then be too late to avoid.

Even the experts in the area of vulnerability did not necessarily focus on those consumers most in need. Research carried out for the Victorian government showed that the group most likely to be vulnerable to financial hardship was not as expected by policymakers and as advocated for by consumer groups. Actual consumption data collected from retailers and distributors showed that financial vulnerability was most likely for dual-income families with mortgages (see Deloitte, 2011). This was further supported by energy retailer AGL's demographic research in 2012, which showed the most common type of customer in its hardship programme was in the 'Family Formation' cohort, with a 'sizeable' monthly mortgage or rental costs and with children who, as 'uncontrollable consumers' used a range of appliances in the household (Simshauser and Nelson, 2012: 21).

Stakeholder moral perspectives

We can see that consumer vulnerability was a complex concept, with multiple, shifting variables that did not allow for a targeted policy response.[7] Further, 'vulnerability' was in itself a precautionary term that signalled *potential* disadvantage, not an actual experience. However, even a focus on actual disadvantage did not materially reduce the scope of the policy problem. Consumer disadvantage could be caused (or reduced) by one or a combination of actions (including no action) by the consumer, government, regulators, retailers, the broader energy industry, other creditors or community groups. For example, the concept of electricity being affordable for vulnerable consumers potentially covered a range of factors: governments providing adequate social welfare payments, concessions and energy efficient public housing; retailers providing flexible payment terms at the right time and the retail market setting prices at their lowest efficient levels; electricity generators and networks setting prices at efficient levels; and the community sector providing advice and direct support. Even when limiting the focus to government alone, potential government failings and support were still spread over various departments (such as education, health, public housing, social security and disability services), and across state and federal governments (state governments paid low-income and pensioner energy concessions and rebates, and the federal government was responsible for income support).[8]

The spread of stakeholder responsibility for influencing consumer disadvantage fuelled ongoing stakeholder debates and policy reform efforts, where

88 *The next thirteen years*

the policy problem could be framed in multiple ways and targeting a solution was a matter of interpretation (and appetite for genuine solution ownership). This was intensified by stakeholder disagreement about what the market was able to achieve in either a normative or practical sense: for example, some low-income consumer advocates viewed a lack of bill affordability for some consumers as a market failure and for retailers to resolve, while others saw this as not a market issue but related to the role of government and its failure to provide sufficient income.

Related to this, stakeholders also held radically differing perspectives on the capacity and rationality of consumers. Retailers viewed consumers as predictably economically rational beings who were responsible for themselves in contractual relationships; the retail model seemed incapable of seeing any other perspective. In contrast, the low-income consumer advocates regularly argued that consumers, particularly vulnerable consumers, were not the rational decision-makers of classical economic theory. Many low-income consumer groups considered that vulnerable consumers needed protection from themselves as well as from retailers.

It seemed that stakeholder views could not be fundamentally reconciled, and debate only served to reinforce the differences. It should be clarified that this is not because the stakeholder organisations were necessarily unimaginative or lacking in the desire or skills to communicate, but because they held strongly subjective moral[9] views. Their perspectives on their own moral standing and the morality of others were intrinsic to their organisational self-talk and their external communications. Importantly, each stakeholder organisation had a self-image that it alone (sometimes also its sectoral counterparts) possessed the key to determining the public interest, and, therefore, to defining right and wrong practices. For example, the apparent self-image of consumer advocacy organisations was that they acted on behalf of consumers, and particularly those who were disenfranchised. This was a moral position, whereby they sought to capture the attention of governments and profiteering corporations to hold them accountable for consumer welfare. As will be shown in later chapters, many low-income consumer advocates were deeply cynical about markets meeting consumer interests and did not believe in retailer self-regulation. Retailer organisations were also highly moral in their collective self-image. Retailers believed that they acted on behalf of their investors, employees and customers. This was a moral position whereby retailers believed that they benefited society by providing returns to shareholders, providing jobs in the community, and giving consumers a choice of service at the lowest price. For retail organisations, it was a given that product choice through markets and less government involvement were in the public interest.

These moral positions tended to immunise the different organisations against learning about and internalising each other's perspectives. (To reiterate: each of the consumer advocacy and retailer organisations believed that *they* represented consumers.) This outcome is not unusual: empirical findings from behavioural economics have confirmed that efforts to induce perspective taking 'can be difficult to implement successfully' due to the natural bias to assume one's own position is objective and exaggerate others' self-interest (Pronin and Schmidt, 2013: 208; see also Sunstein, 2010). Having people go through a process of considering their own and others' views can actually have the opposite of the desired effect and create further self-justification and distrust. This occurred in the retail energy environment, where conflicts about the roles of the retailers and the government were sustained and reinforced through consultation.

Disconnection case studies and consultations

Although vulnerable customers could be disadvantaged in the retail energy market in a range of ways, the primary concern for most low-income consumer advocates was these customers being disconnected from supply for non-payment of a bill. This was framed as a moral issue about the denial of an essential service to someone in financial hardship. While disconnections were allowed by the retail rules, most low-income consumer groups argued that retailers were not doing enough before disconnecting consumers. Thus more rules were required.

Over the years, the consumer advocates published several reports containing case studies of the experience of vulnerable consumers who were in financial hardship and disconnected from supply. The case studies were moral tales that humanised the dry regulatory policy discussions and brought the issues to life. This made them difficult to ignore, even if the probability of harm was low for consumers as a whole (see Sunstein, 2010, for a discussion of these effects of the precautionary principle). As a result, case study reports prepared by low-income consumer advocates were often the trigger for policy debates and consultations. The extract below is from a 2004 case study of a Victorian energy user who was a sole parent with three young children. She was disconnected for non-payment of her gas account several times and was $800 in debt. The story picks up after she has been disconnected for non-payment for a high bill accumulated across two properties.

> Kate was reconnected when she applied for an URG [government-provided emergency relief]. However, her application was unsuccessful because she filled in the form incorrectly. After the reconnection, the [gas] company offered Kate an instalment plan of $60 per fortnight. Although Kate told the company that she could not afford such high payments, the company refused to reduce the amount so Kate agreed to the plan.
>
> Kate fell behind in her payments because they were too high. She contacted a welfare agency and discussed her situation with a financial counsellor, who advised that her current repayment levels were unmanageable. The company still refused to lower her instalment payment amounts and said that it would instead send her another URG application form as the financial councillor [sic] could assist Kate to complete it. Kate never received the new URG application form, despite being told by the company that it had sent the form to her three times. Kate found this difficult to believe as she

90 *The next thirteen years*

continued to receive bills from the company in the meantime. A few weeks later, after having missed two instalments, Kate's gas supply was disconnected again....

Kate described those she dealt with at the company as rude, largely because of the constant insinuation that she was lying about not having received the URG application forms. The company also never informed Kate of the existence of EWOV [Energy and Water Ombudsman Victoria]. Kate went to see her financial counsellor again, who referred Kate to EWOV. EWOV arranged for Kate's household to be reconnected and negotiated a payment plan of $40 per fortnight. In addition, the company agreed to waive $300 if Kate sticks to the payment plan for 12 months. However, Kate continues to have difficulties meeting the payments and has asked the company for another URG application form. The company has refused to send her another application form until her financial counsellor returns from leave.

When we met Kate she was still struggling with her electricity, gas and telephone bills. She receives $850 per fortnight in the pension but her rent alone is $440 per fortnight. Kate has been trying to find part-time work. Some time earlier she had what she described as the perfect job.... However, her employer changed her hours to 8 am until 4 pm and Kate had to resign, as the new hours meant that she could not make sure the children got to school in the morning and she could not make it home on the bus by the time the children returned. She is currently working half a day a week at the local church for $8 per hour.

Kate told us 'a lot of nights I don't eat', as she wants to ensure that she has the money to pay for things that her children need. Kate explained that it is all the little things that many people take for granted that cause her difficulties – she cannot get a hair cut, pay for school excursions (luckily the school is understanding about this) or buy a new pair of shoes (without a car and far from public transport, Kate walks a lot). Kate's house used to have an Internet connection for her children's school work, but Kate had to cancel it. Kate's eldest son in particular gets upset by these conditions and has run away from home numerous times. He tells Kate how sick he is of being poor, asking her 'why don't you pay the bills?' and telling her 'you won't even let me turn the heater on'. Kate worries a lot about him. Kate's 11 year old child is often sick and her 13 year old child is asthmatic and needs expensive allergy medication. The bedrooms are freezing in winter as there is no heating in them, and on cold nights she moves the family's mattresses into the living room so they can sleep in front of the gas heater.

The house Kate currently rents ... has an old ... heater in the living room which Kate believes is faulty and uses excessive amounts of gas.... Kate has made several requests to the landlord about fixing the heater, which Kate suspects triggered a surprise inspection by the owner. A few days after our meeting, Kate was due to attend a tribunal hearing in relation to a Notice to Vacate her residence....

(Rich and Mauseth, 2004: 61–63)

The next thirteen years 91

This case study was from a consumer advocate report *Access to energy and water in Victoria*, which focused on new rules the authors believed were needed to apply to energy providers to support consumers in financial hardship. This report was the trigger for the Victorian wrongful disconnection legislation discussed in Chapter 5. What should be noted at this stage is the emotional pull of the story, as well as the sheer complexity of the consumer's circumstances. It is clear that there were multiple sources of difficulty for the family, including inadequate income and access to state emergency relief, insufficient flexibility from the gas retailer, no family support, employment difficulties, illness, poor rental accommodation, and bill payment pressure from other sources. However, while the authors acknowledged some of these factors, the substance of the report viewed the family's problems through the lens of energy retailer behaviour.

Policy discussions about case studies like this were often narrowly framed to provide the best chance for the energy policymaker or regulator to deliver neat and practical responses (at least, practical for them), which meant focusing only on what further energy regulation could be drafted to make retailers appropriately attentive. There was rarely discussion about whether better enforcement of existing rules was required or whether issues were systemic across the sector, and there was no context provided about the instances of poor or unsympathetic retailer behaviour compared with service delivery the rest of the time. There was never discussion about what might be a reasonable expectation of businesses managing millions of quarterly billed customer accounts via call centres, contractors and mail houses, or what level of error might be acceptable given what consumers were prepared to pay for.[10] Open discussion about the appropriate roles of government and retailers was conspicuously absent. Possible forms of government support were sometimes suggested by consumer advocates, such as improving welfare assistance or energy inefficient housing (particularly public housing), but these were often tangential to the main proposals to improve retailers' processes.

Although the case study approach was the most successful in stakeholder policy advocacy, government responses to these cases were still unpredictable, sometimes resulting in government formal or informal inquiries and sometimes having no apparent effect. Even where a government stated a desire to take action, this provided little indication of the government's genuine appetite to make changes; what looked like action could be more rhetoric than reform. Outcomes of these regulatory policy debates thus showed no real pattern, and depended on a number of contingent factors. Where it felt obliged to act, the logical government response to the challenges of meeting conflicting policy objectives was to pass on the problem to the regulator. Delegating complex decisions to the regulator meant that a government could be seen to do something about an issue when setting the terms of reference.[11] A notable exception to the practice of governments delegating to regulators (and for conflict to be unobserved) occurred in Victoria over 2004 and 2005, when the regulator was publicly undermined and marginalised by the government in order to achieve political outcomes in the area of consumer financial hardship. Chapter 5 discusses that case in detail.

92　*The next thirteen years*

Policy outcomes tended to be more predictable when regulators managed policy debates. Regulators were more closely linked to achieving energy and consumer policy objectives than they were to managing political risk or building reputations (but there were always exceptions). The regulators often created the rules in the first place and therefore felt greater ownership of outcomes, and as enforcers they also had a greater investment in ensuring the rules were sensible and enforceable. In particular, regulators followed their versions of due process for most regulatory issues. However, as with the ESC's development of the Retail Code discussed in Chapter 3, regulatory decision-making nevertheless relied on trading off assertions and finding middle ground: economic tests of benefit and evidential studies of consumer harm were frequently absent. Regulators still needed to engage in political decision-making because there was often insufficient evidence to objectively pick one stakeholder argument over another and it was inefficient (and reputationally risky) to even try.

Retailers responded to the consumer case studies and subsequent consultations with concerned caution. They were risk averse in their public representations: they did not seek to defend themselves, and they did not explain or contextualise the apparent errors identified. When they provided public submissions to consultations, retailers used remote and managerial language to talk about markets, competition and the value of innovation. Why did the retailers behave in this way? There are several likely reasons. First, some of the cases reported were objectively indefensible, demonstrating clear and avoidable faults in retailer judgement or processes that led to a vulnerable consumer being disconnected from supply. Second, where retailer fault was less clear, the industry was still on a hiding to nothing given the discussion had already been framed by the case studies' claims that retailers had done the wrong thing. In the face of emotionally charged stories about families struggling without electricity or gas, retailers were never going to be persuasive about any misrepresentation of the detail or about other factors in the consumer's life and the role of other parties to provide support. Third, it is likely that retailer responses were subdued in the hope that the relevant report or process would go away; there was no need to breathe life into an issue (even to make reasonable arguments) if the government or regulator was unlikely to ultimately take action.

Another reason retailers did not publicly defend themselves is because they were uncomfortable. I observed over the years that many retailer representatives did not seem equipped to discuss the difficult issues related to consumer financial hardship, at least not on the terms of the consumer advocates. The issues and politics were perplexing to people with traditionally rational market beliefs and even more perplexing for those who believed their own processes to be compliant (and in some cases, quite sophisticated). This was amplified when compliance managers were involved in consultative settings; I often found regulatory policy staff (externally focused, dealing with the compliance risk from potential rules) and compliance staff (internally focused, dealing with operational compliance with set rules)[12] to have quite different dispositions, with compliance-oriented people much less likely to engage on policy matters. Further, consumer

The next thirteen years   93

financial hardship was a long-term policy matter, and most retailers did not retain sufficient institutional memory to be able to address and manage the complexity and history of the issue with confidence. I discuss the reason for this in more detail later in this chapter.

Contingency and unpredictable outcomes

The previous sections in this chapter have demonstrated that policy uncertainty was pervasive in the energy retail environment and that this was exacerbated through the inherent politics of meta-regulatory consultation and enforcement. *Most* outcomes in the retail energy regulatory and policy environment were highly politically contingent, in the philosophical sense of contingency as multiple possibilities that are neither necessary nor impossible. In the complex and politically charged energy retail atmosphere, regulatory and policy changes could just as easily occur as not occur; outcomes were the result of often random and minor events and cascading small decisions coming together in particular ways at particular times. The sheer number of factors at play made prediction of political events impossible; everything could always be different, from the broadest policy level through to the detail of specific compliance obligations. This has significant implications for the implicit meta-regulatory assumption that an industry can observe, understand and predict its environment (including the views of its stakeholders) in order to self-regulate and protect its reputation.

At the broad policy level, the uncertainty described in Chapter 3 continued for retailers across the states, with the Queensland government saying it would not privatise or move to a competitive market, but then shifting to both not long after. The government of New South Wales had a privatisation agenda that was discarded and revitalised several times until the retail energy businesses were finally sold in 2010. There were also many different decision-makers over the years: for example, in Victoria during the 17 years between the development of FRC in 1999 to the end of 2015 there were three changes of government (and six changes of Premier), eight energy Ministers, three ESC Chairmen (the head of the Commission) and several ESC CEOs, and all had different capabilities, interests, agendas and opportunities to act on energy retail issues. The attitudes of Premiers and Ministers (and regulators) varied from subdued to evangelical and they also were not necessarily aligned even within the same government. Each national retailer dealt with this kind of complexity across time not only in Victoria but also in South Australia, Queensland, New South Wales, the Commonwealth, and sometimes the jurisdictions of Tasmania and the Australian Capital Territory.

At the level of policy detail, energy retail issues came to light with little predictability, and whether they were acted on was as unpredictable. An issue gaining traction with policymakers depended on many small windows of attention, information and opportunity coinciding. New regulation (or regulatory debate) was often triggered by anecdotes recounted to politicians, government departments or regulators, and on small numbers of individual case studies developed by

94 *The next thirteen years*

consumer advocates at particular points in time. Any of these anecdotes and case studies could just as easily not have eventuated (or been different) at other times or with other people; experiences could have been better or worse, leading to different regulatory outcomes. Issues were pursued based on individuals' or agencies' capacity and perception of the need for action (or the need to be seen to take action).

The news media's reportage of issues was also contingent, which amplified the contingency of political outcomes because the political system could not reliably observe its performance via the lens of public opinion (this also meant that the public could not get a clear view of relevant industry issues). The only energy retail topic that was reported with any predictability was retail price rises, which occurred every year. This topic, which was enthusiastically covered from 2009 onwards, often generated further stories over subsequent days. The industry was aware that several current affairs programmes and tabloid newspapers kept electricity prices as their regular backup for quiet news periods.

The media also tended to accept the media releases provided by governments and other stakeholders and did not investigate or report the issues with any rigour. Reportage in the tabloid media in particular helped perpetuate confusion about the different elements of what was already a complex industry, frequently referring to the greed of 'power companies' without differentiating between the network and retail sectors, and rarely (if ever) raising the responsibility of governments to provide adequate social support through welfare payments and bill concessions. The fact that the network businesses with the highest price increases were government-owned (Queensland and New South Wales) also escaped the community's awareness, with the media helping to perpetuate ignorance about this. For example, in October 2013 an article from a major news agency reported that the then New South Wales Energy Minister had stated his government would be 'banning over-investment by electricity companies' who were seen as 'gold plating' (Wood, 2013). The Minister was further quoted as saying: 'For too long the energy industry has tried to fly under the radar. Well, people are noticing. And it's time to step up' (ibid.). There was nothing in the article that identified the electricity companies in question as specifically network businesses, or as being owned by the Minister's government.

Non-price retail energy news was equally as likely to go unreported as be reported, with domestic and international events and crises overshadowing energy retail matters. Energy as a topic was often too complex and dry for the media to tackle. Sometimes when a retail energy issue was identified or exposed, it was solely about personal events in reporters' or policymakers' lives, making energy relevant to them as a story. There were regular cases where a media focus on energy retail issues arose solely from a reporter or a member of their family being mistreated by call centre staff or a door-to-door sales agent. I was also aware of instances where mundane personal issues, such as a journalist's illness or annual leave, meant there was no reportage of energy issues that would usually be in the news.

None of this bodes well for the meta-regulatory principle of consumers acting in the market to hold industry accountable. In the Australian retail energy markets, consumers did not receive reliable information to act upon – either direct from industry stakeholders or via the news media. However, there was also no evidence that consumers were interested or engaged other than on a superficial level.

The rise and fall (and rise) of the National Energy Customer Framework

A further aspect of the contingency of energy policy and rule-making related to the complexity of the political horse-trading that occurred when multiple states[13] became involved in national market decisions. The primary example of this was the development and implementation of the National Energy Customer Framework, or NECF, which was to replace the separate state energy regulatory regimes and shift responsibility for regulation from state regulators such as Victoria's ESC to the national Australian Energy Regulator (AER), a division of the Australian Competition and Consumer Commission (ACCC).

After strong lobbying from the industry for national consistency in regulation, and after formal government inquiries that supported national energy law, work commenced on this reform in 2004. However, it took several years to have a final agreed version of national law and rules. There were many stops and starts along the way, and most of the states were lacklustre in their engagement on the issues while NECF was being developed. NECF had to be agreed by all Energy Ministers (including the federal Energy Minister), and it was frequently held up as various parochial state-based issues were brought to the fore and Ministers would not agree until their interests were accounted for. The federal government drove the reform and was more enthused, but there was attrition in responsible personnel and gaps in the timeline as new people came on board. This happened several times, and with each change in staff the learning that should have accumulated over time about the range of complex policy issues was lost.

There was also significant public consultation regarding NECF. This was similar to the consultation on retail minimum standards in the states, with by now largely predictable positions taken by all. The Victorian consumer advocates campaigned hard to have the Victorian framework made the basis of NECF so that Victorian consumers would not lose hard fought for protections. By 2010, the view of the NECF officials was that they needed to cater to the specific concerns of the consumer advocates if they were to have NECF implemented at all – Victoria was keen to progress but the other states were starting to lose interest. As a result, and after all consultation had closed in 2010, the NECF officials introduced new and unannounced consumer hardship provisions to NECF in order to get it through the political process and meet the Victorian consumer advocates' needs.

Further changes were made to NECF during the implementation phase, where each state used its parliamentary process to create legal derogations to embed state-specific ways of doing things. Each state government was keen to avoid a public perception that consumers in its state could be 'worse off' in any way,

96   *The next thirteen years*

and so regulation across the states only increased, and not consistently. The final versions of NECF varied on fundamental aspects such as the definition of customer types, and which retailers had to provide offers to which customers. These differences all had systems and call centre implications for retailers that ran the risk of negating the whole point of the national reform. Victoria had the most significant derogations, such as adding substantial smart meter regulations and retaining its 'iconic' legislation on wrongful disconnections, as will be discussed in Chapter 5.

Project teams to implement NECF for 1 July 2012 were established across all relevant governments (state and federal), and within each of the distribution and retail businesses. The AER was heavily resourced and spent two years developing a range of guidelines enabled by NECF, including a performance reporting regime, price disclosure fact sheets and an online price comparison service. However, in the month prior to the planned start date, NECF was significantly delayed in several states. The delays were preceded by an election announcement in Queensland in February 2012 that essentially shut down the Queensland Parliament when it was scheduled to debate the NECF implementation legislation, which meant that NECF was not able to commence on time in that state. The Queensland government took some time to confirm its position, only formally advising the industry that NECF would not be starting on time in Queensland at midnight, 1 June 2012. The next morning, the New South Wales government released a media statement that NECF would also not start in New South Wales on time, and would in fact be delayed until 2014. Victoria followed suit two weeks later, as did South Australia. In the end, only Tasmania and the Australian Capital Territory moved to NECF on 1 July 2012, with these being the smallest and least competitive markets.

These events took everyone by surprise. While the potential delay in Queensland's implementation was expected after the February election announcement, discussions with the Queensland government had still indicated a clear desire to proceed as soon as possible. The New South Wales decision on 1 June 2012, and what came after this, was completely unexpected, with much of the industry (and I suspect the AER and various government departmental staff) in a state of shock. There is no doubt that the last minute abandonment of NECF by the New South Wales government was politically motivated; it was part of its agenda to discredit the federal Labor government and its carbon policy. In late 2011 the then Liberal New South Wales Premier had announced that his government was going to require a message on retail bills to explain the (high) combined cost to consumers of the federal Labor government's carbon pricing mechanism and the previous state government's solar scheme (Sydney Morning Herald, 2011). The message was clearly political propaganda: not only was it generic and combined different schemes, but it also had to be in a prescribed (large) red font and on every page (Coorey, 2012). Making changes to billing systems was time-consuming and expensive and the industry found the New South Wales proposal and its own position as a political pawn unacceptable. Even so, the industry believed it had no choice because it was advised that legislation allowed this kind of government intervention, and the Premier was clearly determined to implement his proposal. There was also a view held by some retailers that acquiescing on this issue put the industry in credit with the government and that other decisions might then be viewed more favourably, such as price deregulation.

However, it turned out that the government did not have a legislative mandate to apply the bill message requirement, and it had not realised this until it was too late to pass new legislation. The only option for the government to enforce the bill message was to create a new retail licence requirement. The problem was that the licensing framework was to be replaced by NECF. Therefore, to get the bill message mandated, NECF had to go. The New South Wales announcement made on 1 June 2012 stated that the government would defer implementing NECF until 'the Government is satisfied that consumer information protection measures are satisfactory' (Hartcher, 2012). This was a clear misrepresentation; the Minister himself had said a week earlier when he had introduced the NECF Adoption Bill into Parliament that there was 'a real need for this national reform' (New South Wales Hansard, 2012: 11829). Calling it 'best practice consumer protection', he said NECF created a 'robust consumer protection framework with particular protections for vulnerable consumers in financial hardship' (ibid.: 11831). The decision to sacrifice NECF for the bill message was even confirmed publicly in August 2012 when a regional newspaper (Smith, 2012) quoted a spokesperson for the Minister saying the government 'planned to sign up to the framework but confirmed it would not be able to enforce the warnings on bills if it had been part of it from the July 1 start date'. This was not picked up by any other media, and the cause for delaying NECF was not the subject of public commentary.

Victoria took a similar politically convenient path, and the Victorian government – which had led the NECF reform, including chairing the jurisdictional governments' NECF implementation group – released a statement in mid-June that it would 'defer its transition to new national laws … to ensure there is no reduction in key protections for Victorian consumers' (O'Brien, 2012a), further stating 'we are not prepared to accept a dilution of key Victorian consumer protections as a result of this reform'. In fact this was not the reason for the delay, at least not in the way this statement was likely to be interpreted. The Victorian government had already made significant state-specific additions to NECF in its reform package, and the coverage of consumer protections was not seen as an issue by government. What actually happened was that the Victorian government and the federal government (which funded the AER) could not reach agreement about how many extra AER regulatory staff would be required for the Victorian-specific regulations (and particularly smart meter regulations), and which government would pay for those additional resources. This was widely known to be a source of frustration for both governments, with each keen to implement NECF. Despite some public sabre-rattling from the Victorian Energy Minister in April 2012 that if the federal government did not provide assurances about AER funding to administer state-specific arrangements, Victoria would 'be left with no alternative but to reconsider its position' (O'Brien, 2012b), the

98 The next thirteen years

industry was repeatedly told by both governments that the issue would be resolved in time. However, this all changed when the Queensland and New South Wales announcements were made – it was easier for the Victorian Energy Minister to align with his counterparts in the other Liberal states than to further try to breach the impasse of AER funding.

South Australia's delay was also politically motivated, but this time by the (Liberal) Opposition, which held up the passage of the NECF Application Bill in the South Australian Parliament for months due to a point of disagreement on solar tariffs that was unrelated to NECF and only relevant because the two issues were covered in the same Bill. This was known to be a game of political brink-manship, and again the industry was told the issue would be resolved in time as the Opposition had no issue with NECF. However, the precedent set by the other states meant it did not need to be resolved.

No version of the public interest was served by these political actions. NECF had the most comprehensive consumer protections of all the jurisdictions (including in Victoria once the Victorian derogations were added). The high cost of the preparations across government and the industry were also already sunk, with cost recovery via tax payers and energy consumers' bills. The states' deci-sions to not proceed incurred further costs from unwinding the almost imple-mented NECF and (potentially) re-implementing it months later. The regulators were in disarray, with the state regulatory frameworks unclear for the rest of 2012 and the various state government departments distancing themselves from assisting in unpicking or resolving the problems experienced. There were also flow-on effects, where a number of extensive national processes to examine other provisions to roll into NECF were delayed or discontinued. Although the events discussed in this chapter were publicly known, there was no further media attention or apparent interest from the community at all.

The disorganised approach to NECF persisted for years. The first of the delayed states to eventually move to NECF was South Australia, where the South Australian government made a surprise announcement in mid-December 2012 that it would adopt NECF early in 2013, giving retailers very little time to redo systems and process changes. South Australia's adoption of NECF coin-cided with its decision to deregulate prices from 1 February 2013, and the last minute timeframe was likely driven by a court case between retailer AGL and the regulator, as discussed in Chapter 6. New South Wales moved to NECF next: after vacillating between various start dates the state adopted NECF on 1 July 2013 in a reasonably uncontentious process (at least in comparison with other states and its own history).

Queensland and Victoria were messier, with Queensland moving to NECF in mid-2015 – three years after it was originally due to be implemented – and Vic-toria never making the move. Queensland announced in early 2013 that it would adopt NECF in the first six months of 2014, then in late September 2013 the government advised stakeholders that NECF would instead commence in mid-2015 to link with proposed price deregulation in that state. Victoria was the worst jurisdiction for NECF uncertainty, with the government stating in 2012 that it would likely move to NECF on 1 January 2014 and then saying nothing more. In the absence of government direction, in early 2013 the Victorian ESC undertook significant consultation to harmonise the Retail Code with NECF based on a comprehensive revised Code it had prepared in late 2012. This was for a start date of mid-2013, which slipped to September 2013 and then October 2014. The Victorian move to NECF was clearly not going to happen when by the end of 2015 the ESC was signalling that it was going to overhaul the NECF-harmonised Victorian Energy Retail Code in line with a Victorian-specific 'modernisation' agenda and it was already proposing changes to harmonised financial hardship provisions.

The story of NECF is astonishing. We must remember that the industry uncertainty about NECF was uncertainty about *who the regulator was and which regulatory regime was in place*. NECF was a comprehensive regulatory regime with hundreds of pages of law and rules that applied to complex systems and processes for millions of customers, and yet no retailer in the key states could effectively plan for compliance. The NECF experience could have, and really should have, been different. Perhaps it would have been different if there had not been Liberal governments in the key states and if the implementation of NECF had not coincided with a Liberal campaign to make the federal Labor government look bad. At the time of the decision to delay NECF, the south-eastern states of Australia had been held by a critical mass of Liberal governments for only a short period: Victoria had a change of government in late 2010, New South Wales in early 2011, and Queensland in early 2012. If any one of these governments had not gained power, there might not have been the eventual result to delay NECF, as there might not have been a critical mass of states not proceeding. It can also be expected that if the federal government had not introduced a policy as contentious as a carbon price (and if it had also been Liberal) the states would not have acted as they did. These were extraordinary circumstances that unfortunately involved NECF as collateral damage. NECF may have predated the various governments and their policies, and it may have been a significant project, but none of this counted compared with the political whims of the time.

The NECF example was clearly a message to retailers to 'be careful what you wish for', because nothing was ever certain despite the assurances from policymakers over the years. The wasted efforts of all involved in NECF since 2004 would have amounted to a significant cost, and the uncertainty that was finally seen as resolved as 1 July 2012 approached was then reinvigorated for the next several years.

The Victorian smart meter debacle

An example that perhaps exemplifies how mundane personal events could change the political environment relates to the 2009 annual leave decision of an industry regulatory decision-maker that may have created (or at least contributed to) a catastrophic political effect for the then Victorian government's smart meter programme.

100 *The next thirteen years*

The benefits said to flow from smart meter capacities were said to be significant, and on this basis the Victorian government mandated a smart meter rollout to all customers between 2010 and the end of 2013, to be run by the distribution businesses. However, the programme was expensive, with costs 'smeared' over the customer base via distribution charges from 1 January 2010. This meant that each Victorian consumer paid for the new meters (and associated communications technology) regardless of whether they wanted a smart meter or already had one installed. The smart meter programme was unpopular with consumer advocates: low-income consumer advocacy groups were concerned about the costs and the potential for consumer disadvantage from new elements, such as remote disconnection and time-of-use pricing (see Mauseth Johnston, 2009). The government's management of the programme had also caused the Victorian Auditor-General (2009) to submit to Parliament a scathing report detailing inadequacies in the department's project governance. Overall, the smart meter programme was extremely fraught for government, and it sought a low profile on the matter. Although the consumer advocates' reports received some media attention, this was not prolonged and the mainstream consumer population did not engage with the topic in any observable way.

It was in this environment that one large incumbent Victorian retailer, Origin Energy, decided to highlight the costs of smart meters. At the start of 2010, it provided to each of its Victorian customers a new bill line item that showed a 'smart meter charge' with a dollar amount. This created pandemonium with consumers, with complaints to government and talkback radio running hot with Origin's customers calling to complain that they did not want the smart meters, and most saying that they refused to pay for something they had not yet received. The government was put on the defence, and the then Energy Minister was extremely upset with Origin, criticising the retailer in Parliament and stating to the media that Origin was trying to undermine public support for the programme (Dunckley, 2010).

The smart meter programme did not recover from the public backlash for some time. The community attention reduced but remained significant, particularly as fringe activists started to occupy media space with wildly inaccurate stories about smart meters causing house fires and about the electromagnetic fields generated by the meters causing significant illness in humans and animals. Again, these claims were not questioned by reporters. By 2011 the community distrust of the programme was so great that a material portion of the population was refusing a smart meter, and violence was reported to have occurred against electrical contractors who tried to replace meters. There were also multiple delays in necessary government policy, with three or so revamps of the departmental decision-making structures and working groups, and several cost-benefit assessments undertaken. Some of the changes were driven by changes in government and political portfolios: a new Liberal Premier came to power in late 2010 after having promised action to re-evaluate, and potentially stop, the smart meter programme as a pre-election promise. Another change in both Premier and

Energy Minister (but not government) in 2013 complicated the policy to support smart meters and time responsive tariffs just as key decisions needed to be made. The smart meter rollout was eventually completed in 2014, behind schedule and with ongoing issues with consumer meter refusal.

It is hard to explain definitively how the Victorian smart meter programme became such a debacle, but it is clear that the smart meter charge on bills acted as a catalyst by bringing the programme into the public consciousness. The government and distribution businesses had previously portrayed the smart meter rollout as a technical system upgrade and had essentially disregarded consumer advocate concerns about pricing outcomes and the need for consumer information. However, the new charge on the bill made it immediately salient for consumers and had them asking what they were getting for their money. This was particularly concerning given the other energy and lifestyle cost increases that applied at the time, and the low consumer confidence levels resulting from the global financial crisis.

Why did Origin Energy segregate and highlight the smart meter charge? Presumably it was seen as a good idea at the time by the marketing staff, and no-one realised that there would be consumer or political upset. Anecdotally, it appears that the key (politically sensitive) internal stakeholder who usually would have been consulted and would have reviewed and potentially argued against highlighting the smart meter charge was on extended leave at the time, and so did not have the opportunity to dissuade the marketers. Therefore, it came as a great surprise to Origin when its decision caused so much concern. While it may seem strange that the eventual political nightmare for government could have snowballed from one person's decision to take leave – or rather, that it might not have happened had that person been available to reject the idea of the bill item – I believe that this type of situation was more the rule than the exception given the complexity of the environment and the many decision-makers and their intertwined and cascading decisions. Every problem and every scandal experienced in the industry had its roots in the many mundane and small decisions that preceded it, whether these were observed or not, and any one of these decisions might just as easily have been different.

When the Queensland Premier went to war with Origin Energy

Origin Energy was the subject of further political drama in 2012, this time regarding retail pricing and an unintended conflict with the then Queensland Premier, Campbell Newman. The Premier was a charismatic ex-Mayor of the City of Brisbane who had announced he was running to be head of the Opposition party before he was even a member of Parliament. 'Can do' Campbell, as he was known, was successful in his efforts, and voted into power as Queensland's Premier in an election landslide in March 2012. Much of his campaign had been about cost-of-living issues, with a pre-election promise to freeze residential electricity prices. In April 2012 he fulfilled this promise and froze the general domestic tariff despite the regulator, the Queensland Competition Authority

102 *The next thirteen years*

(QCA), having decided to allow a price increase to reflect underlying increases in network costs (which retailers had already argued did not recover costs as it was, resulting in an ultimately unsuccessful court action for Origin).

On 29 June 2012 the Premier held a televised press conference (which I watched), where he spoke at some length about a letter that had just been received by his family from their energy provider, Origin Energy. The letter announced a future price rise which Premier Newman believed breached his price freeze. His anger at the press conference was palpable, with him making statements that he was 'crosser and crosser and crosser' about the letter, and about how 'disgusted' he was with the 'outrageous' price increases (see also Newman, 2012a). He said he would start a public awareness campaign against Origin, urging Queenslanders to boycott the company. He also stated that he was going to shift $27 million of government contracts away from Origin and refer it to the consumer law regulator, the ACCC. He brandished his letter in front of the cameras, saying the Origin Energy CEO

> needs to stand up in front of Queenslanders and explain why anyone should use his company after what he's done…. This is just not on. These price increases are not justified…. We've kept our promise and this is an outrage. It's a total outrage.
>
> (Ironside, 2012)

The government subsequently publicised the contact details for all competing retailers, and rushed through legislation to ban exit fees on contracts so that customers could leave Origin without penalty. It even established a website to explain its price freeze and included information about how to switch away from Origin.

Before continuing, I should note that the Premier's outrage and promises in his initial press conference may have come from a misunderstanding about the coverage of the regulatory regime, and thus the coverage of his price freeze. Market contracts – that is, contracts formed between customers and retailers with explicit customer consent – were not price regulated. Price regulation (including the price freeze) only covered the standing offer contracts that came into effect as a default option. Origin's price increase was legitimately applied to market contracts (and only market contracts) which was a fact not communicated by the Premier at the time.

Two other points are also worth noting: First, the price freeze was subsidised by the Queensland government. Retailers were compensated for the difference between the frozen price cap and regulated price cap, so consumers were paying indirectly for the original regulated prices in any event. This was public information but reported on only once to my knowledge. Second, the other incumbent retailer in Queensland, AGL, also increased its prices a few days after Origin, but there was no political commentary and very little media reportage. Everything could have been different for Origin if it had not had Campbell Newman as a customer or if it had not been the first to raise prices, although it did not help

The next thirteen years 103

that Origin's fixed price rise was much higher than AGL's and that Origin was also taking the QCA to court at the time.

The 'war on Origin', as it was known, went on for two weeks, with articles in the Queensland newspapers most days about the government's various efforts to encourage switching away from the company. It came to an abrupt end on 17 July 2012, when the Premier and Origin each released statements to the media that Origin would not impose the market contract price rises after all. Origin's media release implied that the decision was taken because it recognised the cost-of-living issues for consumers, and it stated that its communications with customers and the government 'could have been better' (Origin Energy, 2012). Premier Newman's (2012b) media release stated that Origin had decided to 'adhere' to the price freeze after he met with the Origin CEO, stating it was 'a win for common sense and a win for cutting the cost of living for Queensland families'. The media coverage painted the government's action as a 'fierce campaign' (Daily Mercury, 2012) and Origin's response as a 'massive backdown' (Wardill, 2012), 'buckling' and 'bowing to pressure' from the government (The Australian, 2012). The entire situation was perplexing to observe.

How did consumers actually react to the events in mid-2012 in Queensland? The eventual outcome was that consumer responsiveness to Premier Newman's reputational smearing of Origin was low. Public churn statistics from the technical regulator at the time showed no significant or sustained switching in the state for that period. This is telling: even when reminded on an almost daily basis that Origin was a 'bad' retailer, when actively advised by a trusted leader to switch retailer, when provided with other retailers' contact details and with a ban on exit fees, consumers barely reacted.

As a postscript, in February 2013, it was revealed in the usual public regulatory price setting by the QCA that the price freeze was ending and that it had resulted in high price rises for consumers for the next financial year in order to bring prices to cost reflectivity. This was not the subject of significant media commentary. Four months later the Queensland government further announced that energy prices would be completely deregulated in 2015 (McArdle, 2013), which received a subdued media response. In fact, and continuing the broader theme of contingency, price deregulation did *not* happen as announced, after another surprise election result in February 2015 delayed price deregulation for a further year.

Inside the industry

Chapter 3 showed how retailers responded to perceived risk in their environment by creating business rules and avoiding major decisions where possible. As this chapter has shown, the retailers' environment only became more risky; it was characterised by structural and technological change, and the politics of energy as an essential service for small customers meant that every decision was contingent and potentially political. At various times during the research period – and often for extended periods – retailers were not able to reliably plan ahead about

104　*The next thirteen years*

which markets to enter, how to price their offers, how to manage compliance (because it was not clear which consumer protection regime and regulator would be in place) or which technologies would be present to enable improved service offerings.

The basis for action: commercial drivers and the bottom line

While there has been significant debate in the corporate social responsibility literature on the rights of stakeholders versus shareholders, it is hard to argue against the basic concept that company directors have a fiduciary duty to their shareholders and adopt the functional primacy of the economic system. All retailers that I was aware of in the energy industry primarily used the coding of the economic system, with a need to develop internal economic business cases for various actions to proceed, particularly where finances were tight. Business cases related to anything that required material new expenditure. Compliance was a priority, and most retailers did try to comply with regulation once it was in place, as well as sometimes going 'beyond compliance' as a regulatory buffer.[14] However, these efforts always occurred within the constraints of available economic resources per retailer, which were also in flux. This finding is consistent with the comprehensive research of Gunningham, Kagan, and Thornton (2003) into the effects of the 'economic licence' on corporate behaviour.

There were several complications in the development of business cases for compliance and innovative self-regulatory actions. First, it was never guaranteed that funding at the level requested by a compliance manager would materialise: no matter how good the business case, the compliance function competed with other business functions that were seen as equally, if not more, important to a business's success. Competing functions included necessary IT upgrades for billing, call centre and account manager resourcing, and sales expenditure to increase customer numbers. In the absence of a material risk of a compliance breach it was difficult to show regulatory or compliance improvements were a higher priority. There were also only so many issues a company could prioritise in times of change; if there were more urgent matters (such as mergers and technology upgrades) compliance improvements might be delayed. However, it is worth noting that business cases that were not explicitly marked as compliance could still provide compliance and/or customer benefits by improving systems and staff effectiveness.

Second, compliance and performance innovation to meet perceived political needs (assuming that it was possible to identify these) was sometimes challenging to have approved within a business because of a perspective from senior management that the existing rules and stakeholder expectations were already excessive. I regularly heard a view from retail industry leaders that energy should not be treated differently from other 'essential' services, and in stating this view they demonstrated that they did not buy into much of the political rhetoric at the time. This meant that efforts from within the business to improve already basically compliant business processes were likely to be met with some scepticism from the executive level. This was not necessarily a bad thing; as will be shown in the following chapters, the requirements of retailers continued to grow, with little relationship to demonstrated customer harm. If retail leaders had accepted every demand made by an external stakeholder it is questionable whether they would have remained solvent. Bills were never low enough for many consumer advocates, disconnection numbers were never low enough, and an innovative approach and good reputation appeared to provide no immunity to reputational smearing or the application of new rules.

Third, developing a business case for anything innovative was a challenge because of resource and cognitive limitations within the compliance and operational functions themselves. Where external expectations were unclear (as they generally were), these staff tended to lack the experience, time, energy or inclination to work out where regulators or other stakeholders were coming from; instead, they just wanted rules they could follow. It was efficient for a business to develop rules of thumb, or to make do, in an uncertain environment in order to demonstrate compliance. That the industry behaved like this should not be surprising given the long-standing and extensive international literature on organisational decision-making under conditions of uncertainty. Genuine change in retailer behaviour only happened slowly, and where there was a clear, new strategic benefit (such as products enabled by smart meter technology), or a clear, new cost (such as court action for non-compliance).

Management through risk frameworks

Consistent with the need for a business case for material expenditure (particularly in harder economic times), retailers tended to see compliance and reputational issues through the lens of financial risk. Risk calculations were necessary to understand how to move forward; this was a retailer's way of internalising the world according to its own values within the economic system. Risk management was also expected by the regulatory regimes, in line with the global shift towards managing uncertainty through risk frameworks to meet 'expectations of governance and demands for defendable, auditable process' (Power, 2007: 6).

Risk assessments occurred informally, such as where internal compliance experts and operations staff decided the best means of avoiding or managing the potential costs of breaches. They also occurred formally for those businesses with internal risk reporting that valued regulatory breach and reputational damage at an ostensibly more objective level. However, this is not to say that retailers' risk approaches were traditionally rational or predictable. Both informal and formal approaches were inexact because compliance and regulation did not neatly fit within the risk framework, retailers did not have the time or inclination for detailed probability assessments, and, as already noted, the industry had a significant blind spot when it came to identifying political risk. Retailers' formal approaches also struggled to clearly differentiate between cause and effect in their risk analyses and treatment plans. The conflict in values within every retailer complicated this task, with risk definitions, risk appetites and staff

106 *The next thirteen years*

views on the causes and effects of risk differing across and within operational, corporate and regulatory business units. Further, risk specialists were not the same as compliance specialists, and the differences in language and culture even between these apparently similar disciplines were noticeable.

Within this overall characterisation of decision-making, there were generally two ways that retailers considered reputational risk. The first was to focus on the risk of *costs as a result of compliance breaches*, where these included penalties and the indirect costs of incurring further regulatory scrutiny and potential audits. Managing reputation in this sense was about attempts to positively manage a retailer's reputation for compliance attitudes as perceived by the regulator. From this perspective, retailers responded to the uncertainty in their environment with caution. For example, externally imposed rules were not generally prescribed in the detail required by retailer IT and operations staff seeking to develop detailed process maps. To deal with this, retailers created internal rules that tended towards over-compliance with the basic minimum standards, or at least built in a buffer where possible to avoid errors at the margins. While this way of satisficing was not technically economically efficient, this was a 'middle way' to manage financial risk, particularly in the absence of actuarial analyses of probabilities, which themselves would have been imperfect.

The second way of considering reputational risk was to focus on the risk of *costs of broader reputational effects from perceived poor performance*, by which I mean social performance in line with meta-regulatory expectations. However, while there were attempts to quantify this type of risk, the *value* of this kind of reputation was rarely clear. Although reputation was considered an 'intangible asset' technically, its lack of tangibility made it more a rhetorical device than an asset per se. As noted above, retailers found over time that corporate social responsibility initiatives did not add clear value; they did not protect retailers from reputational smearing by consumer advocates, and similarly did not immunise retailers against government or regulatory intervention. Further, the consumer advocates' views on reputation were not pertinent to business decision-making as they did not affect the bottom line (see Steger, 2008: 563 for similar findings). This is discussed in detail in Chapters 6 and 7.

The *practice* of managing broader reputational risk in any objective or lasting way was also problematic. Reputation is about meeting others' expectations, and in a complex retailer world where there were many 'others' and their expectations were in conflict or unclear (and dynamic even when they could be established), there were rarely practical opportunities to positively manage reputation across the broad stakeholder base. Regulatory and government relations staff engaged with external stakeholders on policy matters but this was on an issue-by-issue basis and was linked more to managing potential compliance risk than anything else. Despite the rhetoric employed by the retail businesses at various times, reputational risk tended to only enter the conceptual frame for retail operational practice when it was linked to proven or imminent material costs. This meant that retailers generally made operational decisions without engaging in guesswork about political risk or non-economic outcomes; decisions were instead based on identifiable short-term economic costs and benefits that aligned with their internal business rules and priorities.

Nevertheless, retailers still perceived a need to address broader reputational risk, where at the very least (and this does not discount other reasons retailers may have had) this was about each retailer building a reputation with its shareholders as caring about its own reputation, and thus about shareholders' investment. Despite the difficulty of managing highly contingent outcomes such as those discussed in this chapter, retailers (like politicians) had to act as if such management was in fact possible. The language of risk provided some assistance in this endeavour: as observed by Hutter and Power (2005: 9–10) 'risk language functions as part of a web of normative framing practices in organizations in which risk management can be conceived as a moral technology for the attribution of responsibility'. Larger retailers also made use of functional specialisation within their business structures, with corporate brand and public relations functions generally filling the broader and long-term reputation risk management role. These functions talked about talk: the brand function was about creative advertising to build a positive reputation with consumers and other stakeholders, and the public relations function was about damage control to protect reputation once scandal occurred. However, these were *not* self-reflective functions that proactively scanned the environment for potential sources of reputational damage in order to learn about and recommend improvements to operational practice; they were generally remote from (and unofficially considered subordinate to) retail operations and regulatory business areas.

The instability of the corporate environment

Organisational responses to the regular environmental changes triggered internal change, with all retailers in cycles of internal reform every 18 months or so. Businesses were bought and sold, commercial outlooks changed over time, and key staff came and went; all of which prompted restructures and sometimes large scale redundancies. The incumbent retailers experienced the most change as these were the ones that tended to buy other businesses and inherit incompatible IT systems and surplus staff. As discussed earlier in this chapter, the three incumbents each embarked on significant IT 'transformation' programmes that involved shifting all customer records on to new IT platforms. These took years to complete and each of the three experienced compliance issues, mostly related to existing data not being suitable for the new IT platform, resulting in late, wrong or duplicate bills to customers. The businesses were also in the grip of various management enthusiasms, and were particularly open to approaches from consulting firms and others who offered better visions of the future.

Corporate brand, compliance and regulatory policy functions[15] were almost always part of organisational restructures as they did not have an obvious home. In the larger and more functionally differentiated businesses the regulatory policy function tended to move between corporate and retail divisions, where the

108 *The next thirteen years*

push/pull was between corporate policy staff who wanted to direct these functions across the whole enterprise but were not familiar with the detail, and the retail business unit that was familiar with the detail and wanted its own voice. The brand function had the same experience. The compliance function tended to merge and then split from regulatory policy as well as move between operations and risk areas. There was never going to be a perfect outcome for a functionally differentiated company, so the shifts continued, and for national retailers these occurred across states as well.

The overall effect of the constant quest for greater rationality and efficiency was that institutional memory was lost, or even disregarded when new leaders came in and assumed they could do better than their predecessors. Many retailers' staff experienced regular periods of uncertainty about their roles and futures, resulting in behaviours that were not conducive to collaboration or innovation. Certainly no one in this kind of environment wanted to draw attention to themselves by taking risks or spending money unless this was clearly consistent with the organisation's ideology at the time.

In summary, the combined effect of external change, financial risk frameworks and internal restructures meant that the sensible response of energy retail organisations was to hunker down into what they already knew within the economic realm and to not extend too far into new and untried practices. Change meant cost, and so operational staff only experimented with new practices when there was a solid financial business case that was sponsored by senior management.

Conclusion

The issues discussed in this chapter have shown that the incompatible stakeholder views and conflicted interactions from the early days of FRC continued over time and across jurisdictions. This was to be expected given that the value of energy as an essential service remained unclear: it was a moral value that had not been (and could not be) translated into meaning for any societal function system. No system could 'see' the issue on its own terms and therefore clearly communicate the value of essentiality. This was a particular problem with the market and the law, leaving the political system to make binding decisions in highly contingent and often hypocritical ways according to government risk perceptions. This was an entirely different phenomenon from the implicit meta-regulatory concept of stakeholder inclusion and discourse bringing different parties together to create consensus.

Further, and consistent with Luhmann (2013),[16] the low-income consumer advocates addressed the political system in their communications, where these communications were not about seeking consensus but protesting against the status quo. Low-income consumer advocates were particularly anxious about the future and most argued that further regulation to support vulnerable consumers was required in line with the precautionary principle, even where there was overall retailer compliance or apparent consumer satisfaction with the market.

The next thirteen years 109

The notion that increased regulation could bring with it more risk, or could mean foregone benefit was not countenanced. This behaviour shows that the meta-regulatory ideal of stakeholders working together to empower organisational self-regulation was not supported. The meta-regulatory literature presumes that meta-regulation can 'reduce the regulatory burden on government, thus freeing up scarce public resources to be allocated to situations where government intervention or assistance is most required' (Gunningham, 1998: 15). As will be explored further in Chapters 5 and 6, consumer advocates *did not want the regulators to do less*. Most low-income consumer advocates argued for government intervention when they felt that regulators were not doing enough publicly to enforce the law.

Governments and regulators were generally receptive to the concerns of the low-income consumer groups, even if this receptiveness did not result in policy change. This was the politics of 'doing something', which is a focus of the next chapter. The governments and regulators could not actually control outcomes or avoid making risky decisions, but they still needed to act as if this was possible. Of course, application of the precautionary principle did not resolve issues, because, by its nature, it was deeply politicised and contested (a finding confirmed by Black (2010) in financial services; see also Heanzle, 2010). Thus conflict continued to play out in ongoing cycles of debate.

This chapter has also shown that governments became committed political players in the retail energy markets for their own sake, or more precisely, to solve separate political problems. The example provided of the delays to NECF commencing demonstrates just how far governments were prepared to go to protect what they saw as their own interests, such as ensuring that political propaganda found its way onto retail electricity bills. NECF experienced collateral damage from a range of unrelated state political issues, leaving the industry unsure of which regulatory regime was in place and how to plan for the future. Government interference in energy prices (such as Premier Newman's price freeze and its true extent) was also unpredictable and left retailers unsure about available margins in price regulated states.

In theory retailers should have put in place cultures and processes that anticipated politics and avoided making politicians look bad, but the problem for the industry was that it was economic, not political, in its nature and was therefore not able to successfully predict which decisions were political and which were not. (It did not help that retailers were themselves in a constant state of organisational flux.) Financial risk frameworks were clearly inadequate for the task of valuing politics, given that they needed to first 'see' politics on *political* terms (such as the political aspects of reputation, which is about anticipating others' use of the political and mass media systems) in order to then translate this into financial risk.

This leads to the next key point for this chapter, which was the basic unpredictability of outcomes as the energy policy environment became more complex and as political interests increased. This resulted in significant uncertainty for retailers and many other stakeholders. Outcomes were politically contingent:

110 *The next thirteen years*

they turned on political perceptions and timeframes within the political system alone. Media attention to issues was also unpredictable, with the timing of reportage often relying on factors that were not able to be observed or anticipated by the industry, such as other news events (or quiet news days) and the personal experiences of the reporters. As with the other systems, the issues that received coverage from the mass media system were determined only within that system. However, media reportage was also closely coupled with the political system. An example provided in this chapter was where the media repeated government media releases that used ambiguous terms to allow governments to distance themselves from their own network cost increases. This should have been examined more closely by reporters if independent coverage 'in the public interest' was to be expected.

The community thus received an inadequate view of the industry, which would also have limited any meaningful activism to compel the industry to serve any broader public interest purposes (assuming these existed). Why did the community not expect something more from the media (or from the industry)? The apparent answer is that the community was not motivated to do so; energy as a topic was dry and complex and the media's weak representation of energy issues was probably a reasonable reflection of the public appetite for more information. The disinterest of consumers is consistent with other findings; as noted by Edelman (1988: 7) writing about the American public:

> Regimes and proponents of political causes know that it takes much coercion, propaganda, and the portrayal of issues in terms that entertain, distort and shock to extract a public response of any kind…. [The public's] apathy, indifference, quiescence, and resistance to the consciousness industry is especially impressive in an age of widespread literacy and virtually universal access to the media.

Further, energy consumers did not know what they did not know; their only source of information was the news media, which employed a form of lazy reporting that can be characterised as 'censorship by mental sloth' (Salter, 2007: 8). Simple scandals were reported but the news quickly moved on, as did consumer attention. Even when consumers were concerned about price rises they did not tend to take action in any noticeable way. An exception to this was the consumer backlash when Origin Energy published its smart meter charge on Victorian consumers' bills and consumers discovered they were paying for something they did not understand and had not yet received. Even then, this was a short-term political effect: consumer dissatisfaction was picked up and nurtured by scandal-seeking radio hosts rather than being a consumer movement of any significance.

Notes

1 The jurisdictions of the Australian Capital Territory and Tasmania were also in the NEM, but these jurisdictions were small and competition was not effective in either state; the market for small consumers had only just opened in Tasmania at the time of writing. Western Australia and the Northern Territory were not in the NEM and were subject to different arrangements.

2 Recall that I use the term 'stakeholder' in this book to potentially mean any party in the regulatory space.

3 Where 'contingency' is meant in the sense that anything could have been different (Luhmann, 2003: 37).

4 Although there was a federal Office of Best Practice Regulation, it was, to my knowledge, never involved with regulatory policy in the energy markets. The federal process for regulatory impact assessment was only a high level and apparently symbolic sign-off that I saw used for the implementation of the National Energy Customer Framework.

5 Despite electricity price rises being a constant topic for stakeholder commentary, the quantum and materiality of the price rises were rarely clear. The cost drivers varied across jurisdictions, network regions and sectors and so could be represented many ways. The Australian Bureau of Statistics (2012) reported that the proportion of real household expenditure on energy was actually at the same level in 2012 as ten years earlier; the issue was more that prices had increased rapidly in recent years. Reports also varied on whether Australian energy prices were high or not relative to the Organisation for Economic Co-operation and Development (OECD) average. A basic comparison of cents per kilowatt hour showed relatively high prices, but an assessment of purchasing power parity showed Australian household electricity prices to be well below the OECD average (Senate Select Committee on Electricity Prices, 2012).

6 The then South Australian Energy Minister Patrick Conlon provided the best quotes on this issue, saying in 2006 that calls to remove price regulation were 'just silliness' and that if the federal government believed it could persuade the states to abandon price capping, it must believe in 'fairies at the bottom of the garden' (Bildstien, 2006). This is despite the inter-governmental agreement to remove price caps that his Premier signed almost five months earlier.

7 The finding that dual-income, mortgage-holding families with multiple appliances were the ones most in need of support was not acted on by governments. This finding was based on reputable sources but was difficult to reconcile with what stakeholders knew about the 'traditional' vulnerable groups such as the elderly and unemployed. It was certainly not helpful to governments wanting to be seen to help the disadvantaged; tax dollars spent to help this customer segment would only raise the thorny issue of middle-class welfare.

8 The Australian state and federal governments also provided significant financial support to consumers who required it, with Australia reported to redistribute more income to the bottom 20 per cent of the population than virtually every other OECD country (OECD, 2014), demonstrating it operated the most 'target efficient' system of social security benefits (Whiteford, 2011).

9 While we could choose to see the various perspectives as ideological or philosophical rather than moral, I am trying to draw out the 'rightness' of the positions. Stakeholders believed themselves to be right and to be good, and thus many were contemptuous towards those stakeholders who did not share their sense of right and wrong.

10 Although this topic was raised by the ESC in a report that cemented its unpopularity with consumer advocates (ESC, 2004) and is discussed further in the next chapter.

11 It also meant that the timeframes involved for the regulator's process and government's consideration of the recommendations could be as long as required to have the issue fall away in the minds of stakeholders or the public. Governments were able to

112 *The next thirteen years*

conveniently disregard the recommendations of the regulator as needed; the regulator was able to be framed as close or distant from government depending on government's preference for handling an issue.

12 Regulatory managers (like me, for much of my career) dealt with all relevant external stakeholders on policy and rules as they were being formed: this was about managing the compliance risk that would ultimately result from policy decisions. Regulatory managers drafted submissions, liaised with other retailers on shared policy issues, attended stakeholder workshops and met with governments and others. The role was often subsumed within external affairs and government relations functions. In contrast, compliance managers dealt with operational compliance with rules once they were in place, including reporting to the regulator. Despite the regulatory engagement, this was largely an internal-facing role. The smaller retailers often had one person undertaking both regulatory policy and compliance roles.

13 Technically this should be 'state and territory' (or 'jurisdiction') because the Australian Capital Territory was part of the NEM. For simplicity, and also because the Australian Capital Territory was such a small player, I will refer only to 'states' in this section.

14 I am not being disingenuous in saying this; I was close to many retailers and did not know of retailers who were intentionally careless about compliance.

15 Recall that regulatory policy staff tended to be externally focused, engaging with stakeholders on any compliance risk that would result from policy decisions that were in train, and compliance staff were internally focused, working closely with retail operations to ensure practices were compliant once policy was locked down.

16 Also consistent with those meta-regulatory writers who see social activism as key to making businesses attentive to reputation (for example, Parker, 2002). However, the implications of using social activism and the further undesirable politicisation of issues as addressed in this book are not identified or accounted for by meta-regulatory theory.

References

Australian Bureau of Statistics (2006) *Adult literacy and life skills survey*, 4228.0 (Reissue).

Australian Bureau of Statistics (2012) *Household energy use*, September.

Australian Energy Regulator (2012) *Senate Select Committee on electricity prices submission*, ref: 49598, 17 September.

Ayres, I. and Braithwaite, J. (1992) *Responsive regulation: transcending the deregulation debate*, Oxford University Press: Oxford.

Bildstien, C. (2006) 'Power bills could be higher for thousands', *The Daily Telegraph*, 27 September.

Black, J. (2010) 'The role of risk in regulatory processes', in R. Baldwin, M. Cave and M. Lodge (eds) *The Oxford handbook of regulation*, Oxford University Press: Oxford, pp. 302–348.

Coorey, P. (2012) 'Voters will decide on power sale: McArdle', *Sun Herald Sydney*, 12 August, p. 9.

Daily Mercury (2012) 'Newman scores win over Origin', *Daily Mercury Mackay*, 18 July, p. 20.

Deloitte (2011) *Advanced Metering Infrastructure customer impacts study, final report. Volume 1*, for Victorian Department of Primary Industries, 18 October.

Dunckley, M. (2010) 'Victoria pauses on move to smart energy meters', *Australian Financial Review*, 4 February, p. 10.

Edelman, M. (1988) *Constructing the political spectacle*, University of Chicago Press: Chicago.

The next thirteen years 113

ESC (Essential Services Commission) (2004) *Disconnections and capacity to pay report on energy retailers' performance*, Melbourne, October.

Gunningham, N. (1998) 'Introduction', in N. Gunningham, P. Grabosky and D. Sinclair (eds) *Smart regulation: designing environmental policy*, Clarendon Press: Oxford, pp. 3–36.

Gunningham, N., Kagan, R.A. and Thornton D. (2003) *Shades of green: business, regulation, and environment*, Stanford University Press: Stanford.

Hartcher, C. (2012) *National Energy Framework to commence in 2014*, New South Wales Government, media release, 31 May (released 1 June 2012).

Heanzle, M. (2010) *Uncertainty in policy making: values and evidence in complex decisions*, Earthscan: London.

Hutter, B. and Power, M. (2005) 'Organizational encounters with risk: an introduction', in B. Hutter and M. Power (eds) *Organizational encounters with risk*, Cambridge University Press: Cambridge, pp. 1–32.

Ironside, R. (2012) 'Premier slams Origin Energy rises and tells families to shop around', *Courier Mail Brisbane*, 30 June, p. 5.

Luhmann, N. (2003) 'Organization', in T. Bakken and T. Hernes (eds) *Autopoietic organization theory*, Abstrakt Forlag: Oslo, pp. 31–52.

Luhmann, N. (2013) *Theory of society. Volume 2*, trans. R. Barrett, Stanford University Press: Stanford.

Mauseth Johnson, M. (2009) *Customer protections and smart meters: issues for Victoria*, report for the Society of St Vincent de Paul National Council, August.

McArdle, M. (2013) *End of electricity price regulation to improve competition*, Minister for Energy and Water Supply, Queensland Government, media release, 17 June.

New South Wales Hansard (2012) *National Energy Retail Law (Adoption) Bill 2012, Energy Legislation Amendment (National Energy Retail Law) Bill 2012*, Second Reading Speech, Legislative Assembly, the Hon Christopher Hartcher, 23 May.

Newman, C. (2012a) *Premier urges electricity customers to shop around*, Queensland Government, media release, 29 June.

Newman, C. (2012b) *Premier welcomes Origin price wind back*, Queensland Government, media release, 17 July.

O'Brien, M. (2012a) *Victorian government defers National Energy Retail Law to safeguard consumer protections*, media release, 13 June.

O'Brien, M. (2012b) *Victorian Government statement regarding the National Energy Retail Law (Victoria) Bill 2012*, media release, 13 April.

OECD (2014) *Social expenditure update: social spending is falling in some countries, but in many others it remains at historically high levels*, Insights from the OECD Social Expenditure database (SOCX), Directorate for Employment, Labour and Social Affairs, November.

Origin Energy (2012) *Origin residential (Tariff 11) market pricing to match Queensland electricity rate freeze*, ASX/media release, 17 July.

Parker, C. (2002) *The open corporation: effective self-regulation and democracy*, Cambridge University Press: Cambridge.

Parker, C. and Nielsen, V. (2009) 'Corporate compliance systems: could they make any difference?', *Administration and Society*, March, vol. 41, pp. 3–37.

Power, M. (2007) *Organized uncertainty: designing a world of risk management*, Oxford University Press: Oxford.

Pronin, E. and Schmidt, K. (2013) 'Claims and denials of bias and their implications for policy', in E. Shafir (ed.) *The behavioral foundations of public policy*, Princeton University Press: Princeton, pp. 195–216.

114 *The next thirteen years*

Rich, N. and Mauseth, M. (2004) *Access to energy and water in Victoria: a research report*, Consumer Law Centre Victoria and Consumer Utilities Advocacy Centre, November.

Salter, D. (2007) *The media we deserve*, Melbourne University Press: Melbourne.

Senate Select Committee on Electricity Prices (2012) *Reducing energy bills and improving efficiency*, November 2012, Commonwealth of Australia.

Simshauser, P. and Nelson, T. (2012) *The energy market death spiral: rethinking customer hardship*, AGL Applied Economic and Policy Research Working Paper No. 31 – Death Spiral, June.

Smith, A. (2012) 'States accused of petty "squabbling"', *Daily Liberal*, Dubbo, 13 August, p. 6.

Steger, U. (2008) 'Future perspectives of corporate social responsibility: where are we coming from? Where are we heading?', in A. Crane, A. McWilliams, D. Matten, J. Moon and D.S. Siegel (eds) *The Oxford Handbook of Corporate Social Responsibility*, Oxford University Press: Oxford, pp. 560–567.

Sunstein, C.R. (2010) *Laws of fear*, Cambridge University Press: Cambridge.

Sydney Morning Herald (2011) 'NSW power bills to display carbon tax cost', 11 November.

The Australian (2012) 'Origin buckles to electricity bill outrage', *The Australian*, 17 July.

VaasaETT (2012) *World energy retail market rankings report 2012*.

Wardill, S. (2012) 'Power grab', *Courier Mail Brisbane*, 18 July, p. 1.

Whiteford, P. (2011) 'How fair is Australia's welfare state?', *Inside Story*, 11 July.

Wood, A. (2013) 'Pledge to cut power prices – NSW Energy Minister Chris Hartcher's keep-it-simple solution', *The Daily Telegraph*, 17 October.

5 Contesting compliance in hardship regulation

The primary problem to challenge energy regulatory policymakers over the years was how to best manage and support energy consumers who could not afford their bills. In one form or another, this was the driver for most of the consumer protection regulation, and it was through the discussions about affordability and customer hardship that energy as an essential service – and thus as a moral issue – was manifested.

Early rules were drafted to ensure that retailers offered a number of payment plans to customers before disconnection of supply, and later rules required customer hardship programmes, where eligible customers would be provided with customised support and be immune from disconnection while they made payments towards their debt. Additional regulatory obligations in some states required on-site energy audits and facilitated contact with community and welfare services. The protection of financially vulnerable consumers was the headline reason for ongoing price regulation across most states, often despite experts' assertions that market competition was effective.

As discussed in Chapter 4, compliance breaches were not reported in any widespread or systemic sense. However, stakeholders' subjective views on performance (such as numbers of disconnections, which were not themselves regulated but were reported on) were more important than proven non-compliance when it came to retailer assistance for customers in hardship. This chapter draws out this issue, describing how the Victorian government and consumer advocates went so far as to marginalise the regulator in 2004 and 2005 when it had arrived at what some saw as inappropriate conclusions about retailer compliance and the regulatory framework. The chapter then moves to how compliance and performance were framed by various parties and how subjective views of performance increasingly outweighed compliance, even the views of the regulators.

The effect of this focus on subjective views of performance meant that the messages to the retail industry about the public interest and the value of compliance were scrambled and therefore unable to provide clear direction.

116 *Contesting compliance in hardship regulation*

The genesis of the Victorian hardship provisions

The states took different approaches to supporting customers in financial hardship in the years before the National Energy Customer Framework (NECF) was finalised, but there was consistency in a general political desire to be seen to be doing something, and a shift towards requiring retailers to provide targeted hardship programmes. This commenced with Victoria, where legislation was passed in 2006 requiring retailers to have hardship programmes. New South Wales created similar obligations in 2010. Issues relating to customer hardship were reinvigorated every few years, based on election timeframes and consumer advocates' (and Ombudsman) publications receiving a political airing. As discussed in Chapter 4, the political cycle became tighter at the end of the decade as electricity prices in each state rose significantly for several consecutive years, and as the media became more finely tuned to the issue of bill affordability and cost of living increases for households. The final NECF package agreed to by the jurisdictional Energy Ministers embedded much of the Victorian approach in the national law and rules, requiring retailers to provide access to hardship programmes and to report on a range of factors related to the provision of those programmes. While the rules relating to customers in financial hardship had several sources across the states, Victoria set the agenda. This section addresses the genesis of the Victorian hardship provisions.

Chapter 3 described how Victoria was the first state to comprehensively consult on consumer protections for retail energy competition. The resulting regulatory provisions through the Victorian Energy Retail Code were widely held to be the most onerous (from a retailer perspective) and evolved (from a consumer advocate perspective). The Retail Code required retailers to undertake an assessment of a customer's capacity to pay when there was reason to believe the customer was experiencing payment difficulties, and the retailer was required to offer payment plans that took this into account. Disconnection of supply was not allowed unless the retailer had provided a bill, a reminder notice and a disconnection notice (with mandated minimum periods before each could be sent), as well as information about payment plans, financial counselling, energy efficiency, energy concessions and other government assistance. Retailers were also required to use best endeavours to contact the customer in person or by telephone. The idea was to make contact with a customer and provide a customised payment plan instead of disconnecting the customer through the usual debt collection processes.

However, people who could not afford to pay their bills were still sometimes disconnected when they should not have been according to the Retail Code's process, and several Victorian consumer advocacy groups stated that the industry was not being held sufficiently accountable. While the ESC tended to find no evidence of significant retailer wrongdoing or a systemic problem of non-compliance, individual cases were often troubling and were used with great political flair by those who sought further limitations on retailer debt collection activity. This included the office of the Energy and Water Ombudsman of

Victoria (EWOV), which was a regular participant in policy debates (even holding its own Hardship Conferences in 2000 and 2009) and which provided complaints figures and case studies to support the arguments for the policy-makers and ESC to 'do more'. Retailers argued in response that there was no issue, and that disconnection rates were much lower than they had been in previous years. There was also concern from retailers that some customers could not be contacted at all; retailers sent letters and made phone calls but with prolonged non-payment and no response from the customer after a certain time it was reasonable to disconnect. Retailers believed that they had a right and responsibility to disconnect to protect shareholders (and ultimately other customers) from bearing the cost of bad debt, and it was sometimes in the customer's interest to be disconnected as this was the action that forced people to re-engage and stop debt spiralling out of control. This perspective on disconnection as forcing re-engagement (assuming the disconnection was undertaken according to the rules) was also supported by some low-income consumer advocates who worked for welfare agencies that regularly dealt with people in financial crisis. Other low-income consumer advocates held the opposite view, believing that no consumer should be disconnected from an essential service because they could not pay, and that the problem was one for the retailer to manage better.

There were three main areas of Victorian hardship regulatory development and discussion through the 2000s: (a) legislation to limit retailer fees and to mandate a $250 a day fee for retailers to pay customers in the event of wrongful disconnection; (b) a collaborative project to determine better practices; and (c) legislation to require hardship policies from retailers. It was this last area that primarily formed the basis for the national Law and Rules through NECF.

Legislative changes in 2004

Although the Victorian ESC and the Retail Code were generally well regarded by low-income consumer advocacy groups, many advocates remained concerned about the possibilities for vulnerable customers to be mistreated by energy retailers. This concern was amplified when the ESC released a draft decision in January 2004 (ESC, 2004b) to allow late payment fees for consumers who had the capacity to pay their bills. The consumer groups responded very strongly against this (for example, Consumer Law Centre Victoria, 2004; Consumer Utilities Advocacy Centre (CUAC), 2004; Victorian Council of Social Service, 2004a), and the then Energy Minister also submitted a letter to the consultation process asking the ESC to reconsider this move (Theophanous, 2004). This was when the ESC started to lose the support of the low-income consumer advocacy groups.

The year 2004 was also when the sunset date approached for both price regulation and the application of the Retail Code. Although the government had shown no desire to remove the Retail Code (and the issue had never been raised as a genuine possibility), the two elements of price and non-price consumer

118   *Contesting compliance in hardship regulation*

protection had been combined in legislative drafting as the energy retail 'safety net', and the safety net was scheduled to cease at the end of 2004. However, the government was able to extend the safety net beyond this date, and so had a decision to make. The ESC carried out a review of the effectiveness of competition as input to the government's decision, triggering concern for the low-income consumer advocacy groups that the ESC would find competition to be effective and so recommend ending price regulation and perhaps even the application of the Retail Code. The ESC's (2004c) finding in June was that competition was generally effective, and it suggested a reduction in the coverage of price regulation to only cover residential customers below a certain consumption threshold. The ESC also suggested a lower customer consumption threshold for the application of the Retail Code. Further, it suggested that the substance of the Retail Code might eventually shift into the jurisdiction of Victoria's more generic consumer affairs regulator – a suggestion that would have alarmed the low-income consumer advocates, who saw the existing Retail Code and an energy-focused regulator as vital.

It was in this environment of low-income consumer advocate anxiety about ESC decision-making that issues related to customers in financial hardship came to a head. In mid-2004 consumer advocates and EWOV lobbied the ESC and government to take action to address increased disconnection rates. The regulator responded by carrying out a special report into disconnections, where it found no issue:

> Neither the Commission's performance data on disconnections, instalment plans and affordability complaints, nor the results of its independent audits of retailer compliance with the code, provide evidence of systematic disconnection of financially vulnerable customers by energy retailers. On the contrary, the Commission's independent audits confirm that energy retailers had a high level of compliance with their Code obligations.
>
> (ESC, 2004a: 2)

In fact, although electricity disconnections had gradually increased from levels reported in 1999 (the lowest disconnection figures in the previous 20 years), by 2004 they were at levels comparable to those achieved by the previous state-owned service providers in the 1980s, which were still relatively low. Further, while the absolute numbers did increase in 2004, the proportion of disconnected customers reconnected in the same name at the same address had decreased from the 1999 level and was also comparable with the performance of the state-owned providers in the 1980s. This was actually the most relevant element, where the metric of reconnections in the same name was used by regulators and consumer advocates as a proxy for the 'wrong' kind of disconnection[1] – that is, a customer who had been disconnected because they could not afford to pay their bill and was in their home and without access to energy. These were the people who were the subject of the consumer advocates' reports about wrongful disconnection.

The ESC did note the consumer advocates' concerns about casework indicating an increase in the number of financially vulnerable customers who were

Contesting compliance in hardship regulation 119

disconnected, and it advised that it would undertake further independent audits of retailers' performance in November 2004. These audits were to focus specifically on the main Retail Code obligations of retailers to assist customers in financial difficulty. The ESC advised that it intended to establish a licence obligation for retailers to 'design and implement hardship policies that conform to objectives and best practice principles that will be specified in the licence' (ESC, 2004a: 5).

Notwithstanding the ESC's findings and stated next steps, the consumer advocates took their concerns to the then Victorian Minister for Energy. The result was that the Victorian government made a number of changes to the legislation for energy retailing, where several of these essentially by-passed the ESC in its own domain. The Energy Minister's renowned legislative changes (which government staff informally referred to as his 'iconic' legislative package) included extending the Retail Code's full application and price regulation until the end of 2007, ignoring the ESC's recommendations earlier in the year. Other changes banned retailers from applying late payment fees to residential customers (further overriding the ESC), gave government the power to regulate early exit fees and prepayment meters, and required publication of retail market offers on the internet. A significant change was a new obligation on retailers to pay a fee of $250 per day to customers who were found to have been wrongfully disconnected – that is, where the retailer was in non-compliance with the disconnection provisions of the Retail Code. This last provision was called the wrongful disconnection legislation and is the focus of the remainder of this section.

It was clear at the time that the range of retail energy legislative changes made by the Victorian Government was a response to consumer advocate concerns, and while it was not obviously stated, it was also clear that the government had accepted the consumer advocates' contention that the ESC was not doing its job as effectively as it could and should have. References were made in Parliament to specific consumer advocacy groups and their support for the legislation, and the political sensitivity was confirmed by the Energy Minister himself when he essentially challenged the Opposition to consider what it would be like to be in government and 'bear the odium of voting against the legislation and facing the consumer groups about the consequences of doing so' (Victorian Hansard, 2004b: 1753). There was one particularly interesting exchange between the Energy Minister and a member of the Opposition on the validity of the new $250 a day wrongful disconnection payment:

Hon. BILL FORWOOD (Templestowe) – The Essential Services Commission has advised us that in the year 2003 there were 14,211 actual electricity disconnections. How many of those were illegal? How many were wrong? How many were because of incapacity to pay as opposed to other reasons?

Hon. T. C. THEOPHANOUS (Minister for Energy Industries) – I do not have figures available here to give the member regarding how many of these might not have followed such a process, but I can inform him that certainly

120 *Contesting compliance in hardship regulation*

the consumer groups have highlighted a number of incidents where they believe processes were not followed and people were disconnected with sometimes fairly severe consequences.

(Ibid.: 1758)

This statement from the Energy Minister is telling, and it is a version of the only reason given in Parliament speeches or debates for the new measure; that is, that consumer groups had expressed concern about disconnections of consumers who were in financial hardship. It would seem from this that legislation was drafted without any specific evidence of systemic issues and thus that there was no objective basis for the legislation in the sense of a regulatory or market failure. There *already were* regulations that applied to disconnection, where breaches of these regulations should have been a matter of enforcement against the relevant retailers. From a traditionally rational or evidence-based perspective some consumer groups 'highlighting a number of incidents where they believed processes were not followed' would not usually be a compelling reason for a government to write new law. This is particularly as the ESC's statistical reports and compliance audits confirmed that there was no evidence of problematic non-compliance, and reconnections in the same name were low compared with historical levels. Parliamentary debate referred to the consumer advocacy report discussed in Chapter 4 (see Rich and Mauseth, 2004) to support the legislation. This report surveyed the experiences of 14 disconnected gas customers, 17 disconnected electricity customers and one restricted water customer, where these people were sourced through EWOV, whom they had contacted to make a complaint after being disconnected. This was obviously not a representative survey (as the authors acknowledged), and little in the report documented specific breaches. Although the ESC and government may have been advised of other cases of potential regulatory breach, these were never referred to publicly. One might imagine that had there been evidence of systemic issues, and specifically of regulatory or market failure, these would have been highlighted and publicised by the proponents of increased regulation.

Regarding the effectiveness of the regulator, the very existence of the wrongful disconnection legislation, which legislated for compliance with existing regulatory provisions, showed that the government had accepted the consumer advocates' claim that the ESC was under-performing. A statement was made in Parliament that 'measures have been included in the bill to make sure that any moves by retailers to disconnect any consumers must be undertaken in accordance with the energy retail code and the process that is outlined there' (Victorian Hansard, 2004b: 1752) and this theme, together with the reference to the consumer advocates' concerns, was the strongest reason given for the new legislative provisions. This was odd if there was already an effective regulator of the Code, which seemed in doubt:

This bill also seeks to address the inadequacies in the Essential Service Commission.... We are strengthening the consumer safety net because the

Contesting compliance in hardship regulation 121

companies are not abiding by it. That is why we have had to put a bit of discipline back into the market with a $250 penalty for illegal disconnection.

(Victorian Hansard, 2004a: 1725)

Parliamentary debate about another initiative announced at the time – a proposed inquiry into the use of pre-payment meters, a means of payment that consumer advocates had lobbied to have banned – showed the government's concern about the ESC more generally, and is worth reproducing:

> Hon. C.A. STRONG (Higinbotham) – The minister has indicated that the government has not made a decision yet as to who will carry out this inquiry. I note that the Essential Services Commission for 2004 has on its work program an inquiry into prepaid meters. Is the minister aware that the Essential Services Commission has that on its work program?
> Hon. T.C. THEOPHANOUS (Minister for Energy Industries) – It is a good question. I can advise Mr Strong that I have discussed this with the essential services commissioner and envisage that an inquiry will be established … and that the essential services commissioner would, rather than continue to his own separate inquiry, provide support to the announced independent inquiry into this important area. He certainly will be able to do analysis, provide statistical information and all the other things the commissioner is able to do for this proposed inquiry, but it will be a separate and independent inquiry, canvassed very broadly and will take in community and industry views.
> Hon. C.A. STRONG (Higinbotham) – The clear implication from that response is that the Essential Services Commission is not competent or trustworthy enough to carry out this inquiry, given that that is its role under the act to carry out such inquiries?
> Hon. T.C. THEOPHANOUS (Minister for Energy Industries) – No, Mr Strong cannot reach that conclusion. The conclusion by the government was that this was such an important issue that we want to have an independent and separate inquiry which takes into account a range of community views and so on. The essential services commissioner accepts that view. He has told me that he will be very happy to cooperate with the government in having this particular inquiry.

(Victorian Hansard, 2004b: 1761)

It is not hard to see a serious problem for the ESC in this exchange, with the Energy Minister implicitly calling into question the regulator's independence and its consultative style. That either should have been questioned was strange, as the regulator had not historically been considered to be captured by the industry (and the industry rarely felt successful in winning its cases), and its behaviour to that point had not given any indication that it lacked independence. It also regularly consulted on issues in some depth, and no less than a government inquiry would have. The issue was more that the ESC had come to some

122 *Contesting compliance in hardship regulation*

unpalatable conclusions in the course of its work in 2004. The ESC's conclusions were well documented and borne out by qualitative and quantitative analysis, but (or perhaps *and so*) they were not politically minded. The political stakes were too high for government to afford to be seen to rely on the ESC's conclusions. The independence of the ESC was sullied in the previous exchange, but it was its very independence from government that caused concern for both the consumer advocates and the government itself. This is highlighted in the following statements from a government parliamentary member earlier in the debate:

> Regarding the late payment fee prohibition, I note that the member for Box Hill said we are politicising the debate by not following the recommendations of the Essential Services Commission, an independent organisation. It is to the credit of this government that it is prepared to say no. We appreciate the work of the Essential Services Commission, but we finally make these decisions. Ultimately it is a political decision – and it is an important political decision. The Essential Services Commission said that a $10 fee should be put on late payments by consumers in hardship as an incentive. We have deliberately said we will not do that. If that is politicising the debate, so be it; if that is saying we are burdening the industry with too much regulation, so be it. What we are ultimately about is ensuring a good outcome for those who are distressed by their inability to meet payments on time. I am very pleased with that.
>
> (Victorian Hansard, 2004a: 1719–1720)

This theme of the greater morality of politicians was present throughout the debate. The usual benefits of regulatory independence and evidence-gathering were reframed as unfortunate limitations on making moral or ethical judgement calls – limitations that needed to be by-passed by the Parliament. The ESC was portrayed as helpless or incompetent in protecting the interests of vulnerable customers, with its views consistently misrepresented, such as the above characterisation of its decision on late payment fees (where the ESC had said nothing of the sort), and in the determined way that some proponents of the new legislation ignored the ESC's findings that there had *not* been systemic non-compliance with the Retail Code. We have only to look at the media release from the Victorian Council of Social Service on the behalf of it and six other consumer advocacy groups to see the way that the situation was framed at the time:

> Protections for Victorian gas and electricity customers are under attack from energy retailers. There has been widespread retailer non-compliance with regulation, including wrongful disconnection.... [We] call on the State government to extend and defend customer protections and call on the regulator, the Essential Services Commission, to start doing its job.
>
> (Victorian Council of Social Service, 2004b)

Contesting compliance in hardship regulation 123

There are three further, and related, points worth drawing out about the debate on disconnections and the wrongful disconnection legislation. First, there was nothing in the legislative changes that specifically addressed the main consumer advocacy report's (see Rich and Mauseth, 2004) core concern that no disconnection should occur for people who did not have the capacity to pay. A recommendation that would have been true to that theme would have been to ban disconnections for all residential customers, or at least for those who may not have had the capacity to pay. This would have truly reflected energy as an essential service, if 'essential' was to be interpreted by its literal meaning. However, this would have been a risky political move; it is not surprising that government might not have wanted to go down that path, and the industry would likely have reacted very strongly.

Second, not even the advocacy report's conclusions were consistent with its implicit theme of no disconnection for vulnerable customers, at least not in a direct sense. The report did not advocate a ban on disconnections; it instead recommended more flexible retailer collection behaviours (including mandating debt waiver in some form) and supported the provisions in the Retail Code. However, nothing in the Retail Code expressly stopped a customer from being disconnected when they could not pay; it was process-based not outcome-based, where a retailer was required to undertake a range of actions before disconnection. If the customer did not respond they could be disconnected. Given that a number of the case study customers in the consumer advocates' report appeared to have not contacted their retailer when they should have, it is not clear that any form of retailer adherence to the Retail Code would have prevented disconnection.

Third, the actions taken by the government through the legislation fundamentally undermined the ESC and its own work programme to identify and resolve the sorts of concerns that were raised by consumer advocates and EWOV in the first place. This pattern extended into the financial hardship legislation addressed in the next section. The time that was used for discussing and debating the new provisions, and then for retailers and the ESC to adjust to them, was time that could have better been used to address the issue at hand, which was the investigation into retailer hardship practices that the ESC had already advised it would undertake.

The various legislative provisions continued on in one form or another in subsequent years, except for price regulation, which ended on 31 December 2008 after another competition effectiveness review. While the wrongful disconnection legislation certainly had the desired effect of reducing disconnections for a time (this was all disconnections, which was a short-term risk-averse reaction from retailers), it turned out to be badly designed, and caused all parties significant issues in the years after its implementation. Regulation of the wrongful disconnection legislation and its unintended outcomes are discussed further later in this chapter.

124   *Contesting compliance in hardship regulation*

The Utility Debt Spiral Project: a collaborative model

Around the same time as the initial discussions about disconnections, in 2004 an organisation called the Committee for Melbourne facilitated an initiative called the Utility Debt Spiral Project. This was led by the ESC and EWOV and was a genuinely collaborative effort with stakeholders from across all sectors to co-ordinate policy and 'explore how utility companies can operate as an early warning system for individuals facing financial hardship' (ESC, 2004a: 41). It was undertaken to fill what was seen as a policy (but not necessarily regulatory) void in the area, and although the private motivations of the key proponents are unknown, it is likely that the project was forged to some degree from the competitive tension at the time between the ESC and EWOV. Each wanted to be seen to take the initiative and 'own' these types of regulatory issues (which is an odd state of affairs for the independent complaints handling body, which will be returned to later).

Funding for the Utility Debt Spiral Project was provided by a consumer advocacy group, an energy retailer, an electricity distributor and a water utility. The work of the group went through several stages, culminating in the development of a Debt Spiral Guideline, which was to provide retailers with guidance on best practice assistance for customers experiencing payment difficulties and on how to avoid customers' debts spiralling out of control. The initial stage, which consisted of mapping the area and developing papers about customer hardship, resulted in a lengthy document (Committee for Melbourne, 2004) that described the issues and the regulatory requirements in some detail. This stage involved senior staff from ESC and EWOV and other stakeholders, with the then Energy and Water Ombudsman herself providing a paper on hardship. However, once the initial excitement of the project had passed and the work shifted to the second stage of developing solutions, interest began to wane and the high-profile individuals were replaced by lower-level stakeholder representatives. The next stage of developing a Debt Spiral Guideline involved a working group comprised mainly of analyst and manager-level representatives from advocacy organisations, utilities, government departments (such as the department that delivered concessions), EWOV and ESC. The state-owned Victorian water sector was seen as a good model, and water industry representatives were looked to for advice. It was also an opportunity for the energy retailers to share information and learn from one another; some of them already had well-regarded hardship programmes, and it was one of these retailers (Origin Energy) that chaired the working group and drafted the Guideline. I worked for Origin and drafted the Guideline based on working group input.

However, not all energy retailers were part of this process, and, in fact, a couple of the retailers were concerned that the outcomes of the process would result in more regulation. This was not an unwarranted concern given that the process had been driven in the early days by the Energy and Water Ombudsman herself, and the senior staffer from the regulator who regularly took the lead to draft more regulation. These retailers are said to have approached the then Minister for Energy and suggested that he intervene in some way to take back control. Apparently this argument found an audience, as in March 2005 the Minister announced the establishment of the Committee of Inquiry into Financial Hardship of Energy Consumers, as discussed below. While the Minister probably already had a desire to do something – he could not allow a group of energy stakeholders to send a message to the public that their initiative was required to fill a policy void, and certainly not where he had a reputation for 'iconic' customer protection legislation to maintain – it is interesting that a possible trigger for the Inquiry (and everything that resulted from it) may well have been industry action rather than consumer advocate activism. Consumer advocates at the time had not lobbied for such an investigation; they had been largely comforted by the Minister's previous actions to reinforce the Retail Code and were actively involved in the Utility Debt Spiral Project and its development of the Debt Spiral Guideline.

This Inquiry had its intended effect on the Utility Debt Spiral Project work: the Inquiry became the new headline act for deliberations on customer financial hardship, and the already waning interest in the Debt Spiral Guideline reduced further. The work on the Guideline continued through 2005 with semi-regular meetings but then limped along for some time with only Origin Energy, which chaired the project, pursuing its implementation. The document *Guiding principles for supporting utility customers experiencing financial hardship* was eventually launched by the next Energy Minister in March 2007, once all the work had been completed for the government's Inquiry, legislation had been passed, and there was a new Minister seeking kudos for good news stories. The Guideline was largely a goodwill document with voluntary uptake, and its actual use by retailers is not clear. The ESC used elements of the document for its own guidelines under the legislation, but stakeholders only referred to it in passing in subsequent years.

The Victorian Hardship Inquiry

In 2005, the then Minister's statement about the Victorian Committee of Inquiry into the Financial Hardship of Energy Consumers said that it was established in response to concerns raised by consumers, consumer groups and the energy industry about the need for a clear direction on the issue of consumer hardship. The Terms of Reference set by the government for the Inquiry were broad, involving an assessment of the 'level and underlying causes of energy consumer hardship' as well as an assessment of the 'impact on consumer hardship of the policies and practices of Victorian energy retailers, government departments and agencies, and financial counsellors and welfare agencies' (Nieuwenhuysen, Huitfeldt and Scarth, 2005: 1). The Committee was to recommend allocation of responsibilities between stakeholders and also to recommend relevant changes to 'policies, programs, regulations and practices' of all parties.

The three-person Committee was chaired by a prominent academic, with the other members being a representative from a welfare agency and a customer benchmarking expert. The Committee had around six months to undertake the

126 *Contesting compliance in hardship regulation*

work, which was little time to investigate, consult and report on a complex set of issues – all the more problematic given that the Committee members were essentially new to the topic. The Committee was guided by a reference group comprising representatives from the various sectors (excluding Origin Energy, which was unpopular with government for chairing the Debt Spiral Guideline work), and used a consultant to carry out the data collection and analysis. An Issues Paper (Milbur Consulting, 2005) was released in May 2005 for public comment, and while the paper was useful in that it brought together literature from across Australia and Great Britain, it lacked depth. Once again, this was to be expected given the limited time available – it can be assumed that after finding a consultant and negotiating the work to be done on the Issues Paper there would have been less than a month to draft the document itself.

Twenty-five submissions were received from across retailers, consumer advocacy groups, government departments and EWOV. A theme common to almost all of the submissions was a concern that government was not setting the required policy standard, and that clarity from government about objectives and coordination of stakeholders was overdue. Consumer advocates tended to reiterate the claims made in the previous year that the ESC was not doing its job and that retailers regularly did not comply with the Retail Code. There was strong support for the Retail Code but a desire from most consumer advocates to see all retailers provide financial hardship programmes for customers experiencing payment difficulties. A ban on disconnections was raised in the Issues Paper and largely dismissed by stakeholders – including consumer advocates – because of the negative effects this would have in terms of debts spiralling out of control.

Nothing more happened for eight months. Then, at the end of May 2006, the government released the Inquiry report and a policy package targeting energy customers in hardship. The 20 recommendations of the Committee were largely uncontroversial and supported work already carried out (see Nieuwenhuysen *et al.*, 2005). The main policy focus was on maintaining the Retail Code, but with the addition of recommending that retailers adopt and publish a 'Best Practice Hardship Policy', and that the ESC strengthen its monitoring of the Retail Code and publish more information on energy hardship issues. There were also recommendations for government to increase funding for concessions and for financial counselling. Overall, the Inquiry supported views put by stakeholders that energy hardship was complex and not easily solved. A key recommendation was for the government to:

> prepare a Statement, based on principles outlined in the Report, on the goals and objects of energy hardship policy, the broad balance of responsibility of all stakeholders (including cooperation between them), plans for new initiatives, and means for assessing the success of the policy over time.
>
> (Ibid.: viii)

An interesting recommendation was for the government to 'establish a small Energy Hardship Policy Working Group ... composed of individuals with

Contesting compliance in hardship regulation 127

expertise and knowledge of energy hardship … to monitor the implementation of the recommendations from this Review' (ibid.). This was a way of embedding further analysis into the process and was possibly an acknowledgement from the Committee that the issues were more complex than could have been addressed in the time provided.

The government's response to the Inquiry's recommendations supported most of the recommendations (see Department of Infrastructure, 2006b). The policy package included a hardship policy statement and new legislation to require retailers to develop financial hardship policies and have them approved by the ESC. The government also announced increased funding for the Department of Human Services' Utility Relief Grants Scheme (including expanded eligibility criteria) and funding for the training of financial counsellors in energy hardship issues. While the government said that it would take up the Inquiry's recommendation to start a working group, this did not eventuate; the tasks associated with that working group were also therefore not progressed. It was known at the time that the recommendations to do more work were a source of frustration for the Minister, who had had higher expectations of the Committee and just wanted the issues resolved. It is therefore understandable that the government did not take further action and let the working group idea (and on a related note, the promised pre-payment meter Inquiry) fade away. Certainly the Minister had already established himself as a man of action and the stakeholders who had sought government intervention seemed satisfied with the approach.

It is worth noting that the new legislation requiring hardship policies, while apparently decisive, was largely symbolic rather than a new idea. The legislation reflected the direction that the ESC had said it would take in 2004, which included consulting on hardship policies and further developing hardship programme performance metrics. The legislation also merely embedded provisions already in the Retail Code and a basic version of what was already the practice of larger retailers. The precise detail was in fact a reflection of the practices of Origin Energy, which had played a key role in the Utility Debt Spiral Project. This would not have been the preferred outcome of the retailers who had originally lobbied the Minister for an intervention in that project's process.

Drawing out the conflict on roles in energy bill management

As shown above, consumer advocate and EWOV statements about how retailers behaved towards customers experiencing payment difficulties garnered significant political attention and subsequently drove much of the legislative approach. The ESC was also seen to have been side-tracked with other projects and therefore it was considered to have neglected its duty to monitor retailer behaviour and respond to non-compliance. Although late 2004 saw a clear government response to these claims with the wrongful disconnection legislation, the arguments continued through to the Hardship Inquiry in 2005. The submissions to the Hardship Inquiry from consumer advocates and industry are worth

128   *Contesting compliance in hardship regulation*

addressing in further detail, as they exemplify the value conflicts that continued to be played out over the years about various parties' roles and customers' rights and needs.

Consumer advocate positions

It was only the low-income consumer advocacy groups that participated in the hardship consultation, with these groups largely the same as those that participated in the Retail Code consultation described in Chapter 3. On the matter of retailer performance and compliance, the general argument from consumer advocates was that retailers had not been flexible enough for customers who needed support, with some retailers said to be actively in non-compliance (Financial and Consumer Rights Council, 2005; St Vincent de Paul Society, 2005) and others said to be perhaps acting in compliance but nevertheless behaving inappropriately towards customers (CUAC, 2005). As with the 2004 consumer advocate study referred to in Chapter 4 (see Rich and Mauseth, 2004, where these authors were from the Consumer Law Centre Victoria and CUAC respectively), many submissions made use of evocative case studies of consumer disconnection.

An interesting point made by one of the authors of the 2004 consumer advocate report in their submission to the Inquiry was that 'While companies may not be breaching the Code, in too many cases there exist breaches of the spirit of the Code' (CUAC, 2005: 5). This reflected a fluid interpretation of non-compliance that included retailers not waiving debts or otherwise subsidising consumption for some customers, and it goes to the heart of the conflicts on this issue. To provide some context, retailer provision of payment plans that allowed for small but regular instalments was the main element of providing support to customers in financial hardship. Hardship approaches thus required payment plans to be offered to customers, and in Victoria two plans had to be offered before a customer experiencing payment difficulties could be disconnected. From its inception, the Retail Code had stated that when an energy retailer offered a payment plan, the amount of the instalments were to 'reflect the customer's consumption needs and capacity to pay' (clause 12.2(a)). The thinking at the time of the Retail Code's drafting was that retailers had a role and responsibility to balance these requirements; there was certainly no implicit expectation that retailers had to take whatever little money a customer was offering. However, this clause became problematic in subsequent years, as stakeholders focused on the inherent conflict between payments to manage consumption and payments to cater to affordability:

> For example, if the customer is a sole parent with four children who needs to consume electricity worth $60 per fortnight but whose income and expenditure (including servicing other debts) may mean that the customer's payment capacity for electricity is at most $20 per fortnight. In addition, the retailer is supposed to include any arrears so the customer gradually pays

Contesting compliance in hardship regulation   129

any outstanding debt to the company.... However due to the lack of clarity in the Code, retailers are not in breach of their obligations as there is no clear direction as to whether 'capacity to pay' or 'consumption needs' should be the guiding principle. This is not the only ambiguous clause in the Code but it serves as an example as it has particularly dire consequences for customers experiencing financial hardship.

(CUAC, 2005: 6)

A number of low-income consumer advocates and EWOV believed that a payment plan that reflected capacity to pay was more important than a plan that reflected consumption, and that retailers needed to accept whatever a customer could manage (including, potentially, no payments). This view was entirely consistent with the perspective that no one should be disconnected from an essential service if they could not afford to pay their bills; obviously a payment arrangement that takes into account a customer's capacity to pay should never result in disconnection.

The ESC was aware of the potential conflict between the elements of clause 12.2(a), and in its 2004 report *Disconnections and capacity to pay* (ESC, 2004a: 3–4) it said the following about an assessment of capacity to pay:

The code is not prescriptive on how this assessment is to be undertaken and, at this time, there is no consensus amongst the stakeholders on what constitutes 'a capacity to pay', how it should be assessed and how differences of view between retailers and customers on this issue should be reconciled. The regulations do not include an objective test for assessing capacity to pay and it is doubtful whether such a test could be developed or would be appropriate. A number of consumer representatives argue against codifying such a test in regulations.

This was not sufficient or appropriate guidance in the eyes of many stakeholders, who claimed in their 2005 submissions that the ESC was not fulfilling its duties. The statements made about the (in)effectiveness of the ESC ranged from a more understanding perspective of the ESC's dilemma in what was seen as a policy vacuum: 'The ESC could be more creative but this may place it possibly at greater risk of taking over part of the government's role' (Kildonan Child and Family Services, 2005: 5), to frank criticisms: 'the Essential Services Commission has failed to monitor and enforce retailer compliance' (Financial and Consumer Rights Council, 2005: 10). Other more specific criticisms went to the way in which ESC interpreted its objectives: several consumer advocates were concerned that the ESC was needlessly and inappropriately economically rational. The ESC was seen to have failed in effectively enforcing the Retail Code by prioritising competitive market outcomes over consumer protections. Further:

It is our view that coordination between the roles responsibilities and expectations on the various parties has eroded over the past 2 years. This erosion

130   *Contesting compliance in hardship regulation*

has occurred due to the activities of the Essential Services Commission and various actual changes and recommendations that have been made to the basic terms and condition [sic] of energy. These actual changes and suggestions have resulted in perverse messages being sent to the energy retail industry. This has resulted in the erosion and fragmentation of the understanding and actual conditions of supply undermining a coordinated response. Some examples of the fragmentations include ... moves to the national market, various reviews of and amalgamation of energy retail codes, approval for the introduction of late payment fees, and other suggestions limiting the protections for all households.

(St Vincent De Paul, 2005: 5)

We can see from this quotation that the decisions of the ESC over the previous two years had set the scene for consumer advocate dissatisfaction, which confirms the observations from the 2004 legislative change debate. Consumer advocates had lost faith in the ESC's ability or willingness to take the consumer perspective, and saw competitive market outcomes as necessarily disadvantageous for low-income and vulnerable customers. This was understood by some as an outcome of having no clear government policy on hardship and of customer protections being left to an economic regulator, as noted by CUAC (2005: 23):

the Victorian regulator has little chance to respond to social policy (if not legislated) as it is likely to conflict with other objectives such as efficiency and promotion of competitive market conduct. To ensure that low-income/ vulnerable consumers benefit from competition does not necessarily equate with assisting consumers in utility stress. It is no surprise that this causes tension within a framework dependent on economic regulators mandated to promote competition.

The Financial and Consumer Rights Council (2005: 8) judged government financial assistance to customers as addressing *market failure*, where presumably the market failure was that anyone was in financial hardship. Retailers and the ESC were said to be 'seeking to target and shift financial hardship low-income customers into Government assistance programs and/or residual markets to accommodate consumers in financial hardship in order to address market failure' (ibid.).

EWOV took a somewhat different tack in its criticism of the ESC, with its submissions stating the number of times that EWOV concerns about retailer behaviour had been provided to the ESC. The implicit criticism was that the ESC had done nothing about EWOV's concerns. EWOV also sought to pursue an ongoing conflict with the ESC, which was how to determine if a problem was 'systemic'. EWOV had often presented problems to the ESC as systemic (and therefore requiring regulatory action and possibly rule change) when there were very few actual complaints, taking the view that if a problem had happened once

Contesting compliance in hardship regulation   131

it was likely to happen again. The ESC had a different perspective, viewing an issue as systemic only if it occurred multiple times and/or had significant impact. EWOV's (2005: 9) suggestion to the Hardship Inquiry was thus to have a:

> clear and transparent licence obligation on energy retailers to report systemic issues to the ESC and to address such issues. The definition of systemic issue should clearly note that just one case, or one customer complaint, may give rise to a systemic issue.

While most consumer advocates explicitly or implicitly supported EWOV's views, some felt that even EWOV had not done enough, with the Institute for Social Research (2005: 8) stating that research found 'the retailer non-compliance issue was not being addressed through this dispute resolution scheme despite the powers it has over its members'.

In summary, the consumer advocate views were largely consistent in their themes of energy retailers needing to be flexible and having to do more to absorb the debt of customers having difficulty paying energy bills, and the ESC needing to do more to ensure this happened. Actual mechanisms of improvement were not agreed – or in most cases not even clarified – and the advocacy groups did not have a shared perspective on the detail of the problems; however, many appeared to agree that retailers needed to accept what customers said they could afford, regardless of the effect on the size of the debt. Indeed, for these stakeholders, ideally the debt would not rise even when consumption was not covered, as the retailer would subsidise use. The argument put to support this view was a moral one, based on a particular interpretation of the policy stance of the time that disconnection was to be a last resort action. The number of instances of non-compliance was not seen as an issue, as from the majority consumer advocate view, even one customer being disconnected when they were in financial hardship was too many, and from the EWOV view even one case should be viewed as a potential systemic problem.

Retailer positions

What did the retailers think about this? Unsurprisingly, the retailer submissions to the Inquiry did not comment on industry compliance or the ESC's competence. Instead, the general retailer theme was to state that as commercial, private sector companies in a competitive market, there was a natural limit to what they should be expected to absorb as social costs. There was concern that having retailers act as the primary support for customers in long-term hardship was not only unsustainable but would also undermine responsive policy development because the extent of any social problem would 'continue to be masked by retailer support' (AGL, 2005: 11; see also TRUenergy, 2005). The argument made by most retailers was that the government had the primary responsibility for funding people in long-term hardship, and there was a need to differentiate these customers from customers who experienced short-term hardship and could

132   *Contesting compliance in hardship regulation*

be assisted through retailer payment plans and hardship programmes to reduce their debts. Retailer AGL (2005: 6) noted that a significant number of its hardship programme customers were paying less than they consumed, and nothing toward their arrears, and that those customers would never clear their debt unless their financial resources improved. Retailers also stated that expecting retailers to waive debts would only increase prices for everyone (for example, AGL, 2005; TRUenergy, 2005).[2]

Other than their similar arguments on these themes, the retailers' submissions were very different, with the three Victorian incumbent retailers reflecting the full spectrum of opinion, even though these were the three retailers that already had voluntarily developed hardship programmes over the previous two years. These programmes varied in the detail, but tended to rely on bespoke payment plans that allowed customers to remained connected to supply as long as they contributed something to their debt. Hardship programmes also sometimes included other forms of assistance, such as in-home energy audits to help consumers better understand their consumption patterns, and free replacement of energy inefficient appliances. Origin Energy and AGL spent the most time describing the thinking behind their own companies' hardship programmes, as well as promoting a 'shared responsibility' model for supporting customers in hardship, where governments, welfare agencies and financial counsellors also had important roles. TRUenergy shared these themes, but focused most on customer responsibility for engaging with retailers and for budget management. Whereas Origin Energy and AGL took a largely conciliatory stance and only made the above argument within a framework of sympathy towards customers in financial hardship, TRUenergy was much less diplomatic. TRUenergy asked the hard questions that other retailers did not want to be seen asking, and put issues on the table that should not have been easy to dismiss, such as the following:

> Notions exist among a number of stakeholders that retailers should become an instrument of social policy, supplementing the incomes of customers who struggle to pay their bills. While the goals of these stakeholders and their hopes for a better society are often altruistic, we must find solutions to issues of affordability that are practical and sustainable and that are more sophisticated than just retailers simply writing off additional debt for the benefit of any particular customer class. In our society, it is generally expected that adult individuals are accountable for their choices and actions. Where customers are the cause of their own financial hardship, we must ask what is the appropriate response that reflects community values and ensures behavioural change. Where customers face hardship purely because of factors beyond their control, we must work together to find compassionate solutions that are cost effective and address the causes of financial hardship.
>
> (TRUenergy, 2005: 6)

TRUenergy was the only retailer that took an interventionist approach to assessing capacity to pay; while AGL and Origin Energy largely took customers at

Contesting compliance in hardship regulation   133

their word, TRUenergy required income statements from customers. Using these data TRUenergy was then able to illustrate in its submission many of its concerns about customer budgeting, noting the following:

> we observe that many of the customers identified as experiencing long term financial hardship are simply not adhering to payment plans that they have the capacity to afford. Others are making spending choices that are inappropriate and not in line with what could be regarded as community standards.
>
> (Ibid.: 10)

TRUenergy went on to provide several case studies to support its argument that customers who stuck to payment plans and made 'responsible' decisions about budgeting and energy consumption were able to meet the costs of their energy usage. TRUenergy's submission also provided examples of what was seen as irresponsible or poor decision-making about energy use and/or budgeting, such as a customer who used four heaters almost 24 hours per day in the winter period and also used her clothes dryer daily for six hours on average because 'the clothes in natural sunlight will not dry as soft as those in the dryer' (ibid.: 28). Another customer ran her gas central heating at 30 degrees Celsius, and then needed to open a window because it became so hot. The customer then continued to run the heating at 30 degrees with the window open (ibid.: 30).

The most confrontational aspect of TRUenergy's submission was its contention that community standards would not support the ongoing subsidisation of many customers said to be in financial hardship, giving examples of a heavy smoker and a drug user who required their bills to be subsidised, as well as customers who had cable television services (reasonably expensive in Australia at the time):

> Recently, TRUenergy conducted a series of free Energy Audits in customer's [sic] homes. Of the 4 properties visited, all 4 had [cable television] packages in their homes. While this doesn't constitute empirical evidence, it does give an indication of what retailers see as they endeavour to assist customers who claim 'hardship' and causes us to question whether community standards would permit additional assistance in these circumstances.
>
> (Ibid.: 22)

These types of statements were seen by many people as provocative and judgemental, and they contrasted significantly with the prevailing tone of most energy retailers (then and to the time of writing) which was more sensitive and collaborative, and only talked about chronic hardship or poor customer decisions in an abstract or principles-based manner. Behind the scenes, many retail staff I spoke with did agree with the TRUenergy perspective, yet retailers were nonetheless uncomfortable publicly questioning customers' experiences of hardship because this tended to look like the industry was defending the episodes of poor retailer behaviour. The case studies of retailer wrongdoing may have been very few in

134 Contesting compliance in hardship regulation

the context of the number of households served by retailers, but they were nevertheless confronting. As a result it was safer for retailers to not enter into challenging debate or test the politics of these situations. TRUenergy was the one party that submitted to the Inquiry that there needed to be clear definitions of hardship; every other submission discussed the complexity of such definitions and the impossibility of making decisions based on objective hardship indicators.

Policy responses and the appearance of action

TRUenergy's statements were not mentioned by the Committee of Inquiry in its final report, and they were not discussed publicly. The problems of defining chronic customer hardship, assessing customers' capacity to pay and establishing a reasonable expectation of retailers regarding customer subsidisation were outlined by the Committee in the final report in the following paragraph about Community Service Obligations (CSOs), which are government-provided social programmes:

> It is true that developing such CSOs is a complex matter. It requires clear definition of hardship, distinction between temporary and permanent hardship, and then raises thorny questions about valuing exactly what is the extent of funding responsibility of different parties. Further, any system needs to ensure that appropriate incentives exist, or at the very least that perverse incentives are not created. As is argued in detail throughout this Report, these are far from easy tasks. But, even though developing CSOs is difficult, it is inherent in the Committee's later recommendations on Government funding for policies to counter energy financial hardship, that efforts be made to create some so as to help define the intentions of the expenditure. They would be useful as part of establishing some goals for energy hardship policy.
>
> (Nieuwenhuysen *et al.*, 2005: 5)

The Committee provided no further guidance on funding roles and responsibilities. Most hardship was seen as a temporary situation that could be managed by more flexible payment plans and emergency relief, and the Committee merely encouraged retailers and other stakeholders to collaborate to understand future customer requirements. This appeared to meet the key stakeholder needs in a political sense. From a government perspective, it was convenient to accept this outcome because although it would require an injection of funds for financial counsellors and emergency grants, this would be a once-off and would effectively draw a line under what would be required from the government budget. The Victorian Energy Minister was able to announce that once again he had protected consumers, this time through 'the most comprehensive and far-reaching consumer hardship package since the deregulation and privatisation of the energy sector in Victoria during the 1990s' (Department of Infrastructure,

Contesting compliance in hardship regulation   135

2006a: 3).[3] Retailers (with the exception of TRUenergy) were also comfortable with the outcomes, as they were grateful that the recommendations had not been more onerous, such as a requirement to identify customers in hardship through systems changes or a ban on disconnections (both of which were unworkable but had potentially been on the cards). As long as there were not too many customers who were in chronic hardship, many retailers were apparently happy to foot the bill for their ongoing support through hardship programmes. Further, consumer advocacy groups seemed comfortable: first, there was an increase in funding; and second, even though the hardship policy outcomes were what the ESC had suggested some time earlier, this time the consumer advocates felt they had been listened to, and they saw the government embed a requirement for retailer hardship programmes in legislation rather than through ESC regulatory processes. Several consumer advocates had also wanted retailers to bear the ongoing costs of service provision because they recognised that the government was not going to contribute more in the form of income support.[4]

The outcomes of the Inquiry may have been bland but this was, and is, completely understandable: the Committee's recommendations were the best that could be asked of lay-people who were asked to answer complex and politically loaded questions in a short period. The only problem was that the troublesome issues identified by the Committee and through submissions were never resolved; as noted above, no working group was formed, there was never a rational or statistical analysis of the causes of hardship or an assessment of the prevalence and cost of chronic hardship, and no clarity was ever reached about the appropriate role for a commercial business in subsidising the provision of an essential service. The question of what should be done for customers who could never pay their bills was not addressed, and neither was the resulting problem of customers' hardship increasing as their consumption continued. A further problem that came up time and time again in later years related to what retailers needed to do, or should be expected to do, when customers did not respond to letters, telephone calls or even home visits. As will be discussed in the next section, the ESC and EWOV interpretation of the wrongful disconnection legislation, in combination with the belief that payment plans had to meet a customer's capacity to pay, meant there were many regulatory outcomes that were not anticipated in 2004 and 2005 by the industry, or, it seems by the government, politicians and the ESC itself.

However, the Victorian legislative outcomes continued to be held up as best practice by the Victorian government (including after a change of government) and consumer advocates, even leading to the Victorian model being used for NECF. The legacy of the political compromises made by Victorian stakeholders in 2005 was thus felt by all stakeholders in one way or another for many years after the Inquiry and across several Australian jurisdictions. Although this may have been bearable while prices were regulated only lightly (as they were in Victoria at the time) and while there was limited pressure on household budgets, in later years the problems were more apparent as prices rose and the expectations of retailers increased. Retailers continued to be looked to as the managers of energy customers

136 Contesting compliance in hardship regulation

in both short- and long-term hardship and while consumer advocates had wanted hardship support to be provided on a case-by-case basis (as had most retailers), the reality of such discretion for so many bill and payment plan transactions (potentially millions per annum in Victoria alone) was often unpalatable to people who also sought consistency in customer service and zero errors.

Before concluding the discussion of the Inquiry, we should note that the Committee was agnostic about the consumer advocate claims about retailer performance and compliance, repeating some of the claims made but saying 'it is hard to direct accusations of non-compliance against one or all retailers as there is insufficient data to indicate which retailer was non-compliant, and at which point in time this occurred' (Nieuwenhuysen *et al.*, 2005: 42). The final report made no mention of the ESC's 2004 findings that retailers *had* been compliant. The ESC did not provide a submission to the Inquiry, was not on the Committee's reference group and was not listed as having had a hearing with the Committee. The views of the ESC do not seem to have been accounted for other than an initial meeting held with the ESC on the Inquiry's Terms of Reference. It is not clear why this is the case, but it may be supposed that the Inquiry was expected to be independent from the ESC. The ESC's lack of involvement may have been to keep a low profile in what must have been a difficult time, or perhaps key staffers felt disgruntled to some degree about the way the regulator had been represented and so stayed away from the proceedings.

The compliance of retailers seemed to have been irrelevant to the policy and legislative outcomes at the time, as was the opinion and analysis of the regulator. The nature of what was compliant was contested and a subject that led to particular conflict between the ESC and EWOV.

Conflicts between the ESC and EWOV and wrongful disconnection referrals

EWOV was an alternative dispute resolution mechanism that all small Victorian customers had a right to use if they had tried to resolve a dispute with their retailer and had been unsuccessful in doing so. Any customer call to EWOV cost the industry money (paid to EWOV), and so represented a penalty for customer dissatisfaction. In 2005, the Hardship Inquiry published the costs, which showed that the EWOV complaints process required retailers to pay $84 for each enquiry, and $620 if the matter was escalated to a complaint. An enquiry could be anything from a customer calling to ask a question about the industry, to a genuine complaint. However, EWOV did more than resolve disputes. As discussed above, EWOV also involved itself in public policy debates, regularly arguing for more regulation in response to what it deemed to be 'systemic' issues, and publishing regular reports on complaint statistics. EWOV's views were often critical of the industry and the ESC.

As part of the hardship and disconnection debates, in mid-2005 EWOV wrote to the ESC identifying a number of disconnection cases where retailers may not have complied with their obligations under the Retail Code. In response to this,

Contesting compliance in hardship regulation 137

the ESC (2006) undertook a review of the EWOV cases and found that there was actually a high degree of compliance by retailers. However, the ESC noted that recent audit findings and the review of the EWOV cases showed that in many instances retailers had allowed customers' debt to build up over a long period. This was said to be for two key reasons. On the one hand, debt accumulated where retailers asked customers to pay more than the customer could manage, and so the customer further defaulted; on the other hand, payment plan instalment amounts were sometimes found to be too low, and so debts were rising as further bills became due. Retailers were also said to accept small and sporadic payments or sometimes no payments at all, over a number of account cycles. Importantly, the ESC noted that payment arrangements negotiated through assistance from EWOV reduced the instalment payment arrangements to less than 10 per cent of the debt for 65 per cent of the customers (ibid.: iv). This goes to the heart of the conflict between the policy principles of providing for capacity to pay but not allowing debt to spiral out of control; a conflict that was rarely acknowledged by most of the low-income consumer advocates or by EWOV. Welfare expert People First Total Solutions provided advice to the ESC for its review, noting that:

> While some of the cases analysed were straightforward, many of the cases were very complex involving negotiations and transactions over two or more years. As a result, there were a number of cases which were difficult to determine. It needs to be acknowledged that this increases the complexity for the retailers in assessing clients when customer complex life histories and needs are factored in.
>
> (Ibid.: 27)

People First also showed how different payment plan levels were able to clear debt, showing that an EWOV recommended payment amount for a customer would mean that the customer would never clear their debt, given that consumption would continue to add to the amount owing (ibid.: 16).

This investigation of the issues received no further attention, and in the years that followed the expectations of EWOV and most consumer advocates continued to focus on low payment plan repayment amounts over all else. The issue was most played out in the wrongful disconnection cases that EWOV managed, such as a case from 2011 where EWOV referred a customer's case to the ESC for a finding on several regulatory issues, including a claim that the retailer (Lumo Energy) had not assessed the customer's capacity to pay prior to disconnection and not used its best endeavours to contact the customer prior to disconnection. On the first matter of the assessment of capacity to pay, an extract from the ESC's public findings is below, where both the situation and the ESC's perspective on the issue are explained:

> On 29 January 2009, Lumo agreed a payment plan of $10 per fortnight with The Complainant, for both the electricity and gas accounts. At the time, the

138 *Contesting compliance in hardship regulation*

account arrears were approximately $915. EWOV considered that Lumo breached this clause because 'there were no notes about the discussion with The Complainant regarding the financial circumstances or the affordability of the arrangements'. At the time of entering this payment arrangement, The Complainant was on a Centrelink [welfare] payment of $280 per fortnight and had no rental or mortgage commitments. The $10 per fortnight payment amounted to approximately 1 per cent towards the dual fuel accounts and approximately 3.5 per cent of the fortnightly income. There were various references in the call centre notes to the assistance provided by Lumo staff and The Complainant was referred to the hardship program. The call centre notes also stated that The Complainant 'could only afford $10 per fortnight'. In light of the above, it is considered that Lumo took The Complainant's capacity to pay into account when agreeing the fortnightly payment. It is not agreed therefore that Lumo was in breach of the regulatory requirements.

(ESC, 2010b: 3)

EWOV should have had access to the same notes on the case as the ESC, and given these notes it is difficult to see how EWOV deemed Lumo to be noncompliant with its capacity to pay obligation. Even without the notes it is hard to see why a payment amount of $10 a fortnight could or should have been lower, particularly as it represented only 1 per cent of the amount owing. EWOV had also claimed that Lumo had not sufficiently attempted to contact the customer. In contrast, the ESC found Lumo to have 'made many telephone calls requesting contact if financial difficulties were experienced' (ibid.: 4), but the phone number was disconnected. There were further efforts to contact and promises made by the customer that were not kept. The ESC did not support EWOV's view.

This case was also brought to the ESC on the claim that Lumo had not notified the customer prior to disconnecting them on a dual fuel contract, and on this matter the EWOV concern was upheld. The Retail Code specified that separate disconnection warnings were required per fuel, with different minimum times prior to disconnection (electricity notices gave more time, reflecting the more essential nature of electricity compared with gas). However, Lumo's first warning and a subsequent letter referred instead to the disconnection of both fuels. Lumo sent three notices about gas and three notices for electricity in total, more notices than required by the Code and giving the customer more time to pay than the mandated minimum for each fuel. Nevertheless, the final result of this case for Lumo was compensation for the customer of $35,357 for gas (disconnection for five months, one day, 10.27 hours) and $14,170 for electricity (two months, 16.30 hours) on this issue of the disconnection notice not separating gas from electricity.

This case was sobering for the industry as it set a new precedent for wrongful disconnection amounts. However, all retailers had stories like this one; EWOV was known for stringent attention to technicalities in the customer's favour, and there were apocryphal tales of customers who had been disconnected in

Contesting compliance in hardship regulation 139

technical breach who were unaware of the disconnection but were still seen to require compensation of $250 a day for the period of disconnection. These were customers with uninhabited holiday homes, or customers in gaol, or customers with separately metered swimming pools over winter, and they were owed tens of thousands of dollars for their 'inconvenience'. These cases tended to not go to the final payment, but the process of negotiating the issues with EWOV was itself costly both in terms of time and money. The wrongful disconnection legislation was strict and did not grant the ESC leeway; if a case was referred to the ESC and the retailer was found to be in any technical breach, the ESC had to calculate compensation as per the Lumo case. This was viewed as deeply inequitable by both the industry and the ESC, as it went against any reasonable interpretation of the Retail Code. As one of the drafters of the original Retail Code I personally found these outcomes to be astonishing. The efforts that many retailers made to contact customers, such as Lumo's example in the case described, were far in excess of what was contemplated in the drafting of the Retail Code. The hardship and disconnection clauses of the Retail Code were written to avoid retailers disconnecting customers without notice and with no allowance for a customer's intent to pay. They were not written to be interpreted as providing a customer a $50,000 windfall when they had repeatedly not honoured their promises to their service provider and had been contacted multiple times to negotiate an alternative to disconnection.

There is no doubt that a number of disconnections were truly wrongful, in that retailers did not comply with the Retail Code, but the Lumo case – and others like it – did not seem to fit the criteria for wrongful behaviour, at least not to the degree to which the retailer was penalised. This was recognised by the government, and the ESC was asked to review the legislation in 2009. In January 2010 the ESC (2010a) recommended that government limit the compensation payment for customers who did not respond, and to move the details of the policy from statute to regulation to enable greater flexibility to respond to different circumstances. The government took almost two years to respond. In late 2011, it legislated to cap wrongful disconnection payments to $3,500 if the customer did not contact the retailer about the disconnection within 14 days of the disconnection. However, the changes to the legislation did not grant the ESC the flexibility it sought.

Third parties such as EWOV and the other jurisdictional energy industry Ombudsman schemes played an important and positive role in the consumer protection regime. However, the issues above draw out other aspects of these schemes, where it can be seen that some of EWOV's decisions were contrary to any sense of reflexive or responsive regulation. The irony is that EWOV was an industry scheme. Within a meta-regulatory framework that merely called for retailers to be members of an independent dispute resolution scheme, the industry had established EWOV to act in this capacity. EWOV's Board comprised industry and consumer representatives, and in theory the industry could have done more to manage its risks from EWOV. However, it did not. In my years of asking why this was the case, it appeared that the answer was that no retailer

140 *Contesting compliance in hardship regulation*

wanted to complain about EWOV (and certainly not the formidable Ombudsman, who was in place for 16 years until early 2012) in case this inflamed the situation and had negative repercussions for their business.

The implications for compliance and performance

A recurring theme in the previous sections is that compliance was a contested concept. Not only were the rules open to interpretation in a basic sense, but they were also more fundamentally disputed by consumer advocates (and EWOV) according to their own perspectives on what a rule *should* have meant and therefore what compliance/non-compliance should have looked like. This extended to a claim that the regulator was not doing its job if the regulator did not enforce the rules a certain way. The normative case thus became thoroughly intertwined with the practical realities of compliance enforcement.

The result of this was that the regulator's performance and compliance reports on the industry were rarely acknowledged by the consumer advocacy groups, as we saw earlier in this chapter where the ESC's reports that retailers were in compliance had no effect on political lobbying to enact new laws, and in fact only resulted in the ESC being discredited. Instead, the consumer advocates used their own assessments of performance and compliance, on their own terms. The studies developed by consumer advocacy groups for lobbying on regulatory changes frequently claimed regulatory breaches had occurred, and some claims described behaviour that was clearly in breach of both the letter and the spirit of the law. However, a number of alleged breaches were not non-compliant in the technical sense, and perhaps not even in principle if one were to take a different perspective on terms such as disconnecting as a 'last resort' or or a payment plan 'reflecting' a customer's capacity to pay. These were the cases where retailers did not disconnect as late in the process as the report's authors thought appropriate, or did not reduce payment plans to payment amounts as low as report's authors believed they should be. Even the various consumer advocacy groups had different views on some of these issues: as noted previously, groups with links to frontline welfare support tended to oppose disconnection that was delayed because this merely caused debt to grow, whereas groups that did not have frontline welfare agents tended to take a more ideological position that all disconnection was bad.

The consumer advocate reports also described incidents as 'breaches' when they had not been investigated and verified as breaches by the regulator. My own experience in Victoria with at least two of these consumer reports that claimed breaches was that I could not verify or resolve the alleged breaches when I tried to follow up the claims against my retailer employer; actionable information was never provided to the regulator and sometimes the claimants could not be located by the report's authors. This is not to say that the poor retailer behaviour did not occur, but again, it is also possible that 'breaches' were sometimes the result of consumer stories being framed by normative story tellers focused more on what they believed should have happened than on technical non-compliance. In this way we can see that the matter was perhaps less about compliance and

Contesting compliance in hardship regulation   141

non-compliance and more about subjective views of *performance*. This was also the natural outcome of the principles-based regulatory approach, which in its lack of prescription opened up the rules to debate around interpretation and, therefore, politicking by those who wished to see their own interpretation prescribed and enforced. Indeed, the debates were never really about compliance and enforcement, but *always* about how satisfactory the rules were in promoting a certain type of performance. Inevitably the rules were seen to be unsatisfactory at guaranteeing specific outcomes, so it was necessary for regulators and governments to continue to tweak them.

Reactions to formal and informal performance reporting

Across all the jurisdictions, the industry reacted to these circumstances with confusion and significant denial that there was an issue. The retailers did not accept the version of the industry that was presented to them by the consumer sector; they believed that retailer practices were largely compliant and ethical, with several retailers going well beyond basic compliance with their hardship programmes. The informal performance reporting of the consumer advocates (again, this was mainly in Victoria) was not absorbed in any detail by the businesses as far as I could tell; responses to these reports were often left to individual regulatory and communications managers to deal with as a risk management or public relations exercise, particularly if there was any media attention. As noted above there were some efforts by retailers to discover their points of non-compliance and remedy them, but the lack of reliable information about the alleged breaches made this a challenge.

In contrast, retailers were attentive to the Ombudsman reports in each jurisdiction and prepared for their public release. The retailers were given the reports confidentially ahead of time so they could understand and respond to any errors, and these reports also gave each retailer the first chance to see how they compared with others. Featuring statistics for every company and commentary on customer service complaints and trends, the reports were taken seriously; they also featured in the local newspapers without fail.

Formal compliance and performance reports from the regulator were generally more subtle than the consumer advocate or Ombudsman reports on the industry. Regulatory reports were procedural and captured levels of detail that were ambiguous in terms of real customer or business harm. The performance reports showed small annual changes in metrics like customer numbers, call waiting times and customers on direct debit arrangements, and presented these in tabular form by retailer as well as industry trends over time. These reports also included the controversial metrics related to disconnections and customer participation in hardship programmes.

Compliance reports, which employed more narrative than performance reports, described the main compliance breaches identified by retailers in the reporting period, and the means by which these breaches were being rectified by the retailer, including any action taken by the regulator. A review of the various

142   *Contesting compliance in hardship regulation*

regulators' compliance reports across the country from 2003 to 2015 show three types of reported non-compliance: (a) transactional, such as system errors with bill processing; (b) third party, such as door-to-door salespeople misleading consumers; and (c) other internal non-compliance, such as reporting and call centre breaches. Compliance breaches were generally framed by retailers as the result of system errors or rogue operators. The regulators' reports on both compliance and performance documented the issues and their treatment plans in a reasonably bland manner and rarely pointed to any overwhelming issue or concern on the relevant regulator's behalf. They also tended to not form judgements on what was good or bad unless this was clearly required; the data were recognised as being ambiguous or open to interpretation and regulators were careful about absolute statements. Thus formal regulatory reports acted less as a mechanism for retailer learning and reputational regulation than as a basic compliance obligation and discussion between the industry and regulator's compliance staff.

There was never any evidence that the general customer population read either the formal or informal performance and compliance reporting, a finding consistent with other research on consumer responses to regulatory disclosure initiatives (van Erp, 2011). While Ombudsman reports and the occasional consumer report were picked up by the media, this rarely went on for more than a day. As discussed in the previous chapter, the real power of consumer advocate (and Ombudsman) informal performance reports was more in how they could capture the attention of a regulator or government that wanted to be seen to take action on something. However, the likelihood of this proceeding depended on political personalities and other competing issues, and so was impossible to predict.

Consumer advocate naming and shaming

An interesting aspect of consumer advocate reporting on the industry is that they rarely named the wrongdoers or the good performers. This was probably seen as unnecessary, because often the case being made was that the whole industry was at fault and required further regulation. It was also probably a matter of good manners; despite the conflicting views and some strain, the relationship between retailer and consumer advocate staff was always civil and did not get personal, and there seemed to be a concern that even naming the better performers was playing favourites. While it could be argued that criticisms of the industry as a whole could inspire all retailers to do better, in practice this just worked against the already high performers and alienated them from the consumer lobby. Recall that the three incumbent retailers had voluntary hardship programmes in place in 2004 and 2005, yet the consumer groups were criticising all retailers for non-performance and compliance breaches. The fact that these retailers waived debt, provided payment plans and free home energy efficiency audits, and accepted low repayments was not highlighted by advocates at the time.

Even when specific retailers were named by the regulator this made little difference to how consumer advocates responded. For example, the increase in disconnections that occurred in 2004 and drove the subsequent wrongful disconnection debate was primarily linked to two retailers only. A performance report published by the ESC in 2005 about the 2004 calendar year showed that electricity disconnections for the industry were skewed by one large retailer in particular, which advised that it was 're-establishing collection procedures' from a business it had bought in 2002 and so disconnections almost doubled (ESC, 2005: 29). The retailer had added several stages to the disconnection process to give consumers additional opportunities to pay. This retailer was not named by the consumer advocates; instead, and as we saw, all retailers were criticised and the ESC was also criticised for not doing enough.

Regulatory focus on performance

As rising energy prices became more of a political issue, regulators became increasingly interested in energy retailer performance indicators on disconnection and hardship programmes. The Australian Energy Regulator's (AER's) preparation for NECF involved a prolonged consultation on performance indicators over 2010 and 2011, where a key focus was on customer outcomes from hardship programmes. This was a frustrating process for the industry and could be given a chapter of its own. In short, the AER made a number of statements about hardship performance indicators that demonstrated no clear objective for performance data, and little assessment of what was genuinely within retailers' control and so could be called retailer 'performance', compared with unpredictable customer behaviours or broader societal trends. For example, the AER suggested that a customer being disconnected within two years of exiting a hardship programme reflected badly on the retailer. However, this had never been the perspective of the drafters of the rules and was not supported by any evidence that a retailer and its hardship programme could have permanent effects on a customer's financial situation, or that a customer's situation and willingness to deal with a retailer were static or predictable. The complexity of the issues underpinning this broad assumption was not even contemplated by the AER, and yet at the time it planned to publish reports on what was superior and inferior retailer 'performance' for this measure and many others. (By late 2013 the AER's view had changed: its first performance report was careful and devoid of significant commentary. The process of receiving significant quantities of data on unclear issues had probably forced the AER's staff towards a more pragmatic view.)

The Victorian ESC pursued a similar line of thinking to the AER in 2011. The ESC Chairman wrote a letter to all retailers' CEOs advising them of a consultant's report his office had procured, where vulnerable and low-income customers of water and energy businesses had been interviewed about how their needs were met by the businesses. Despite the energy industry having been found to be compliant with the Retail Code in recent audits, and despite there being no evidence of breaches or compliance issues, the ESC appeared concerned about performance; there had been an increase in disconnections in the previous reporting period and a slight decrease in hardship programme

144 *Contesting compliance in hardship regulation*

participation. Each business was asked a range of questions about how it dealt with various situations, with the focus sometimes on much more than compliance. For example, the businesses were asked how they 'ensured' that payment terms under customer payment plans were 'set in line with customer capacity to pay' (ESC, 2012: 3), which was a misreading of the Retail Code's balancing of capacity to pay against consumption payments, and also contradicted the ESC's previous statements that it would not form a view that capacity to pay was more important than paying for consumption. Interestingly, the ESC also stated that the study indicated that some businesses needed:

> to do more to ensure they are providing appropriate support to customers experiencing hardship, and by extension, to ensure they satisfy and exceed the intent of the Commission's Customer Service Codes and guidelines in relation to their approach to hardship.[5]

The energy retailers were troubled by the implications of the ESC's statements. The Hardship Inquiry may as well not have happened, and the ESC's own findings of previous years seemed to be forgotten. The idea that industry needed to ensure it *satisfied and exceeded the intent of the rules* was certainly perplexing; although several retailers went well beyond basic compliance, surely all that could be required was compliance with the rules as they were written. A further problem was that the performance statistics on hardship programmes and disconnections that sat behind the ESC's beliefs about the industry had apparently not been examined to discover their causes, and the performance trends were not common to all retailers. The retailers responded to the ESC on these issues and the matter appeared to then be closed.[6]

The approach of the AER and ESC during the period 2010–2011 is likely to have been in some part a reaction to political pressure at the time to 'do something' about energy price rises and their effects on consumers. As discussed in Chapter 4, this pressure was felt by all energy-related government and regulatory staffers in one form or another, and the adequacy of hardship programmes was raised in several states and in several forms. This was definitely the concern underpinning the ESC's consultation on hardship programmes. There was also a genuine unease expressed by the ESC's Chairman about the fitness of the regulatory framework, where he was not sure that it was equipped to deal with the underlying market conditions regarding pricing (see Ben-David, 2012). This issue will be returned to in Chapter 6. The point made here, however, is that the regulator–retailer interaction in 2011, and in particular the ESC–retailer interaction, seems to demonstrate that even the regulator was able to put aside compliance and enforcement as core values when it was seen as necessary. For this period the ESC focus was on performance according to (unstated) criteria that went beyond the compliance obligations in the Retail Code.

The creation of retailer hardship programmes

It has come up several times in this chapter that at the time of the Victorian Hardship Inquiry the three incumbent retailers had financial hardship programmes in place for consumers who were struggling to pay their bills. Hardship programmes for residential consumers were eventually mandated for all retailers and across all jurisdictions, but in 2005 they were provided entirely at retailers' discretion and focused on Victoria. This is a key example of the sort of positive and innovative behaviour that meta-regulation seeks to embed, and so it is important to consider the circumstances that were conducive to such voluntary performance improvements. The discussion below considers the period leading to 2003–2004 when the retailers created their hardship programmes.

First, it is likely that the retailers in question were put under pressure from the ESC and EWOV to develop their hardship programmes, based on precedents from the water sector. The ESC and EWOV also covered the Victorian water utilities and regularly portrayed these businesses' relatively new (at the time) hardship policies as reflecting best practice in managing consumer hardship (although the water businesses' environment was very different, as they were, and to the time of writing still are, government-owned monopolies). It is also possible that retailers believed this was all they needed to do to manage the criticisms from consumer advocates and EWOV; the incumbent energy retailers may have believed they had 'solved the problem' of consumer hardship, at least insofar as energy retailers were held to be responsible. This was before retailers started to see the trend for ever increasing retailer responsibility for filling the social welfare gap.

Second, the period during which the retailers developed their programmes seems to have been relatively free of financial and resource pressure compared with later periods. The years 2003–2004 were before several of the larger business acquisitions and well before IT transformations were required. This was also a time when retailers said they wanted retail price deregulation but did not actively pursue this objective, which would imply that financial positions were strong. This timing provided a window for social innovators within the businesses:[7] they were able to receive funding and support at a time when business decision-makers were not otherwise distracted or managing budget cuts.

Third, two of the three retailers relied heavily on advice, staff training and customer in-home energy audits provided by a particular financial counselling agency that also worked with some water businesses, specifically those which were viewed positively by the ESC and EWOV. The blurred line between the financial counselling agency's role as contractor to the industry and its social welfare advocacy role was conveniently exploited by both the agency and the retailers. The relationship lent further social (and regulatory) legitimacy to the retailers' approach, and it provided revenue to the agency. The retailers stated that there was economic value to them from the relationship but the truth of this was not clear; it was perhaps one of the rare episodes where a business case requirement was not heavily enforced and action was taken more to pursue

146 *Contesting compliance in hardship regulation*

social or reputational objectives. There was also a degree of faddishness to retailers' ready adoption of the agency's language and concepts; the feel-good factor of being seen as socially accepted seemed hard to resist.

On a related note, the retailer that did not use this provider was not viewed as positively as other retailers by the low-income consumer advocates. As discussed earlier, TRUenergy undertook its own assessments of its customers' capacity to pay and so did not use financial counsellors. It recast the concept of a hardship programme to meet what might be considered more rigorous operational and economic criteria. The fact that TRUenergy had a hardship programme that exceeded the standards prescribed in the Retail Code should, in theory, have been viewed positively by low-income consumer advocates. However, this appeared to make little difference because the form of TRUenergy's approach did not match low-income consumer advocates' view of what a hardship programme *should* look like. In fact, the hardship programmes that were viewed favourably by these consumer advocates actively espoused forms of debt waiver, which, as we saw earlier, were not aligned with TRUenergy's philosophical approach.

The obvious conclusion from this brief discussion of the circumstances for noted performance innovation – and specifically related to the fact that it is so brief – is that such innovation did not happen often, or in any particularly observable sense. The most that can be said is that retailers undertook clear 'beyond compliance' social responsibility initiatives when they still thought this would make a difference, when the economic conditions were positive and when they were faced with fewer competing objectives. These conditions were not present for very long in the Australian retail energy industry. This is not to say that retailers did not innovate constantly in smaller ways; for example, some retailers had exceptionally high standards of customer service, which included innovative ways to assist consumers in their energy management and bill payments. However, these were rarely recognised (or even 'seen') as valuable by observers of the industry, and so were not discussed. Of course, this chapter has shown that, over time, even the significant step of voluntary hardship programme creation was also forgotten as the requirements of retailers continued to climb. In the hardship debates in 2005 and to the time of writing the *only* thing that mattered to many low-income consumer advocates (and the policymakers they were able to influence) in any long-term sense was that any disconnections for non-payment might occur for vulnerable consumers.

A surprising turn of events: the ESC proposal to abolish hardship programmes

Despite the years of repeated conflict on the same issues – and, perhaps, *because* of the conflict – the Victorian regulator took the hardship policy issue in a new direction in late 2015. According to the usual cycle of being seen to investigate and 'do something' about consumer hardship, the ESC commenced a review of retailers' hardship programmes. This originated with the ESC's own desire to address increased disconnection rates in 2014, and morphed into a full hardship inquiry in 2015 as a result of a new Minister issuing broader terms of reference.

It might be imagined that this investigation would have proceeded down the same path as the other processes in previous years; certainly while I was writing this book I did not anticipate a change to the narrative. However, the ESC went on to show a remarkable change in approach, identifying that the soft terms of payment plans 'reflecting a customer's capacity to pay' and a customer 'being in hardship' were essentially unmeasurable and unenforceable. In September 2015 the ESC (2015) argued that retailers should not be responsible for assessing a customer's capacity to pay, and that the retailers' basic inability to do this effectively was understandable. The ESC proposed some startling alternatives, such as abolishing hardship programmes and instead prescribing different bands of payment plans that customers were entitled to when they met certain criteria, such as being able to pay for ongoing consumption but not debt. The ESC also essentially mandated that consumers who could not pay for their ongoing consumption would be disconnected after prescribed processes had been followed (including extensive efforts at assistance).[8] This ultimately put the social responsibility for consumers in chronic hardship back onto government and the welfare sector.

This change was extraordinary given the years of previous experience, and all stakeholders seemed unnerved. Most stakeholder submissions to the ESC's draft decision paper began with congratulating the ESC for taking a new perspective, then went on to criticise the approach as unworkable. The low-income consumer advocates were concerned about the proposed approach for a range of reasons, with the standout argument being that retailers *should* be responsible for assessing capacity to pay, and that flexibility was required. They also fiercely disagreed with the more explicit regulatory provision for customers to be disconnected when they could not pay for consumption, which was consistent with their philosophy from the early days.

Retailers did not like the proposed approach because they did not agree there was a problem, at least not to the degree identified by the ESC. In fact, many retailers wanted to keep their hardship programmes, despite this meaning that they accepted the challenging social policy role that this entailed. While there were definitely valid concerns about the possible interpretations of the ESC's new model (it was ambiguous in parts and potentially did not sufficiently account for operational practices and consumer preferences), the retailers' dislike was far more intense than a matter of mere interpretative differences. Some retailers were known to have lobbied the then Minister for Energy to argue against the ESC's proposal, even though that Minister was known for her distaste for retailers and she had recently introduced legislation that doubled the wrongful disconnection penalty (among other things) with no consultation. The ESC read the political winds and delayed its final decision by two months to provide for more consultation, with its final decision endorsed by the Minister in March 2016.

The retailers' initial response to the ESC's proposed revamp of industry hardship obligations would seem to be at odds with the years of previous arguments

148 *Contesting compliance in hardship regulation*

put to policymakers that the industry just wanted direction and should not have been responsible for filling the social welfare gap, particularly for customers in chronic hardship. However, this perspective becomes more comprehensible when we account for the tendency for business organisations to be rule-followers, to be resistant to change and the risk it brings, and to hunker down around what they already know. The retailers had developed their systems and processes and wanted to keep the rules they had established for themselves, regardless of whether these met the principles of arguments they had put to the regulator in the past, and certainly compared to the new and somewhat unclear rules proposed by the ESC.

Further, the direction taken by the ESC was the opposite to that of the AER on the same topic, which reinforced the difference in compliance obligations, and thus compliance risk, across jurisdictions for most retailers. Following a review of hardship programmes in 2014 that had found 'many community concerns about hardship assistance and payment plan affordability are not symptomatic of widespread non-compliance' (AER, 2015: 3), the AER released in 2016 a voluntary 'good practice framework' to assist retailers in assessing their customers' capacity to pay (AER, 2016).

As a postscript, the programme of transforming the hardship approach of the Retail Code was ongoing at the time of writing, with a policy revamp proposed in October 2016 that did not change the fundamental approach from 2015 but much of the surrounding detail. The entire project had turned out to be far more problematic than anticipated, for reasons that can collectively be characterised as the ESC underestimating the complexity in the changes it was seeking to make. The ESC's consultation through 2016 was also a source of concern for both the industry and the consumer groups. However, the conditions in September 2015 were before any of this came to light, and before the fundamental problems in the detail had become apparent.

Conclusion

The moral issue of energy as an essential service for small consumers was most demonstrated in the area of consumer financial hardship, and more precisely with the use of disconnections for non-payment. Debt collection activity and disconnections were allowed by law and determined within the retailer organisations according to economic system coding, which was moral according to the retailers. However, this was irrelevant to other systems that valued consumer outcomes on different criteria. As a result, conflicts were inherent in the energy policy debates and could not be resolved through meta-regulatory discourse or consultation. Stakeholders' cognitive limitations and basic values meant that consultation just appeared to reinforce their existing views rather than encourage learning about new ones.

A key manifestation of the ongoing value conflicts in the retail energy industry was that retailer compliance with regulations seemed to be largely a matter of perspective for many stakeholders rather than an objective fact. The finding of

Contesting compliance in hardship regulation 149

the ESC in 2004 that the industry was compliant with the Retail Code was irrelevant to the stakeholders who claimed that the industry was breaching its obligations. The ESC was sidelined by consumer advocates, and then the government, because these stakeholders did not like the outcomes of consumers being disconnected if they could not afford to pay. This is despite the Retail Code providing for these disconnections if the correct process was followed (the legal system found disconnections to be legal in principle), despite the Retail Code itself being supported and despite there being no evidence that retailers were not following the processes in a material sense. What retailers saw was in fact the prominence of perceptions of *performance* over compliance, where the concept of performance was flexible enough to account for subjective normative views of regulation rather than black letter law. While compliance with the Retail Code was about processes being followed, performance was about moral views of consumer outcomes for an essential service, and the regulation (and legislation) by case study approach was entirely about specific outcomes framed a particular way.

Meta-consensus turned out to be fragile, with the legitimacy of the regulator in the eyes of its stakeholders never assured. The ESC's legitimacy to act in a range of ways was contingent on it making the 'right' decisions, which has some precedent in the academic literature (see Hawkins, 2002; Brunsson, 2003). As Black (2010: 329) comments in the context of financial regulators in the global financial crisis, 'even independent regulators need a "political licence" to operate' (see also Parker, 2006).

The government's behaviour during the period where it sidelined the ESC and industry in 2004–2005 was deeply hypocritical (in the sense used by Brunsson, 2003). The interpretation issues about consumer outcomes could actually have been regulated away if there had been political appetite to do so. Either the government or the regulator could have developed rules that stated 'no disconnection for non-payment above X per cent of the customer population' or 'no disconnection for Y type of customer'. Most obviously, if government truly valued energy as an essential service it could have decided that small customer disconnections were illegal. None of these solutions would have been a good idea; they would have been arbitrary and would have caused significant problems in the economic system as retailers considered how to manage non-payment (and this would have reflected back to politics). Nevertheless, they still would have been purer interpretations of energy as 'essential'. Instead, political (and later legal) communications ambiguously referred to disconnection as a 'last resort' option, implying that more than Retail Code compliance was required. However, there was no logical programme for 'last resort' other than the Retail Code, with the convenient misunderstanding about the Retail Code's process-based approach protecting consumers from disconnection persisting until the ESC's revised approach was proposed in late 2015.

The 2005 Hardship Inquiry example particularly illustrated stakeholders' inability to have objectively rational discussions about difficult topics. Almost no-one wanted to deal with the thorny issues on consumer hardship that might

150   *Contesting compliance in hardship regulation*

have actually provided more responsive and sustainable policy outcomes, such as unpicking problems of inadequate consumer income, poor consumer decision-making and the role of government to directly subsidise those in chronic hardship. This is not unexpected: these were issues that went beyond the scope of any stakeholder group (including the state government, which was not responsible for primary income support) and a holistic view was beyond any communicative system. The only party that sought rational analysis was widely condemned for being politically incorrect, which is itself a telling phrase; TRUenergy was not political where it needed to be. Rational analysis of a complex suite of consumer and policy issues was not practical or politically palatable, and so the government was necessarily hypocritical in its response. The main purpose of the 2005 Hardship Inquiry seemed to be to demonstrate that government had 'done something' through its 'iconic' actions (and that it had achieved more than the ESC/EWOV-led Utility Debt Spiral Project).

Conflicts not only occurred at given times; they also occurred *through* time as organisations changed their views about policy issues. Of course the key example from this chapter is the ESC's 2015 view that the Retail Code's 'capacity to pay' and hardship provisions were essentially unenforceable, which was clearly an important shift from the approach over the previous years. From this point the regulatory conversation seemed likely to change, albeit still within the parameters of meta-regulation. It is important to recognise that until late 2015 the Retail Code was considered the gold standard of consumer protection regulation, with the regulator not questioning its overall approach (note this not the same as the ESC Chairman's concern about competition and prices), and stakeholders previously only seeking clarification on specific issues. The ESC view from late 2015 marked a change to this and a recasting of the cost to regulatory clarity of the trade-offs made in the Retail Code in 1999–2000 and the outcomes from the 2005 Hardship Inquiry. This shows the contingency and time dependence of what is even considered good regulation.[9]

This chapter also showed that key low-income consumer advocates did not support the meta-regulatory enforcement model. The responses to the ESC in 2004 illustrate that no enforcement was good enough if it was not public, was not managed by the state, and if it did not enforce stakeholders' views of adequate industry performance (despite actual compliance). By this stance they also did not support responsive regulation (as per Ayres and Braithwaite, 1992), because if enforcement was not public and not at maximum levels it was seen to be inadequate. The wrongful disconnection legislation was the opposite of responsive regulation, with no discretion afforded to the regulator. Further, while some form of co-regulation through the Utility Debt Spiral Project seemed like a good idea to start with, interest fell away when actual participation was required.

Retailers responded to their environment with bewilderment. The industry was generally found to be compliant by the regulator (notwithstanding the ESC's conclusions in late 2015 about the problems with the Retail Code), and yet all retailers were regularly criticised by consumer advocates and the government for unproven breaches. Those with sophisticated hardship programmes were not

Contesting compliance in hardship regulation   151

publicised or given credit for their efforts; instead, retailers were collectively tarred in order to argue that more rules were required. Retailers were also essentially told by several major consumer advocacy organisations that they should subsidise consumers who did not pay at all, so that no person would be disconnected for non-payment. If these were the cues that the industry was to learn from to improve its performance then they were of limited use given the lack of commercial considerations, and thus value, in the economic system. While some retailers did waive significant debts, to expect all retailers to absorb all debt could not be justified to shareholders, and it also let government off the hook for its social responsibilities. Further, there was ambiguity about the moral status of disconnection; as discussed in this chapter, some low-income advocacy organisations supported disconnection as a means of prompting customer engagement whereas others were vehemently against disconnection. Even if a retailer were to (hypothetically) seek to directly import a consumer advocate view, there was no clarity about which view to adopt.

Notes

1 Other disconnections occurred when people moved residence (this was usual) and for reasons such as illegal use.
2 Consumer groups had been silent on this, with the exception of the Institute for Social Research (2005: 2), which stated that retailers were 'basically agents of wealth redistribution' and 'quasi tax collectors'.
3 This was a Labor government Minister: the difference between this statement and his Labor predecessors' statements about the reform in 2000 (as discussed in Chapter 3) were marked.
4 Noting that this was the state government, which did not have responsibility for welfare other than to fund concessions for concessions card holders and emergency assistance. The federal government had responsibility for welfare payments and other forms of social security.
5 As quoted by Origin Energy (2011: 12) in its public submission.
6 At least until later in the year when the ESC then proposed changes to the Retail Code on various issues across four different consultation processes. These consultations were a further source of frustration for the industry (and the Victorian government) because they required business systems changes in the months prior to the intended commencement date of NECF. The proposed changes were also not based on any evidence of problems. Most of the ESC's proposed Retail Code changes were suspended and were never revisited.
7 I do not believe the hardship programmes were cynical exercises in public relations; for example, the manager of the hardship programme in the retailer I worked for was a true believer in the programme he created and a strong consumer advocate within the business.
8 The Retail Code had always implicitly allowed for the disconnection of these customers, but the new framework appeared to actively require it. It did this through valuing the avoidance of debt more than maintaining connection to supply.
9 Although I should note that at the time of writing (October 2016) the ESC's revised approach was not itself clearly considered good regulation (by any stakeholder) either.

152 *Contesting compliance in hardship regulation*

References

AER (Australian Energy Regulator) (2015) *AER review of energy retailers' customer hardship policies and practices 2015*, January.

AER (Australian Energy Regulator) (2016) *Sustainable payment plans: a good practice framework for assessing customers' capacity to pay*, Version 1, July.

AGL (2005) *Submission to the Committee of Inquiry into financial hardship of energy consumers*, Australian Gas Light Company, 20 June.

Ayres, I. and Braithwaite, J. (1992) *Responsive regulation: transcending the deregulation debate*, Oxford University Press: Oxford.

Ben-David, R. (2012) *Retail energy markets: a case for economics redux*, presented to Consumer Utility Advocacy Centre, 7 March, Essential Services Commission: Melbourne.

Black, J. (2010) 'The role of risk in regulatory processes', in R. Baldwin, M. Cave and M. Lodge (eds) *The Oxford handbook of regulation*, Oxford University Press: Oxford, pp. 302–348.

Brunsson, N. (2003) *The organization of hypocrisy: talk, decisions and actions in organizations*, second edition, trans. N. Adler, Copenhagen Business School Press: Herndon.

Committee for Melbourne (2004) *Utility Debt Spiral Project*, Melbourne, November.

Consumer Law Centre Victoria (2004) *Submission to the Essential Services Commission on the Draft Decision on its review of the electricity and gas Retail Codes*, letter to Katherine Koesasi from Chris Field and Anna Stewart, 27 February.

CUAC (Consumer Utilities Advocacy Centre) (2004) *Submission to the draft Energy Code*, letter to Katherine Koesasi from Kerry Connors, 27 February.

CUAC (Consumer Utilities Advocacy Centre) (2005) *Submission to the Committee of Inquiry into financial hardship of energy consumers: Issues Paper*, May, May Mauseth Johnston.

Department of Infrastructure (2006a) *Government energy consumer hardship policy statement*, May.

Department of Infrastructure (2006b) *Government response to the Hardship Inquiry*, May.

ESC (Essential Services Commission) (2004a) *Disconnections and capacity to pay report on energy retailers' performance*, Melbourne, October.

ESC (Essential Services Commission) (2004b) *Review of electricity and gas retail codes: a draft Energy Code*, Draft decision, January, Melbourne.

ESC (Essential Services Commission) (2004c) *Special investigation: review of effectiveness of retail competition and consumer safety net in gas and electricity*, Final report to Minister, Overview report, 22 June, Melbourne.

ESC (Essential Services Commission) (2005) *Energy retail businesses: comparative performance report for the 2004 calendar year*, Melbourne, August.

ESC (Essential Services Commission) (2006) *Regulatory audit of electricity and gas retailers 2003/04: review of Energy and Water Ombudsman, Victoria cases July–December 2004*, Melbourne, March.

ESC (Essential Services Commission) (2010a) *Review of wrongful disconnection payment: final report*, Melbourne, January.

ESC (Essential Services Commission) (2010b) *Wrongful disconnection payment dispute Lumo Energy and the Complainant, statement of reasons*, Melbourne, December.

ESC (Essential Services Commission) (2012) *Improving approaches to customer financial hardship: summary of business responses to commission request for information on hardship policies and procedures*, Melbourne, February.

Contesting compliance in hardship regulation 153

ESC (Essential Services Commission) (2015) *Supporting customers, avoiding labels: energy hardship inquiry, draft report*, Melbourne, September.

EWOV (Energy and Water Ombudsman of Victoria) (2005) *Re: Committee of Inquiry into financial hardship of energy consumers – issues paper for consultation with stakeholders*, 23 June, letter from Fiona McLeod.

Financial and Consumer Rights Council (2005) *Financial and Consumer Rights Council Victoria Committee of Inquiry into Financial Hardship of Energy Consumers submission*, Melbourne, June.

Hawkins, K. (2002) *Law as last resort: prosecution decision-making in a regulatory agency*, Oxford University Press: Oxford.

Institute for Social Research (2005) *Submission to the Committee of Inquiry into Financial Hardship for Energy Consumers*, 20 June, Andrea Sharam.

Kildonan Child and Family Services (2005) *Submission by Kildonan Child and Family Services to the Issues Paper*, Marie Stivala-Andrews, June.

Milbur Consulting (2005) *Committee of Inquiry into Financial Hardship of Energy Consumers issues paper for consultation with stakeholders*, May.

Nieuwenhuysen, J., Huitfeldt, J. and Scarth, C. (2005) *Committee of Inquiry into the Financial Hardship of Energy Consumers: main report*, September.

Origin Energy (2011) *Re: Commission research into customer experiences of the water and energy retail business approaches to hardship*, 29 July, letter to Ron Ben-David from Graeme Hamilton.

Parker, C. (2006) 'The "compliance trap": the moral message in responsive regulatory enforcement', *Law and Society Review*, vol. 40, no. 3, pp. 591–622.

Rich, N. and Mauseth, M. (2004) *Access to energy and water in Victoria: a research report*, Consumer Law Centre Victoria and Consumer Utilities Advocacy Centre, November.

St Vincent De Paul Society (2005) *Committee of Inquiry into Financial Hardship of Energy Consumers*, June, Gavin Dufty.

Theophanous, T. (2004) *Review of electricity and gas Retail Codes: Draft Decision Energy Retail Code*, letter to Dr John Tamblyn from Theo Theophanous MP, Minister for Energy Industries and Resources, 27 February, Ref: MBN003322, File: RDN/2003/00008.

TRUenergy (2005) *Committee of Inquiry into Financial Hardship of Energy Consumers – TRUenergy Submission*.

van Erp, J. (2011) 'Naming and shaming in regulatory enforcement', in C. Parker and V. Lehmann Nielsen (eds) *Explaining compliance: business responses to regulation*, Edward Elgar: Cheltenham, pp. 322–342.

Victorian Council of Social Service (2004a) Untitled submission in response to the *Draft decision: review of Electricity and Gas Retail Codes*, letter to Katherine Koesasi from Cath Smith, 27 February.

Victorian Council of Social Service (2004b) *VCOSS media conference: customer protections in electricity and gas – what's happening and what needs to happen?*, media release, 5 October.

Victorian Hansard (2004a) in Hansard Parliamentary debates, fifty-fifth Parliament, first session, *Energy Legislation (Amendment) Bill*, Legislative Assembly, 18 November 2004, Book 7.

Victorian Hansard (2004b) in Hansard Parliamentary debates, fifty-fifth Parliament, first session, *Energy Legislation (Amendment) Bill*, Legislative Council, 2 December 2004, Book 7.

6 Conflicting views of market competition

As discussed in Chapter 2, normative meta-regulatory theory depends on markets to make an industry attentive to the public interest. At its most basic level, this occurs through the behaviour of transactional stakeholders such as customers, who are expected to use their purchasing decisions to send messages to the industry about appropriate behaviour. Certainly the language of consumer activism to promote reputational damage is geared towards markets providing the ultimate discipline on business. Despite this reliance on markets, normative meta-regulatory theory does not seek to question or determine the effectiveness of markets in this role, and empirical studies have similarly not considered the issue. In an attempt to start to resolve this problem, this chapter explores and describes the Australian retail energy markets and consumer purchasing behaviour. Did the markets 'work'? How did customers behave? What did the industry respond to?

Unsurprisingly, given the previous chapters, stakeholder discussions about retail energy market effectiveness were characterised by conflict. One metric for market assessment was the rate at which customers switched retailers, also called customer churn. According to switching rates, the Australian state of Victoria was considered the most competitive market in the world for several years, and other Australian jurisdictions were also highly competitive. Industry (and some governments) regularly declared the high rates of customer churn as proof of effective markets. However, this view was not shared by other stakeholders, including many in the consumer sector and even some economic regulators.

This chapter describes the issues that complicated competition assessments, particularly in later years as policy discussions on behavioural economics and questions about the traditionally 'rational' consumer gained momentum. This chapter also examines the effectiveness of competition from the perspective of the political system and explores the policy shift toward retail price deregulation. This was part of a new narrative about empowering consumers to participate in the market and make more informed decisions. However, beneath the political rhetoric there were important policy questions that remained unanswered, and consensus on the issues seemed to become only more remote over time.

This chapter also explores one of the problematic areas of the market: the door-to-door sales channel. This was the industry's most effective channel and drove the high switching rates that were said to demonstrate the effectiveness of

Conflicting views of market competition 155

competition. As described in Chapter 4, it was also a source of compliance concerns, with consumer advocates asserting that consumers were regularly misled about their options by unscrupulous sales agents. Retailers attempted self-regulation of door-to-door sales activity, which eventually led to the strongest self-discipline of all, when the incumbents chose to stop using the channel for residential customers in 2013. However, despite consumer advocates' claims about their influence in this decision, the industry's reasoning was far more to do with business-as-usual assessments of financial risk.

Economic assessments of competition

The effectiveness of competition was reviewed in most of the competitive markets, with the Essential Services Commission (ESC) reviewing the Victorian market twice and the Australian Energy Market Commission (AEMC) reviewing the Victorian, South Australian, New South Wales, Queensland and Australian Capital Territory markets. The AEMC reviews were technically the most important, with a commitment from all Energy Ministers in 2006 to deregulate prices once competition was found to be effective by the AEMC (although, as discussed in Chapter 4, this did not mean that deregulation actually occurred).

The AEMC was traditionally economically rational, with a view that market forces would by definition protect consumers from inefficient prices in competitive markets: 'Where competition is effective and retail price regulation is removed, market forces should prevent retailers from charging inefficiently high prices and profit margins should approach an efficient level' (AEMC, 2013b: 62). The assessment framework used by the AEMC tended to focus on three interrelated features: market structure (independent rivalry, ability of suppliers to enter the market), market conduct (the exercise of market choice by customers, customer switching behaviour) and market performance (price and profit margins and differentiated products and services). Except for the Australian Capital Territory, the various findings on structure were always positive, with retailers able to enter and exit the relevant market and an adequate degree of rivalry present. Assessment of performance was limited to product differentiation given that it was hard to discover and value profit margins in an environment where these were not reported. Conduct indicators were viewed as particularly relevant, with consumer awareness of their ability to choose their retailer generally very high. Switching statistics at each review prior to deregulation were also high for the markets found to be competitive (all markets but the Australian Capital Territory),[1] with percentages of relevant customers who had switched retailers on an annual basis as follows:

- South Australia (2007–2008) at 23 per cent for electricity and 13 per cent for gas, but regional gas was a concern (AEMC, 2008);
- Victoria (2007) at 26 per cent for electricity and 21 per cent for gas (AEMC, 2007);

156 *Conflicting views of market competition*

- New South Wales (2012–2013) at 21 per cent for electricity and 14 per cent for gas (AEMC, 2013b); and
- Queensland (2013) at 17 per cent for electricity and 11 per cent for gas (AEMC, 2014).

There was validation for the AEMC's positive assessments through international switching studies. A Finnish organisation called the VaasaETT Global Energy Think Tank collated switching rates from competitive retail markets, and its findings were regularly referenced by the industry and governments. According to VaasaETT reports, the Australian states of Victoria, New South Wales, South Australia and Queensland were regularly in the global top ten. Victoria's level of switching was the highest in the world between 2005 and 2011 inclusive, and VaasaETT even created a new category of 'super hot' market for the 2009 Victorian market to describe a market with more than 20 per cent switching for three years in a row (VaasaETT, 2010). This was viewed favourably by the Victorian government, with the then Energy Minister releasing a statement to the media announcing the VaasaETT findings and quoting ESC data that consumers could save 10 per cent by switching from the standing offer (O'Brien, 2010). In 2012 Victoria's record was broken when it was overtaken by New South Wales (new global number two) and New Zealand (new global number one) (VaasaETT, 2013).

So what drove customer switching? In all Australian competition reviews (and surveys carried out by other stakeholders), consumers were found to respond most to prices. For example, research for the 2013 New South Wales competition review found that 78 per cent of switchers in the previous two years had switched because of a perception of paying a lower price (Newgate Research, 2013: 3). The main trigger for switching was an approach by an energy retailer (or their agent) at the consumer's premises: the door-to-door sales channel was the primary means of customer acquisition for retailers. Consumers reported that other 'low-level' triggers for switching were moving house or business premises (5 per cent), dissatisfaction with service from their current supplier (4 per cent, but mostly business consumers) and receiving several higher than expected electricity bills (1 per cent, despite price being the main trigger for switching) (ibid.: 33). In Victoria, a 2013 survey (Wallis Consulting Group, 2013: 38) found that only 13 per cent had approached a retailer proactively (compared with 81 per cent approached by a retailer) with consumers mostly telephoning retailers (80 per cent). These statistics were consistent with consumers in other states.

The New South Wales research also compared electricity switching rates with other consumer services, finding that electricity switching was much higher (based on self-reporting by consumers, although this was also found by Simshauser and Laochumnanvanit, 2011, in a nationwide assessment). Thirty-four per cent of respondents said they had switched their electricity company. Gas switching was lower, with 10 per cent switching retailer. In comparison, only 21 per cent had changed their car insurance or mobile phone provider, 12 per cent

Conflicting views of market competition   157

had changed their home insurance provider, 8 per cent had changed banks and 7 per cent had changed their health insurance provider (Newgate Research, 2013: 30).

Complicating factors in identifying effective competition

The positive industry and government perspective on the value of switching statistics was not shared by other stakeholder groups. Low-income consumer advocates claimed that switching statistics were misleading; for these stakeholders, proving effective competition was more about demonstrating consumer satisfaction and better consumer outcomes. Switching rates also did not address the question of whether consumers were even capable of making decisions in their own interest. Several low-income consumer advocacy groups claimed that it was incorrect to assume consumers were predictably rational and were capable of making the decisions expected of them without further assistance. It was argued that the market was too complex and that consumers made incorrect decisions based on subconscious biases.

The value of switching also depended on one's perspective of the main driver of customer churn: the door-to-door sales channel. This sales channel was said to be plagued by bad practices and was deeply disliked by consumer advocates and policymakers. If the door-to-door sales channel could not be trusted to provide consumers with the information they needed to make an informed decision, this put into jeopardy any reliance on switching as a proxy for effective competition. The validity of switching rates was also called into question with the belief held by some in the industry that the door-to-door channel largely changed the same group of customers regularly, so the churn statistics counted the same consumers multiple times.

A further complication in addressing the competitiveness of energy markets was in understanding how competition met the needs of customers on the highest priced standing offers; these were the customers who had not switched retailer or made a choice to shift to their existing retailer's market contract. The perceived 'stickiness' of the standing offer customers was behind the significant prices paid by retailers to governments in the privatisation processes and made being an incumbent retailer worth the effort; sticky customers were not expected to switch from the standing contract and so did not require discounted offers. The reasons for customer stickiness varied significantly: sticky customers could be apathetic and making a rational choice to not engage with the market, but they also could be people who were financially or socially disadvantaged and not able to actively engage with the market.

The highest standing offer prices in the Australian markets were in Victoria, where prices were deregulated for the longest period. What makes this particularly interesting is that Victoria was also the world's only 'super hot' market during the research period. This combination of high prices and high competition caused concern for the Victorian ESC and some consumer advocates – if the

158 *Conflicting views of market competition*

most competitive market in the world could sustain high prices, then what did that mean about competition and efficiency?

This range of complicating factors in the assessment of competition is now discussed in detail.

Behavioural economics and 'rational' consumer choice

The Australian competition policy assessment frameworks as described earlier in this chapter remained resolutely economically rationalist. Traditional economic analysis includes the notions that economic decision-makers have access to adequate information (and potentially perfect information), that the search or transaction costs involved with making choices are low (and potentially costless), and that decision-makers will make self-interested, predictable decisions that maximise their expected utility. Therefore, an awareness of retailer choice combined with high switching rates were seen by the AEMC as adequate consumer engagement with the market, and the quality of consumer decision-making was not in itself addressed in the competition assessments through to 2015.

In contrast, consumer advocates argued that competition assessments needed to take a broader view of consumer decision-making and the presumption of rationality underpinning it. From around 2010 several organisations took a strong interest in behavioural economics, which they used to explain what they saw as the dysfunctional consumer behaviours that actually lay beneath the positive headline statistics on consumer awareness and churn. The field of behavioural economics addresses consumer decision-making that is 'predictably irrational' (Ariely, 2009), where consumers are subject to a range of biases and use decision-making heuristics that do not adhere to the traditional model of expected utility (see Shafir, 2013). Founded on earlier work in the 1960s and 1970s by Tversky and Kahneman (see Kahneman, Slovic and Tversky, 1982; Gilovich, Griffin and Kahneman, 2002), behavioural economics introduces us to several concepts, such as limited consumer capacity, where a consumer cannot process the amount of information available, and the availability heuristic, which is a biased assessment of risk based on examples that come readily to mind. Other empirically observed phenomena include loss aversion, where people value things that they have more than things that they do not, and time inconsistency, where consumers make decisions based on short-term benefits despite longer-term costs. The status quo bias is particularly relevant to the sticky customer phenomenon, where consumers stick with what is familiar (even if it is more expensive) rather than go through the process of analysing or taking the risk on alternatives.

Much of the behavioural economics literature investigates the interactions of these effects with how decisions are framed, where it has been found that people make different decisions with the same information, depending on how the information is presented and the consumer's reference point. Consumers make choices based on limited offers so they do not miss out; they also like to compare

Conflicting views of market competition 159

themselves to other consumers and conform to others' decisions, so frames that represent a desired behaviour as 'everyone is/is not doing it' are more likely to encourage copying (Sunstein, 2003). The default position for any choice is important to understand, as this not only provides an anchor for decision-making but is also what many sticky customers 'choose' by merit of not making an active choice. Insurance decisions and superannuation schemes are often used as the examples where consumers 'choose' defaults through inaction that may leave them worse off than the 'rational' outcome (Thaler and Sunstein, 2009; Shafir, 2013).

What this means is that consumers can be led to make different decisions, or at least be left with different outcomes, when the 'choice architecture' (Thaler and Sunstein, 2009) is constructed in particular ways. This can be used to improve people's decisions, such as where policymakers set default policies that inherently protect consumers at some basic level, or be used for consumer detriment, when service providers frame their services and products to exploit consumers' predictably irrational behaviour. Within behavioural economics there are 'hard' and 'soft' paternalistic interventions that policymakers can use to better assist consumers in their decision-making. Hard paternalism is action to limit choices, and soft paternalism (or libertarian paternalism in the language of Thaler and Sunstein, 2009) merely 'nudges' consumers to make better choices from the existing array.

The energy consumer protection framework was indirectly developed in response to behavioural economics concepts. Despite behavioural economics not being referenced by energy policymakers, many of its tenets were supported by the consumer protections, such as the cooling-off period for contract entry (which supports the behavioural finding that consumers make decisions in 'hot' states and benefit from subsequent time to re-evaluate when in a 'cooler' state) and the variety of standardised product disclosure information provided to consumers. The existence of the standing offer as a default was itself part of a soft paternalistic behavioural economics approach, particularly when governments regulated prices to low levels.

However, these consumer protections were not seen as going far enough, and some low-income consumer advocates lobbied policymakers in Australia based on behavioural economics precedents in Great Britain. The British regulator Ofgem had embarked on a programme of hard paternalism in 2013–2014 after concerns were raised about the state of the British energy market; Ofgem not only required significant enhancements to product and price disclosure, but also limited the number of energy contract choices to consumers (per retailer) to four. The consumer advocates proposed this approach in Australia, but hard paternalism was not given a hearing by any energy policymaker. The unwillingness of Australian policymakers to go down the same path as Great Britain (at least by the time of writing) seemed to be because it was in their interests to stay with the rational actor model rather than risk the uncertain world that a full acceptance of behavioural economics presented. The AEMC was the rule-maker for the NECF states and the assessor of competition in the jurisdictions. Its

160   *Conflicting views of market competition*

Commissioners were also seen as the architects of the wholesale market. The AEMC's views were clearly in favour of markets and competition, and these views did not countenance the messy and unpredictable world of 'irrational' consumers. The AEMC could see the need for consumers to have information but did not go too far in developing a view about what that information should be or what consumers would do with it, even when developing its information blueprint for the New South Wales competition review in 2013, as discussed later in this chapter. Similarly, it suited politicians and governments to see consumers as essentially predictably rational. At the least, this was because the story of high churn rates (and therefore claims of strong competition) suited politicians; they could claim a role in improving choice and keeping prices efficient, and there was also a good story to tell about being 'the most competitive market in the world', as was the case in Victoria for several years. If politicians or their departments took the view that consumers were not making the right decisions this would have unravelled the story of competition and its benefits, and potentially could have led to a significant programme of costly and unpopular policy work. This action also would not necessarily have been effective given the unproven nature of hard paternalistic intervention, and particularly given later claims about the detrimental effects of Ofgem's approach, which were published in a review of the British energy market by the Competition and Markets Authority.[2]

This is not to say that further attention to the issues of consumer rationality was not warranted. There was no clarity about consumers' true preferences and whether these were being met, and if we were to fully subscribe to the behavioural economics perspective, even the consumers' self-reports could not be trusted because individuals tend to have blind spots about their objectivity and their own biases (Pronin and Schmidt, 2013). Surveys of past consumer behaviour consistently showed that consumers were highly aware of choice, were highly satisfied, and changed retailers frequently. However, they also showed that consumers did not know why they switched, did not know if they were on a 'better' deal once switching, and did not know other key aspects about their decision to switch:

> For those who had recently switched provider or plan, knowledge of the plan they were on was primarily framed in terms of the percentage discount they had been offered. Note that, when probed, virtually all admitted they were not clear on what was being discounted.
>
> (Newgate Research, 2013: 23)

> Just over half (55%) of those who had switched or changed their arrangements with their retailer reported that they had checked their rates. The majority (70%) of these believed they were competitive, while only one in fourteen (7%) believed they were not and just under a quarter (23%) were unsure.
>
> (Wallis Consulting Group: 2013: 26)

Conflicting views of market competition 161

Perhaps these were rational outcomes because many consumers' primary preference was to not be bothered with the market (and not remember their interactions with it) and they were as engaged as they were ever going to be. There were definitely consumers who could have made a better choice but were too apathetic to do anything. However, there were also consumers with more significant cognitive limitations, and with this in mind the fact that consumers were not really aware of their choices could demonstrate a far more concerning reality for the state of competition. For example, we recall the vulnerable consumer statistics from Chapter 4 that showed almost half of the Australian population had limited literacy.

Several retailers did not help the case for consumer rationality and could be said to have exploited consumer biases. Some retailers used discounts without establishing the reference point, and so let consumers think it was a discount off their existing bill, which was not necessarily the case. Others signed consumers on to evergreen contracts with fixed benefits that automatically rolled on to higher prices after the benefit ended (with no notice, which was legal at the time), which was also a clear exploitation of consumers' predictable lack of engagement or low level of understanding. Further, energy contracts were dense, complicated and legalistic. This was largely the result of all stakeholders wanting more and more added to the regulated information provided and was not solely driven by retailers per se, but the end effect for the consumer was still alienating.

So what does the field of behavioural economics mean for assumptions about the state of competition? Fundamentally, it causes us to question the validity of assuming that consumer decision-making is in any way based on a traditionally rational comparison of options, and/or an assessment of actual costs. Behavioural economics raises a number of profound questions about consumers' decision-making, and no clear direction for answers. Questions for retail energy markets include: What is 'informed consent' really and what should be a reasonable expectation of various consumer types? (Even if we assume that policy settings could be modified to help the non-vulnerable 'mainstream' consumer with the usual cognitive biases, what could be assumed about the largely undefinable vulnerable customer group?) If energy consumers made their choices on something other than a rational assessment of costs, what did they depend on and how could this be planned for? Would this even be possible? (As noted by Shafir (2008: 12): 'People's preferences are typically constructed, not merely revealed, during the decision-making process, and the construction of preferences is influenced by the nature and the context of decision'). Despite these questions being important and interesting, the challenge of providing answers does not bode well for evidence-based policymaking. The soft to hard paternalistic spectrum also provides for very different policy prescriptions depending on one's view about markets and the need for government intervention.

162   *Conflicting views of market competition*

The door-to-door sales channel driving churn rates

The previous discussion was about consumers making wrong decisions with correct information, albeit potentially limited information. A more fundamental problem occurred in the industry where consumers made decisions, or were expected to make decisions, based on the *wrong* information.

Energy is a low-involvement purchase, with contract take-up generally needing to be driven by specific events that capture consumers' attention and make energy a salient issue. For this reason, the channel that was considered the most effective was the door-to-door sales channel, which was the main driver of in-situ consumer switching. However, it was also seen as the most problematic channel. Tales of poor sales practices in the door-to-door sales channel were endemic, reaching a point of heightened community awareness from around 2009, which corresponded with the increased focus on price rises and bill affordability. News articles described door-to-door sales agent behaviours such as 'intimidation, lies, posing as government employees, raiding householders' mail boxes to obtain their personal details and even forging the signatures of customers on contracts' (Neighbour, 2009). It was reported that sales agents would tell householders that they were just checking that a government rebate had been received, and then ask the householder to sign a form to prove that the check had been made. The form would actually switch the consumer's energy supply (ibid.).

Consumer advocacy groups also released reports about door-to-door sales, with the Consumer Action Law Centre and the Financial and Consumer Rights Council (2007: 36) finding from a sample of 28 case studies that consumers reported behaviours such as those quoted above. Two years later, the Financial and Consumer Rights Council (2009: 24) also found potential compliance breaches that specifically affected low-income consumers, including failure of the sales agent to gain explicit informed consent to enter a market contract and failure to provide a contract copy on a customer's request when signing up. This was reinforced by a further survey of 327 people carried out in 2011 by CUAC (2011b: 7), which stated that:

> 87 per cent of survey respondents indicated that they had been approached by a door-to-door salesperson. Of these, 31 per cent indicated that the most recent seller had told them that the whole neighbourhood was changing energy supplier and 11 per cent reported that the seller indicated that they had come as the representative of a government agency.

Consumer advocate reports claimed that sales agents would even target vulnerable consumers, such as those in public housing areas or areas where recently arrived refugees had made their homes. Agents were said to coerce people who were clearly not able to understand what was being sold to them as this provided higher sales strike rates. For example, in 2009 a report was released by the Footscray Community Legal Centre (2009) that claimed door-to-door salespeople were signing up African migrants in Melbourne's west to energy contracts they did not understand.[3]

Conflicting views of market competition   163

Before discussing why this sales channel was such a problem, it should be recognised that despite the case studies, systemic consumer detriment from the channel was unproven. There were definitely compliance breaches, but these were hard to address and contextualise in any objective way, given the extent of the industry's activity in the area. In late 2010, the industry reported that approximately 40,000 homes were door-knocked per working day by energy retailers and their representatives (Energy Assured Limited, 2010: 5), with approximately 1,600 sales agents operating at any one time (Energy Retailers Association of Australia, 2010). If we compare the Ombudsman complaints for 2013 the rate of complaints to approaches is around 0.1 per cent.[4] Complaints are also not the same as non-compliance.

The main cause of non-compliance seemed to be the incentive structure required for sales agents: most retailers contracted out sales to companies that paid agents on commission. This was seen as key to achieving results and my own exploration into this with sales experts was that the channel would be ineffective without commissions. It also meant that despite training on appropriate behaviour, some agents found it more lucrative to do whatever was required to get the sale, including telling consumers they weren't really entering a contract, or that they should sign up even if they weren't sure and just cool off during the cooling off period. Doorstep sales was hard work, with sales agents trudging the streets through all weather conditions to sell a service few were interested in. In addition, it did not represent a long-term career: the job attracted transient people, such as international students who could use the job to get around their visa working hours (as the work was paid on commission not hours worked). Turnover was high, with agents lasting around three months on average (Frost and Sullivan, 2012: 49). Many were therefore not likely to be in a position themselves to understand the industry and product in real detail; this involved complexity that even those with long-term employment within the sector found challenging.

Importantly, door-to-door sales agents (although not necessarily energy sales agents) interviewed by a consultant for the Australian Competition and Consumer Commission (ibid.: 60–61) told of a particular sales technique they used called GIFTS, which stood for:

- Greed, to appeal to the consumer's sense of greed; sales agents were to repeat the benefits from discounts or savings.
- Indifference, where the sales agent implied that they received no benefit from the sales attempt (which was not true given all agents operated on commissions or incentive payments).
- Fear of loss, where the consumer would be advised that they were missed last time the agents were in the neighbourhood (whether this was true or not) and that this was their last chance to sign up.
- The Jones theory, where the sales agent mentioned (whether this was true or not) that everyone else in the neighbourhood signed up 'thereby creating a sense of pressure for some to follow the herd'.

164   *Conflicting views of market competition*

- Sense of urgency, where the sales agent implied (whether this was true or not) that the offer was limited and the consumer was to act immediately to not miss out.

These tactics clearly aligned with the consumer decision-making biases addressed in the previous section, such as appealing to consumers' loss aversion and need to conform. Further, statements about savings were not likely to be accurate if the reference point was not the consumers' own past bill (ideally past four quarterly bills given seasonal differences). Some agents (again, note these were not necessarily energy salespeople) even admitted to outright lies (ibid.: 63):

> You just use the word 'government' as many times as you can ... so then it feels like you are working for the government (implying trust). You would use similar language or techniques of the intelligence industry or you could just tell them lies like I am not going to gain any advantage by selling this as I am not on commission – it is all very psychological what you are doing and there are neuroscience techniques.... You may keep using the word agree (suggestively, over and over). It is really just bullying.

I describe the response from the energy retailers to regulate the channel later in this chapter, including the eventual decision by the incumbent retailers to stop using doorstep sales agents for residential sales.

The quality of competition and unresolved issues about policy expectations

The complications with assessing competition discussed so far have presumed that competition could still be found to be economically effective if only certain further actions were taken. The behavioural economics perspective is generally a hopeful one in that it believes that consumers could make the 'right' choice, or at least a better choice, with support from the choice architecture. The issues with door-to-door sales could also be resolved with improvements in compliance or even a cessation of the channel (as discussed in the next section).

However, there are more fundamental questions: What if reaching a state of effective competition was not just a matter of tweaking consumer engagement or ensuring retailer compliance? What if the market itself did not behave as expected? These were reasonable questions to ask: Victoria was the world's most competitive market through 2005–2011 and yet also had the highest retail prices of the states (during that period and after it) and specifically had the highest retail cost component. This appeared to be for both standing and market contracts (however, see the later research below), and had been demonstrated by independent research by the AEMC on retail price movements (AEMC, 2013a) and by consumer advocate St Vincent de Paul Society (St Vincent de Paul Society and Alviss Consulting, 2013). The then Chairman of the Victorian ESC,

Conflicting views of market competition   165

Ron Ben-David, also published a number of papers that questioned the market and the effectiveness of the regulatory framework to support competition. This started with a controversial address to the retail association's (Energy Retailers Association of Australia, or ERAA) 2011 industry briefing where he suggested that the Victorian retail energy market was an oligopoly with retailers making 'super profits'. While he was not certain about the super profits, he did say that the oligopolistic nature of the market raised in his mind 'questions about whether the extant regulatory environment is designed suitably' (Ben-David, 2011: 4). The issues were not taken further, the speech was reported on once in the media and otherwise went largely unnoticed by the energy industry and its stakeholders.

Ben-David reinvigorated the issue in 2013, with a speech and research released from the ESC on Victorian retail electricity margins (Ben-David, 2013). Stating that he was 'increasingly perplexed' about rising electricity prices in Victoria, Ben-David asked the question: 'What might prices be telling us about the state of competition in our local electricity market?' (ibid.: 20). He illustrated his case with a comparison of prices between Victoria and other states, noting that Victorian prices had continued to increase at the same rate as other jurisdictions from 2008–2009 despite wholesale prices reducing and Victoria not being subject to the same increased network cost drivers as the other states. It was particularly surprising given Victoria's then claim to be the world's most competitive retail market, so he suggested that there was insufficient competition:

> 'What?' you might be gasping. 'But Victoria has the most competitive market in the country!'
>
> Maybe so. Maybe so. But … [author's pause]
>
> Is it *sufficiently* competitive? Is it *sufficiently* competitive to push retail operating costs towards their long-run margins and prices towards those long-run marginal costs? After all, *that* is the definition of a competitive market – not customer churn rates, or the number of offers in the market place, or the number of retailers vying for custom, or low barriers to entry.
>
> (Ibid.: 24, author's emphasis)

Despite Ben-David's concerns, market effectiveness was formally a matter for the AEMC, not the ESC, and the AEMC's (2014) *2014 Retail competition review* avoided committing to a view on whether prices and/or margins were too high, despite being asked to specifically investigate the issue by the Victorian government (Victorian Department of State Development, Business and Innovation, 2014). The AEMC viewed competition in Victoria as effective, and the retail cost and margins issue was explained as possibly related to different wholesale energy and operational costs, or measurement of these costs, in Victoria compared with other jurisdictions. The AEMC also stated a need for caution, saying that an analysis of retailer margins needed 'to be carried out over a sufficiently long period to understand the profitability of the industry through multiple business cycles and changes in market conditions' (AEMC, 2014: 179).

166 *Conflicting views of market competition*

This was not an unreasonable position given the complexity of the issues, but it did not give the clarity that stakeholders sought (see CALC, 2014). The St Vincent de Paul Society and Alviss Consulting (2014: 15) stated in a subsequent report about the market that while they appreciated the complexity of the analysis:

> we do not understand how the AEMC can be tasked to undertake an effectiveness of competition review without assessing retail costs/margins. The cost of retail in deregulated markets has become the elephant in the room that governments and regulators continue to ignore.

The ESC's Chairman tackled the issue publicly again in 2015, with his paper *If the retail energy market is competitive then is Lara Bingle a Russian cosmonaut?*. Ben-David suggested in this paper that the logic used by the AEMC and others to claim the Victorian retail energy market was effectively competitive could also be used to show an Australian minor celebrity was in fact a Russian space traveller. This deliberately ridiculous outcome was said by Ben-David to be evidence of syllogism fallacy, 'whereby two perfectly true premises lead to an unquestionably false conclusion' (Ben-David, 2015: 21). Again, this paper did not prompt debate or a response from the AEMC.

In contrast with Ben-David's argument, economists from energy retailer AGL (Simshauser and Whish-Wilson, 2015: 28) demonstrated through a comprehensive theoretical and empirical analysis that competition in Victoria was economically efficient. They analysed the efficiency of pricing for standing offer contracts compared with market contracts. Standing offer prices in Victoria were found to be about 10 per cent above the industry average total cost of supply. This was not in itself an inefficient outcome:

> price discrimination of this kind is known to distribute a firm's cost recovery from strong (less-price sensitive) customer segments to weak (more-price sensitive) customer segments, and in this sense frequently displays positive distributional efficiency effects because the former are usually high-income households.
>
> (Ibid.: 28)

However, there was a valid public policy issue in the fact that there were vulnerable customers on standing offers, an outcome said by the paper's authors to be a 'misallocation'. Using a broad definition of vulnerable customers to cover those in receipt of government concessions, the authors found that around 4.9 per cent of AGL's household accounts were both vulnerable and on standing offer contracts. This prompted AGL to pilot a shift of these customers on to discounted standing offer contracts.

Retail profits on market contracts were another matter, with the lowest priced market offer[5] providing zero profit margin and priced at 20 per cent below the industry average total cost of supply (ibid.). The AGL findings thus called into

Conflicting views of market competition 167

question the claims of high retailer margins on market contracts (which had been prevalent as commentators tended to blur the standing offer and market contract types). They could also be interpreted as supporting a view that retailers were using their Victorian standing offers to subsidise their market offers, which some smaller second tier retailers had been concerned about. Overall, the issues raised by AGL were less about the effectiveness or efficiency of competition from a pure economic perspective and more about observers' perspectives on the fairness of these outcomes.

The different views about competitive outcomes as described above were not limited to Australian markets. In late 2013 the Chief Executive of the British energy regulator Ofgem was quoted as saying that Ofgem could not describe competitive market outcomes. When asked to define what success would look like, he said 'The cop out answer is we are just starting a programme of work ... to answer that question' (Gosden, 2013). The active disagreement *between* economic regulators was also present in the UK, with the 2014–2016 energy market review undertaken by the Competition and Markets Authority (CMA) drawing out deep divisions between past and present regulators, and ultimately conflict between past regulators and the CMA itself. In a public letter to the CMA the previous regulators of Ofgem (and its predecessors)[6] questioned Ofgem's approach to competition, suggesting Ofgem's interventions to limit tariffs may have reduced competition in the market (Littlechild, McCarthy, Marshall, Smith and Spottiswoode, 2014).[7] Previous Ofgem Board Member George Yarrow was also scathing about how the regulator had made policy changes that had effectively stifled competition (Yarrow, 2014; see also Littlechild, 2014). In a later submission critiquing the CMA's own analysis, Littlechild (2016: 9), pointed out that the term 'well-functioning market', which was used regularly in British competition evaluations had 'no well-defined economic meaning', similar to 'effective competition'.

Given that meta-regulation depends on 'harnessing the market' it would seem fundamental that the market being harnessed works as expected by economists and economic policymakers[8] – that is, on its own terms within an economic frame. We should not underestimate the fact that energy market experts in Australia and the UK could not agree on the way to consider and measure competition, despite years of experience (including observing the most competitive energy markets of the past) and significant qualifications (including acting as the regulator). This has serious implications for meta-regulatory theory, as discussed in the next chapter.

Political views of market effectiveness

While the discussion in this chapter so far has focused on assessments of competition through a (broad) economic lens, the *political* assessments of competition were the most important because these determined policy outcomes. Governments made the decisions to regulate and deregulate prices, and the policy debate on price deregulation in each state set the stage for each government to play out

168 *Conflicting views of market competition*

its political narrative on the effectiveness of the market. Price deregulation decisions sometimes referenced economic assessments, but the political focus was more on whether deregulation might cause vulnerable consumers to be worse off (which the market did not value), and what might be the resulting level of political risk. The irreconcilable policy objectives for retail energy markets specifically required political decision-making: as outlined in Chapter 3, the economic need to have higher standing offer prices to provide for competition clashed fundamentally with the social need for lower prices for an essential service. Over time, the environmental need to price energy high enough to allow for renewable energy and to penalise high carbon-emitting generation sources also played a major political role, as did the need for higher prices to cover the costs of new technology such as smart meters.

This section explores how the political system identified and responded to market and pricing issues as they became politically salient. The political winds shifted over time: while governments had been concerned about the risk of prices being too high in a deregulated market they also started to experience the political cost from being in charge when prices had to increase for unavoidable reasons, such as to provide for necessary infrastructure upgrades. The question thus moved from '*do* we deregulate?' to '*when* do we deregulate?', with an accompanying change in the political narrative about the value and effectiveness of the retail energy markets.

How Victoria deregulated prices

Victoria deregulated energy prices from 1 January 2009, followed a few years later by the other states. While the main theme of this section is about the policy windows for the other states it is worth describing the factors that allowed Victoria to deregulate when it did, as these identify some of the many factors that could lead to fundamental policy shifts.

First, Victoria had the longest history of privatised energy assets. This meant that there was a clear distinction between the owners of energy businesses and the political interests of government. There was also little to no union involvement in energy policy. By the mid-2000s the network and retail businesses were also completely separate corporate entities and not the pseudo ring-fenced network-retail entities that persisted in other states for some years. These cultural factors made a difference to government enthusiasm for innovation.

Second, the form of price regulation assisted in the path to deregulation. The other states applied price regulation through an independent economic regulator (albeit working with government terms of reference), which used a transparent method for cost evaluation and provided public consultation processes. In contrast, price regulation in Victoria had always been an opaque annual agreement between government and the retailers, with the ESC not involved after 2002. This allowed for headroom to be built into prices as considered necessary. Related to this, the Victorian pricing framework delivered profits to retailers across all regions and consumer types, which was not possible in the other states.

Conflicting views of market competition 169

The states of New South Wales and Queensland had entire regions and customer groups for whom retailers could not even recover costs, which was also related to state government ownership of network assets. To get the relevant customer tariffs to the point of cost recovery – let alone to make a profit – meant price increases that these governments could not countenance in one step, and so deregulation was delayed as prices were slowly brought to cost recovery (as per government terms of reference for the relevant state regulators).

Third, Victoria was the most competitive market in the world in 2008 according to switching statistics, and had led the world since 2005, so it was hard to justify a view that competition was not yet effective. Of course this was related to the previous points: Victoria's status as the most competitive market was possible because of the headroom in prices.

Fourth, the Victorian government had a unique mix of political and departmental staff members who were open to the idea of price deregulation and even championed it. This is despite Victoria having the most vocal anti-deregulation consumer advocates in the country. The Victorian officials' openness was also very much in contrast to the more wary perspective of the other state governments toward price deregulation. For example, South Australia could have taken a similar approach to Victoria in 2009: while South Australian retail competition was slightly less evolved than in Victoria, privatisation was not an issue (the assets had been leased years earlier) and the state's regulated prices were cost-reflective. Yet the South Australian government was still not inclined to deregulate prices even when the AEMC gave it a reason to do so by deeming retail energy competition in the state to be adequately competitive. Victoria's approach was also notable because it was not led by a conservative government with a free market ideology: Victoria was deregulated by a Labor government, on advice from a senior bureaucrat with a strong social conscience and deep experience in energy consumer protection. Further, the politicians and staff who eventually deregulated prices in Victoria were not the same people who established the price regulation framework or provided the circumstances for deregulation; this was not a matter of long-term planning. The relevant Minister and his advisors just happened to be the decision-makers at a time that provided for the decision to be made and implemented. This comes down to the contingency of the many small decisions that brought the relevant people together at a particular time.

Finally, Victoria deregulated just before price rises became a national media and community issue, and so the government avoided being held responsible. The community and political focus on energy prices from 2009 made price deregulation politically risky for the other states and essentially closed the policy window. While it makes sense that the other states were going to take longer than Victoria to deregulate prices for many of the reasons listed above, they could have acted earlier than they eventually did if the political circumstances had been favourable.

170   *Conflicting views of market competition*

Drivers for deregulation in the other states

Four years after the deregulation policy window closed in 2009, it reopened when the South Australian government announced in December 2012 that it would deregulate retail energy prices in February 2013. The South Australian version of deregulation was a price agreement between government and the incumbent retailers that was to fall away after two years. This was the South Australian government's way of avoiding a political tangle between the then regulator (Essential Services Commission of South Australia, ESCOSA) and the industry: energy retailer AGL was in the process of taking the regulator to court about its calculation for wholesale costs. The government's solution provided for higher prices than ESCOSA would have allowed for, but at lower prices than those at the time, so it had something positive to announce.

In April 2014 the New South Wales government announced it would deregulate its retail energy prices from 1 July 2014, following a similar approach to South Australia in agreeing to lower transitional prices with the incumbent retailers. This came after a positive review of competition from the AEMC, and was also known to have been a preferred philosophical position of the government for some time since the retailers had been sold to the private sector in 2010 and prices had become cost-reflective. Similarly, the Queensland government announced in 2013 that it would deregulate prices in South East Queensland from mid-2015.[9] It was claimed that the extended timeframe was required to provide for tariff reform across retail and network tariffs, and to analyse the state of competition and consumer engagement (a process that had not yet occurred for Queensland).

Why did the policy window for retail energy price deregulation re-open? The opening of the policy window was largely about how the philosophy of deregulation took hold; even some low-income consumer advocates started to support market outcomes. Public attention to electricity price rises may have closed the policy window for deregulation, but it can be argued – somewhat paradoxically – that the subsequent public pricing debates contributed to the window opening again as government risk perspectives changed. A flood of government energy policy reviews and debates resulted from the price rises post-2009, with diverse stakeholder voices then converging on and prioritising the principle of cost-reflective energy prices to consumers. This indirectly set the scene for an acceptance of price deregulation.

To explain, prior to 2009, cost-reflective energy pricing was not a priority for anyone; in contrast, cross-subsidies were desired, ignored, or at least tolerated by all parties.[10] This even included retailers when regulated prices were high enough to allow for acceptable profits. Governments actively promoted cross-subsidies, whether this was via retail price regulation or the range of heavily subsidised renewables and energy efficiency schemes ('green schemes') that proliferated from around 2007. Solar feed-in tariffs were a particular example of this, where various state governments sought to encourage the uptake of solar photovoltaic rooftop panels by paying consumers for the electricity they exported to the grid,

Conflicting views of market competition   171

and sometimes even the electricity they generated and used within the home. Federal schemes compounded the benefits for customers by paying further subsidies for solar installations. The rates paid by governments were generous: for a while in New South Wales it was uneconomic for a household to not buy solar photovoltaic panels (valued at several thousand dollars) for the rebates and tariffs received, combined with reduced consumption costs. As a result, the various solar schemes experienced high uptake, and their budgets were quickly overwhelmed. Most were recalibrated to lower payback levels, which then created political discontent with the new solar industry that had been created and the solar consumers who had benefited from the billions of dollars of subsidies.

The costs of these schemes were passed through to all consumers via electricity bills. However, most of the costs were opaque (and so politically palatable), and governments were not blamed for price rises. This changed from late 2010 to early 2012 when governments in several states changed from Labor to Liberal governments, and the new governments sought to make the (then) federal Labor government and their state Labor predecessors look bad by demonstrating the true extent of the green schemes. It did not help that the impact of green schemes on bills was increased by the carbon pricing mechanism implemented by the federal Labor government in mid-2012; this increased average household bills by a further 9 per cent. In 2012, Liberal governments in Queensland and New South Wales even sought to highlight the costs of the various Labor schemes to a typical household by requiring retailers to put political messaging on bills, as discussed in Chapter 4.

While the cost of government green schemes was significant, the main driver of the price rises in the key states was actually the state-based networks, which were embarking on major infrastructure upgrades. The government-owned network assets in New South Wales and Queensland were behind the cost increases in those states, and the cost of the network-led smart meter rollout was a major contributor to Victorian price rises. This is likely to have had a role in the political point-scoring over green schemes; for state governments the federal and previous state government green schemes provided a welcome distraction from acknowledging the role played by their own networks in the price rises.

Networks thus also came under considerable scrutiny as the blame game continued: they were accused by many commentators of 'gold plating' their capital works and of being in need of discipline to have network prices be efficient and more cost-reflective. The networks became the focus of multiple reviews from industry and consumer associations, as well as from the national AEMC and Productivity Commission. The review fever peaked in mid-2012 when the federal Labor government formed a Senate Select Committee into electricity prices. The Committee's creation seemed to be about being seen to be doing something and to reframe the debate: it was known to be a sop to the influential Green Party, which supported the green schemes. The timeframe for exploration of the many issues it raised was short and the group was under-experienced, resulting in weak recommendations. However, it shifted the public focus from the federal carbon pricing mechanism back to the states' network costs and the

172 *Conflicting views of market competition*

perceived need for cost-reflectivity in network prices, which was likely to have been the real aim of the federal politicians who supported it.

The politics of the environment was contagious, even appearing to spread to notionally independent policymakers. The most significant consultation on customer (demand side) issues during 2012 was the AEMC's 'Power of Choice' review, which was a comprehensive assessment of the whole electricity value chain in order to develop policy to reduce the costs to consumers and promote more cost-reflective prices, as well as active customer participation (known as 'demand response'). This was a high-profile review and employed a strong rhetoric of action. However, it was not particularly effective in resolving the complex matters facing the industry: after tens of hours of stakeholder meetings and several stages of written consultation, the final report (AEMC, 2012) was long but generally lacking in new insights into the existing issues. Among other things, the AEMC proposed two fundamental market reforms on the basis of what was clearly insufficient analysis, where the politics of the situation seem to have prompted the AEMC to be seen to be doing something at the cost of a scientifically robust assessment of the issues.[11]

Other reviews addressed how cost-reflective pricing and demand response could be promoted through smart meters, which was also a priority of the AEMC's Power of Choice review. Smart meters provided the technological foundation for cost-reflective prices, as they delivered actual data to retailers about each customer's use per half-hour, rather than the proxy used previously. The combination of smart meters, time-of-use pricing and communications innovations like internet portals was the best hope for consumers to break through the opaque nature of the industry and better control their energy costs. Importantly, the near real-time feedback on consumption provided by these innovations would mean no more 'bill shock' for consumers receiving high bills three months in arrears. As discussed in Chapter 4, the Victorian smart meter rollout was a political nightmare, which meant that in 2012 the other state governments were unwilling to do much more than talk about customer benefits from *future* smart metering. However, the talk was still all that was required to fuel the push for cost-reflectivity and the value of getting consumers into the market in the non-Victorian states.

To summarise, the political propaganda wars had made key cross-subsidies more apparent, and stakeholders became concerned. The cumulative effect of the many political statements and policy reviews was that, despite their flaws, they laid the foundation for a broader political and community acceptance that consumers would be better off if they could choose their own products and control their own costs. This general push for cost-reflectivity thus provided space for governments to deregulate energy prices and reframe the markets as effective.

When the market became the safety net

The price deregulation policy window that had started to unstick with the new policy language of consumer empowerment and energy cost-reflectivity was

Conflicting views of market competition 173

emphatically pushed open by a shift in stakeholder discourse about the value of price deregulation. The year 2013 marked a time where it became clearer to governments and the consumer sector that price regulation gave consumers a false sense of security that they were on the best price.[12] Indeed, because standing offer prices were the 'prices to beat', they were by definition the most expensive offers. This seemed to have not been understood by non-industry stakeholders. Research by energy retailer AGL released in mid-2013 (see Nelson and Reid, 2013) showed that even if consumers bore the full suite of additional fees and charges from market contracts (such as late payment fees, which were often seen as the reason to stay on the standing offers) their bills would still be lower than if they were on standing offer contracts, with the exception of premises with very low consumption. The research also found that financial assistance providers from the community sector (and particularly financial counsellors) rarely, if ever, advised their clients to move from standing offer contracts to market contracts, even though consumers could save hundreds of dollars. This appeared to be because the financial assistance providers did not know about market contracts or which contract clients were on. While the blame for this level of ignorance was said by the AGL paper's authors to lie across government, consumer groups and industry, it is worth specifically considering the role of the consumer advocacy peak bodies who dealt with front-line community sector staff such as financial counsellors. It was common knowledge across the industry that many low-income consumer advocates (particularly in Victoria) believed that consumers should stay on the standing offer contract as the 'safety net'; their distrust of the market (or perhaps their trust in regulated outcomes) was such that they would not engage with the concept that consumers might benefit relative to the default standing offer.[13] The notion that the market was not the worst of all worlds for consumers seemed to be an ideological block that many consumer advocates could not pass. An exception to this was the work of consultant May Mauseth Johnson, who undertook tariff analysis across the jurisdictions over several years with welfare agency St Vincent de Paul. The clear message from this analysis (which the St Vincent de Paul representative shared across all sectors, including the media) was that consumers were better off switching from the standing offer.

The governments in New South Wales and Queensland were openly talking about their intentions to deregulate by 2013, with consumer advocates in those states also cautiously optimistic. By this time the majority of the Australian state governments had recognised that price regulation did not protect consumers from hardship, and it certainly did not protect governments when prices needed to rise to recover network costs (a problem further amplified by state government ownership of the networks). In fact, the long-standing retailer argument that price regulation inhibited competition (because it implicitly restricted headroom) started to be made by some policymakers, where the conclusion was that they should stop looking for effective competition and just deregulate prices. The issue then became one of how to engage consumers to enter the market and make decisions about better offers.

174   *Conflicting views of market competition*

The AEMC's consumer engagement blueprint

In order to implement its recommendation to the state government that New South Wales should deregulate energy prices for small consumers, the AEMC (2013c) carried out additional research into consumer engagement strategies to have the consumers on standing offers enter the market. The AEMC's concern was that while consumers were aware of their ability to choose a retailer, its research had found that consumers were not confident they could actually make a choice that would suit their needs. There was also low consumer awareness about the support services available, such as the independent federal government (AER) comparison website Energy Made Easy. The AEMC recommended a 'consumer engagement blueprint' be developed for New South Wales, with the main components being:

- a government public information campaign to advise the existence of Energy Made Easy and let people know they could save money by choosing an energy plan; the campaign would also use different channels to target specific consumer segments as well as the broader community;
- refinements to Energy Made Easy, which was also subject to an AER work programme; and
- training services for community organisations to communicate the key campaign messages and work with the consumers they assisted to use comparison tools such as Energy Made Easy.

The AEMC (ibid.: 8) did not see its remit to be about creating more information; there was already significant information in the market. It stated that it was addressing the 'communications challenge' for consumers to be able to find the right information, to compare offers on a like-for-like basis and to be confident about making an informed decision. The AEMC also sought to better understand the socio-economic and demographic characteristics of consumers on regulated prices, although it said very little about this in its report, noting data confidentiality as an issue. The most the AEMC provided on this issue was a three point overview, from which it was difficult to draw conclusions. Customers in the Sydney area and particular regional areas were found to be less likely to be on a regulated tariff. These areas were correlated with economic advantage, an older population, higher levels of education and smaller households. The regional areas with a greater proportion of customers on regulated tariffs were associated with greater economic disadvantage, lower levels of education and lower levels of mortgages or rent (ibid.: 16).[14]

The engagement programme mentioned but did not expand on what the AEMC's own consultants had found to be consumers' reasons for staying on the standing offer, which were inertia (because of no incentive to switch) and customer satisfaction:

> When asked why they had not changed energy company or plan in the last two years, more than a third (37%) said they were satisfied with their

Conflicting views of market competition 175

existing energy company. A quarter said 'no particular reason' or (23%) or didn't know (2%). A further one in five (19%) said it was either 'too much hassle/can't be bothered' (12%) or they were 'too busy/don't have time' (7%).

(Newgate Research, 2013: 3)

In fact, Newgate Research found that 'most people don't have any real contact with their energy company unless they have an interruption to supply or a billing issue … as long as the power is running, they generally feel satisfied with the level of service' (ibid.: 27). Satisfaction with the current retailer was considered by Newgate Research to be a 'key barrier to switching' (ibid.). These outcomes were consistent with Victorian consumer research undertaken at the same time as the New South Wales research. Wallis Consulting (2013) found that almost a quarter of Victorians remained on a standing offer and were unlikely to be proactive to switch retailer. Wallis Consulting (ibid.: 40) noted that 43 per cent of people on standing offers 'cannot see the benefits in changing, saying that they have not switched or entered an agreement because they have just stayed with the same retailer', with 25 per cent who 'could not be bothered entering an agreement'. Further, while Victorians said that electricity constituted a high proportion of their household running costs, 40 per cent still had not switched retailer because it was 'not worth the effort' (ibid.: 21).

The hope behind the AEMC's engagement blueprint was that all (or most) consumers would be in the market if they only knew they might save some money and had more information and potentially face-to-face interaction regarding how they could proactively use a government switching website. By focusing on use of Energy Made Easy as the consumer's link to the market, the AEMC set an extremely optimistic target: awareness of existing longer-term independent or government switching websites was at that time very low; when unprompted it was zero per cent (Newgate Research, 2013: 46). Further, despite heavy promotion for commercial and other comparison sites at the time, 73 per cent of respondents in New South Wales could not name a single comparison website (ibid.) These statistics were aligned with consumer survey findings in Victoria (see Wallis Consulting Group, 2013: 32).

The data and analysis in the AEMC's consumer blueprint had other limitations. There was no assessment of whether economically disadvantaged consumers responded to government information campaigns or of whether they used the internet. The AEMC provided no evaluation of consumer apathy, such as how the quarter of consumers who said they had not switched for 'no particular reason' or they 'didn't know' might be interpreted, and there was no assessment of whether the likely savings to consumers from switching would be salient enough to overcome this apathy. It was not clear to what degree apathy overlapped with the economically disadvantaged regional consumers and those who might have been subject to community outreach, or whether they had other reasons for not switching (such as not being doorknocked). In addition, a consumer segmentation model developed by the AEMC's consultants did not crossreference its consumer segments against location or socio-economic status, with

176   *Conflicting views of market competition*

the apparent assumption that everyone was equally able to switch and that the only variables related to motivation and potentially life stage.

There were also policy questions left unexamined – or at least unexamined in public. These questions related to the reasonable expectations of the outcomes of a public engagement campaign or other engagement approach, such as what would be an acceptable level of knowledge in the consumer base and what would be an acceptable level of ignorance. Consistent with the apparent belief that all consumers were potentially economically rational in the traditional sense, the issue for policymakers was instead a much easier matter (in theory) of just finding the right policy buttons to push to have consumers seek out their own deals and respond rationally. The models for engagement thus avoided the tricky issues of accessing what might actually be unreachable consumers, both in a cognitive and physical sense. While the engagement approaches did provide for enlisting community and welfare agencies to reach certain pockets of the community, it was still assumed that all consumers could be reached through their public life or community connections to help them be better off and that they would be motivated to respond (and capable of doing so). Not only was this inconsistent with past experience with consumers but it was also inconsistent with the past reality of the influence of both government and the community/welfare sectors.[15]

While it may be easy to observe the gaps in the engagement work from a distance, we should note that discovering the answers to any of the unresolved issues described above would probably have required more from the AEMC than it was able to determine through reliable data, manage in its reporting timeframe, or defend politically. Even with a belief that anyone could be 'made' economically rational (or at least more economically rational) with more information and access to the internet, this was a complicated task. The problem of engagement would have become infeasible under usual time and budget constraints if the AEMC had also overlaid a behavioural economics perspective on consumer decision-making that fundamentally questioned consumer rationality.[16] In-depth analysis based on behavioural economics would have discovered even more complexity (again, what does 'no particular reason' for not switching mean?) and provided no clear solution. This is all before any questions could be asked about whether the market itself 'worked' as per policymakers' expectations, which AEMC had assumed it did.

The contradiction of the sticky consumers, and particularly the economically disadvantaged consumers, being on the high standing offer price that effectively subsidised the rest of the consumer base was not able to be resolved through the market (even assuming the market was effective).[17] Instead, most parties conveniently subscribed to the notion that all it would take was the 'right' engagement programme to move everyone off the standing offer and into the market.

In the end, the New South Wales government ran an advertising campaign for 11 weeks at the end of 2014. The campaign featured advertising across multiple media, including a campaign website, and the incumbent retailers were also asked to provide brochures about Energy Made Easy with customer bills.

Conflicting views of market competition 177

Although consistent with the AEMC's blueprint, this was not a segmented approach and did not grapple with the issues discussed above. This was to be expected given the likely cost of a larger campaign and the lack of evidence that more could be achieved. The AEMC (2015: 37) reported that there was a 60 per cent increase in traffic to Energy Made Easy over the length of the campaign. However, the effectiveness of the campaign in the sense of positive consumer outcomes was not clear (in the sense that it was not reported on), and the AEMC's (2015, 2016) competition reviews in 2015 and 2016 showed very low unprompted consumer awareness of Energy Made Easy.

Co-regulation, self-regulation and external enforcement of door-to-door sales

We will now return to the most vexed issue for competition, which was the door-to-door sales channel. Of the three main complicating factors for assessing competition as discussed earlier, this was the one related specifically to retailer non-compliance with the law and rules, and it reveals some of the problems associated with assuming consumer rationality. The message to the industry from many consumer advocates was simple: do not use door-to-door salespeople to sell energy. So how did the industry respond to this message? It was a challenging issue given that the industry depended on doorstep sales as its most effective customer acquisition channel and the very factors that made it successful also made it vulnerable to exploitation and misbehaviour.

Self-regulation under Energy Assured Limited

After a couple of attempts at self-regulating retail energy marketing in the early days – these failed due to lack of interest (including lack of consumer advocate interest in co-regulation) and a lack of discipline – industry self-regulation returned as a serious concept in 2010. The new approach was focused on door-to-door sales only and was known to be a formal response to threats from the Victorian government that the industry needed to do something about the channel or the government would intervene in some way. Given that this could be implied as a ban on door-to-door selling (which had been lobbied for by some consumer advocates) and that retailers depended on the channel, this threat provided sufficient impetus for the retailers to overcome their earlier inability to organise themselves on self-regulatory issues.

An ERAA member working group hired consultants and created a formal code and scheme called Energy Assured Limited (EAL), which was a non-profit company limited by guarantee that operated within the corporate structure of ERAA. The EAL framework was based on a scheme from Great Britain called EnergySure, which had been in place since 2002, albeit in an environment that was less regulated than the Australian energy markets. EAL operated across all jurisdictions and was created to provide a standard for door-to-door marketing activities, to develop and facilitate training programmes, to administer a register

178 *Conflicting views of market competition*

of accredited sales agents, to implement monitoring and assessment procedures for the conduct of sales agents, and to manage a complaints process. EAL was intended to lead industry self-enforcement of appropriate sanctions on sales agents and members when necessary. Nothing in the scheme reduced the existing regulatory framework or proposed to do so; it was intended to improve retailer practices to better comply with existing regulation. As such, it was a behind-the-scenes attempt to manage the known problem areas for the industry, such as training sales agents and managing the salespeople who misrepresented the service moving on to another retailer once they were found out.

Under the federal *Trade Practices Act 1974* regulated by the ACCC (later amended to the *Competition and Consumer Act 2010*, and containing the Australian Consumer Law), EAL needed to be approved by the ACCC, or at least the ERAA believed this would be prudent. Authorisation from the ACCC effectively granted immunity from legal action for anti-competitive conduct that might otherwise breach the Act, and was sought because EAL limited the behaviour of competitors. The initial EAL application to the ACCC outlined the reasons for developing the Code, stating that there was 'still some perception that door-to-door marketing of energy lacks the necessary level of regulation to ensure the integrity of sales and marketing activities in the energy retail industry' (Energy Retailers Association of Australia, 2010: 2). Noting that sales agents were screened and trained by retailers and their third party marketing companies, ERAA advised that nevertheless 'training is not standardised throughout the industry' and 'additional support and consistent training for Sales Agents is desirable' (ibid.). The application also noted the then Victorian Energy Minister's concerns.

In November 2010, the ACCC commenced a formal consultation process in response to the EAL application, inviting stakeholders to submit their views on the proposed arrangements. Early views from the ACCC to ERAA had been positive about draft material presented,[18] so the industry did not expect the process to be problematic. However, submissions to the ACCC complicated the matter. Stakeholder views were clearly divided, with retailers and the New South Wales and Victorian state Ombudsman schemes supporting EAL, and low-income consumer advocacy groups opposing it. There were two significant themes that characterised all consumer advocate submissions: first, a perceived lack of effective consultation with consumer groups; and second, a strong view that the commission and incentive payment structure for agents created pressure sales tactics at the door and needed to be stopped. Consumer advocates' concerns also related to details of the EAL package, including EAL's focus on individual agents more than energy retailers, and the accessibility of the scheme, with a view that consumers would be confused by it without a brochure provided at the door.

The first significant theme of consultation was a particular sticking point, with the Consumer Utilities Advocacy Centre (CUAC) stating that a 'fundamental failure is that the EAL Code of Practice was not drafted with any consumer input' (CUAC, 2010: 5). On the basis of this inadequate attention to consumer

Conflicting views of market competition 179

advocate input, CUAC advised that EAL should withdraw its application and resubmit only after seeking consumer and regulatory participation in the process. It further stated that 'In the event that this does not occur, CUAC requests that the ACCC reject the Application on the basis that the lack of consumer involvement in the EAL framework calls into question the likelihood of public benefit' (ibid.: 6). This view was supported by other consumer advocates, such as the Consumer Action Law Centre (CALC, previously known as the Consumer Law Centre Victoria), which stated that while it 'would welcome effective initiatives to address the problems associated with door to door energy marketing' it did 'not consider that the EAL proposal in this matter is such an initiative' (CALC, 2010: 1). CALC (ibid.: 2) highlighted 'the failure of EAL to consult stakeholders, particularly consumer representatives, in the development of the Code to date'.

ERAA/EAL (for ease of reference referred to from here on as EAL) responded that it had, in fact, consulted with consumer advocates prior to its request for authorisation to the ACCC. For example, during September 2010, EAL had invited various consumer groups to a briefing at the CUAC premises (which CUAC must have been invited to and authorised). EAL also noted that CALC had requested to attend the briefing and had been invited. This session was held at CUAC on 6 October 2010. No one from CALC attended. CUAC then invited EAL to present at a consumer roundtable the next week on 14 October, which it did. CUAC and CALC were among those who attended. EAL goes on to say:

> Despite the various briefings, no consumer group formally approached the ERAA/EAL to discuss the proposed EAL Scheme. Only limited comment was received from consumer groups consulted in response to the briefs provided on the proposed EAL Scheme. However, all feedback was considered and, where possible, incorporated into the EAL Scheme.
>
> (EAL, 2011a: 3–4)

CUAC (2011a: 2) responded with its perspective on the above:

> CUAC was provided with a copy of the Energy Retailers Association of Australia's (ERAA)'s press release and EAL's Code of Practice on 6 October 2010.... Following this CUAC ... invited [ERAA] to present the EAL Code of Practice at the Roundtable meeting on 14 October 2010. For most Roundtable members, this was the first time that they had heard about EAL's Code of Practice. No process for input or modification was suggested. The EAL lodged its Application on 29 October 2010.

The ACCC seemed to listen to the views of the consumer advocates, and what had commenced as a simple approval exercise started to unravel for the industry. Following the initial application from EAL, the ACCC raised a number of detailed concerns about the scheme. EAL responded by significantly redrafting

180 *Conflicting views of market competition*

the EAL approach, making changes such as providing a brochure to consumers at the door. Nevertheless, the ACCC's response to the revised EAL application was comprehensively negative, and its draft decision in April 2011 was to not authorise the EAL scheme. A point raised by the ACCC was that the door-to-door sales framework itself was a problem:

> the effectiveness of a self regulatory regime in addressing the conduct of door to door sales agents is difficult because both sales agents and retailers face a conflict of interest. In the first instance, sales agents have a conflict of interest between whether to provide clear and appropriate advice to potential consumers which may mean they do not entice a consumer to switch supplier, or use high pressure sales techniques so that they entice the consumer to switch and get paid commission. Retailers also face a conflict of interest between ensuring that their sales agents behave in an appropriate and compliant way which may mean fewer sales, rather than generating additional sales through promoting aggressive marketing strategies.
>
> (ACCC, 2011: 21)

The ACCC stated that it was fundamentally concerned that energy retailers who benefited from the activities of door-to-door sales agents were not sufficiently accountable for the actions of their agents, and it was also concerned that the scheme did not 'offer protection above the current regulatory environment' (ibid.: 31).

EAL again sought to make changes in response to the ACCC's comments. It also responded to the ACCC's views on self-regulation, arguing that the concerns expressed about the channel itself went beyond the scope of the ACCC's assessment of whether the public benefit of the self-regulatory scheme outweighed any anti-competitive outcomes (EAL, 2011c). It noted that the concern the ACCC raised about a conflict of interest between self-regulation and benefits from increased sales, if true, applied to all industries and all sales channels, not only energy retail. Privately, many in the industry had by now had enough of being held to ransom on issues outside the scope of what was being requested for an industry-proposed additional layer of regulation.

After some delays and more submissions from all parties to the Draft Decision that were consistent with the previous submissions, the ACCC approved the scheme. This was despite its concerns about commissions, conflicts and improvements on the current regulatory environment not being specifically addressed by the revised EAL documentation. The reasons for the ACCC's (second) change of heart are not clear, but it might be speculated that the ACCC realised the industry was not going to budge further and was at risk of walking away. The ERAA had no obligation to proceed: not only was EAL a voluntary scheme, but the Victorian politicians who had pushed the industry in the first place had moved on by the time of the ACCC's decision-making. Retailers could effectively abandon EAL if required, which was possibly recognised by the ACCC. The industry giving up a self-regulatory scheme on door-to-door sales because

Conflicting views of market competition   181

the ACCC made it too hard was not a good story for the ACCC. Further, although its distaste for the channel (which it was publicly campaigning about, as discussed in the next section) and its preference for a different form of self-regulation may have been understandable given the tales of poor behaviour, the ACCC was in fact acting outside its remit to not approve the scheme on the basis that it did not contain the consumer protections or sales agent remuneration provisions the ACCC wanted.

Soon after the ACCC approved EAL, CALC (2011) provided a media release about the EAL Code and ACCC process, calling it a 'lame duck':

> Self-regulation is just not appropriate in an environment where industry relies on sales commissions to switch customers who are often better off with their current deal.... Each time a sale is made, not only the retailer but the salesperson reaps a financial benefit, so there's an incentive for agents to pressure sell or mislead consumers.... This is why a code focused on individual door knockers won't work, and why we need stronger enforcement by regulators where miss-selling [sic] occurs.

This media release clearly implies that the regulators were not doing enough to enforce existing laws for door-to-door sales (which they did go on to do, as discussed next). It gave no credit to the industry for seeking to improve the sales channel and made it clear that self-regulation was not a valid possibility with the sales industry structured as it was (which, it should be noted, was legal and not limited to energy sales).

The story of the approval process of EAL is complicated, and the retelling here has been necessarily truncated. The main point worth noting is that it was clear that the key consumer groups were never going to support the type of scheme that was being suggested because they wanted a fundamentally different approach. Their claims of inadequate consultation did have some validity given that consumer advocates were not part of the Code's initial drafting, but this was a self-regulatory scheme for retailers to better comply with existing regulation, not an outward facing approach or replacement for existing consumer protections. However, it was misleading for the consumer advocates to be so adamant about having not being consulted when they were briefed but appeared to do nothing about it. The timeframes reported by both EAL and CUAC are telling: CUAC did little to nothing with a draft over three weeks (one week less than most formal regulatory submission periods), and CALC asked to be invited to a briefing and then did not attend. Perhaps these consumer groups did not want to be seen as supporting the concept at all, which is why they did not provide comment. There may also have been an issue with resourcing; there was no doubt that all the consultations on foot at any time were taxing for any organisation, let alone small and under-funded consumer groups. Whatever the reason, this kind of inaction was common: over the years I repeatedly saw certain vocal low-income consumer advocacy organisations agitate for inclusion in decisions and then fail to attend meetings or provide substantive input.

182 *Conflicting views of market competition*

EAL formally commenced in January 2012, launched by the then Victorian Energy Minister (from a different government to the one who pressed the industry to do something in the first place). At the time, the majority of energy retailers and energy marketers that sold energy were members. EAL had an independent Code Manager to carry out the administration and day-to-day supervision of the Code and a Code Panel to hear appeals from members regarding sanctions imposed upon them by the Code Manager. Members of the Code Panel included the former Energy Ombudsman of South Australia, the former Energy and Water Ombudsman of Queensland and a prominent consumer advocate from the St Vincent de Paul Society.

The story of EAL ends with a whimper, which should not be surprising given the contingency of outcomes and low support for self-regulation. As a result of the incumbent retailers pulling out of door-to-door sales in 2013 (as described in the next section), EAL became unsustainable. Without the incumbent retailers there was no critical mass of EAL members to fund the organisation at the level required (funding was based on market share). In April 2015, EAL submitted to the ACCC that it was going to be deregistered and so should be deauthorised by the ACCC. The ACCC started a consultation process, and invited submissions 'from approximately 100 potentially interested parties including energy retailers and marketers, industry associations, small business representatives, government regulators and ombudsmen and consumer associations and representatives' (ACCC, 2015b: 1–2). No party provided a submission and so EAL was deauthorised and deregistered. There was no public commentary about this, and it barely made a ripple in industry discussions behind the scenes.[19]

Regulatory enforcement and further retailer self-regulation

The previous discussion was about door-to-door self-regulation within an existing regulatory framework. What about enforcement by the relevant regulators? As noted by the consumer advocates, the regulatory framework itself was not publicly enforced for many years, although there were private discussions held between individual retailers and regulators about breaches. The first public action taken by a state regulator was when the Victorian ESC responded to the Footscray Community Legal Centre's (2009) report claiming that door-to-door sales teams targeted vulnerable people from non-English speaking backgrounds. The ESC released a series of papers to respond to the claims made in the Footscray report and held workshops with the community and retailers. However, very few issues were actually raised by consumers when given the opportunity:

> One person described a possible breach of a regulatory obligation through a retailer's actions, that is, transfer of her account without explicit informed consent. Another described a possible misleading conduct breach in 2008. However, that matter was quickly remedied by the customer and the retailer.

Conflicting views of market competition 183

Otherwise, customers identified no significant issues or breaches of regulatory obligations in the marketing of energy.

(ESC, 2009: 4–5)

The ESC also commenced a programme to review retailers' marketing materials, including scripting for sales agents. The review 'found no concerns', but noted that such a desktop review could not establish sales agents' actual compliance with the materials. The ESC then undertook to include marketing conduct obligations in the independent audits of the retailers scheduled for 2010 (ESC, 2010a: 1). Similarly, the ESC (2010b) reviewed retailers' complaints handling procedures to see if they were compliant and if retailers provided adequate access and information to non-English speaking customers and others with special needs. Again, there were no concerns.

It is difficult to evaluate the effectiveness of the ESC's approach. The ESC's papers seemed tokenistic at the time, as there was no evidence of wrongdoing. The 'breaches' identified in the Footscray report could not be followed up: I was part of discussions at the time to understand what had gone wrong and I found that the people in the report's case studies could not be located and the stories could not be verified. The ESC also could not find evidence of wrongdoing, even after holding its community workshops. However, door-to-door practices *were* a problem: anecdotal stories around the industry and most people's personal experience bore this out to some degree at the time. What was missing was a sense of materiality.

In contrast with the ESC's apparently lenient approach to door-to-door sales, the ACCC took a strong interest, putting the industry on notice in 2011 that it would be targeting the use of the door-to-door channel. It did this via a comprehensive media campaign in 2012, with community presentations and a coordinated approach to information provision across various regulatory websites. The ACCC also filed proceedings in the Federal Court against several energy retailers, which seems to have driven the most fundamental self-regulation the market had seen: during 2013, the three incumbents announced they would cease using the door-to-door sales channel for residential consumers. The precedent was action taken against a second tier retailer, Neighbourhood Energy, which was fined $1 million by the Federal Court (together with its sales agency) in September 2012 for illegal door-to-door sales (ACCC, 2012a). AGL was also taken to court in March 2012 because, among other things, its door-to-door salespeople did not clearly advise consumers about why they were at the premises or who they worked for (ACCC, 2012b). It was later fined $1.555 million (ACCC, 2013e).

What followed was an interesting series of events for the incumbents. Other than AGL, which was taken to court before making its announcement that it would stop using door-to-door sales agents, each company's announcement that it would end its use of the channel for residential consumers foreshadowed an announcement of impending legal action from the ACCC. AGL went first after its court case had commenced, but it did not leave its most lucrative states.

184 *Conflicting views of market competition*

It only did this later – the day after EnergyAustralia (2013b) made its announcement on 25 February 2013 (AGL, 2013b). Two weeks after EnergyAustralia announced it was leaving the channel, the ACCC then announced it had instituted proceedings against the company for door-to-door sales people making misleading statements that there was a mandated tariff and that EnergyAustralia was affiliated with the government (ACCC, 2013d). The behaviour occurred 'variously' across three states between July 2011 and August 2012, and resulted in a fine of $1.2 million (ACCC, 2014). It was just a matter of time before Origin's (2013) June announcement that it would cease using the channel for residential consumers, and there was no surprise about the ACCC's (2013c) announcement three months later that it had filed proceedings against Origin, this time for house visits to 13 customers across various states between September 2011 and December 2012. Among other things, consumers were allegedly told they had been overcharged by their current retailer and that there was a government requirement to switch to Origin. Origin was subsequently fined $2 million in May 2015 (ACCC, 2015a). AGL was also taken to court twice more in 2013: on one occasion for selling discounts that were later eroded (ACCC, 2013b) and on another for conduct where a sales agent ignored a 'Do Not Knock' sign at one consumer's premises ($60,000 in penalties) (ACCC, 2013g). The ACCC also took further action against the second tier retailers, with the Australian Power and Gas Company required by the Federal Court in November 2013 to pay a penalty of $1.1 million for illegal door-to-door selling practices. This business had since been taken over by AGL, which bore the fine. Second tier retailer Lumo was required to enter an enforceable undertaking in 2013 for conduct related to sales agents not being clear about their reason for being at the premises 'at least four times in Victoria' (ACCC, 2013a). No second tier retailer ceased using the door-to-door channel.

The reasons for the incumbent retailers leaving the channel can be reasonably assumed. There were several reports in the media that they did this due to 'widespread community backlash and a major "Do Not Knock" campaign from consumer advocates' (Collier, 2013; see also Evans, 2013; Roberts, 2013). This was a story fed by the incumbent retailers (and by consumer advocates who sought credit) as the retailers' reason for leaving but is unlikely to be the entire truth. Not only had consumer advocates been fighting door-to-door sales for *years* (and the community 'backlash' been undocumented) but the timing of the ACCC's announcements was too coincidental. It is more likely that the outcome came from two interrelated factors that were catalysed by the ACCC's actions (where these actions were likely discussed between the ACCC and the retailers for months prior to the point of the ACCC announcing court action). First, two of the incumbent retailers were experiencing profit losses from reduced demand, customer losses and retail price regulation. For example, the day after its announcement about leaving the door-to-door sales channel, EnergyAustralia reported a 42 per cent drop in full-year earnings, with this delaying the prospect of listing the company on the stock exchange for the second time in two years (Macdonald-Smith, 2013). Around the same time, Origin announced it was in the process of cutting 850 jobs from its workforce to reduce costs, and it had downgraded earnings forecasts for the second time since November 2012 (Robins, 2013). AGL was not doing as badly as its competitors, mainly because it was obtaining the customers lost from EnergyAustralia and Origin in New South Wales after an extremely aggressive marketing strategy that it had announced in 2010 (including door-to-door sales) when it was not a successful purchaser of the two government retail businesses.[20] Of course, it meant AGL was a target of the ACCC more than the other two retailers.

Second, the door-to-door channel was expensive, and although it was the most effective customer acquisition channel the anecdotal evidence was that the customers who used it most were not profitable; they had a reputation for switching regularly (and often leaving debt) and switching again before the retailer could recover the cost of the acquisition. As the incumbent retailers came to terms with the need to cut costs, this would have made them re-evaluate the sense of chasing unprofitable customers with an expensive channel. What they really needed to do was focus on retaining the customers they already had. It would have been far more cost effective to spend money on programmes to protect these customers from second tier retailers and one another; for example, Origin had been providing 'Do Not Knock' stickers to its own customers to place on their front doors, with some success.

While a need to prioritise retention should not have been news for the incumbent retailers, the culture of chasing customer numbers was hard to break. It is likely that commercial analysis about the real costs of the door-to-door channel was not seriously undertaken until it became a salient issue for senior decision-makers, which it did when the ACCC won its court cases against Neighbourhood Energy and AGL. While the first AGL fine of $1.5 million may not seem like a significant sum, the fact is that it (and the other proceedings) were for specific instances and there were likely to be more given the number of doors knocked and the known existence of bad practices. It is not hard to see why the incumbent retailers decided that it made sense to leave the channel.

This left the second tier retailers in an invidious position. On the one hand, it was positive, as they had free reign to chase the incumbents' customers (assuming these customers did not use 'Do Not Knock' stickers). On the other hand, there was a chance that with a critical mass of retailers not using door-to-door, the second tier retailers would have been under pressure to also stop using the channel. The incumbents were helping to build this pressure to some degree (which, if successful, would have been a highly effective retention strategy), such as when an AGL senior executive 'called on the industry to withdraw from doorknocking' when AGL's first court case was heard (see also EnergyAustralia, 2013a):

> This case demonstrates how difficult it is to control what salespeople do when they are at people's premises. Even if a company puts significant training and compliance mechanisms in place, doorknocking remains a risky sales technique. Doorknocking also preys on susceptible segments of the

186 *Conflicting views of market competition*

community, such as the elderly and migrants. Those companies still undertaking the practice are doing harm to the energy sector's reputation.

(AGL, 2013a)

Broader acceptance of this view could have been the death of the second tiers, as they relied on customer acquisition, and door-to-door was the most effective acquisition channel. However, staying with the channel in the environment of million dollar fines for specific cases could be expensive and wipe out the benefits.

Given the above, there are three further points worth discussing. First, the door-to-door sales channel was certainly seen as an issue but this was never based on anything more than case studies and anecdotes. As noted earlier in the chapter, complaint numbers did not demonstrate systemic breach when compared with the stated tens of thousands of doors knocked per day. It is too hard to know how material the problem was; the consumers who never complained may have not known they could, not been bothered, or not realised they were being misled. Perhaps upon learning that they had been misled, they may have not have cared (depending on the point they were misled about). Responding to the rather opaque data thus required interpretation from regulators, and we saw regulators acting at both ends of the enforcement spectrum. For example, when confronted with case studies, the ESC's response was to attempt to collect views but then do little more than behind-the-scenes light-handed enforcement because it could see no evidence of systemic breach. In contrast, when confronted with case studies, the ACCC used these to publicly prosecute the businesses as far as it could to dissuade them from using the channel. This would also have been connected with the ACCC's high profile public campaign about doorknocking, where it was very much in the mode of 'doing something' about the issue.

Second, and related to the first point, despite surveys showing that consumers did not like the channel,[21] consumers' behaviour (that is, their actions in engaging with retailers) did not send clear messages to the industry that the door-to-door sales channel was not in their (the public's) interest. It was not just about customer complaints: if we were to assume that consumers were rational (as retailers did), then they would have stopped signing up through the channel once they found they were being misled, or they would have used the cooling off period in greater numbers. The fact that they did not – again, assuming they were rational – could imply that they did not care about the way they were sold to, or even preferred the channel, despite survey results suggesting otherwise. Even if we assume that consumers were misled in fundamental ways and so took some time to realise, they would still have discovered this at some stage, as there would have been some form of harm experienced.[22] Of course, there was no evidence that consumers were particularly rational, but there was also no evidence that they were not.

Third, the reduction in the use of the most effective customer acquisition channel had an effect on churn, as would have been expected. Victoria and the

Conflicting views of market competition 187

other Australian states dropped further down the VaasaETT global switching ladder as switching rates dropped, echoing the experience of Great Britain, which was once the most competitive market but had dropped to twelfth place by 2013 (VaasaETT, 2013). While the door-to-door channel would not have been entirely responsible for the drop in churn in Australia or Great Britain it had a key role to play. This is likely to be the reason why door-to-door sales were tolerated by policymakers and regulators until the ACCC took enforcement action. Up to that point, governments and regulators had been responsible for establishing the market, and the good news stories from consumer switching were valued, as we saw from the Victorian Energy Minister's press release from 2010 supporting the VaasaETT research and Victoria's 'super hot' position (O'Brien, 2010).

Conclusion

The previous chapters showed sustained stakeholder conflict on social policy aspects of the retail energy markets, such as the roles of the retailers and the government, whether compliance was as important as performance, and what constituted 'good' performance on social criteria. No degree of stakeholder consultation or engagement created consensus on these issues. This chapter has demonstrated conflicts on more fundamental economic market definitions, such as what a competitive market might look like and how to identify an informed, or 'rational', consumer. Judgements on these issues came down to the assumptions made about which consumers mattered, what benefit should look like, and the way that consumers made decisions. There was also no stakeholder agreement on the consumer benefit or detriment from the market contracts or the sales channels used.

The conflict on these matters was not just between regulators and their stakeholders, but also between economic agencies in the regulatory and policy space, both in Australia and in the UK. This point is significant and needs to be reiterated: *economic specialists – that is, those who are expert in the operations of markets – could not agree about what effective markets looked like.* This has implications for theories based on an expectation for consumers to play a clear and unambiguous role in regulating industry on non-economic issues, such as compliance and social performance. In this case study there was no agreement about whether consumers (or which consumers) knew how to value and act on their own *economic* interests in assessing cheaper offers, let alone whether they could meaningfully act on any non-economic interests.

Further, the ultimate conclusions on whether competition was effective were formed within the political system not the economic system, and were therefore subject to the usual political contingency. Governments chose to tell the story of competitive markets to suit their own agendas and appetite for political risk at particular points in time, where decisions about the timing of retail market price deregulation were often shaped by unrelated political issues. This would not have been clear to an external viewer: casual observers of the process might have

188   *Conflicting views of market competition*

considered price deregulation as the natural outcome of competition evolving to an objectively agreed level, with rational policymaking based on solid economic evidence.

This chapter has also described the conflict about the main customer acquisition channel: the door-to-door sales channel. As with previous chapters, we found that the consumer advocates did not trust the industry to regulate itself and some even actively campaigned against increased industry self-regulation because they did not support the way the channel worked. Campaigns from consumer advocates against the channel did not stop the industry using door-to-door sales, and neither did the soft regulatory approach of the ESC. The actions taken by the industry to constrain itself were taken only in response to direct threats that were able to be translated into financial risk; EAL was created to offset the risk of government intervention of some type, and the incumbents gave up the channel because the ACCC made the financial risk untenable. This was not corporate social responsibility or self-regulation in the normative meta-regulatory sense but a response to old-fashioned deterrence measures where retailers were able to observe events through their economic construction of reality and value them accordingly.

Despite the reported community concern about door-to-door sales, governments did not take action to curb the practice (although there was the occasional threat). The governments appeared to like the churn statistics and the story these told about their energy markets. Consumers apparently wanted to exercise their ability to switch energy retailer, because they did so in significant numbers. The answer to the question of what consumers wanted was a matter of perspective rather than objective 'truth', and all that governments could be sure of was that there was no good news in examining the market too closely. This was particularly as governments went down the deregulation path to reduce the greater political risk of retaining control of energy prices; they needed to believe that the markets worked in consumers' interests and that consumers were traditionally rational. To do otherwise would have resulted in highly complex and likely impossible policy prescriptions; the markets and the law would not have been of any assistance because they did not recognise and account for consumers who were not traditionally or in some way predictably rational. Governments (and the AEMC) thus employed necessarily hypocritical policy responses to manage the apparently conflicting evidence that consumers engaged with the market while not understanding it, and that profits appeared highest in the most competitive markets.[23] It also led to an apparent belief that the previously unreachable 'sticky' customers could change their behaviour and become proactive in what was primarily a reactive market.

Given the cases discussed in this chapter, what might the retailers have learned from their experiences with consumers and consumer advocates? First, and as already discussed, the retailers valued commercial outcomes within the economic system and so pursued the door-to-door sales channel because this delivered the best outcomes in terms of customer numbers (although it was not always a cost-effective decision, which relates to the imperfect economic

Conflicting views of market competition 189

decision-making of retailers themselves). The message sent by consumers in taking up offers at the door was that they wanted these offers. Comparatively speaking, it was not all that relevant what consumer advocates said about the channel (other than where this influenced policy intervention), as the anti-doorstep selling sentiment of the consumer advocates had no direct financial effect on the businesses.

Second, the retailers were clearly shown that even developing self-regulatory mechanisms to supplement the existing framework was not supported by the most vocal consumer advocates. In attempting to consult with the consumer advocates on EAL, the industry learned that this was risky and potentially not worth it. The EAL example demonstrated that there was not even consensus on what was valid consultation: industry believed it had consulted, but the consumer advocates' perspective on the same events was quite different.

Notes

1 Switching for the Australian Capital Territory in 2011 was at 6 per cent for electricity (AEMC, 2011).
2 See Competition and Markets Authority (2016: 569–577, 646). Previous Ofgem regulators had also raised concerns about Ofgem's decisions (Littlechild *et al.*, 2014; see also Littlechild, 2014; Yarrow, 2014), suggesting that the Ofgem move to limit tariff choices for consumers may have resulted in the withdrawal of tariffs without standing charges – tariffs that were viewed extremely positively by older and lower income customers.
3 It should be noted that this behaviour was illegal under Australian Consumer Law and the energy provisions relating to explicit informed consent under both NECF and the state regulatory regimes. However, it was not only about illegal behaviour: even where the sales agent did not actively misrepresent what they were offering, consumers at the door were said by consumer advocates to feel pressured into entering contracts.
4 This number is based on 1,884 marketing 'issues raised' with EWOV in 2013 (Energy and Water Ombudsman, Victoria, 2013: 21) or 2 per cent of complaints in Victoria, and 2,501 marketing complaints in New South Wales (Energy and Water Ombudsman, New South Wales, 2013: 7). If we extrapolate these numbers out to cover all the states and view as a percentage of doors knocked in a year, the formal complaints raised with Ombudsman schemes is around 0.1 per cent. Of course, this analysis is flawed in the detail because not all dissatisfied consumers would necessary have complained to an Ombudsman scheme, but we still get a sense of publicly available complaints data and can see that the numbers are very small.
5 Note this was not an outlier but part of a number of highly discounted market offers.
6 This was a very well-credentialed group, including: Stephen Littlechild, Director General of Electricity Supply and Head of the Office of Electricity Regulation (Offer) 1989–1998; Sir Callum McCarthy, Chairman and Chief Executive of Ofgem and the Gas and Electricity Markets Authority (GEMA) 1998–2003; Eileen Marshall CBE, Director of Regulation and Business Affairs, Offer 1989–1994, Chief Economic Adviser and later Deputy Director General of the Office of Gas Regulation (Ofgas) 1994–1999, Managing Director, Ofgem and Executive Director, GEMA 1999–2003; Stephen Smith, who held senior executive positions at Ofgem 1999–2002 and 2003–2010, including Managing Director, Markets, 2004–2007 and Executive Board Member, GEMA 2004– 2010; and Clare Spottiswoode CBE, Director General of Gas Supply and Head of Ofgas 1993–1998.

190 *Conflicting views of market competition*

7 Ofgem's approach was briefly commented on by the AEMC in its 2014 competition report, where the AEMC then noted: 'Intervening in a competitive market based on inconclusive evidence can lead to unintended outcomes and reduce the effectiveness of competition' (AEMC, 2014: 180).

8 Noting that Littlechild (2015) has stated that Ofgem's executives from around 2008 were not economists.

9 However, a subsequent change in government delayed price deregulation for a further year. The new Energy Minister had no Parliamentary or energy experience, and despite being committed to price deregulation he was apparently uncomfortable with the 2015 date because there had been no community education. Of course, it was the change of government that stopped the comprehensive education campaign that had been developed, but it was not good politics to roll out the previous government's approach.

10 Except consumers, who we can expect would not have wanted to subsidise other users or market players, but who remained ignorant of existing cross-subsidies because their representatives and the media had not publicised the issue sufficiently.

11 Discussion of these reforms (with both ultimately shown to result in net cost to consumers) wasted substantial stakeholder time over the next four years, with regular revitalisation from the federal government, which also wanted to be seen to 'do something'.

12 It also gave governments a false sense of security, with analysis of media reports carried out by energy company AGL showing that governments kept political risk from regulation that they did not have with deregulation (Simshauser and Laochumnanvanit, 2011). This research would have presumably been noted and retained by the New South Wales and Queensland governments until the 2013 policy windows opened following the New South Wales competition review and Queensland interdepartmental review.

13 While this might seem to be in the industry's interest, I observed that the retailer staff who managed hardship programmes and sought to engage with community groups found it perplexing that they could not get the message through that this was not the best outcome for consumers.

14 Similarly, the UK Competition and Markets Authority (2016: 448) found that consumers who were less likely to have switched retailer in the previous three years in Great Britain were people: with low household incomes; living in rented social housing; without qualifications; over 65 years' old; with a disability; or registered on the Priority Services Register, which included aged pensioners, disabled people and people with chronic illness.

15 It is worth recalling the AGL research (Nelson and Reid, 2013) that found that financial counsellors did not advise financially disadvantaged consumers to consider changing contracts from standing offers despite their peak bodies knowing this was not the best value.

16 Although I note that in 2016 the AEMC *did* address behavioural economics in its 2016 competition review (but not to the degree of fundamentally questioning consumer rationality), enlisting the services of an economic consulting firm to address the retail energy markets from a behavioural economics perspective (see Oxera, 2016). The shared Oxera and AEMC view on behavioural economics was very light-touch, noting that some decision-making heuristics make sense because they are efficient for the consumer: 'Behavioural biases do not necessarily result in worse consumer outcomes' (AEMC, 2016: 12). The AEMC's stance on behavioural economics was still aligned with a more traditional economic perspective that valued customer choice and agency, in stark contrast with some consumer advocates' (and Ofgem's) hard paternalistic perspective. It is also worth noting that the AEMC's 2016 review considered vulnerable customer qualities in much greater depth than previously. The combined effect was still a view that competition was effective, but that governments needed to do more to educate consumers (with a reference to the AEMC's 2013 blueprint).

Conflicting views of market competition 191

17 A committed government could have managed this issue outside the market with welfare payments, but this would not have been appealing from a budget perspective.

18 As explained in a public letter dated 11 February 2011 to Richard Chadwick from EAL's Ramy Soussou (EAL, 2011b: 2–3).

19 A much smaller organisation called Sales Assured replaced EAL, with only five second tier retailers (where two were from the original ERAA group) and some marketing companies as members. This version focused on retailer commitments to sales agent screening and use of a central agent register (as well as compliance with existing regulations and law). Very little information was publicly available.

20 AGL's (2010: 17) strategic vision was to 'acquire 400,000 to 500,000 mass market electricity customers in NSW' with a view that acquisition of these customers at $150 per customer was a better deal than purchasing them from the government at around $1,300 per customer.

21 See Boreham (2013) for a statement from energy retailer AGL that a survey had shown 70 per cent of householders had a negative view of the channel, also Consumer Action Law Centre (2012) where CALC found that 77 per cent of respondents stated unequivocally that they disliked door-to-door selling. However, it was not clear whether these included people who used the channel, and the findings also did not differentiate between expected consumer disdain for interruptions at home and a greater concern about something more sinister.

22 By definition, no harm experienced would indicate the effects of being misled were not material, even though the fact of consumers being misled was unethical and illegal.

23 Although I note that whispers about a potential Victorian review into margins persisted into 2016 and at the time of writing it remains to be seen whether Victoria will take action, such as pursuing the model proposed by the UK CMA that all customers who had been on the equivalent of standing offer contracts for more than three years needed to be on a database managed by Ofgem and provided to competitors for marketing purposes (Competition and Markets Authority, 2016).

References

ACCC (Australian Competition and Consumer Commission) (2011) *Draft Determination: Applications for authorisation lodged by Energy Assured Limited in respect of a scheme to self regulate door to door energy sales*, Authorisation no.: A91258 and A91259, Public Register no.: C2010/970, 11 April.

ACCC (Australian Competition and Consumer Commission) (2012a) *$1 million in penalties for door-to-door sales*, media release number 207/12, 28 September.

ACCC (Australian Competition and Consumer Commission) (2012b) *ACCC takes court action against energy retailers for door-to-door sales tactics*, media release number 056/12, 27 March.

ACCC (Australian Competition and Consumer Commission) (2013a) *ACCC accepts undertaking from Lumo Energy over door-to-door sales*, media release number 161/13, 10 July.

ACCC (Australian Competition and Consumer Commission) (2013b) *ACCC takes action against AGL South Australia for alleged false or misleading representations*, media release number 274/13, 5 December.

ACCC (Australian Competition and Consumer Commission) (2013c) *ACCC takes action against Origin Energy and Salesforce for door-to-door selling*, media release number 220/13, 27 September.

ACCC (Australian Competition and Consumer Commission) (2013d) *ACCC targets door-to-door sales tactics*, media release number 48/13, 8 March.

192 *Conflicting views of market competition*

ACCC (Australian Competition and Consumer Commission) (2013e) *AGL ordered to pay $1.5 million for illegal door-to-door sales practices*, media release number 104/13, 21 May.

ACCC (Australian Competition and Consumer Commission) (2013f) *Australian Power and Gas ordered by consent to pay $1.1 million for door-to-door sales conduct*, media release number 263/13, 28 November.

ACCC (Australian Competition and Consumer Commission) (2013g) *Court imposes penalties for ignoring 'do not knock' sign*, media release number 302/13, 13 December.

ACCC (Australian Competition and Consumer Commission) (2014) *EnergyAustralia ordered by consent to pay $1.2 million for unlawful sales tactics*, media release number 77/14, 8 April.

ACCC (Australian Competition and Consumer Commission) (2015a) *Origin to pay $2 million for unlawful door-to-door sales tactics*, media release number 45/15, 30 March.

ACCC (Australian Competition and Consumer Commission) (2015b) *Determination: Application for revocation of authorisations A91390 and A91391 lodged by Energy Assured Limited in respect of its Code of Practice for face-to-face electricity and gas sales*, A91390 and A91391, 13 May.

AEMC (Australian Energy Market Commission) (2007) *Review of the effectiveness of competition in electricity and gas retail markets in Victoria*, first final report, 19 December, Sydney.

AEMC (Australian Energy Market Commission) (2008) *Review of the effectiveness of competition in electricity and gas retail markets in South Australia*, first final report, Appendix D, 19 September, Sydney.

AEMC (Australian Energy Market Commission) (2011) *Review of the effectiveness of competition in the electricity retail market in the ACT*, Stage 2 final report, 3 March, Sydney.

AEMC (Australian Energy Market Commission) (2012) *Power of Choice review – giving consumers options in the way they use electricity*, final report, 30 November, Sydney.

AEMC (Australian Energy Market Commission) (2013a) *2013 Residential electricity price trends report*, 13 December, Sydney.

AEMC (Australian Energy Market Commission) (2013b) *Review of competition in the retail electricity and natural gas markets in New South Wales*, report, 3 October, Sydney.

AEMC (Australian Energy Market Commission) (2013c) *Review of competition in the retail electricity and natural gas markets in New South Wales, supplementary report: Increasing consumer engagement*, 31 October, Sydney.

AEMC (Australian Energy Market Commission) (2014) *2014 Retail competition review*, final report, 22 August, Sydney.

AEMC (Australian Energy Market Commission) (2015) *2015 Retail Competition Review*, final report, 30 June, Sydney.

AEMC (Australian Energy Market Commission) (2016) *2016 Retail Competition Review*, final report, 30 June, Sydney.

AGL (2010) *NSW electricity organic growth to deliver higher shareholder returns*, Michael Fraser, Managing Director and CEO, 14 December, provided to the ASX 15 December.

AGL (2013a) *AGL breaches law and calls on industry to stop doorknocking*, 21 May.

AGL (2013b) *AGL withdraws from unsolicited door-to-door sales*, media release, 26 February.

Ariely, D. (2009) *Predictably irrational*, HarperCollins Publishers: New York.

Conflicting views of market competition 193

Ben-David, R. (2011) *Next steps for the regulator of Australia's most deregulated retail energy market*, presented at industry briefing hosted by Energy Retailers Association of Australia, 21 July, Essential Services Commission: Melbourne.

Ben-David, R. (2013) *Regulating retail energy markets in the long term interests of consumers*, presented at Power and Pricing 2013 Conference, 23 May, Essential Services Commission: Melbourne.

Ben-David, R. (2015) *If the retail energy market is competitive then is Lara Bingle a Russian cosmonaut?*, 22 June, Essential Services Commission: Melbourne.

Boreham, T. (2013) 'Utility stops pestering customers at home', *The Australian*, 28 February, p. 23.

CALC (Consumer Action Law Centre) (2010) *Energy Assured Limited applications for authorisation A91258 and 91259 – interested party submissions*, letter to Gavin Jones from Janine Rayner and Nicole Rich, 13 December.

CALC (Consumer Action Law Centre) (2011) *New energy sales self-regulation scheme fundamentally flawed*, media release, 24 June.

CALC (Consumer Action Law Centre) (2012) *Door to door sales: consumer views*, March.

CALC (Consumer Action Law Centre) (2014) *Energy market failing Victorian households, annual market report shows*, media release, 22 August.

CALC (Consumer Action Law Centre) and the Financial and Consumer Rights Council (2007) *Coercion and harassment at the door consumer experiences with energy direct marketers*, November.

Collier, K. (2013) 'Origin Energy to scrap controversial doorknocking sales methods', *Herald Sun*, 19 June.

Competition and Markets Authority (2016) *Energy market investigation: final report*, London, 24 June.

CUAC (Consumer Utilities Advocacy Centre) (2010) *Energy Assured Limited applications for authorisation A91258 and A91259 – interested party consultation*, letter to Richard Chadwick from Jo Benvenuti and Deanna Foong, 23 November.

CUAC (Consumer Utilities Advocacy Centre) (2011a) *Energy Assured Limited Applications for Authorisation A91258 and A91259 – interested party submissions*, letter to Richard Chadwick from Jo Benvenuti and Deanna Foong, 10 January.

CUAC (Consumer Utilities Advocacy Centre) (2011b) *Improving energy market competition through consumer participation: a CUAC Research Report*, CUAC: Melbourne.

EAL (Energy Assured Limited) (2010) *Energy Assured Limited applications for authorisation A91258 and 91259*, letter to Gavin Jones from Ramy Soussou, 21 December.

EAL (Energy Assured Limited) (2011a) *Energy Assured Limited applications for authorisation A91258 and 91259*, letter to Gavin Jones from Ramy Soussou, 11 January.

EAL (Energy Assured Limited) (2011b) *Energy Assured Limited applications for authorisation A91258 and A91259*, letter to Richard Chadwick from Ramy Soussou, 11 February 2011 (erroneously dated 11 February 2010).

EAL (Energy Assured Limited) (2011c) *Energy Assured Limited applications for authorisation A91258 and 91259*, letter to Richard Chadwick from Ramy Soussou, 13 May.

Energy and Water Ombudsman of New South Wales (2013) *Annual Report, 2012–2013*.

Energy and Water Ombudsman of Victoria (2013) *Energy and Water Ombudsman (Victoria), 2013 Annual Report*.

Energy Retailers Association of Australia (2010) *Submission in support of application for authorisation, Energy Assured Limited Door-to-door energy sales self-regulatory scheme*, 23 October, to the ACCC from Ramy Soussou.

194 Conflicting views of market competition

EnergyAustralia (2013a) *Energy customers do not want door knocking*, media release, 10 July.

EnergyAustralia (2013b) *Knock knock ... who's there? Not EnergyAustralia*, media release, 25 February.

ESC (Essential Services Commission) (2009) *Respecting customers: energy retail businesses, status report*, Melbourne, December.

ESC (Essential Services Commission) (2010a) *Energy retailers' marketing to vulnerable customers*, Melbourne, March.

ESC (Essential Services Commission) (2010b) *Respecting customers: energy retailers' complaint-handling procedures*, Melbourne, March.

Evans, J. (2013) 'Electricity and gas supplier EnergyAustralia axes "intrusive" door knockers after customer complaints', *Herald Sun*, 25 February.

Financial and Consumer Rights Council (2009) *Still an Unfair Deal: Reassessing the impacts of energy reform and deregulation on low income and vulnerable consumers*, report by the Financial and Consumer Rights Council (FCRC) for the Consumer Utilities Advocacy Centre (CUAC).

Footscray Community Legal Centre (2009) *The African consumer experience of the contestable energy market in the west of Melbourne*, Footscray Community Legal Centre and Financial Counselling Service, Melbourne, March.

Frost and Sullivan (2012) *Research into the door-to-door sales industry in Australia*, report by Frost and Sullivan for Australian Competition and Consumer Commission (ACCC), August.

Gilovich, T., Griffin, D. and Kahneman, D. (eds) (2002) *Heuristics and biases: the psychology of intuitive judgement*, Cambridge University Press: Cambridge.

Gosden, E. (2013) 'Competitive energy market? We can't define that, Ofgem admits', *The Telegraph*, 5 November.

Kahneman, D., Slovic, P. and Tversky, A. (1982) *Judgement under uncertainty: heuristics and biases*, Cambridge University Press: Cambridge.

Littlechild, S. (2014) *Promoting or restricting competition? Regulation of the UK retail residential energy market since 2008*, response to the Competition and Markets Authority's Statement of Issues, 15 August.

Littlechild, S. (2015) 'Regulation of retail energy markets in the UK and Australia', paper for the Energy Supply Association of Australia, September.

Littlechild, S. (2016) *The CMA energy market investigation, the well-functioning market, Ofgem, Government and behavioural economics*, submission to the Competition and Markets Authority, 8 February.

Littlechild, S., McCarthy, C., Marshall, E., Smith, S. and Spottiswoode, C. (2014) Letter to Competition and Markets Authority in response to its Statement of Issues, 7 August.

Macdonald-Smith, A. (2013) 'Early EnergyAustralia float called off', *Australian Financial Review*, 26 February, p. 22.

Neighbour, S. (2009) 'Fraudsters target energy contracts', *The Australian*, 1 July.

Nelson, T. and Reid, C. (2013) *Reconciling energy prices and social policy*, AGL Applied Economic and Policy Research Working Paper No. 37 – Energy and Social Policy.

Newgate Research (2013) *NSW consumer and stakeholder research report, prepared for the Australian Energy Market Commission to inform the communications blueprint associated with a review of competition in the retail electricity and natural gas markets in NSW*, final report, 20 September.

O'Brien, M. (2010) *Victoria leads the world in electricity switching*, Victorian Government, media release, 21 December.

Origin Energy (2013) *Origin to withdraw from door to door sales*, ASX/media Release, 19 June.

Oxera (2016) *Behavioural insights into Australian retail energy markets*, report to the AEMC, March.

Pronin, E. and Schmidt, K. (2013) 'Claims and denials of bias and their implications for policy', in E. Shafir (ed.) *The behavioral foundations of public policy*, Princeton University Press: Princeton, pp. 195–216.

Roberts, G. (2013) 'Dodgy selling claims land Origin in court', *Adelaide Advertiser*, 28 September, p. 75.

Robins, B. (2013) 'Origin flags job cuts as profit dives', *Sydney Morning Herald*, 21 February.

Shafir, E. (2008) 'A behavioural background for economic policy', in Productivity Commission, *Behavioural economics and public policy*, Roundtable Proceedings, Canberra, pp. 9–26.

Shafir, E. (ed.) (2013) *The behavioral foundations of public policy*, Princeton University Press: Princeton.

Simshauser, P. and Laochumnanvanit, K. (2011) *The price-suppression domino effect and the political economy of regulating retail electricity prices in a rising cost environment*, AGL Applied Economic and Policy Research Working Paper No. 20 – Domino Effect.

Simshauser, P. and Whish-Wilson, P. (2015) *Reforming reform: differential pricing and price dispersion in retail electricity markets*, AGL Applied Economic and Policy Research Working Paper No. 49 – Differential Prices.

St Vincent de Paul Society and Alviss Consulting (2013) *The National Energy Market: is there a devil in the retail? Observations from the Vinnies Tariff Tracking Project*, G. Dufty (St Vincent de Paul Society) and M. Mauseth Johnston (Alviss Consulting), December, Melbourne.

St Vincent de Paul Society and Alviss Consulting (2014) *The National Energy Market – wrong way, go back? Observations from the Vinnies' Tariff Tracking Project*, G. Dufty (St Vincent de Paul Society) and M. Mauseth Johnston (Alviss Consulting), September, Melbourne.

Sunstein, C. (2003) *Why societies need dissent*, Harvard University Press: Cambridge Massachusetts.

Thaler, R.H. and Sunstein, C.R. (2009) *Nudge: improving decisions about health, wealth and happiness*, revised and expanded edition, Penguin Books: New York.

VaasaETT (2010) *World energy retail market rankings report 2010*.

VaasaETT (2013) *The most active energy markets in 2013*, media release, 16 December.

Victorian Department of State Development, Business and Innovation (2014) *Submission to the AEMC 2014 retail competition review*, Approach Paper, p. 2.

Wallis Consulting Group (2013) *Victorians' experience of the electricity market 2013*, final report, August, Reference Number: WG4092.

Yarrow, G. (2014) *Energy market investigation: Response to the CMA's Statement of Issues*, August.

7   Rethinking meta-regulation

This book has explored whether a clear sense of the public interest (the interest that regulation was designed to to serve) developed over time in the Australian retail energy industry. The key question for this exploration relates to what the industry observed: Was the industry enabled and incentivised to self-regulate to meet the public interest as expected by normative meta-regulatory theory? The short answer is 'no'.

Normative meta-regulatory theory anticipates that inclusion of more stakeholders in regulatory policymaking and enforcement will help regulators and regulated industries better meet the public interest. What happened instead in the Australian retail energy sector was that every decision became contested and politicised. There was no single public interest or, in other words, no clear set of moral outcomes or norms for industry to work towards. Stakeholders were also not oriented towards reaching consensus, and consensus only became more remote the more that discussions on controversial issues occurred and new risks were discovered. The signals that retailers were to rely on to determine appropriate self-regulation were lost in the political clamour between stakeholders, and the industry was not programmed to absorb and learn from political messages in any event. Further, the reputation mechanism as a form of regulation was unreliable. Not only did most consumers tend to respond to price only (and were not predictably rational in doing this) but the messages to the community about business behaviour were skewed and inconsistent, meaning that even consumers who might conceivably have changed their purchasing decisions based on their view of the integrity and compliance of a company were not given the appropriate or correct information to act upon.

The regulatory and retailer organisations were also not rational in the traditional sense of the term. They did not have access to sufficient information to make truly rational decisions, nor did they have the cognitive capacity or the inclination. More importantly, they made decisions based on their own (limited) constructions of reality, which related to meaning as determined by their dominant function systems. The limitations to rational decision-making were not recognised by these or other organisations, with their virtual realities including an apparent belief that rationality in some predictable sense was probable in others and as well as in their future selves (see Brunsson (2006) for more on this phenomenon). This allowed for planning and was behind the reform measures undertaken by all (and particularly the retailers) apparently in the hope that future risks could be better managed.

The following sections draw out two key themes. First, at a theoretical level I argue that the normative meta-regulatory theory has an inadequate view of society. It does not 'see' the societal functions of politics, economics and the law, and so does not recognise the natural limitations that they impose on any direct input/output relationships between the organisations that reference them. Second, meta-regulation in practice is most challenged in a complex and contested environment. The meta-regulatory elements of principles over prescription and of stakeholder participation in debates only increased the contest over meaning. The resulting environment was highly politically contingent and, as such, overtaxed governments, regulators and the industry.

The political need to 'do something'

This book has shown that governments and their agencies, including independent policymakers and regulators, were often driven to act (or talk about action) in order to manage their perceptions of political risk. This was the politics of 'doing something', where a government or its agency sought to communicate that it was managing (and ideally resolving) the issues that politically influential stakeholders were concerned about.[1]

Normative meta-regulatory theory does not account for the politics of doing something; it does not appear to explicitly acknowledge politics at all.[2] Systems theory provides greater assistance in understanding the politics of doing something, where we see the political system's self-presentation of societal control – and thus as doing something – as paramount. This influences all organisations within public administration, such as the regulators and entities such as the Australian Energy Market Commission (AEMC). As discussed below, despite a putative independence from departmental energy policy-setting, none of these organisations were independent from the political system itself.

Not only is the existing role of politics within the regulatory environment not addressed in the normative meta-regulatory theory, the prescriptions of the theory implicitly enhance the role for political communications in regulation. It can be argued that by viewing regulation as a process of dynamic decision-making on principles and processes and, further, by introducing stakeholder participation in this decision-making, meta-regulation is *particularly* political. Osborne (2009: 98) notes 'the entire reason for politics is that our conceptions of "the public interest" differ'. In this study there were many private interests that defined issues and risks in different ways, with all competing for their view to be reflected as the public interest.

198   *Rethinking meta-regulation*

Risk perceptions were amplified under meta-regulation

A clear theme in this book is how risk was defined and discussed by different parties. Risk had specific properties: for retailers, it was about financial risk, where the industry faced an uncertain and unpredictable policy environment that might not support commercial requirements; for consumer advocates, risk was related to the risk of consumers experiencing undesirable outcomes in the market. Luhmann (2002) draws a distinction between risk and danger, where risk is a result of one's own decisions in an uncertain environment, and therefore potentially controllable, and danger is the result of others' decisions. Using this distinction we can be more precise, noting that the retailers saw danger in the behaviour of consumer advocates and the policymakers they were able to influence; danger was in policy changes that could mean commercial loss. Consumer advocates saw danger in the freedom of the industry to price and deliver an essential service on its own terms, where commercial decisions could disadvantage vulnerable consumers, such as through disconnection. Many low-income consumer advocates did not welcome experimentation or moves toward business self-regulation: they wanted certainty and public, formal enforcement.

Linked to this, the time dimensions of how parties considered issues varied. Retailers were generally backwards-looking when it came to considering issues and taking action. They needed to see harms and costs in clear and definite ways before they changed their approach – a phenomenon discussed further later in this chapter. In contrast, low-income consumer advocates focused on preventing harm and so sought precautionary actions from the industry and policymakers, including regulators. They sought bans rather than penalties, prohibition over compensation.

Perceptions of risk and danger did not decrease with greater examination. Instead, the more that questions were asked about stakeholders' concerns, the more concerned stakeholders became about potential problems that needed to be managed through regulation. This concern was heightened by the consumer advocates' use of the precautionary principle, which required anyone proposing change to demonstrate the change would be *harmless*, a phenomenon that Heanzle (2010: 61) points out 'requires us to know what cannot be known'. This nature of how parties perceive risk and danger has implications for meta-regulatory programmes of consultation that intend to make decisions about policy through rational discourse: there are no risk-free decisions (from an actuarial or any other perspective) and so stakeholder satisfaction may be elusive or short-lived. While not anticipated by the normative meta-regulatory theory, this has been observed by regulatory scholars (for example, see Hutter and Power, 2005; Black, 2010: 340). It is also expected by systems theory: 'the more we know, the better we know what we do not know, and the more elaborate our risk awareness becomes' (Luhmann, 2002: 28). Further:

> Is it not an illusion to expect more communication (or as variations: more information, more knowledge, more participation, more learning, more reflection) to provide the remedy? Will not more of all these things rather

Rethinking meta-regulation 199

contribute decisively to widening the gap between decision makers and those affected? All the more so, since for both parties the future, being in the probability/improbability mode, remains in the last instance indeterminable – and since the only thing that is certain is that the other side, too, cannot offer certainty?

(Ibid.: 111)

The dual problems of apparently irreconcilable risk perspectives and ever-present, uncontainable, risks were exacerbated by the strong value conflicts in the Australian retail energy markets and the moral tone taken by consumer advocates. In his writing on ecological communication, Luhmann (1989: 130) wrote of the way that anxiety 'infuses ecological communication with morality', where 'whoever suffers anxiety is morally in the right'. It is in this same way that low-income consumer advocate anxiety infused energy issues such as disconnections and marketing methods with a morality according to the advocates' perspective on energy as an essential service. Consumer case studies used by the low-income consumer groups were moral tales that sought to capture the political agenda. It did not matter if these tales could not be proven or were in the minority, or even if they were far more complex than just tales of energy retailer failure; the point is that they provided meaningful narratives for undesirable circumstances that had been made possible through the policy framework. However, like risk, anxiety resists contradiction and rational debate: anxiety is 'not empirical but transcendental' (Luhmann, 1989: 128).

Many of the examples in this book thus showed the apparent impossibility of consensus, or of an objectively rational examination of the issues at stake, at least where anyone other than the examiner would agree the process was objective. This meant that the governments and organisations in the political system often had to communicate hypocritically to present a view that they had everything under control and had aligned previously inconsistent norms in the environment (Brunsson, 2003). Writing about the political system and its response to ecological issues, Luhmann (1989: 120) states that it 'relies on the effectiveness of illusions', and in effect passes problems to other systems, such as law and the economy:

> The system enables and promotes loose talk. As we can read in the newspapers, nothing prevents a politician from demanding, proposing or promising the ecological adjustment of the economy. But a politician is not obliged to think and act economically, and so does not operate at all within the very system that his or her demand will ultimately bring to ruin. Political communication is always concerned exclusively with which political programs will or will not help the government and the opposition to take over from the other. This is its code.

The politics of doing something not only jeopardises other systems, but also causes problems for the political system itself. The illusion of control maintained

200 *Rethinking meta-regulation*

by the political system creates expectations in stakeholders that risk-free decisions are possible (Luhmann, 2002) and that further decisions can and should be made (see Brunsson, 2003), which we also saw in the energy industry. The need for governments to respond to the risk that arises from never meeting stakeholder expectations in any sustained way creates a self-perpetuating cycle for reform to bring talk and actions back into alignment. For Luhmann, this brings complications in that the political system is pressured into politicising risks of all kinds, and its self-referral of problems 'for which it cannot be held accountable and which it cannot resolve' undermines its own symbolic and practical legitimacy (King and Thornhill, 2003: 85).

Political behaviour from the regulators was amplified under meta-regulation

I have stated that regulators and other public agencies are part of the political system, and that the energy regulators in this study were *required* to act politically to support meta-regulation. It is worth exploring these statements in more depth.

Chapter 3 showed that prior to the market opening, the Victorian Essential Services Commission (ESC) acted as an arm of the political administration when it created the Retail Code. Although the ESC operated within the political system, it did so in a policy vacuum, where government was remote from the issues at hand and so did not seek to intervene. This granted the ESC a certain degree of leeway to pursue decisions as it saw fit, which at the time was based on a philosophy of due process and evidence-based decision-making where possible. There was a need for trade-offs and symbolic regulation, but this was limited in scope and the legitimacy of the regulator was not questioned by any stakeholder.

The ESC continued in this vein for the next few years, but increasingly made decisions that caused concern for some low-income consumer advocates. As we saw in Chapter 5, this ultimately led to the ESC's reputation being tarnished by consumer advocates and politicians. Subsequent years saw a somewhat more reflective and politically aware ESC, and by 2011, in a politically charged environment of rising energy prices, it had transformed into a much more political entity (noting this is not the same as saying it was not independent). This later incarnation valued compliance but valued the politics of performance more, with the ESC's Chairman also heading into new areas questioning the fabric of the market (albeit not a particularly politically palatable action in the views of the government at the time). The regulator was very much in the mode of being seen to 'do something'. In 2015, and once the community concern about energy prices had died down to some extent, its version of 'doing something' was to renovate the Retail Code protections for consumers in financial hardship.

The energy regulators in the other eastern Australian jurisdictions tended to be less publicly active than the ESC. However, they were also in far less politicised environments, with a much less involved consumer advocacy sector. These were also the jurisdictions where government ownership of assets remained for far longer (and so it did not do to be involved in criticising government businesses). The national Australian Energy Regulator (AER), which by mid-2014 had replaced the energy regulatory duties of many of the jurisdictional regulators (note this did not include the ESC), was a more political entity than the regulators it replaced. This regulator was not able to make rules (a function allocated to the AEMC) but it used its full discretion in interpreting the existing rules, including creating comprehensive Guidelines that were effectively treated as rules.

The politics of doing something was not limited to Australian energy regulation, with the British energy regulator Ofgem criticised for its behaviour during a period of price rises much like that experienced in Australia. After resigning from Ofgem's supervisory board in 2008 because of his concern about the policy directions being taken, George Yarrow claimed that Ofgem and its board was politicised (Pagnamenta, 2009). Writing to the Competition and Markets Authority (CMA) for its review of the energy market in late 2014, he explained his perspective on what had happened:

> It is a common experience across jurisdictions and over time that regulatory tasks in the energy sector become more challenging when underlying cost pressures are strongly upward. The public, the media and politicians (reasonably) want to know *why* prices are rising. One job of a regulator is to discover and explain why.
>
> Less reasonably, vociferous sections of the public, the media and politicians start to ask who is to blame and what is to be done about it. The regulator's tasks are then subject to a step-increase in difficulty because it may (and often will) be necessary to try to explain that those are not necessarily sensible questions to ask: nobody may be to blame and 'doing something about it' may (and often will) make matters worse. Moreover, challenging the sense of these questions invites the inference that, in the absence of simple answers to simple questions, it is the regulator who is to blame and that something should be done about the regulator.
>
> (Yarrow, 2014: 4–5, author's emphasis)

Yarrow portrays Ofgem and its board as abandoning appropriate regulatory boundaries from 2008 when it started to point 'the finger of blame for the higher prices that energy consumers were facing':[3]

> The general shift can be characterised as a move towards a regulatory world of smoke and mirrors, where attention is drawn away from consideration of substantive issues toward how the regulator appears in the media ('how do we look?') and a preoccupation with being seen to be 'doing something about it', almost irrespective of the particular features of the 'it', of the 'something' or of the relationships between the two.
>
> (Ibid.: 5)

202 *Rethinking meta-regulation*

After it had released some unexpected preliminary views (at least from an economic perspective) the views of the CMA itself were also portrayed as political, with the UK electricity regulator from 1989 to 1998 Stephen Littlechild (2016) showing through comprehensive evidence that the British government, Ofgem and CMA were very clearly aligned on policy issues.

Political behaviour from regulators (and independent regulatory review and policy bodies) is difficult to understand and account for within normative meta-regulatory theory,[4] as the theory lacks a conceptual framework for the regulator other than as an agent for the public interest that uses law to achieve its goals. This is an important point to note: regulatory theory tends to see state regulators as proxies for the law, and thus implicitly within the legal system. The only conclusion that could be drawn from a normative meta-regulatory perspective on regulatory politics is that regulation in practice is messy, complex and depends on the circumstances. This interpretation does not assist in explanation but retains the hope that next time it could be different, that regulators too can improve.

Systems theory offers a much deeper understanding of the effects observed. If we consider that regulatory organisations serve an administrative function within the political system, their behaviour becomes more explicable. According to systems theory, the role of the administration is to unburden the politicians from detailed and complex decision-making. We saw the Australian energy regulators regularly used for this purpose, both in their basic regulatory role and in additional roles such as in price regulation and providing market reviews and special reports. The regulators were considered independent, but this was independence from energy departments, not from government itself.

As a self-referencing organisation, each regulatory agency had its own preferred mode of operating at any point in time; regulatory values and communications were decided by the organisation alone. Sometimes, regulatory behaviour was clearly aligned with the more traditional expectations of regulators, such as behaviour to support due process, evidence and accountability. However, each regulatory organisation also needed to value its reputation and legitimacy within the political system. The regulators may not have valued politics on the same terms as politicians, but as public organisations they were still vulnerable to changes in government ideology, funding and political views on their performance. This research found that political stress – the need to be seen to be doing something – created a stronger need for the regulator to focus on politically urgent decisions than on evidence or due process, and as such, evidential and procedural aspects of decision-making were able to be discounted when required. As per the quotations from Yarrow above, this phenomenon has also been considered as an explanation for similar events in Great Britain.

Of course, meta-regulation – with its focus on issue and stakeholder inclusion, consultation, and learning for regulators and the industry – only increased political stress.[5] Regulators in the energy industry were expected to make (political) binding decisions on complex and little understood issues, such as the optimal assistance to consumers in financial hardship, and the information needs of consumers with unknown rationality. They were implicitly expected to trade

Rethinking meta-regulation 203

off competing claims provided by self-selected and self-validated stakeholder representatives from different sectors, and the competing claims were often based on irreconcilable values. As described above, stakeholder perceptions of risk increased and anxiety could not be relieved, which set in action a cycle of hypocritical regulatory reform.

As consultation cycles became tighter and more politically contested, the energy regulators depended less on in-depth analysis and more on simply trying to find a middle ground between competing stakeholder claims. This finding does not support the meta-regulatory expectation that regulators are more able or willing to process information under meta-regulation (in a political and complex environment) than under command and control. Even when a regulator was disposed to value evidence over its own legitimacy with its political masters, this was increasingly difficult given the noise in the environment and the apparent impossibility of ever finding the 'truth' from competing claims and discourses. We can also see the risk to regulators when they did focus on evidence and were not sufficiently political: the hardship policy experience of the ESC in 2004 should be a cautionary tale for regulators in a politicised environment.

It is useful to briefly compare the regulatory regime in Australia with the approach taken in New Zealand. The New Zealand electricity market was very different from its Australian counterpart, with a lighter-handed regulatory approach. The electricity regulator (the Electricity Authority) in New Zealand was primarily responsible for competitive outcomes;[6] although regulation for vulnerable customers was in place, it did not appear to drive policy change. Unlike Australian energy regulators, the Authority ran cost-benefit assessments of regulation, where new regulation had to reflect a net economic benefit in order to be implemented. Importantly, the Authority ran consultation processes in a very different way from the regulators in Australia. The consultation carried out by the Authority was primarily based on the use of advisory groups which included representatives from across industry and consumer advocacy organisations. Each advisory group was itself responsible for consultation documents, including the drafting of papers. These advisory groups were expected to work towards the greater good for the consumers of New Zealand rather than represent their organisation's views[7] – an approach that was viewed positively by the regulator and stakeholders.[8] The New Zealand example shows us that the inclusive aspect of meta-regulation can be designed to reduce the need for politics. By not making the energy regulator responsible for managing social issues (consumer protection was managed by the general consumer protection regulator), and by having regulatory stakeholders adhere to higher goals and be accountable for outcomes, the New Zealand processes avoided some of the worst political behaviour observed in Australia.

Harnessing the market?

This book has shown that the retail energy market and policy environment did not provide clear messages to retailers about what consumers valued. There was

204 *Rethinking meta-regulation*

not only stakeholder conflict about the use of the market to provide an essential service – which was a political and moral issue – but even within an economic paradigm there was no consensus on desirable market processes and outcomes. According to a traditional economic perspective the market was effective, with consumers regularly choosing alternative products. However, the behavioural economics perspective questioned the rationality underpinning consumer decision-making, and thus cast doubt on whether the market could be said to be operating in an economically efficient manner or in the best interests of consumers. Further, the situation in Victoria where the high levels of switching (taken to indicate strong competition) appeared to coincide with the highest prices (implying inefficient competition), remained anomalous in the eyes of policymakers, most of whom chose to not address the issues too closely. These outcomes are not anticipated by normative meta-regulatory theory, which implicitly expects that a market will be effective on its own terms (note this is not the same as saying that markets are virtuous).

The ambitions of normative meta-regulation to harness the market for achieving non-price regulatory and performance improvement outcomes were also not met, with consumers not valuing what they were expected to value in the sense of 'moral' outcomes in retailer behaviour. Energy customers acted on price only (a finding confirmed by multiple other studies, as discussed in Chapter 2), not on their views of retailers' performance on non-price matters. Systems theory helps explain this outcome, noting that the economic system is self-referential and self-reproducing, and that its code of payment/non-payment provides for the main programme of price. Economics does not inherently find meaning in non-economic factors, by definition. What the economic system observes from its environment is determined within the economic system alone and according to whether economics can reproduce itself in its own terms. Economics does not require legitimacy and does not have a need for 'social licence' in the way that politics does; the economic system proceeds on the basis of the constant reallocation of money, and money 'does not remember why it was paid out' (Luhmann, 2002: 172).

It follows that businesses as primarily economic organisations respond to social messaging where the financial costs or benefits to them of doing so are sufficiently valuable. In the energy industry the value of social innovation was generally low or unclear, with major 'socially responsible' operational changes observed only rarely. (This does not mean that retailers did not regularly improve their operational standards and practices, but that these activities were not the subject of commentary and so went unseen by outsiders.) The examples of major change included where innovators in the early days of competition developed hardship programmes to manage risk, and where legal action against door-to-door sales tipped an already expensive marketing channel from being manageable into being unsustainable for large energy retailers.

Although the economic system can value norms in its environment (on its own terms), it is important to note that the economic system does not *create* norms, at least not in any stable or predictable sense. We saw this in Chapter 3, where the industry was unable to create the rules required for full retail competition. The retailers were not programmed to value non-economic or unquantifiable service requirements, and their preparedness to invest or divest at any time based on their perception of the current economic value meant that planning ahead was risky. This should not be surprising; the problem of expecting market participants to act 'as if' competition were in place was discussed in detail by Hayek (1979) and the Austrian school some decades ago. Despite econometric constructs of market equilibria, competition is about unpredictable change (including possible failure), not stability. As discussed by Renner (2011: 107), the 'never-ending process of re-allocation' is fundamental to the economic system, and this dynamic requirement means that the notion of the economic system 'internalising the generation of normative expectations ... is bound to fail as the market process ultimately aims at enhancing normative uncertainty; not at reducing it'.

The reputation mechanism was highly unreliable

The most that can be hoped for from the economic system is that it internalises an existing norm and builds it into its processes at a point in time. The reputation mechanism has been implicitly proposed by normative meta-regulatory theory as a means for this to occur: it provides for an industry's stakeholders to transmit their expectations and perceptions of the industry to the industry via market transactions. This allows for learning and ultimately behaviour change within the industry that aligns with stakeholder norms, at least until this alignment becomes commercially unviable. However, this study found that the reputation mechanism was *not* sensitive, consistent or salient enough to be of any particular or predictable value to retailer self-regulation. Retailers instead followed their own logic within the economic system.

I described the detailed assumptions related to the reputation mechanism in Chapter 2, where these anticipate direct input/output relationships and are as follows:

a   Price/product (economic) and non-price/product (non-economic) stakeholder expectations:
    i   exist and are articulated/acted on by stakeholders (including consumers in the market);
    ii   can be accessed and understood by business;
    iii   are largely static and technically possible for the business to meet through self-regulation even if they are idealistic and/or onerous;
    iv   are commercially valid from the business's perspective and, further, the business perceives a material financial loss from negative reputation effects if it does not take action; there must be a net perceived cost of not responding; and
    v   are responded to by the business in a way the stakeholders recognise, value and accept.

206　*Rethinking meta-regulation*

b The market and reputation mechanism provides the right outcomes in the temporal dimension:

  i stakeholders observe business performance and communicate their views or concerns to the business and/or others;

  ii these communications are then observed, prioritised and responded to by business in a timely fashion; and

  iii the business's communications about its responses to stakeholder concerns are observed in a timely fashion by the stakeholders and are seen to meet expectations, ending potential or actual reputational damage.

These criteria were not met in the Australian retail energy environment. In contrast, reputational messaging to energy retailers from the various stakeholders was scrambled, subjective and not well aligned with retailers' own perspectives on reputational risk or danger.[9]

Starting with criterion (a), we have already discussed how retailers' customers acted on economic grounds only. Certainly customers did not demonstrably act in the market based on compliance or non-financial performance values. Investors and other potential transactional stakeholders were also silent on non-economic issues. The question is then whether non-transactional stakeholders such as consumer advocates could *enlist transactional stakeholders to act in the market on non-economic grounds* and so activate the reputation mechanism. There was no evidence of this occurring over the research period. At their peak, the risks and anxiety communicated by the consumer advocates in the political and policy debates did percolate to the community, but they did not appear to change consumer or investor behaviour in the market. The influence of governments and the mass media (such as the Queensland Premier's plea to voters to shift from Origin Energy in 2012) and regulators (through performance and compliance reports) was also negligible in transactional stakeholders' decision-making. Therefore, retailers did not generally perceive material risk from reputation loss relating to compliance or non-financial performance. The 'social licence' to operate that can come into play as a reputational mechanism to bestow (or withdraw) legitimacy had no bearing in this case study. This is because there was no evidence that compliance or non-financial performance translated meaningfully into economic terms for the retailers. I return to this issue later in this chapter.

Addressing the non-transactional stakeholders in more depth, these parties also had minimal direct influence on retailers. While economic and non-economic expectations existed in this group and were strong (particularly for low-income consumer advocates), these were not consistent across stakeholders or through time and so were hard to conceptually grasp in any simple way. Stakeholder views were also generally not expressed directly to retailers but to governments and regulators via case study reports and submissions to consultations. This meant that the stakeholder views were not accessible to retailer organisations as a whole: only retailer employees who managed policy and

Rethinking meta-regulation 207

government relations (or had some interaction with them) were involved in the policy debates that elucidated consumer advocates' concerns. Some operations staff who managed hardship programmes also had direct contact with consumer advocacy organisations,[10] but the degree to which this occurred depended on their organisational perspective on the value of building these relationships. Understanding of the issues within retailer businesses – at least on the consumer advocates' terms – was thus also low. Those who dealt with the issues may have understood the intent of the low-income consumer advocates (or a selected subset), but struggled to translate this intent into a valid business perspective and so enlist broader business support. This was particularly as the consumer advocates' views were often not commercially feasible or salient to a business's corporate identity or view of the world. Most of the consumer advocates were protesting about what they saw as societal problems, such as the provision (and disconnection) of an essential service by the private sector. They were not specifically motivated or required to help retailers do better within the existing paradigm. The only actions acceptable within many consumer advocates' precautionary frame related to retailers taking extreme steps, such as stopping disconnections and door-to-door sales, which was not a valid commercial approach for most retailers.

These issues, combined with the lack of an apparent economic business case for change based on potential reputational damage from transactional stakeholders, meant that businesses were generally not in a position to prioritise and respond to consumer advocates' expectations. When retailers *did* respond to issues as raised by consumer advocates this was often seen as not meeting expectations anyway: we saw in Chapter 5 that even the retailers with voluntary hardship policies were criticised by consumer advocates, and Chapter 6 showed that the self-regulatory direct sales initiative was not welcomed. When the industry did act in more social ways it did this on its own terms, which were not necessarily the terms of those who called for change. Governments and regulators possessed more influence in changing retailer behaviour, but retailers responded to governments and regulators not on reputation but on retailer assessments of more direct financial and regulatory cost.

The temporal dimension as described under (b) was also problematic. Even where there were issues that the retailers were able to observe as requiring a response, there was little to no alignment in response times to potentially offset reputational damage. Retailers were generally slow to take action, needing to see sustained and material financial cost (or a direct threat from government or a regulator) before changing direction on an issue. This was a fundamental mismatch with the consumer advocacy precautionary timeframe. Preventative actions were inefficient from a retailer perspective; it did not do to pick winners from future regulatory environments given the complexity involved and ever-changing stakeholder views.

Putting aside for the moment the finding that consumers and investors did not engage on non-economic issues, it is worth drawing out how the *strength* of stakeholder opinion might have affected the effectiveness of the reputation

208 *Rethinking meta-regulation*

mechanism. As discussed in Chapter 2, it is my contention that the meta-regulatory theory, insofar as it expects stakeholders to effect reputational damage, is underpinned by the potential for controversial conflict. I have argued that the reputation mechanism relies on passionate views, where some form of scandal must be possible if reputational damage is to be inflicted. The Australian retail energy market was a perfect example of a market that mattered: it was an essential service, so all but a very small proportion of the community had a relationship with a retailer, and as an essential service it also inspired strong opinion. The fact that there were consumer advocates who specialised in energy policy, let alone government departments dedicated to energy, demonstrates that energy could be expected to be salient to most people, at least relative to many other topics and industries. Therefore, the stage was set for interested consumers to receive communications about good/bad outcomes and to take action. However, the strength of opinion required to draw industry issues to the attention of the public in order to create reputational damage had the paradoxical effect of undermining the reputational mechanism. This is because issues that were subject to strong conflicting views became politicised. The stakes were high, so communications to the community about the industry from all parties (that is, governments, energy networks, energy retailers, regulators, Ombudsman schemes, consumer advocates and others) were inconsistent and used self-serving rhetoric that did not promote genuine understanding. If energy consumers and investors had actually responded in any transactional sense (that is, through purchases in the market) to what they observed from retail energy performance and compliance debates, the responses would not have been consistent or normatively meaningful.

The mass media system was the primary delivery mechanism for information, which amplified the potential for observer confusion. Not only did the news media not question or analyse the rhetoric used by various entities, they essentially replicated media releases and opinions in their original form, despite inconsistency in the language used about even basic matters. Based on the media representations, an actively interested consumer would not have made sense of the industry or understood how to take action. This problem was only made worse by the fact that the mass media system alone decided *when* to report on an issue and so energy issues were not reported with any consistency. Energy stories competed with all other news, and coverage depended on a range of variables that could not be observed from outside the media system, or even from outside any one media organisation. It is likely that a major scandal would receive coverage, but scandals were rare, and even ample media coverage did not appear to change consumer behaviour.

Retailer learning was heavily constrained

We have seen that the reputation mechanism did not show demonstrable value as a means of regulating retailer compliance and non-financial performance via the market. So how *did* retailers learn about and reflect upon stakeholder

Rethinking meta-regulation 209

expectations on these matters? What were the organisational dynamics within retail businesses?

Consistent with systems theory, it is useful to see 'learning' as the process of the energy retailer refining its internal construct of its environment; it was not about discovering information that was 'out there' in some objective sense. We can say this because there is no evidence that any of the organisations in this study saw their environments on anything other than their own terms: their environments were subjective virtual worlds given meaning by the decision-making and communicative orientation of each organisation. The energy retailers were not naturally learning organisations, at least not in the sense expected by normative meta-regulatory theory. Instead, the events discussed in this book indicate that the normative meta-regulatory expectation that businesses have the capacity to see and internalise plural and conflicting stakeholder expectations is somewhat heroic.

In effect, the energy retailers excelled at *not seeing*, and at *forgetting* the past in order to move forward. To explain, we have already noted the way in which investigations of risk breed more perceptions of risk, and the same can be said about decisions, which according to Luhmann (2005) are the form of self-reproduction for organisations. Decisions breed decisions, and 'rational' analysis of complex issues in the pursuit of action can have a paradoxical effect of creating paralysis (Weick, 2001; Brunsson, 2003, 2007). This effect is heightened where conflict must be managed and somehow accounted for; Brunsson (2003: 33) draws a distinction between political and action oriented organisations, where 'it is not possible to be good at both politics and action'. We saw this throughout this research, where the political organisations (the governments and regulators) specialised in hypocritical talk to manage conflict through communicating that 'something was being done', although real action could take time or might be illusory. The action organisations (the businesses) focused on market growth and financial management and were not particularly adept at politics.[11] Retailers operated according to their specific organisational ideologies, which reduced the range of decisions to be made,[12] a phenomenon explained by Brunsson (ibid.: 17). They satisficed to keep moving, hunkering down with the rules as they understood them and their normative views about regulation, markets, the rationality of consumers, and the role of industry to fill the social responsibility gap for consumers in financial hardship. The fact that their views on these issues were not shared by other stakeholders went unobserved by most people within the energy businesses. Even though retailers were primarily oriented within the economic system (or perhaps *particularly* because of this), they had a blind spot on market effectiveness and tended not to see that consumers might not be rational and that markets might fail.

Politics was a challenge for the industry because retailers could not predict which of their decisions would be viewed according to a political agenda or which agenda would be in play. That is, retailers could not predict how others developed their own virtual worlds. For example, if we look at the Queensland Government's 'war on Origin' from Chapter 4, how was Origin Energy supposed to know that the Queensland Premier would not recognise that his price freeze

210 Rethinking meta-regulation

did not extend to market prices? How was the company to predict his response? We could say that the retailer should have seen the environment as a risky (dangerous) one and managed it accordingly, but how can we say what the retailer should have seen or what was ever going to be within its control? For any retailer its environment was not an actual thing that was out there to observe objectively, but a construct created by the retailer. So regulatory, government and consumer advocacy organisations were only seen as part of a retailer's internal virtual reality and not necessarily as per the self-image of any of the organisations in question (or as per the desires of any second-order observer). Retailers at an organisational level managed political uncertainty by not seeing it; this alone allowed for necessary action. This is the opposite effect to what is anticipated by normative meta-regulatory theory, which expects regulated businesses to become politically rational and observe themselves and their stakeholders in their environment, be cognitively open to conflict, and acknowledge and plan for dynamic and politically contingent outcomes.

However, action and political models can still co-exist in the same organisation, which was also demonstrated in this book. Czarniawska (2005: 132–133) describes three strategies that are practised in organisations to manage the paradox of managing conflict in order to act: *temporisation*, which shifts conflicts into the future; *spatialisation*, which separates the issue into different areas such as creating multiple committees; and *relativisation*, which attempts to redefine an issue relative to a particular observer. These were all used by Australian energy retailers (as well as by governments and regulators), with the most common strategy for retailers being spatialisation, which was essentially the further functional differentiation within each business that created regulatory policy areas and corporate functions dedicated to brand and public relations. These areas specialised in talk while the operational parts of the retailers were able to get on with running the business. Risk management was also sometimes used to link a business's perception of its environment (specifically the reputational and political aspects) with its action orientation, but objectively effective risk management formulations were elusive. There was recognition within the businesses that talk and action occasionally needed to be reconciled, with regular organisational restructures fuelling the hope that the future could be more rational and efficient. However, the cycle always continued because internal value conflicts between different business functions were difficult to reconcile, similar to the broader value conflicts in retailers' environments. The instability of the corporate environment further contributed to a lack of responsiveness and self-reflection for most retailers and the industry as a whole, with the organisational restructures discouraging innovation and limiting institutional memory.

Overall, there was little evidence to support a model of retailer learning about non-economic stakeholder concerns in a general sense. Learning did occur at a localised level; it tended to be limited to regulatory and compliance units. This learning was also easily lost with usual staff turnover. Further, what these retailer staff learned over time was to 'not poke the bear': engagement with regulators and consumer advocates seemed like a good idea but rarely ended well. The mere mention of a risk or a proposed solution re-started the cycle of debate to uncover more stakeholder perceptions of danger.

Learning that led to change at a whole-of-retailer or industry-wide level was unlikely, requiring non-economic issues to be identified as potentially salient, agreed across often inharmonious organisational divisions, and translated into commercial (economic) terms that reflected sufficient cost for senior decision-makers to contemplate a change in behaviour. There were very few issues that met these criteria over the research period, with the key example being when the incumbent retailers ceased their use of the door-to-door sales channel after they incurred legal penalties as discussed in Chapter 6. As noted above, costs or scandals also tended to need to happen *before* retailers took action; retailers could then observe how others reacted and measure the commercial impact.

None of this is promising for normative meta-regulatory hopes that businesses have the capacity to observe themselves in their environments and to observe and proactively learn about (and respond to) how others in their environments are observing them (let alone whether any business response is even recognised as valid by external observers). Meta-regulation appears to pass the challenges of understanding societal complexity to business organisations, with no recognition that businesses might not function on these terms.

The role of the law

Having addressed the political and economic systems, we will now turn to the legal system. As discussed, I am suggesting that regulatory organisations are not inherently legal organisations despite the fact that their duties include interpretation of the law and despite their capacity to impose penalties on regulated businesses. Regulatory decisions depend upon more than strict legal interpretations. The regulatory organisations in this book had the capacity to be more political than legal, particularly when the political stakes were high; in these cases, communications through the political system took precedence. This perspective would appear to be fundamentally contrary to normative meta-regulatory theory, which, while it does not associate organisations with societal function systems, does appear to consider regulators as representing the law.

If we take the view that regulators are primarily legal entities, a problem emerges. This problem relates to understanding the role of the law and how regulators support that role within a normative meta-regulatory framework. The normative meta-regulatory literature sees the law and regulators as being able to learn and adapt, with an important role to enable stakeholder participation in regulatory consultation and enforcement. Regulators are considered able to identify the right issues and stakeholders, in order to promote and embed the right values and public interest outcomes. Looking at the Australian retail energy markets, we can see there was a range of stakeholder groups with different values and views on social responsibility, and the values and views varied even within stakeholder groups. To see the management of conflict across these stakeholders as an inherently legal act is challenging and potentially overtaxes

212 *Rethinking meta-regulation*

any reasonable expectation of the law. This is all the more so because conflicts were often about risks and dangers – that is, a future that no one could be certain about. Writing about this phenomenon King and Thornhill (2003: 198) note that:

> Any attempt to make consequences more certain and so more amenable to regulation through law is fraught with difficulties, since certain knowledge about the future simply is not available. So law may be faced with conflicting versions of what the consequences might be without any sound way of choosing between them. Arbitrariness in decisions is likely to increase, and any attempts to invoke principles ... or formulas such as 'equalising', 'balancing' or 'proportionality' can be achieved only arbitrarily. In resorting to 'technically informed arbitrariness' law may succeed in resolving conflicts, but at a cost to its own integrity ... because such solutions are not specifically legal ones.

According to Luhmann's systems theory, law's function is to provide stability about normative expectations; it maintains norms (such as those related to legal process) despite disappointment through any individual case. However, law's performance against its self-image is distorted by the use of law to manage risk, with 'a danger of law taking upon itself the regulation of expectations which go beyond the normative and in doing so finding that the stability of such expectations are disappointed by events over which the legal system has no control' (ibid.: 200). If regulators are seen as predominantly acting within the legal system then it would seem that meta-regulation creates this problem for law.

My own argument is that meta-regulation is not really about law but about embedding politics (and a faulty view of the market) *instead of law*. This has a negative effect on politics, as already discussed, because the political system is continually faced with risks (or, more precisely, dangers) that it cannot eliminate but for which it must maintain an illusion of control.

More importantly, attempts to replace the function of law cannot be successful by definition. Luhmann argued that only the legal system can perform law's function, and that:

> A functionally differentiated society cannot provide for alternatives to its functional subsystems. All functional equivalents are part of the functional subsystems because these are organized in view of their functions.... The political system cannot replace the economic system, the economic system cannot replace the educational system, the educational system cannot replace the legal system, the legal system cannot replace the political system, *because no functional subsystem is able to solve the core problems of another system.*
>
> (Luhmann, 1988: 120, author's emphasis)

This is important to note as we consider the defining thesis of meta-regulatory theory to allow for norms to be internalised by businesses through the market

Rethinking meta-regulation 213

and the involvement of special interests (politics). It is my contention that neither the market nor politics are able to set the *stable* norms required by businesses to guide their behaviour towards any putative public interest. Not only can the economic and political systems not act 'as if' they were law (by definition), but purely market-based or political norms are volatile, meaning that any action a business may take that appears to be in the public interest based on some alignment with the market or special interest views can quickly be found to be inadequate as economic factors, interests, or views on ethical choices change. The legal system does change over time, but as the provider of stable norms it is not subject to the same dynamism and thus is not a source of uncertainty for rule followers.

Assessing the effectiveness of meta-regulation in the Australian energy markets

The previous sections in this chapter have addressed the industry experience of meta-regulation through this study. What does this experience tell us about the effectiveness of meta-regulation for the Australian retail energy markets? It may help to return to the core elements of meta-regulation and summarise how these played out. Table 7.1 is repeated from Chapter 4, but with an additional (shaded) column which summarises the findings.

Table 7.1 confirms that the Australian retail energy regulatory environment demonstrated all the characteristics of meta-regulation as I have defined it. The components of the meta-regulatory machinery were thus in place. Was this enough? The answer must surely be 'no'. Not only is it logical to judge a programme by its *outcomes*, or effects upon a problem, but the shaded column in Table 7.1 gives us evidence that the outcomes identified here require closer scrutiny (which was of course the premise for this book).

So what are ideal or even acceptable outcomes according to the meta-regulatory canon? How *do* we assess the events discussed in this book? The problem we encounter is that the meta-regulatory canon does not provide clear guidance about ultimate objectives, and where it does, objectives may not be practically observable. Of course, this is not limited to meta-regulation: measuring the success (or failure) of regulation is already challenging (Hawkins, 2002; Baldwin and Black, 2008; Sparrow, 2008). However, the challenge of assessing success is increased where there are multiple regulators, such as the additional parties brought in by meta-regulation (Van der Meer and Edelenbos, 2006).

In his writing on environmental meta-regulation, and consistent with the broader regulatory literature, Gunningham (1998: 26) suggests measures of regulatory success include *effectiveness* (contributing to improving the environment), *efficiency* (minimum cost, administrative simplicity) and *equity* (fairness in burden sharing, also includes political acceptability, meaning liberty, transparency and accountability).[13] These are eminently sensible from a theoretical standpoint, and perhaps also in practice where the regulatory space is simple and uncontroversial. However, these measures are difficult to apply meaningfully to

Table 7.1 Effectiveness of meta-regulation in the Australian retail energy markets

Core elements of meta-regulation	How these were demonstrated in the retail energy markets	Effectiveness as observed
i Formal rules are based on principles, not prescription.	The regulatory frameworks used principles and set out processes. Outcomes were not prescribed.	The lack of prescribed (and proscribed) outcomes was not seen as acceptable by many stakeholders. Processes became highly regulated.
ii Law is reflexive and responsive.	If we take the law as the regulators, they were reflexive and responsive: regulation and its interpretation were regularly assessed and reconsidered in light of compliance outcomes as well as stakeholder concerns.	Regulators seemed constantly concerned about the market but did not often develop a deep or shared understanding; responsiveness tended towards political behaviour.
iii Third parties such as non-government organisations and activists support regulation by acting as 'civil regulators', via	Larger retailers had customer consultative committees, and many retailers also developed informal relationships with consumer advocacy organisations.	Retailer relationships with consumer advocacy organisations did not seem to add value to either group in any general sense. Retailers tended to quarantine relationship management to their external affairs functions.

• consultation for policy formation, to make sure that the right values are embedded in rules; and
• enforcement, in
  a monitoring, and
  b using reputation in markets to force industry self-reflection and culture change.
	The regulators engaged in public consultation for regulatory development and change, including comprehensive meetings that involved all relevant stakeholders. Low-income consumer advocates were particularly represented in regulatory consultation. The advocates also regularly published reports about retailer performance (outcomes); most were taken up by the media in some form.	Consultation never ceased; it was not good enough for any party unless and until their own values were codified.
		
		No agreement on what was even compliant behaviour.
		
		Reputation also seemed to not be a meaningful regulatory tool.

iv	Business self-regulates within the above context (and is also reflexive and responsive).	Energy retailers self-reported breaches as below; they were proactive in identifying issues. Compliance was generally found to be high. Energy retailers existed in a competitive retail market with high consumer switching rates.	No apparent problems found with self-reporting, but there was stakeholder concern about the degree to which the market effectively sent messages to retailers about consumer needs and values.
v	Transparency in business performance is promoted, specifically compliance and performance reporting (both self-reporting and regulatory reporting) to provide for industry self-reflection under (iii) above, and third parties to have information to act upon under (iv) above.	The retail energy businesses self-reported compliance breaches and reported on performance indicators. Retailers were also required by regulation to periodically bring in external auditors to audit on set criteria. Auditors' reports were also provided to the regulators, and reported on publicly.	No apparent issues with transparency of corporate information.

216 *Rethinking meta-regulation*

the complex and contested consumer protection regime in the Australian retail energy markets. We could argue that the regulatory regime was effective because it did provide consumer protections, but were these the right protections at the right time for the right consumers? Certainly many consumer advocates still did not find the regulatory regime to be adequate, and the energy retailers argued that it stifled innovation. The regulators seemed generally unsure. Efficiency is also difficult to prove, with the retailers arguing that regulatory financial and resource costs were needlessly burdensome. These costs may have been appropriate, but with no direct link to consumer outcomes it is hard to prove efficiency either way. Equity was the most challenging measure, with significant conflict between stakeholders about each element addressed by Gunningham. There was strong disagreement about fairness in burden sharing, as well as the degree to which regulatory outcomes promoted liberty, transparency and accountability.

Gunningham notes that no assessment of successful regulation is value-free, and that effectiveness and efficiency may not always sit easily with equity. I agree with this but think the criteria as proposed are *particularly* open-ended, both in terms of the detailed problem-solving they leave to others in identifying details and trading off competing concepts, and in their operation across time.[14] For example, in what industry *could* it be proved that a regulatory approach was least cost, or that it fairly shared the burden across all parties? What about future parties who we do not yet know about but who may bear the costs of today? Also, isn't regulation about depriving some people and organisations of their liberty to act as they want? What is the reasonable trade-off between liberty and restriction? Further, how transparent does corporate information need to be while maintaining reasonable commercial confidentiality? (And what is reasonable?)

I suggest that we should also consider some more immediate measures of meta-regulation for assessing the retail energy regulatory regime, where these are linked to the specific claims of meta-regulation itself. The theory is ambitious about improving corporate morality and stakeholder satisfaction, and so these should be tested explicitly (despite their exhibiting the same ambiguity regarding value and temporal judgements as the measures above). Compliance outcomes also warrant further exploration, as does a comparison of meta-regulatory limitations against the criticisms most often aimed at command and control regulation.

Meta-regulatory outcomes

As a start, if we were to be true to the normative intent of much of the meta-regulatory literature then some change in *corporate morality* would need to occur as a result of meta-regulation if it were to be considered effective. However, applying the lens of morality does not help us to understand and explain the outcomes described in this book. There was no objective basis from which to judge organisational morality and attribute virtue or vice. None of the organisations in this research was inherently or observably 'good' or 'bad' (including those who breached their compliance obligations),[15] and none of the

Rethinking meta-regulation   217

debates discussed in this book were able to clarify unambiguously what the public interest might be for any topic discussed. Judgements on morality depended on who was doing the judging at certain points in time. Morality was not transcendental; it provided no access to deeper truth about right and wrong and had no capacity to unite different perspectives. Instead, this research showed that morality created *negative* effects within the regulatory environment. The liberal use of moral proclamations in consultations and the media inflamed conflict, distracted from the issues that *could* be resolved, and damaged the trust between stakeholders. Some degree of morality in society is unavoidable, and is also necessary. It does not escape me that I could also be considered to be making moral statements about the use of morality. However, it has been said that morality in large doses can be dangerous and should be handled carefully (Moeller, 2009, referencing Luhmann). The large doses of morality in the energy industry – and particularly the low-income consumer advocate focus on the assumed immorality of the private sector – were not helpful in improving policy and regulation.

We should also recognise that even if the public interest was clear and it was possible to design better corporate morality (and I do not believe it is), it would not be able to be observed. As I noted in Chapter 1, effective meta-regulation that causes a business to internalise previously external values will by definition be presented by the business as a sensible corporate decision taken on its own terms. This could not be reasonably challenged because no one can stand outside the societal or organisational systems and claim to observe cause and effect in an objective sense. Further, meta-regulation in the sense of genuine culture change would take years to be effective, and, as such, potential causes for effects would be increasingly remote and difficult to argue.

The next proxy for meta-regulation's effectiveness in practice could be the acceptability of outcomes to the stakeholders involved in regulation. Meta-regulation thus 'works' where stakeholders are happy with the performance outcomes of the regulated businesses. I raise this possibility given that the principles of third party stakeholder inclusion and potential stakeholder anti-market/business activism (which would occur where activists' needs are not met) are defining features of meta-regulation compared with traditional command and control approaches.[16] If we were to measure the effectiveness of the regulatory approach by observing stakeholder happiness, the question is then: *which stakeholders and at what point in time?* This study has shown that for the energy industry these were difficult questions to answer. It was not possible to please everyone at the one time, even when stakeholder organisations shared broad values. As discussed in Chapter 5, some low-income consumer advocacy groups supported consumer disconnection for non-payment of a bill because disconnection might encourage a customer to seek help and it would also stop debt from growing. Other low-income advocates believed that no one should be disconnected when they could not pay. Each group had a moral argument to support it, depending on the values of the observer. Who would have been justified to inflict reputational damage (should such a thing be possible)?[17] We could argue that the

218 *Rethinking meta-regulation*

market itself would determine this; consumers would act according to their values. However, while this seems reasonable, it does not help us understand whether the machinery of meta-regulation is working as intended. If the community does not respond to activism, is it because it does not share activists' views (which would not by itself suggest meta-regulation isn't working), or it is because it *cannot* respond because of some undesirable constraint in the meta-regulatory machinery? Who would we believe if we asked, and what policy measures could be put into place to ensure the 'right' values were met through meta-regulation? We again find that subjective states of morality and entitlement cannot assist in determining whether regulation is achieving what was intended on any objective basis. My own experience was that subjective views of 'what was intended' could not even be reconciled, with parties recalibrating the past to match their perspective of what they thought *should* have happened. While this does not mean that third party or activist stakeholder views are not relevant, it does mean that these views cannot be the primary means of assessing the effectiveness of regulation if we are looking for objective measures of success.

Of course, no metrics of success appear perfect in complex meta-regulatory cases, and objectivity may be an impossible measure under any circumstance. Systems theory would suggest this is the case as well: there is only ever one's own interpretation of reality rather than a 'truth' that is objectively out there. It is therefore reasonable that some scholars might consider stakeholder views to be vital to meta-regulatory success despite the problems encountered. I do not take issue with this. However, if this is the approach adopted, the role of politics should be acknowledged, particularly if it is acceptable for communications to businesses to be via political channels rather than through the market. The theory needs to reveal and explain the political process that may be set in motion as a form of regulation, as well as noting the political contingency in outcomes. The current void in the meta-regulatory literature regarding politics and the role for government needs to be filled.

There may also be a useful future research direction regarding the difference between political and market-based 'social licence' influences and where these have the greatest effect on corporate outcomes. My research found the social licence held little value in the energy consumer protection regulatory space, at least insofar as we construct the social licence as a market response to corporate social performance. Other research has found the social licence concept to be meaningful in environmental cases (albeit constrained by the economic licence), with grassroots community activists and local communities perceived by business to exert real power in the *political* sphere (Gunningham, Kagan and Thornton, 2003; see also Haines, 2009). I could have written a completely different book about this even within the energy industry; the politics about the extraction of coal seam gas ran very high during the research period. However, coal seam gas as a social licence topic was never about the market and consumers making different product choices; it was about locally affected voters making representations to their local Members of Parliament.[18] The meta-regulatory research programme could differentiate between these types of social movement and focus on the required salience of an issue for consumers or the community to take action. It would seem logical that the threshold for consumer action is much lower when it relates to a person's perceived personal loss instead of a broader social responsibility; this is perhaps where reputation has more of a role to play in business regulation.

The third and final measure of regulatory success or failure is the view of the responsible regulator (or regulators) about business compliance outcomes, and specifically the frequency and materiality of compliance breaches. This is arguably the best measure, and is also a version of harm as proposed by Sparrow (2008) and of Gunningham's (1998) notion of regime effectiveness. My version of compliance breach is focused more on technical breaches of existing rules and according to the entity officially tasked with enforcement. This traditional position has value because it avoids the contested nature of compliance based on stakeholder moral positions. Regulatory agencies are the entities that are explicitly accountable (even under meta-regulation) and therefore incentivised to design and enforce regulatory programmes that result in public benefit. The approach runs the risk of relying on potentially self-seeking or incompetent regulatory agencies, but this is unavoidable. The legal and political systems at least have a broader role to play in mitigating this risk: the legal system in the event of appeals and court cases, and the political system where government exercises oversight of regulatory agencies and is also in turn held to account by voters.

When observing the meta-regulation of the Australian retail energy markets through the lens of corporate compliance (in the view of the regulators, who I believe were generally competent), the positive compliance outcomes might indicate that meta-regulation was successful. But is this a logical conclusion? To take this perspective means ignoring the finding that the industry was *not* enabled and incentivised to self-regulate to meet the public interest as expected by normative meta-regulatory theory. The underlying findings that (a) third parties such as consumer advocacy organisations had little effect on retailers' operations, and (b) the market sent no messages to retailers about consumer social values, indicate that the machinery of meta-regulation did not work as intended. Business compliance may have been unrelated to the fact that the regulatory regime had the hallmarks of meta-regulation. We certainly do not have any evidence that the markets or third party involvement enhanced compliance. Retailer reporting and self-regulation may have positively influenced compliance, but this is only my feeling based on personal experience.

This does not weaken the point that compliance outcomes (or harms) are all we can observe to form a view about the effectiveness of regulation, in whatever form regulation takes and in whichever timeframe. We have seen that to this point in time the Australian retail energy industry has been largely compliant, which might indicate that something is working for now. But I am saying that we cannot attribute this to meta-regulation in its current form. If we were to do so, we would need some evidence that the machinery of meta-regulation played a meaningful role. The compliance we saw was perhaps more related to the

220   *Rethinking meta-regulation*

command and control threats that lay beneath the veneer of meta-regulatory flexibility. I return to this in the next section.

As a final point on compliance, it is possible that some scholars may argue that regulatory programme success could lie not only in general compliance but also in an absence of significant or scandalous breaches. I raise this possibility given that many scholars seem to consider tragedy and scandal as clearly demonstrating regulatory failure, whether self- or state-based. The absence of scandal might lead to the assumption that the reputation mechanism is working in a preventative sense where the meta-regulatory machinery is in place. However, an absence of scandal seems to be a very low threshold for claiming success, as well as creating a problem for meaningful measurement. (Is regulation considered effective until something bad happens? How do we view the self-regulatory capability of a business the day after a scandal compared with the day before?) A scandal is also not necessarily a demonstration of a failed regulatory approach, despite post-scandal narratives that reinterpret the past in this way. In practice, major breaches can arise from a coincidence of many small decisions within a business, and good or bad luck plays a role in how (or whether) harm eventuates. Breaches need to be observed and identified, whether within the affected business or externally, and the stories we hear about major breaches often also report the many near misses that no one would otherwise have known about. A major breach turning into a scandal is also a rare and chaotic event that depends on windows aligning across industry, non-government organisations, the news media, consumers and the community in general. Of course there are disasters where the transformation from breach into scandal does not matter; where the harm was clear and public, and scandal was expected. The Union Carbide gas leak in Bhopal and the BP Deepwater Horizon oil spill readily come to mind as examples. However, and fortunately, these kinds of terrible accidents happen so infrequently that they are the exception rather than the rule. For these reasons, I consider the 'example by scandal' approach to be highly problematic for prescribing regulatory values and processes or as a means for understanding regulatory programme success.

A comparison with command and control regulation

At the start of this book I noted that the Australian policymakers did not explicitly aim to develop a meta-regulatory framework for the energy retail sector, and that they did not reference regulatory theory. There was no debate about whether to pursue command and control regulation or meta-regulation. Instead, meta-regulation developed naturally, albeit in an environment that already supported market principles. A further reason for this, but one we can only really construct in hindsight, is that retail energy minimum standards were not amenable to precise codification. Unlike command and control regulation for the environment where environmental protection agencies arrive at figures for pollution types that businesses must not exceed, there was no corollary for energy retail compliance, such as maximum disconnection figures. Prescribing these

Rethinking meta-regulation 221

types of business behaviour may have been technically possible but was never seen as logical, as discussed in Chapter 5. This meant that the obvious alternative was a meta-regulatory focus on principles and process, which brought problems of its own. A lack of codification on the statistics that stakeholders valued meant that the issues were constantly debated and the focus was on subjective perceptions of performance rather than compliance. The spectre of command and control continued to lurk; governments and regulators may not have enacted the 'command' in the form of precise maxima or minima but the need to be seen to be doing something was manifested in other ways.

Moving from the command to the control, normative meta-regulatory theory promotes the use of markets and third parties as to support regulatory resources in enforcement. This is where meta-regulation of the Australian energy market also became problematic, as stakeholder inclusion meant the introduction of political behaviour, and the public interest as a concept became increasingly blurred. Businesses responded best when breaches were converted into financial costs, such as when the retailers ceased using doorstep sales after the ACCC took them to court. However, this is difficult to claim as a meta-regulatory victory – it was not really anything other than deterrence through command and control. The normative meta-regulatory hope for markets to regulate on non-price/product (non-economic) aspects was absolutely unsupported, with questions remaining about whether the markets were even effective at regulating on customers' economic preferences.

Table 7.2 shows how meta-regulation in this research addressed the recognised flaws of command and control regulation as described in Chapter 2. It shows that the usual criticisms of command and control regulation were not removed by meta-regulation but instead morphed into other forms. The general theme is that the requirement for regulators to be increasingly political brought its own problems of resource drain, risk of regulatory capture by *more* interests, and increased complexity and uncertainty.

What can we make of this? At the least we can see that meta-regulation brings its own problems, which may or may not be preferable to the problems experienced with command and control regulation. We are left with a discomforting but unsurprising conclusion: both meta-regulation and command and control regulation have their drawbacks, and these drawbacks may be impossible to eliminate. My own view is that we *cannot* eliminate the drawbacks because to do so would imply a control that no entity or system possesses. As closed systems, politics, law and the economy will continue to reproduce themselves on their own terms, as will the organisations that reference them. The notion of telling or coercing a government to be less political is nonsense, as is the notion of telling a commercial business to place less value on profits. This is not to say that there is not more we can do as observers of regulation. At the least, we can adjust our expectations, which should then be reflected in more meaningful theories of, and prescriptions for, regulation, particularly meta-regulation.

222 *Rethinking meta-regulation*

Table 7.2 Command and control versus meta-regulation

Recognised flaws of command and control regulation	*How the flaws are dealt with under meta-regulation*
Informational requirements of regulators are very high.	Informational requirements of regulators to manage compliance in a day-to-day sense are reduced but the inclusion of more views and the political cycle speeds up the need for the regulator to review issues and be seen to respond. Public reporting is also a drain on regulatory resources.
Need for a close relationship between regulator and regulated business makes the regulator vulnerable to manipulation. 'Regulatory capture' where regulation itself is seen as a commodity that is traded between industry and the regulator.	The regulator remains equally vulnerable to manipulation, but now by more parties; the politics inherent in meta-regulation also exposes the regulator to a legitimacy deficit with government.
Over-abundance of unnecessarily complex and inflexible regulation.	Regulation is not limited in complexity: plural values require regulation to continue to be revisited and regulated businesses require clarification to progress. Flexibility brings uncertainty.
Loss of trust between the regulator and the regulated business. The legalistic style of command and control regulation leads to an unhelpful adversarial style.	Loss of trust between the regulator and the regulated business, where the regulator needs to be seen to be doing something and therefore acts politically. Political behaviour that undermines the market creates in industry a perception of sovereign risk.

A different perspective on meta-regulation

In this study there was no stakeholder consensus on issues and no predictably rational outcomes. Instead, politics was pervasive and everything was contingent. The study showed that the meta-regulatory approach amplified and reinforced the need for politics. This was inevitable given the inclusion of stakeholders in regulatory decision-making whose needs could never be met except through episodic and necessarily hypocritical communications from governments and regulators. On this basis, meta-regulation was a flawed concept for the complex and contested Australian energy markets. Even if one does not accept the legitimacy of my conditions for effective meta-regulation (although I ask what the alternative conditions might be), the observed outcomes of increased political pressure on regulators and unclear public interest messages to self-regulating entities would appear to be unintended and undesirable, to the point of undermining the promise of meta-regulation in the first place. Of course this is just one industry example, but I suggest that there is little reason to believe the conditions for effective meta-regulation in the normative case would be

Rethinking meta-regulation   223

better met anywhere else given the common societal and organisational elements discussed in this chapter.

The bad news is that meta-regulation may still often be the better option compared with the pure command and control alternative. The good news is that there are other ways of seeing meta-regulation, but this means revising our expectations of markets and stakeholder participation. Based on the discussion above, I propose that if meta-regulatory theory is to be of greater practical value we need to:

i   Give up the idea of designing regulation with the aim of creating corporate 'morality' and focus instead on compliance outcomes. We need to create regulation for *responsive* businesses (and really, what else is there – unresponsive businesses will be penalised and/or go out of business) and move away from subjective judgements on virtue or otherwise.
ii   Acknowledge the problems presented by complex and contested environments. Any future hope for meta-regulation in a practical sense probably needs to lie in how complexity and conflict can be *limited* more than in how they can be embraced, in order to relieve regulatory resources and provide clearer direction.
iii Question the role of the market and be more precise about what a market might achieve for a given regulatory issue. My own sense is that markets do not hold the value hoped for by normative meta-regulatory theory, at least not where reputation is to influence business behaviour in a mass market (that is, a market with mass appeal and broad coverage).

The first of these elements has already been addressed: we cannot recognise a 'moral' entity in any objective way, so the concept of morality holds no specific value.

We can flesh out the second and third elements of the proposed approach by considering some questions about a hypothetical regulatory environment, where these relate to how certain conditions exist in the regulatory space. The first set of conditions relates to how political stakeholders (governments and regulators) perceive their environment according to where it lies on two spectra: (1) high to low contest over values and meaning; and (2) high to low environmental or issues complexity. Figure 7.1 shows how regulatory behaviour may need to adjust to the different scenarios.

As Figure 7.1 shows, circumstances where there is the lowest contest over values and meaning are most amenable to regulation in the general sense. These are the shaded quadrants. These circumstances provide freedom for the regulator to act within its legal remit and be less distracted by politics, which in turn hopefully reduces the likelihood of undesirable knee-jerk regulatory actions. An environment of low contest over values and high complexity may make meta-regulation a better way to regulate than command and control regulation, where the meta-regulatory approach would make use of businesses' self-audits, and reporting (including the usual environmental/safety cases which have been found to be an effective way of managing complexity).

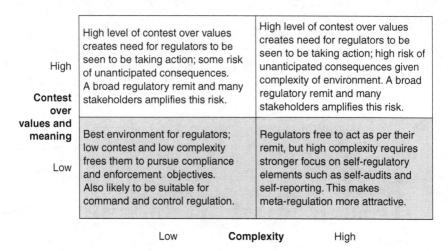

Figure 7.1 The regulatory matrix for complex and contested environments.

The worst case scenario is an environment with a high level of contest over values and meaning as well as a high level of complexity. This not only requires regulators to be seen to be doing things, but the complexity of the environment also increases the likelihood of unforeseen and unintended consequences of regulatory action for both the political system and other systems. Opening up the regulatory space to further contest through the involvement of third parties only amplifies the political pressures for the regulator and thus the risks to other systems such as law and the economy.

So what is a regulator to do when its environment falls into one of the top two quadrants? There is no easy answer; as already noted, we cannot control whether issues become political nor expect something other than political behaviour from political (or protest) organisations. We also cannot make complex issues somehow simple, other than refocusing on reducing identifiable harm, but this can still be complex and contested. However, there is an alternative to expecting regulators and/or businesses to collect and assimilate views from unaccountable and unrepresentative special interests. The New Zealand example provides some direction, and based on this I posit that when stakeholder numbers are limited in consultation (perhaps to peak bodies who have constituencies) and when these stakeholders are held accountable for outcomes in the broader interest (assuming they will agree to this, which is far from guaranteed),[19] there should be less contest and unresolved conflict. Being selective in how stakeholders are formally brought into the regulatory space means that regulators of complex and contested regimes need to be *less*, not more, responsive if they are to have some chance of avoiding the worst of these circumstances. Policymakers at the point of creating regulatory remits should also be cautioned against requiring the regulator(s) to address too many issues – once that genie is out of the bottle it may be too difficult to put it back in.

Rethinking meta-regulation   225

The next set of conditions to assess in a regulatory environment relates to the market and the reputation mechanism. The questions to be asked are as follows:[20]

i Do consumers (and other transactional stakeholders in the market) value the non-price (or product) issues that are valued by the policymaker as the subject of regulation, such as performance on social criteria or compliance? If relevant parties do not value these, then 'harnessing the market' to regulate through the reputation mechanism is unlikely to be rewarding. (The market will only be of use in this situation where non-economic issues can be translated into the currency of price by political or legal means, such as valuing externalities like environmental pollution. This has been studied comprehensively elsewhere, so there is nothing I will add here other than to raise the possibility that no market's effectiveness is set in stone, even on its own terms.)
ii If consumers (and I will refer only to consumers for the sake of convenience) *do* value the desired non-economic issues, the next question is: Do consumers have access to meaningful information about what they value, and are they likely to value those issues enough to take action? If consumers do not have the will or ability to effectively send messages about non-economic issues through the transactions in the market, the reputation mechanism is a non-starter.
iii In the event that consumers are found to sufficiently value non-economic issues *and* they are able to demonstrate their values through the marketplace, the question is then: Is business responsive to the messages received? Again, for the reputation mechanism to have some chance of effectiveness, business needs to perceive a material financial benefit or risk from its responsiveness (or lack of responsiveness) to messages received through the markets on non-economic issues.

If we have reached a point where the answer is again 'yes', then the next stage is to address the degree of contest over values and meaning and the degree of complexity in the regulatory space, but this time from the perspective of the effectiveness of the reputation mechanism. As this book has shown, complexity and contest have particular relevance for how messages about the public interest might be communicated and received by all relevant parties. Figure 7.2 shows the likelihood of the reputation mechanism being effective for high and low environmental complexity and high and low contest over values and meaning.

We can see from Figure 7.2 that the top left quadrant (shaded) represents the best environment for the reputation mechanism. This is where contest over values is high and complexity is low. As discussed above, controversy appears to be a necessary foundation for the reputation mechanism in the market. However, even as a best case scenario this is still problematic as the contest over values means there may be a range of conflicting interpretations (and potential misrepresentations) about what is good and bad. This means that there is unlikely to be a clear and singular 'public interest' value to communicate to consumers

Contest over values and meaning	Low complexity	High complexity
High	Necessary controversy to attract attention but this also means that the stakes are high and messages to stakeholders are likely to be inconsistent. However, low complexity means messages clearer (albeit plural).	Necessary controversy to attract attention but this also means that the stakes are high and messages to stakeholders are likely to be inconsistent. High complexity amplifies problem of getting clear messages out.
Low	Low contest may mean insufficient controversy to attract attention; however, this at least means any messages have greater chance of being clear. This is assisted by low complexity.	Low contest may mean insufficient controversy to attract attention. While this means any messages have greater chance of being clear, clarity of messaging may be offset by high complexity.

Figure 7.2 The reputation matrix for complex and contested environments.

(and of course consumers would not necessarily share values either). The benefit of a simpler environment (low complexity) should at least mean that there is a lower likelihood of consumer confusion, even though there are plural values. The more complex the environment is, the more likely it is that messages sent from third parties and via the media to consumers and other transactional stakeholders will be unclear and thus too hard to grasp.

Linked to the previous discussion on scandals and their contingent and exceptional nature, we might also ask how often consumers could be relied upon to act *even when the circumstances are favourable.* Surely regular boycott action is unlikely: the mass media system is quick to move on from an issue, as are consumers, who may well suffer from controversy-fatigue. It is plausible that meaningful 'social licence' reputation effects in an enforcement sense would only occur as (or less) frequently as formal regulatory action at the top of the enforcement pyramid, such as actual (legal) licence suspension or revocation (see Ayres and Braithwaite, 1992). This might also explain why examples of the effectiveness of the reputation mechanism in the meta-regulatory literature are generally found in the same set of case studies.

In conclusion, the market reputation mechanism is unpromising as a regulatory tool. The paradox that it requires conflict and passion to animate it, but that these also distort its performance, seems unable to be resolved. In any event, there is substantial evidence that consumers in general do *not* value non-economic outcomes other than at the highest level of scandal, and so any reliance on reputation would be limited from the outset. This leaves the regulator as the primary means of giving businesses direction about self-regulation within a meta-regulatory environment. As already discussed, it will be best able to do this where it is not expected to also respond to and satisfy a large number of competing and unaccountable stakeholder needs.

Some final thoughts

Much of the meta-regulatory scholarly literature proposes that meta-regulation is an efficient and effective response to the problems encountered by command and control regulation. However, this claim has been made with little to no assessment of the regulatory costs and side effects of meta-regulation itself. An analysis of the meta-regulatory machinery and its effectiveness *on its own terms* has been neglected by theory and research to date, which would seem to be a major failing.

This book has shown that meta-regulation creates its own problems when the regulatory environment is complex and contested. However, we can still go further than this: meta-regulation in complex and contested environments can be seen to fundamentally bring command and control regulation back into play. This occurs through the need for stakeholder conflict to be managed by politics, where the political system then applies power to be seen to be in control. This selective form of command and control regulation specifically undermines the concept of 'responsive' regulation as it was intended (including use of market mechanisms), creating instead *responsive politicisation of regulatory issues, on the terms of the political system*. As noted above, this may be *more* onerous for regulators and stakeholders compared to the old-fashioned version of command and control regulation reflecting intimate regulatory involvement in business operations.

This book has also shown that objectively assigning moral values to businesses and their stakeholders is fraught with difficulty. The notions of virtue and vice were largely meaningless in the energy sector; 'good' and 'bad' were mostly subjective terms used by entities to label themselves and others. This outcome is not isolated: we have only to be reminded of Reich's (2008) examples and the Brent Spar case discussed in Chapter 2. The conclusion to be drawn from this is that scholars should be less accepting of moralistic stereotypes, and particularly the salvationist mindset that assumes businesses will always become objectively better from meeting the demands of third parties such as activists. My own moral position is that open and meaningful sociological enquiry should not tolerate such naïve prejudices.

I have argued that the inability to identify entities as good or bad arises from the plural versions of the public interest – that is, what is good for society. Society is complex, with competing perspectives unable to be reconciled across functional and organisational system boundaries. Luhmann says that systems are operationally closed, meaning that they do not have direct inputs and outputs to one another, they cannot steer one another, and they do not share perceptions of events or time. This concept complicates regulatory theory and is a specific problem for meta-regulation, which relies on achieving consensus and ignores any impediments to this.

Whether or not one wants to accept the full ramifications of Luhmann's theory, I suggest the academy must still evolve its position if the meta-regulatory approach is to have practical value. A recalibrated theory and research

228 *Rethinking meta-regulation*

programme that engages with the issues raised here is likely to be more useful to practitioners than wishful thinking about applying societal control to enforce a particular version of corporate morality. To this end, I have provided some ideas about how meta-regulation could work better with the grain of modern society. Naturally, I do not have a solution to the apparent problems of inter-system communications.[21] Contingency in the face of complexity will also continue to disrupt the best laid plans. There is no guarantee that outcomes from this version of meta-regulation will meet any one conception of the public interest, that politics will not still run rampant, or that regulated businesses will be inclined to internalise the values of others. Measuring regulatory 'success' will also be limited to assessments of material known compliance breaches at a given point in time. However, these outcomes are perhaps the most we can reasonably hope for.

Notes

1 As an aside, being seen to do something had the most value when it was about holding someone else to account. Chapter 5 discussed government intervention in hardship debates to hold businesses to account; in this case the energy retailers were an easy target for action and this helped avoid a focus on the (in)adequacy of government support. In contrast, the market issues addressed in Chapter 6 were harder to define and pin to any one stakeholder. Being seen to do something in this environment was far riskier for governments given the higher possibility of unintended consequences (such as market failures) that could have political costs. In these circumstances governments were more careful; the most that could be done was to choose to not see problems and, when pushed, pass problems to the regulator or other entity to undertake a review.

2 Social activism is an important element of the machinery of meta-regulation, but this is not as a political process; activism is primarily intended for activists to communicate with consumers in the market.

3 See also Littlechild (2014), where he describes the UK regulatory environment in some detail and suggests Ofgem made its decisions in order to be seen to be doing something.

4 Unless we choose to see these behaviour changes as a responsible and logical regulatory reaction to legitimate community values. I hope that by this stage of this book this is not the automatic response of readers.

5 We should also consider whether this kind of political environment affected regulators' focus on compliance enforcement; being pulled in so many directions was surely a distraction.

6 The Authority's statutory objective was to 'promote competition in, reliable supply by, and the efficient operation of, the electricity industry for the long-term benefit of consumers' (section 21, *Electricity Industry Act*, 2010).

7 For example, the Retail Advisory Group's Terms of Reference required the Group to 'reconcile divergent views and interests in ways consistent with the Authority's statutory objective and in a manner that achieves wider stakeholder "buy in"' (Electricity Authority, 2013b: 4).

8 This was as advised to me by senior leaders of the Authority in early 2014 and was supported by public stakeholder views (Electricity Authority, 2013a).

9 As discussed earlier in this chapter, where risk is a result of one's own decisions in an uncertain environment, and so is potentially controllable, and danger is the result of others' decisions.

Rethinking meta-regulation 229

10 This includes where retailers had consultative committees, but these were not widespread and even where they existed their value was unclear.

11 I note that Haines (2009: 411) suggests that the fact that businesses need to manage 'risks to their legitimacy' from communities (under meta-regulatory styles of regulation) makes them *political organisations* as defined by Brunsson. I do not agree with Haines's characterisation: in my view, businesses are clearly action organisations. And this is where the problem lies: businesses are expected to be political when they are not.

12 We can see a similarity here between organisational decision-making and individual decision-making as per behavioural economics. Recall that behavioural economics addresses the 'choice architecture' of decision-making, and the hard paternalist strand even reduces the number of options in a choice decision.

13 Effectiveness and efficiency are the pre-eminent criteria for Gunningham (1998: 27), with the view that these will tend to be the primary concerns of policymakers. There is no further discussion of equity other than an acknowledgement that it would be at the top of *others'* lists, such as proponents of environmental justice.

14 Gunningham (1998: 29) acknowledges this to some degree, saying that the 'complex normative dilemmas' and arguments about measurement timeframes may be avoided by 'putting ourselves in the position of policy advisers' to support any given policymaker with its *own* defined policy goals. In my view this may be over-stating the capacity of policymakers, particularly in a meta-regulatory environment.

15 Recall from Chapter 4 that compliance breaches were often because of IT issues and call centre staff saying the wrong thing, or not saying enough. It is hard to consider a large and complex organisation to be 'immoral' on the basis of the types of breaches in evidence. The door-to-door sales area is a little less clear but I stand by my view that the entities that used this channel were not immoral, even when found to be in breach.

16 As I have argued already, the normative meta-regulatory concept of activism to effect reputational damage implicitly considers that: (a) material reputational damage *can* be effected through the mechanism; (b) activists' values are right and reputational damage is a reasonable 'enforcement' measure to take; and (c) reputational damage will cease once activists' needs are met. If we put aside my own findings and assume for the moment that (a) and (b) are true, then (c) is inevitable if meta-regulation is to serve a meaningful purpose. If this were not the case, then meta-regulation would not be *regulation* but mere vandalism of corporate brands.

17 When I worked at the regulator's office in 1999–2002 the common internal view was that one was doing a good job in setting regulatory policy if everyone was equally *unhappy* with regulatory decisions (assuming the legitimacy of the regulator was not in question); this at least meant that policy did not unfairly favour any party. This concept becomes problematic for state regulators in political environments who also need to show they are 'doing something' to satisfy politically influential stakeholders. It becomes impossible when applied to *self*-regulation within the normative meta-regulatory model, as stakeholder unhappiness is implicitly endorsed as a reason for unaccountable organisations to inflict punishment in the market as they see fit.

18 It is useful to note that this kind of action could lead to market losses, perhaps with employees or partners withdrawing support from businesses in affected communities. However, I do not think this should be confused with the broader, financially damaging market outcomes from consumer boycotts that the normative meta-regulatory literature tends to focus on.

19 As discussed in Chapter 2, stakeholders may not want this accountability. My research confirmed this was broadly the case for the Australian energy industry.

20 These reflect a shorter version of the criteria I have already outlined in this chapter and in Chapter 2 because I am not trying to establish where reputation *will* work but the basic conditions where it *might* work. The conditions also need to be observable by a policymaker, which naturally reduces their number.

230   Rethinking meta-regulation

21 I say 'apparent' because a systems theorist would not consider operational closure to be a problem; it is operational closure that provides for a system to operate in the first place, and system development has been a natural evolution to manage societal complexity.

References

Ayres, I. and Braithwaite, J. (1992) *Responsive regulation: transcending the deregulation debate*, Oxford University Press: Oxford.

Baldwin, R. and Black, J. (2008) 'Really responsive regulation', *The Modern Law Review*, vol. 71, no. 1, pp. 59–94.

Black, J. (2010) 'The role of risk in regulatory processes', in R. Baldwin, M. Cave and M. Lodge (eds) *The Oxford handbook of regulation*, Oxford University Press: Oxford, pp. 302–348.

Brunsson, N. (2003) *The organization of hypocrisy: talk, decisions and actions in organizations*, second edition, trans. N. Adler, Copenhagen Business School Press: Herndon.

Brunsson, N. (2006) *Mechanisms of hope: maintaining the dream of the rational organization*, Copenhagen Business School Press: Liber.

Brunsson, N. (2007) *The consequences of decision-making*, Oxford University Press: Oxford.

Czarniawska, B. (2005) 'On Gorgon sisters: organizational action in the face of paradox', in D. Seidl and K.H. Becker (eds) *Niklas Luhmann and organization studies*, Advances in Organization Studies, Volume 14, Liber: Copenhagen, pp. 127–142.

Electricity Authority, New Zealand (2013a) *Review of advisory group administrative arrangements: summary of submissions*, 18 June.

Electricity Authority, New Zealand (2013b) *Terms of reference for the Retail Advisory Group*, 791315–1.

Gunningham, N. (1998) 'Introduction', in N. Gunningham, P. Grabosky and D. Sinclair (eds) *Smart regulation: designing environmental policy*, Clarendon Press: Oxford, pp. 3–36.

Gunningham, N., Kagan, R.A. and Thornton, D. (2003) *Shades of green: business, regulation, and environment*, Stanford University Press: Stanford.

Haines, F. (2009) 'Vanquishing the enemy or civilizing the neighbour? Controlling the risks from hazardous industries', *Social and Legal Studies*, vol. 18, no. 3, pp. 397–415.

Hawkins, K. (2002) *Law as last resort: prosecution decision-making in a regulatory agency*, Oxford University Press: Oxford.

Hayek, F.A. (1979) *Law, legislation and liberty. Volume 3: the political order of a free people*, Routledge & Kegan Paul: London.

Heanzle, M. (2010) *Uncertainty in policy making: values and evidence in complex decisions*, Earthscan: London.

Hutter, B. and Power, M. (2005) 'Organizational encounters with risk: an introduction', in B. Hutter, and M. Power (eds) *Organizational encounters with risk*, Cambridge University Press: Cambridge, pp. 1–32.

King, M. and Thornhill, C.J. (2003) *Niklas Luhmann's theory of politics and law*, Palgrave Macmillan: Basingstoke.

Littlechild, S. (2014) *Promoting or restricting competition? Regulation of the UK retail residential energy market since 2008*, response to the Competition and Markets Authority's Statement of Issues, 15 August.

Littlechild, S. (2016) *The CMA energy market investigation, the well-functioning market, Ofgem, Government and behavioural economics*, submission to the Competition and Markets Authority, 8 February.

Luhmann, N. (1988) 'The self-reproduction of law and its limits', in G. Teubner (ed.) *Dilemmas of law in the welfare state*, Walter de Gruyter: New York, pp. 111–127.

Luhmann, N. (1989) *Ecological communication*, trans. J. Bednarz, Jr., University of Chicago Press: Chicago.

Luhmann, N. (2002) *Risk: a sociological theory*, trans. R. Barrett, Introduction: N. Stehr and G. Bechmann, Aldine Transaction: New Jersey.

Luhmann, N. (2005) 'The paradox of decision making', in D. Seidl and K.H. Becker (eds) *Niklas Luhmann and organization studies*, Advances in Organization Studies, Volume 14, Liber: Copenhagen, pp. 85–106.

Moeller, H.-G. (2009) *The moral fool: a case for amorality*, Columbia University Press: New York.

Osborne, E. (2009) *The rise of the anti-corporate movement: corporations and the people who hate them*, Stanford University Press: Stanford.

Pagnamenta, R. (2009) 'Privatisation expert George Yarrow attacks Ofgem for "failing to protect consumers" ', *The Times*, 8 October.

Renner, M. (2011) 'Death by complexity', in P.F. Kjaer, G. Teubner and A. Febbrajo (eds) *The financial crisis in constitutional perspective: the dark side of functional differentiation*, Hart Publishing: Oxford, pp. 93–111.

Sparrow, M. (2008) *The character of harms: operational challenges in control*, Cambridge University Press: Cambridge.

Van der Meer, F.-B. and Edelenbos, J. (2006) Evaluation in multi-actor policy processes: accountability, learning and co-operation, *Evaluation*, April, 12, pp. 201–218.

Weick, K. (2001) *Making sense of the organization*, Blackwell Publishing: Malden.

Yarrow, G. (2014) *Energy market investigation: response to the CMA's Statement of Issues*, August.

Index

Page numbers in *italics* denote tables, those in **bold** denote figures.

AGL: 2005 Hardship Inquiry submission 131–2; anti-doorknocking statement 185–6; ceased door-to-door sales 184; court cases for door-to-door sales 183–4; customer acquisition approach 185, 191n20; incumbent retailer 79; South Australian court case 98, 170; voluntary hardship programme 145–6

AGL research: consumer advocate contract recommendations 173, 190n15; hardship programme demographics 87; political risk 190n12; prices 166–7

Ariely, D. 44, 158

Australian Bureau of Statistics 86, 111n5

Australian Capital Territory: adopted NECF 96; competition 155, 189n1; NEM 11, 111n1, 112n13

Australian Competition and Consumer Commission (ACCC): EAL consultation 178–81, 182; energy retailer court cases 183–4

Australian Consumer Law 178, 189n3

Australian Energy Market Commission (AEMC): behavioural economics 176, 190n16; competition assessments 155–6, 160, 165; engagement blueprint 174–7; Power of Choice review 172

Australian Energy Regulator (AER): consultation on performance guidelines 143; Energy Made Easy 175–7; funding issue for enforcement of Victorian NECF 97–8; hardship guidance 148; role under NECF 12, 95, 201

Ayres, I. 1, 2, 5, 10, 14, 17n6, 23, 43, 81, 150, 226

Baldwin, R. 1, 4, 13, 27–8, 43, 74, 213

Banerjee, S.B. 41

Bardach, E. 1–2, 74

Bauknecht, D. 24, 26

behavioural economics: AEMC use of 176, 190n16; definition of 44, 158–61; foundations in consumer protections 159; implications for decision-making 204, 229n12; implications for policy 176; perspective taking 88; retailer exploitation of biases 161, 163–4; UK Ofgem approach 159, 167, 201

Ben-David, R. 144, 165–6

bills: affordability 115, 135; low customer engagement 135; political messaging 96–7, 171; smart meter charge 100–1; system errors 81; *see also* payment plans

Black, J. 21, 43, 50n12, 109, 149, 198, 213

blind spot: consumer 160; retailer 105, 209; systems theory definition 9

Borch, C. 8, 17n9

Braithwaite, J. 1–3, 5, 10, 14, 17n6, 23, 26, 43, 49n4, 81, 150, 226

Brent Spar 32–7, 227

Brunsson, N. 29, 44, 51n24, 149, 196, 199–200, 209, 229n11

Campbell, K. 42

capacity to pay: AER guidance 148; concerns about interpretation 128–9, 140, 147; ESC view 129, 144, 147, 150; EWOV view 137–8; late payment fee application 117; Lumo wrongful disconnection case 137–8; means of assessment 70; no disconnection for incapacity 123, 129; Retail Code requirement 116, 128, 147; TRUenergy view 132–3, 146

Index 233

carbon pricing mechanism 82, **84**, 96, 99, 171
Carroll, A.B. 21, 24
Cave, M. 1, 4
certification schemes 21, 49n1
civil regulation 3, 32, 34, 49n1
Coglianese, C. 2, 17n4, 21, 23
command and control regulation: comparison with meta-regulatory outcomes 221, *222*; criticisms of 1, *222*; political version 227; rational actor 23
Committee for Melbourne 124
Committee of Inquiry into Financial Hardship of Energy Consumers 125–7, 134–6
communicative possibilities 7, 24; *see also* meta-regulation, machinery of
Community Service Obligations (CSOs) 134
competition: assessments of 73, **84**, 155–6, 173; concerns about 157–7, 187; *see also* consumer/customer switching statistics; full retail competition
Competition and Markets Authority, UK (CMA): as political 202; divisions between regulators 167; finding on sticky customers 190n14, 191n23; review of UK market 160, 167; stakeholder views of Ofgem 160, 167, 189n2, 201
compliance: contested nature of 140–1; door-to-door sales channel 157, 162–4; outcomes 12, 79–81; reporting 80–2, 140–2
Conley, J.M. 31, 37, 51n21
consensus: meta-consensus on Retail Code outcome 65, 75, 149; meta-regulatory assumption of 4–6, 25–6, 39, 45, *46*; no consensus 8, 34, 74–5, 78, 108, 154, 187, 189, 196, 199, 204; *see also* public interest
Consumer Action Law Centre (CALC) 162, 166, 179, 181, 191n21; *see also* Consumer Law Centre Victoria
consumer advocates **26**; different perspectives within sector 68–9, 117, 140, 151; involvement in creation of Retail Code 67–8; *see also* low-income consumer advocates; vulnerable consumers
Consumer Law Centre Victoria 117, 128, 179; *see also* Consumer Action Law Centre (CALC)
consumer protection: definition 12, 58;

prior to Retail Code 59; public interest goals 13–14; *see also* precautionary principle; price regulation; Retail Code; standing offer contract
Consumer Utilities Advocacy Centre (CUAC) 69, 117, 128–30, 162, 178–9, 181
consumer/customer **26**; boycotts 4, 22, 32–3, 37, 39, 102, 226; capacity to act on reliable information 94–5, 110, 196, 208; competition engagement blueprint 174; concern about door-to-door sales 184, 186, 188, 191n21; definition 18n11; engagement on bills 117, 135, 151; engagement on compliance reporting 142; inertia 174–5; rationality 88, 160–1, 175–6, 186, 196, 206; stickiness 157–9, 161, 176, 188; switching statistics 155–7, 186–7; views on price 156, 175; *see also* hardship; vulnerable customers
contingency/contingent outcomes: decisions and events 78, 93, 103, 107, 109, 169, 182, 187, 222; definition 10, 111n3; ethical consumerism 41; 'good' regulation 150; government response to lobbying 91, 108; NECF 95–9; news reportage 94; observations of socially responsible behaviour 45; price deregulation 169, 187; Queensland Premier war on Origin 101–3; regulatory learning 31; regulatory legitimacy 149; regulatory practice 14, 108, 197, 218; Victorian smart meter rollout 99–101
corporate social responsibility: commonality with normative meta-regulatory theory 24–5, 37, 49n6, 50n11; definition of 24; problems with 41, 47, 106; similarity to systems theory 42; strategic management and business ethics literature 37, 50n17; timing of observations 45; *see also* reputation; social licence; 'win–win' school of thought
customer consultative committees *80*, *214*, 229n10
Customer Issues Working Group (CIWG) 64–6
Czarniawska, B. 210

Debt Spiral Guideline 124–6; *see also* Utility Debt Spiral Project
Deetz, S. 41

234 *Index*

deliberative democracy 2–3, 5, 26
Department of Treasury and Finance 69
disconnections: as driver for political intervention 116; as moral issue 89, 115, 117, 131, 148–9, 198, 207; competing consumer advocate views on 117, 140, 151; last resort for an essential service 89, 123, 131; process 65, 116; rate 118; retailer perspective 117; *see also* wrongful disconnections
door-to-door sales channel: ACCC court cases 183–4; affecting competition analyses 157; behaviour of sales agents 162–4; concern from consumer advocates 157, 162, 177, 181, 182; consumer/customer views 184, 186, 188, 191n21; effectiveness of 162; ESC investigation 182–3; industry activity 163; role of commissions 163; *see also* Energy Assured Limited

economic function system 8, 42, **47**; on non-economic matters 39, 74, 204–5; retailers within 42, 48, 74, 104–7, 109, 204–6, 212–13; unable to create norms 74, 204, 213
Edelman, M. 29, 110
Electricity Authority, New Zealand 203, 228n7, 228n8
Electricity Retail Code 65, 71, 75; *see also* Retail Code
Elfenbein, H.A. 41
Energy Assured Limited (EAL) 163, 177–82, 188–9, 191n18, 191n19
energy efficiency audits: provision by consumer advocate agency 145; role within hardship programmes 115, 132, 133, 144
Energy Ombudsman of South Australia 182
energy retailers: business case for change 104–5, 108, 145, 207; compliance overview 79–81; concern about policy uncertainty/politics 78, 82–3, 99, 144, 150; corporate instability 107–8; creation of hardship programmes 145–6; exploiting customer biases 161, 163–4; framing of compliance breaches 142; inability to set up Victorian market 58, 60, 74; integration over time 79; involvement in the creation of the Retail Code 64–7, 74; learning 108, 188–9, 198, 205, 208–11; performance overview 81–2; perspective on

consumer advocates 206–7; perspective on disconnection 117; position in 2015 Hardship Inquiry 147–8; positions in 2005 Hardship Inquiry 131–4, 135; pre-FRC perceptions of risk 60–3; rationality 92, 105, 108, 148, 188, 198, 204, 207, 209–11; reactions to reporting 141; regulatory versus compliance functions 92, 112n12, 112n15; risk aversion in public 92; risk management approach 105–7, 198, 207; role of 11; self-image of 88; within economic system 42, 48, 74, 104–7, 109, 204–6, 212–13; *see also* incumbent retailers; risk; second tier retailers; self-regulation
Energy Retailers Association of Australia (ERAA) 163, 165, 177–80, 191n19; *see also* Energy Assured Limited
Energy and Water Ombudsman of Victoria (EWOV): clashes with ESC 130, 136–9; concerns about disconnections 117, 118, 129; costs in 2005 136; Hardship Conferences 117; involvement in Retail Code creation 65; Lumo wrongful disconnection case 137–9; negotiations of payment plans 90; Utility Debt Spiral Project 124; view on systemic issues 130, 131, 136; wrongful disconnection referrals 136–7
EnergyAustralia 79, 184–5: ceased door-to-door sales 184; court case for door-to-door sales 184; incumbent retailer 79; voluntary hardship programme 132, 145–6; *see also* TRUenergy
enforced self-regulation 2
essential service: conflict with commodity perspective 73, 75, 168, 204; definition of 11–12; (im)morality of disconnection 89, 115, 117, 131, 148–9, 198, 207; no disconnection for inability to pay 68, 123, 129, 135; no system orientation 108; public interest goals 13–14; *see also* Essential Services Commission, Victoria
Essential Services Commission of South Australia (ESCOSA) 170
Essential Services Commission, Victoria (ESC): created Retail Code 58, 64–71; marginalisation of 117–23, 136; objectives 12, 18n13; on capacity to pay 129, 137–8, 144, 147, 150; political behaviour 144, 200; proposal to abolish hardship programmes 146–8, 150

Index 235

Financial and Consumer Rights Council 128–30, 162
Footscray Community Legal Centre 162, 182–3
Frost and Sullivan report 163–4
full retail competition, Victoria: ideologically motivated 75n1; origins of 58–9; retailer role to implement 59; *see* competition
function system 8–9, **47**; economic 42, 74; legal 30–1; mass media 35; political 28

Gilad, S. 2, 21, 23
Gilovich, T. 44, 158
'good' regulation 12–13, 150, 151n9
government **26**; change of **84**; hypocrisy of 29, 108, 149–50, 188, 199, 203, 209, 222; in meta-regulatory theory 27; intervention in the market 71–3, 75, 82–3, 91, 93, 119; *see also* New South Wales government; politics; price regulation; Queensland government; South Australian government; Victorian government
Grabosky, P.N. 1–2, 16n2, 27
Greenpeace 32–4, 37
Griffin, D. 44, 158
Griffiths, D. 68
Gunningham, N. 1–2, 16n2, 21–3, 27, 41–2, 49n6, 104, 109, 213, 216, 218–19, 229n13, 229n14

Habermas, J. 50n9; Habermasian communicative rationality 25
Haines, F. 2, 21, 23, 27–8, 31, 218, 229n11
Hancher, L. 2, 27
hardship: 2005 Victorian Inquiry 125–36; 2015 Victorian Inquiry 146–8; creation of voluntary programmes 145–6; rules 116; state approaches 116; *see also* capacity to pay; vulnerable consumers
harnessing markets: implications for 167, 187, 203–5; meta-regulatory reliance on 2, 13, 17n7; outcomes 41, 204, 219, 223; pre-conditions 39, 167; *see also* reputation mechanism; 'win–win' school of thought
Hawkins, K. 149, 213
Heanzle, M. 109, 198
Henderson, D. 31, 34, 51n21
Holzer, B. 25, 33–4, 37
Hood, C. 25, 27, 29, 74

Huitfeld, J. 125–6, 134, 136
Hutter, B. 22, 107, 198

incumbent retailers: created Victorian FRC 60–7; door-to-door sales regulation 155, 183–5; IT problems 81, 107; national retailers 79; problems with price regulation 83; profit losses 184–5; sticky customer benefits 157; voluntary hardship programmes 132, 142, 145; *see also* AGL; energy retailers; EnergyAustralia; Origin Energy; TRUenergy
Institute for Social Research 131, 151n2

Jones, C.J. 22

Kagan, R.A. 1–2, 22–3, 41–2, 49n6, 74, 104, 218
Kahneman, D. 44, 158
Kemp, R. 24, 26
Kildonan Child and Family Services 129
King, M. 8–10, 17n9, 18n10, 29, 200, 212
Kuhn, T. 41

Laochumnanvanit, K. 13, 156, 190n12
late payment fees 117, 119, 123, 173
Lazer, D. 2
legal function system 8, **47**; learning 30–1, 43; norm stabilisation 30–1, 212; regulators within 31, 211; role in meta-regulation 212–13
Lehmann Nielsen, V.L. 23, 49n3, 51n23; *see also* Nielsen, V.L
Lenoble, J. 26, 49n7
Littlechild, S. 167, 189n2, 189n6, 190n8, 202, 228n3
Livesey, S.M. 33
low-income consumer advocates: against industry self-regulation 88, 109, 150, 181, 188–9, 198, 207; concern about capacity to pay 70, 123, 128–9, 140, 147; concern about consumer rationality 88, 157; concern about disconnections 89, 116–17, 123, 140, 143; concern about the door-to-door sales channel 157, 162, 177, 181, 182; concern about ESC 117–19, 122, 126, 129–30, 200; conflict on disconnections 117, 140, 151; focus on performance 140, 149; influence on retailers 206–7; involvement in the creation of the Retail Code 67–8; perspective on the market 67–8, 109, 157; self-image of 88; support for standing offer 173;

236 *Index*

low-income consumer advocates *continued*
use of case studies 89–91, 120; use of
politics 108; *see also* precautionary
principle
Luhmann, N. 8–10, 17n9, 51n24; functional
differentiation 17n10; on anxiety 199; on
economics 42, 204; on law 30–1, 212; on
mass media 35–6; on morality 217; on
operational closure 8, 47, 227; on
organisations 9, 209; on politics 28–9,
35–6, 199–200; on protest movements
34–5, 108; on risk and danger 198;
orthodox position 10; *see also*
contingency; function system
Lumo Energy: door-to-door undertaking to
ACCC 184; wrongful disconnection
case 137–9

Maesschalck, M. 49n7
management-based regulation 2
March, J.G. 9, 43–4, 51n24
Margolis, J. D 41
mass market 22, 41, 223
mass/news media **26**; ACCC doorknocking
campaign 183; effectiveness of 94–5,
206, 208; function of 35; link to politics
28, 109, 110, 201; moralising talk 36;
poor reportage 94–5, 97–8, 100, 102–3,
110, 142, 165, 184, 208; protest
movement use of 35; reputational
enforcement via 27; role of the truth 35,
36; self-image 35; system of 35, **47**,
110; unpredictability 94, 226; *see also*
contingency
Mauseth, M. 90, 120, 123, 128
Meidinger, E. 2, 21, 49n1
Mendelson, E. 17n4, 21
meta-regulation: assessment of 6, 13,
21–2, 213–20; basic version 2, 223;
commonality with corporate social
responsibility 24–5, 37, 49n6, 50n11;
commonality with reflexive
governance 24–5, 49n6, 50n11;
definition for book 3; energy market
elements of *80, 214–5*; harnessing
markets 2, 13, 17n7, 39, 154, 167, 187,
203–5, 223; machinery of 6–7, 23–4,
218–19, 227; regulator, impact on
29–31, 43, **47**, 197, 202–3; response of
regulated business 36–42; scandal 220,
226; self-regulation as basis of 2–5,
17n3, 21, 24–5, **26**, 29, 31, 43, *80; see
also* rationality; reputation; self-
regulation; social activism

meta-regulatory theory: normative
assumptions 4–5; role of government
27; role of regulator 29–31, 202; role of
third party advocates and activists 31–2;
see also morality; rationality; social
activism
Minimum Standards Working Group 65–7
Moeller, H.–G. 9, 10, 17n9, 35, 217
morality: anxiety as moral 199; as
inhibiting learning 88; case studies as
moral tales 89–91; consumer advocate
self-image 88; consumer/customer view
204; difficulty in identifying better
morality 35–6, 47; disconnection as
moral issue 89, 115, 117, 131, 148–9,
198, 207; for essential service 108, 148,
151; media selection of issues 36; of
politicians 122; retailer self-image 88;
risk management as moral 107; role in
normative meta-regulatory theory 4–6,
31, 45, 223, 227; role in regulatory
studies 22–3; third party morality 4–5,
17n7, 31, 34–5; value as means of
assessing regulatory success 216–7;
vulnerable customer needs 87–92,
198–9; *see also* meta-regulation,
machinery of
Moran, M. 2, 27

National Electricity Market (NEM) 11, 78,
83, 111n1, 112n13
National Energy Customer Framework
(NECF) **84**; delays in adoption 96–9,
109; initiation of 95; reflection of
Victorian approach 116, 135; role of the
AER 95–6, 143
Neighbourhood Energy 183, 185
Nelson, T. 87, 173, 190n15
New South Wales government:
communications campaign 176–7; delay
in adopting NECF 96–7; NECF
commencement 98; networks driving
price rises 171; opened market 70;
political messaging on bills 96–7, 171;
price deregulation 170, 173, 190n12;
price regulation 169; privatised retail
assets 79, 93; stifling FRC 62, 67; use of
media 94, 97
New South Wales Hansard 97
New Zealand: approach to consultation
203, 224; Electricity Authority 203
Newgate Research 156, 157, 160, 175
Newman, Campbell (Queensland Premier)
101–3, 109

Nielsen, V.L. 21, 79; *see also* Lehmann Nielsen, V.L

Nieuwenhuysen, J. 125–6, 134, 136

Northern Territory 111n1

O'Brien, M. 97, 156, 187

Office of the Electricity Industry Ombudsman 65; *see also* Energy and Water Ombudsman of Victoria (EWOV)

Office of the Regulator-General 12, 58; *see also* Essential Services Commission, Victoria (ESC)

Office of State Owned Enterprises 59

Ofgem: effects on UK market 167; political behaviour 201; use of behavioural economics 159, 167, 201

Organisation for Economic Co–operation and Development (OECD) 111n5, 111n8

organisation systems **47**; action organisations 209–10; in systems theory 9; political organisations 209–10; rationality 43–5, 196; role of decisions 209; *see also* consumer advocates; energy retailers; low-income consumer advocates; regulators

Origin Energy: 2005 Hardship Inquiry submission 131–2; ceased door-to-door sales 184; court case for door-to-door sales 184; incumbent retailer 79; outcomes of 2005 Hardship Inquiry 127, 132; role in Debt Spiral project 124–5; smart meter charges on bills 100–1, 110; voluntary hardship programme 132, 145–6; war with Queensland Premier 101–3

Osborne, E. 46, 49n5, 197

Owen, P. 33

Parker, C. 2–5, 7, 10, 17n3, 21, 23, 26, 30, 32, 47, 49n3, 49n4, 49n6, 50n8, 50n13, 50n16, 51n23, 79, 112n16, 149

Paterson, J. 10

payment plans: basis for hardship programmes 132; components of consumer protections 65, 115, 116; reporting 81; *see also* capacity to pay

People First Total Solutions 137

performance: outcomes 81–2; reporting 141–4

political function system 8, 28–9, **47**; administration 28; legitimacy 28; public opinion 28, 35–6, 75, 94; regulators within 31, 197, 200–3, 224

politics of 'doing something' 29, 109, 116, 171, 172, 186, 197–202; responsive politicisation 227

Power, M. 34, 37, 44–5, 105, 107, 198

precautionary principle 68, 87, 89, 108–9, 198, 207

price deregulation: New South Wales 169, 170, 173; push for cost-reflective prices 170–2; Queensland 169, 170, 173; role of price rises 170; South Australia 169, 170; Victoria 168–9; *see also* price regulation

price regulation: political risk 187, 190n12; pre-FRC Victoria 72–3; Queensland price freeze 101–2; standing offer contract 83, 102, 168; structural constraint 83; *see also* price deregulation; standing offer contracts

prices: cost–reflectivity 170, 172; green schemes 170–1; networks 171; Queensland price freeze 101–2; retailer profits 165–7; rises 82, 111n5, 171; Senate Select Committee on Electricity Prices 171; spot price 11, 62; standing offer 157; *see also* price deregulation; price regulation

privatisation 58, 59, 79, 83, **84**, 93, 168–9

process-oriented regulation 2

Pronin, E. 88–9, 160

protest movements: and consensus 108, 199, 207; use of politics 108; within systems theory 34–5, **47**; *see also* consumer advocates; low-income consumer advocates

public interest *46*; competing interests 197, 227; meta-regulatory assumptions 25; *see also* consensus of values

Queensland Competition Authority (QCA) 101–3

Queensland government: delay in adopting NECF 96, 98; delay to FRC 62, 67, 79; NECF commencement 98; networks driving price rises 94, 171; opened market 70; political messaging on bills 171; Premier's war on Origin 101–3, 209; price deregulation 103, 170, 173, 190n12; price regulation 103, 169; privatised retail assets 79; use of media 94, 97

rationality *46*; assumption of meta-regulatory theory 4–6, 40–1, 51n23;

238 *Index*

rationality *continued*
   consumer/customer 88, 160–1, 175–6,
    186, 196, 206; energy retailer 92, 105,
    108, 148, 188, 198, 204, 207, 209–11;
    Habermasian communicative rationality
    50n9; Luhmannian perspective 10;
    organisational 43–5, 47, 196; regulator
    43–5, 196–7, 203; timing of observation
    45
reflexive governance 49n7; commonality
   with normative meta-regulatory theory
   24–5, 49n6, 50n11
reflexive law 10
regulator **26**; creation of Victorian rules
   64–5, 69–71; focus on performance over
   compliance 143–4; learning 31; political
   behaviour 144, 200–3; rationality 43–5,
   196–7, 203; reporting on industry
   140–2; under meta-regulation 29–30,
   43, **47**, 223–4, *224*; within legal system
   211; within political system 202, 211;
   see also Australian Competition and
   Consumer Commission; Australian
   Energy Regulator; Essential Services
   Commission, Victoria
regulatory capitalism 2
Reich, R.B. 32, 36, 41–2, 227
Reid, C. 173, 190n15
Renner, M. 205
reputation: conceptual challenges 45, 109;
   evidence for value in self-regulation 22,
   37–8, 41–2, 51n22, 219; role of social
   activism 3, 26, 112n16; threat of
   damage 3–4, 7, 22, 24, 26, 34, 37, 154,
   229n16; *see also* competition;
   consumer/customer boycotts; corporate
   social responsibility; risk; social
   activism
reputation mechanism **40**, *46*; assessment of
   6; conditions for 38–9, 205–6, 225–6,
   226; market as effective 39, 204;
   outcomes 48, 93, 105–7, 142, 196,
   205–8, 223; possibility of success 225–6;
   scandal 39, 207–8, 220, 226; timeframe
   38–9; under normative meta-regulation
   38–41; *see also* self-regulation
responsive regulation: enforced self-
   regulation 2; enforcement pyramid 14,
   17n6, 23, 81, 226; likelihood of success
   5; tripartite version 5, 17n6; *see also*
   morality
Retail Code: 'capacity to pay' payment
   plans 70, 116, 123, 128–9, 137–8, 144,
   146–7; changes proposed in 2015

146–50; content 65, 116; development of
   64–71; disconnections 65, 116, 123;
   harmonised with NECF 99; non-academic
   origins 70; regulation to manage risk to
   legitimacy 71; *see also* disconnections;
   Essential Services Commission, Victoria;
   hardship
Rice, T. 33
Rich, N. 90, 120, 123, 128
risk: compliance risk 83, 62, 99, 144, 148;
   from reputation loss 32–4, 37, 50n17,
   155, 206–8; government aversion to 73,
   83, 197; low-income advocate concern
   68, 88, 198; pre-FRC retailer
   perceptions of 60–3; retailer aversion to
   60–4, 92; retailer management of 103,
   105–7, 109, 141, 148, 155, 198, 209;
   timeframes 198, 207; to regulators 71,
   119, 203, 211–12, 224; versus danger
   198, 206, 228n9; *see also* precautionary
   principle; price regulation
Rogowski, R. 10
Rothstein, H. 27, 74

Salter, D. 29, 110
Scarth, C. 125–6, 134, 136
Schmidt, K. 88–9, 160
second tier retailer 79; activity in pre-FRC
   consultation 66–7; court cases for door-
   to-door sales 183–4; risks in market 83,
   167, 185–6; *see also* energy retailers
self-regulation: basis of meta-regulation
   2–5, 17n3, 21, 24–5, **26**, 29, 31, 43, *80*;
   door-to-door sales 155, 177–85;
   inability for retailers to create market
   74; no consumer advocate support for
   88, 109, 150, 181, 188–9, 198, 207;
   outcomes 196, 205, 207, 219, 226,
   229n17; role of morality 4, 6–7, 22–4,
   49n4, 88; voluntary hardship
   programmes 145–6; *see also* energy
   retailers; reputation mechanism
Senate Select Committee on Electricity
   Prices 111n5, 171
Shafir, E. 158–9, 161
Shell 32–4, 37
Simon, H.A. 9, 43, 51n24
Simshauser, P. 13, 87, 156, 166, 190n12
Sinclair, D. 1–2, 16n2, 27
Slovic, P. 44, 158
smart meters: cost of rollout 168, 171;
   disruption to industry 83; Origin charge
   on bills 100–1, 110; role in price
   deregulation 172; role in Victorian

NECF delay 97; rules added to NECF 96; value of 83, 172; Victorian rollout 83, 99–101
smart regulation 2; role of the market 2; role of government 16n2, 27
Smith, N.C. 41
social activism: outcomes 110, 217–18; within normative meta-regulation 3, 26, 112n16, 154, 228n2; within reputation mechanism 40–2, **40**
social licence: economic perception of 204; outcomes 206, 218; political versus economic drivers 22, 218; value of 3, 226
South Australian government: delay in adopting NECF 96, 98; delay to FRC 62; NECF commencement 98; opened market 79; price deregulation 170; price regulation 169, 111n6; privatised retail assets 79
Sparrow, M. 213, 219
St Vincent de Paul Society 130; St Vincent de Paul Society and Alviss Consulting 164, 166, 173
stakeholder: definition 16n1, 76n5; expectations 38–9, *46*, 198–200, 217–18; involvement in meta-regulation 2–6, 21, 24–6, 33–4, 37, 196, 205–6; regulatory management of 17n3, 30–1, 202–3, 211, 224; studies of involvement in regulation 21–2, 41–2; *see also* consensus; consumer advocates; consumers/customers; politics; reputation mechanism
standing offer contracts: as a safety net 73, 159, 168, 173; preference of consumer advocates 173; price regulation of 72, 83, 102; prices of 83, 157, 164–7; to promote competition 73, 168; *see also* price deregulation
State Electricity Commission of Victoria (SECV) 59–60
Steger, U. 41, 47, 106
Sunstein, C.R. 89, 159
systems theory: communications not individuals 9; functional differentiation 17n10; key systems 8–9, **47**; reducing societal complexity 8; *see also* contingency; function systems; Luhmann, N.

Tanner, L. 56
Tasmania: adopted NECF 96; competition 111n1; NEM 11, 111n1

Teubner, G. 10
Thaler, R.H. 159
Thornhill, C. 8–9, 10, 17n9, 18n10, 29, 200, 212
Thornton, D. 23, 38–9, 41–2, 49n6, 104, 218
TRUenergy 79; hardship programme 146; 2005 Hardship Inquiry submission 131–4; *see also* EnergyAustralia
Tversky, A. 44, 158
Tyler, T.R. 23

Utility Debt Spiral Project: Debt Spiral Guideline 124–5; formation of 124–5, 127, 150; influence on 2005 Hardship Inquiry 125

VaasaETT 13, 58, 79, 156, 187
van Erp, J. 42, 51n22, 142
Vick, D. 42
Victorian Council of Social Service 67, 69, 117, 122
Victorian government: 2005 Hardship Inquiry 125–7, 134–6; 2015 Hardship Inquiry 147; changing political priorities 93; concern about prices 165, 191n23; delay in adopting NECF 96–9; last minute changes to NECF 95; marginalisation of ESC 2004–2005; 115, 119–23, 149; policy environment pre-FRC 58–60; price deregulation approach 168–9; price regulation 72–3; response on wrongful disconnection outcomes 139, 147; smart meter rollout 99–101; support for switching statistics 156, 187
Victorian Hansard 119–22
virtual realities: energy retailers 74, 196, 209–10; mass media 36; prediction of others' 209–10; regulators 196; systems theory 9
Vogel, D. 21, 41, 49n1
Vos, J.–P. 45
Voss, J.–P. 24, 26
vulnerable consumers: categories of 86; definitions 68, 85–92, 111n7, 161, 166; driver for regulations 68, 115, 168; effect of disconnection 89–91; needing protection from themselves 88, 190n16; on standing offer tariffs 166; targeted by doorknockers 162, 182; *see also* hardship; low-income consumer advocates; precautionary principle

240 *Index*

Wallis Consulting Group 156, 160, 175
Walsh, J.P. 41
Weber, M. 17n10, 25, 44, 76n6
Weick, K. 44–5, 51n24, 209
Western Australia 111n1
Whish-Wilson, P. 166
Williams, C.E. 31, 37, 51n21
'win–win' outcomes 5, 37, 41

wrongful disconnections: further
government intervention 139, 147;
legislation 117–25; Lumo case 137–9;
outcomes 136–9, 147

Yarrow, G. 167, 189n2, 201

Zadek, S. 32, 34